GOLFING in New England

The Essential Guide for the New England Golfer

by John da Silva

New England Cartographics
1997

Copyright * 1997 by John da Silva

Published by New England Cartographics, Inc. All rights reserved. No part of this book may be reproduced or transmitted in any form or by any means, electronic or mechanical, including photocopying and recording, or by any information storage or retrieval system, except as may be expressly permitted by the 1976 Copyright Act or in writing from the publisher.
Requests for permission should be addressed in writing to:
New England Cartographics, P.O. Box 9369, North Amherst MA 01059.

Cover design by Bruce Scofield
Cover photo: Bretwood Golf Course, New Hampshire

Text and photographs by John da Silva
Text editing and layout by Valerie Vaughan

Publishers Cataloguing in Publication

da Silva, John
 Golfing in New England : the essential guide for the New England golfer / by John da Silva.
 200 p. Includes maps.
 ISBN 1-889787-00-0
 Library of Congress catalog card number 97-67647
 1. Golf--Guidebooks. 2. Golf courses--New England.
 796.352

Printed in the United States of America
10 9 8 7 6 5 4 3 2 1

01 00 99 98 97

Preface

My wife Marcia and I started playing golf 3 years ago and really enjoy it. We are not great golfers by any stretch of the imagination -- breaking 100 is still a cause of celebration. We live in North Tewksbury which has many golf courses nearby - both in Massachusetts and New Hampshire. As we became better golfers, we started playing more golf and trying new courses. However, with so many great courses in the area, finding a single source of information on all the courses was next to impossible. In order to solve this problem, I started collecting information on golf courses from a variety of sources including state tourism agencies, local and national course guides, golf associations, golf magazines, and the Internet. As I collected more and more information, I realized that no one source had all of the courses listed because some guides (1) were outdated (new courses were built after the guide was published), (2) only covered small geographic areas (3) included only 18 hole courses or the better courses, or (4) did not include resort or semi-private courses. Once I had an initial list of courses, I contacted each golf course (mail and telephone) to fill in the information blanks and to get up-to-date greens fees and yardages.

As I did my research, I found and included in the book other golfing information that makes the book a complete resource for all golfers in New England. This includes information on topics such as local off-course driving ranges, golf retailers, private golf courses, golf touring clubs, golf schools, national golf association and societies, discount golf cards, rules for typical golf situations, golf museums, golfing magazines, golf history, golf course design, golf ball and club history, choosing a golf ball that is right for you, oldest courses in New England, famous course architects, handicap calculation, derivation of course pars, unusual courses in the world, typical club yardage for an average player, and more.

I believe this book is the most comprehensive guide to golfing in New England. Even so, I will be updating, expanding, and improving the book each year to make it more useful. I welcome your feedback on how the book can be improved, courses missing, incorrect information, or general comments.

Now, the challenge is to play as many of these courses as I can. See you on the fairway!

Table of Contents

How to Use This Book	5
Quick Guide to N.E. Golf Courses	7
Short History of Golf	21
Golf Timeline	22
Golf Course Design and Construction	23
Unusual Golf Courses	25
Golf Balls	25
Golf Clubs	27
Building Your Own Clubs	29
Golf Rules	30
Calculating Your Handicap	31
Short Games Statistics	31
Discount Golf Cards	31
Tournaments	32
Golfing Records	33
Publicly Traded Golf Companies	33
Golf Sites on the Internet	34
National Golf Associations & Societies	35
Golf Museums	37
Glossary of Golf Terms	37
New England Golf Courses	39
Greens Fees, Slope & Yardage	40
Connecticut	41
Greens Fees, Slope & Yardage	41
Top Ten Courses, Oldest Courses	42
Private Golf Courses	42
Golf Schools & Instruction	43
Retailers	43
Driving Ranges	44
Associations & Touring Clubs	44
Course Indexes	45
Locator Map	48
Course Listings	49
Maine	67
Greens Fees, Slope & Yardage	67
Top Ten Courses, Oldest Courses	68
Golf Schools & Instruction	68
Associations & Touring Clubs	68
Private Golf Courses	68
Retailers	69
Driving Ranges	69
Course Indexes	70
Locator Map	72
Course Listings	73
Massachusetts	93
Greens Fees, Slope & Yardage	93
Top Ten Courses, Oldest Courses	94
Golf Schools & Instruction	94
Associations & Touring Clubs	94
Private Golf Courses	95
Retailers	96
Driving Ranges	98
Course Indexes	99
Locator Map	102
Course Listings	105
New Hampshire	143
Greens Fees, Slope & Yardage	143
Top 10 Courses, Oldest Courses	144
Golf Schools & Instruction	144
Associations & Touring Clubs	144
Retailers	144
Private Golf Courses	145
Driving Ranges	146
Course Indexes	146
Locator Map	148
Course Listings	149
Rhode Island	165
Greens Fees, Slope & Yardage	165
Top 10 Courses, Oldest Courses	166
Golf Schools & Instruction	166
Associations & Touring Clubs	166
Private Golf Courses	166
Retailers	167
Driving Ranges	167
Course Indexes	167
Locator Map	170
Course Listings	171
Vermont	177
Greens Fees, Slope & Yardage	177
Top 10 Courses, Oldest Courses	178
Golf Schools & Instruction	178
Associations & Touring Clubs	178
Private Golf Courses	178
Retailers	179
Driving Ranges	179
Course Indexes	180
Locator Map	182
Course Listings	183
Bibliography	194
New England Cartographic Order Form	197
Readers' Comments & Additions	199

How to Use This Book

This book is divided into two sections. The first section provides general golf information including a short history of golf, golf course design, golf ball and club history, national golf association and societies, discount golf cards, rules for typical golf situations, golf museums, golfing magazines, handicap calculation, derivation of course pars, unusual golf courses, typical club yardage for an average player, and more.

The next section presents information on golfing in New England. This section includes all public, semi-private, and resort golf courses and is organized alphabetically by the six New England states and New England as a whole. At the beginning of each state's section is a description of general state golf course statistics which can be compared from state to state. These statistics are described below.

Public Courses: The number of public, semi-private, and resort golf courses in the state.
Private Courses: The number of private golf courses in the state.
Total Courses: The number of total golf courses in the state.
Percent Public Courses: The percentage of total courses that is open to the public.
18 Hole Public Courses: The total number of public, semi-private, and resort golf courses in the state that are 18 hole courses.
9 Hole Public Courses: The total number of public, semi-private, and resort golf courses in the state that are 9 hole courses.
Golfers Per Course: The total number of golfers divided by the total number of golf courses. This is a measure of how crowded courses are in each state.
Courses Per 100 Square Miles: The total number of golf courses divided by the total square miles of land area in the state. This is a measure of golf course density in each state.
Average Weekend Fee: The average greens fee for one person on the weekend. Includes all 18 and 9 hole courses. Cart fees are included for those courses where carts are mandatory.
Average Weekday Fee: The average greens fee for one person during weekdays. Includes all 18 and 9 hole courses. Cart fees are included for those courses where carts are mandatory.
Average Weekend Fee w/Power Cart: The average greens fee plus one half of the cart fee for one person on the weekend. Includes only 18 and 9 hole courses where carts are available.
Average Weekday Fee w/Power Cart: The average greens fee plus one half of the cart fee for one person during weekdays. Includes only 18 and 9 hole courses where carts are available.
Average Slope: The average slope for all 18 and 9 hole courses in the state that have a slope rating. The slope ratings are from the white or men's tees.
Average Yardage: The average yardage for all 18 and 9 hole courses in the state. The yardage ratings are from the white or men's tees.

Summary information on all the public courses in the state follows the state course statistics. Included are average, minimum, and maximum fees, yardages, and slopes. Also provided is information on top rated courses, oldest golf courses, golf schools, and golf associations and touring clubs, private golf courses, retailers, and driving ranges in the state.

Next, there is a map of the state that includes the location of each course. The location is marked by a number that corresponds to the number by each course in the course descriptions.

Following the map, there are several course indexes. The indexes include lists of golf courses organized by town, hardest, easiest, most expensive, least expensive, longest, shortest, and open year-round.

There are several ways to find courses. If you know the name of the golf course you are interested in and the state it is located, you can turn to the state section and locate the course quickly since courses are listed alphabetically. If you want to find courses in a geographical area, you can find all courses in that area by examining the locator map at the beginning of each state section. All courses on the maps are identified

INTRODUCTION

by a number. Once you locate a course, you can find the course listing by matching the number of the course shown at the beginning of the course's name. Each course is in numerical order in the course listings. If you are interested in finding the least expensive courses or the hardest courses in a particular state, you can find them quickly in the indexes provided at the beginning of each state section. Also, there is a quick guide to all the courses alphabetically by state along with associated course parameters at the end of this section.

Each course described in this book has a number of parameters associated with it. These parameters are described below using the Airways Golf Course as an illustration.

1 Airways Golf Course
1070 South Grand Street, Suffield, CT 06078
203-668-4973

Weekend Fee	$20	*Weekday Fee*	$19
Power Cart Fee	$20	*Pull Carts*	Yes
Putting Green	Yes	*Driving Range*	No
Season	Mar 15 - Nov 15	*Credit Cards*	No
Pro	Wayne Leale	*Tee Times*	7 days
Comments	Flat, easy to walk, lots of water		
Directions	Hartford, I-91N, exit 40, Rt 20W, East Granby, 4th light right on East St		

Tee	Holes	Par	Rating	Slope	Yards
Red	18	71	65.0	103	5,154
White	18	71	65.0	103	5,493
Blue	18	71	66.0	106	5,845

1 Airways Golf Course: The name of the golf course. The 1 signifies it is the first listed course in this state and that it can be found in the Connecticut location map labeled "1".
Weekend Fee: Greens fee for one person on the weekend. Fee covers 18 holes on 9 hole courses.
Weekday Fee: Greens fee for one person on weekdays. Fee covers 18 holes on 9 hole courses.
Power Cart Fee: Cost for power cart rental for 2 people. Fee covers 18 holes on 9 hole courses.
Pull Carts Allowed: Whether pull carts can be used or the course walked.
Putting Green: Existence of a putting green for practice.
Driving Range: Existence of a driving range for practice.
Season: Time of the year course is open.
Credit Cards: Whether credit cards can be used to pay for greens fees.
Pro: Name of golf pro at the course.
Tee Times: Days to call in advance to reserve tee times for the weekend.
Comments: Short description of the course or unique features.
Directions: Directions to the course from a major highway.
Tee: Tee boxes. Some courses use other designations such as Women's for Red, Men's for White, and Championship for Blue.
Holes: Number of individual holes available at the course.
Par: Par for the course for each tee box. For 9 hole courses, the par covers an 18 hole round. NA designates that the information is not available or applicable.
Rating: Course rating from each tee box. For 9 hole courses, the rating covers an 18 hole round. NA designates that the information is not available or applicable.
Slope: Slope for the course for each tee box. NA designates that the information is not available or applicable.
Yards: Course yardage from each tee box. For 9 hole courses, the yardage covers an 18 hole round. NA designates that the information is not available or applicable.

Quick Guide to All Public New England Courses

Connecticut

Course	Town	Holes	Weekend	Weekday	Par	Rating	Slope	Distance
Airways GC	Suffield	18	$20	$19	71	65.0	103	5,493
Alling Memorial GC	New Haven	18	$25	$24	72	68.0	119	5,884
Banner Lodge CC	Moodus	18	$23	$20	72	68.9	118	5,950
Bel Compo GC	Avon	18	$27	$22	72	70.1	125	6,304
Blackledge CC - Anderson/Gilead	Hebron	18	$26	$24	72	69.6	118	6,173
Blackledge CC - Gilead/Links	Hebron	18	$26	$24	72	NA	NA	6,015
Blackledge CC - Links/Anderson	Hebron	18	$26	$24	72	NA	NA	6,058
Brooklyn Hill CC	Danielson	9	$17	$15	70	NA	NA	5,760
Bruce Memorial GC	Greenwich	18	$28	$28	72	69.3	120	6,093
Buena Vista GC	W. Hartford	9	$20	$18	64	NA	NA	3,664
Canaan CC	Canaan	9	$20	$20	70	67.0	113	5,586
Candlewood Valley CC	New Milford	18	$27	$22	72	70.3	120	6,295
Canton Public GC	Canton	9	$23	$20	72	68.0	116	5,798
Cedar Knob GC	Somers	18	$20	$18	72	70.3	116	6,298
Cedar Ridge GC	E. Lyme	18	$17	$13	54	NA	NA	2,958
Chanticlair GC	Colchester	9	$18	$16	70	69.8	117	5,983
Connecticut Golf Land	Vernon	18	$6	$6	54	NA	NA	980
Copper Hill CC	E. Granby	9	$22	$18	72	69.0	116	5,772
Crestbrook Park GC	Watertown	18	$23	$21	71	71.1	125	6,367
East Gaynor Brennan GC	Stamford	18	$30	$25	71	71.0	122	5,868
East Hartford GC	E. Hartford	18	$23	$21	71	68.6	114	6,076
East Mountain GC	Waterbury	18	$20	$18	67	67.0	113	5,701
Eastwood CC	Torrington	9	$21	$19	72	67.8	113	5,866
Ellington Golf Center	Ellington	9	$12	$12	54	NA	NA	1,716
Elmridge GC	Pawcatuck	18	$29	$26	71	69.5	117	6,082
Fairchild Wheeler GC - Black	Fairfield	18	$23	$18	71	71.0	124	6,402
Fairchild Wheeler GC - Red	Fairfield	18	$23	$18	72	72.0	122	6,382
Farmingbury Hill CC	Wolcott	9	$19	$19	72	68.7	117	6,078
Fenwick GC	Old Saybrook	9	$14	$14	70	NA	NA	5,722
Gainfield Farms GC	Southbury	9	$22	$20	56	NA	NA	2,768
Goodwin GC - Goodwin	Hartford	18	$21	$18	70	66.7	108	5,638
Goodwin GC - North	Hartford	9	$19	$16	70	NA	NA	5,088
Grassmere CC	Enfield	9	$22	$20	70	69.1	111	6,130
Grassy Hill CC	Orange	18	$28	$21	70	69.4	119	5,849
H. Smith Richardson GC	Fairfield	18	$27	$22	72	70.2	124	6,323
Harrisville GC	Woodstock	9	$18	$14	70	NA	NA	5,928
Highland Greens GC	Prospect	9	$10	$8	54	NA	NA	2,796
Hillside Links	Deep River	9	$12	$10	54	NA	NA	1,864
Hop Brook CC	Naugatuck	9	$20	$17	72	67.8	109	5,774
Hotchkiss School GC	Lakeville	9	$25	$15	70	69.2	111	6,008
Hunter Memorial GC	Meriden	18	$22	$20	71	70.3	123	6,243
Indian Hill CC	Newington	18	$30	$30	72	69.6	121	6,120
Indian Springs GC	Middlefield	9	$24	$20	72	68.9	116	6,000

QUICK GUIDE TO COURSES

Connecticut (Continued)

Course	Town	Holes	Weekend	Weekday	Par	Rating	Slope	Distance
Keney Park GC	Hartford	18	$20	$16	70	67.7	116	5,678
Laurel View CC	Hamden	18	$23	$20	72	70.8	124	6,372
Lisbon CC	Lisbon	9	$16	$14	66	65.5	102	4,700
Lyman Orchards GC - Jones	Middlefield	18	$49	$42	72	70.0	124	6,200
Lyman Orchards GC - Player	Middlefield	18	$49	$42	71	71.2	131	6,269
Manchester CC	Manchester	18	$32	$28	72	69.8	120	6,167
Meadowbrook CC	Hamden	9	$14	$12	70	NA	NA	5,442
Millbrook GC	Windsor	18	$24	$21	71	69.5	121	6,074
Mill Stone CC	Milford	9	$12	$10	72	NA	NA	5,820
Miner Hills GC	Middletown	9	$18	$14	60	NA	NA	3,400
Minnechaug GC	Glastonbury	9	$23	$21	70	67.0	111	5,386
Norwich GC	Norwich	18	$27	$24	71	68.1	117	5,927
Oak Hills GC	Norwalk	18	$30	$26	71	68.0	120	5,920
Orange Hills CC	Orange	18	$30	$22	71	69.8	119	6,084
Patton Brook CC	Southington	18	$18	$14	60	58.5	93	4,056
Pequabuck GC of Bristol	Pequabuck	18	$31	$31	69	67.6	119	5,692
Pequot GC	Stonington	18	$24	$18	70	67.2	108	5,903
Pilgrim's Harbor GC	Wallingford	9	$29	$22	72	72.6	127	5,898
Pine Valley GC	Southington	18	$26	$22	71	69.5	121	6,039
Portland GC	Portland	18	$27	$23	71	68.5	121	5,802
Portland GC West	Portland	18	$22	$19	60	60.4	79	3,620
Putnam CC	Putnam	9	$20	$16	72	69.6	112	6,140
Quarry Ridge	Portland	9	$36	$32	72	69.3	115	5,608
Raceway GC	Thompson	18	$22	$18	71	68.6	116	5,916
Richter Park GC	Danbury	18	$44	$44	72	71.1	126	6,325
Ridgefield GC	Ridgefield	18	$27	$27	70	68.1	119	5,919
Rockledge CC	Hartford	18	$25	$21	72	68.6	119	6,010
Rolling Greens GC	Rocky Hill	9	$25	$20	70	72.0	131	6,258
Shennecossett GC	Groton	18	$26	$22	72	69.5	118	6,142
Short Beach GC	Stratford	9	$13	$11	54	NA	NA	2,540
Silver Spring CC	Ridgefield	18	$50	$35	71	70.3	125	6,142
Simsbury Farms GC	W. Simsbury	18	$25	$21	72	68.3	118	6,104
Skungamaug River GC	Coventry	18	$24	$21	70	68.6	118	5,624
Sleeping Giant GC	Hamden	9	$18	$15	70	NA	NA	5,641
Southington CC	Southington	18	$24	$21	71	67.0	113	5,675
South Pine Creek Park	Fairfield	9	$18	$16	54	NA	NA	2,146
Stanley Municipal GC - Blue/Red	New Britain	18	$23	$19	72	68.9	119	6,067
Stanley Municipal GC - White	New Britain	9	$23	$19	70	68.4	NA	5,612
Sterling Farms GC	Stamford	18	$33	$28	72	69.7	123	6,082
Stonybrook GC	Litchfield	9	$30	$24	70	68.6	122	5,548
Sunset Hill GC	Brookfield	18	$21	$17	69	62.6	100	4,720
Tallwood CC	Hebron	18	$25	$23	72	69.0	117	6,126
Tashua Knolls GC	Trumbull	18	$24	$20	72	69.3	122	6,119
Timberlin GC	Kensington	18	$24	$21	72	70.0	123	6,342
Trumbull GC	Groton	18	$15	$13	54	NA	NA	2,660
Tunxis Plantation CC - Green	Farmington	18	$27	$23	72	68.1	117	5,958

Connecticut (Continued)

Course	Town	Holes	Weekend	Weekday	Par	Rating	Slope	Distance
Tunxis Plantation CC - Red	Farmington	9	$27	$23	72	68.8	119	6,152
Tunxis Plantation CC - White	Farmington	18	$27	$23	72	69.2	117	6,241
Twin Hills CC	Coventry	18	$24	$22	71	68.6	116	5,954
Twin Lakes GC	N. Branford	9	$10	$9	54	NA	NA	1,702
Western Hills GC	Waterbury	18	$20	$18	72	69.6	122	6,246
Westport Longshore GC	Westport	18	$26	$22	69	66.7	113	5,676
Westwoods GC	Farmington	18	$21	$17	61	58.6	85	4,407
Whitney Farms GC	Monroe	18	$42	$37	72	70.9	127	6,262
Willimantic CC	Willimantic	18	$35	$35	71	69.2	119	6,003
Woodhaven CC	Bethany	9	$27	$22	72	70.6	123	6,384
Woodstock GC	Woodstock	9	$16	$13	66	63.4	104	4,180

Maine

Course	Town	Holes	Weekend	Weekday	Par	Rating	Slope	Distance
Apple Valley GC	Lewiston	9	$15	$15	70	64.3	108	5,037
Aroostook Valley CC	Fort Fairfield	18	$22	$22	72	69.9	113	5,977
Bangor Municipal GC - 18	Bangor	18	$19	$18	71	67.9	112	6,345
Bangor Municipal GC - 9	Bangor	9	$19	$18	72	69.6	128	6,006
Bar Harbor GC	Trenton	18	$24	$24	71	70.2	122	6,437
Bath CC	Bath	18	$25	$25	70	67.8	123	5,748
Bethel Inn and CC	Bethel	18	$35	$26	72	69.6	124	6,330
Biddeford and Saco CC	Saco	18	$30	$30	71	68.2	119	5,835
Birch Point GC	Madawaska	9	$15	$15	70	NA	105	5,900
Boothbay Region CC	Boothbay	9	$22	$22	70	66.1	118	5,630
Bridgton Highlands CC	Bridgton	9	$35	$30	72	68.1	116	5,940
Brunswick GC	Brunswick	18	$25	$25	72	70.0	123	6,251
Bucksport GC	Bucksport	9	$16	$15	72	70.6	117	6,704
Cape Arundel GC	Kennebunkport	18	$30	$30	69	67.0	117	5,869
Caribou CC	Caribou	9	$15	$15	72	68.8	116	6,320
Carmel Valley GC	Carmel	9	$10	$10	54	55.7	NA	2,416
Castine GC	Castine	9	$20	$20	70	68.1	116	5,954
Causeway GC	SouthWest Harbor	9	$22	$22	64	60.8	95	4,604
Cobbossee Colony GC	Monmouth	9	$10	$10	68	62.0	102	4,702
Country View GC	Brooks	9	$15	$15	72	66.4	115	5,770
Dexter Municipal GC	Dexter	9	$15	$13	70	65.7	115	5,172
Dutch Elm GC	Biddeford	18	$25	$25	72	67.4	115	5,882
Fairlawn GC	E. Poland	18	$16	$14	72	69.3	119	6,300
Fort Kent GC	Fort Kent	9	$18	$18	70	69.0	111	6,224
Foxcroft GC	Dover-Foxcroft	9	$20	$20	72	NA	107	6,250
Freeport CC	Freeport	9	$15	$12	72	68.2	113	5,884
Frye Island GC	Raymond	9	$20	$15	72	68.7	113	6,046
Goose River GC	Camden	9	$20	$20	71	68.7	115	6,098
Gorham CC	Gorham	18	$20	$20	71	68.3	116	6,334
Great Chebeague GC	Chebeague Island	9	$25	$20	66	62.1	106	4,468
Great Cove GC	Jonesboro	9	$10	$10	60	NA	84	3,388

QUICK GUIDE TO COURSES

Maine (Continued)

Course	Town	Holes	Weekend	Weekday	Par	Rating	Slope	Distance
Green Acres Inn and CC	Canton	9	$10	$10	62	NA	NA	3,600
Green Meadow GC	Farmingdale	18	$20	$20	70	67.1	123	5,525
Greens at Eaglebrook	Scarborough	9	$10	$10	72	66.8	106	5,768
Green Valley GC	W. Enfield	9	$11	$11	72	63.0	101	5,248
Grindstone Neck GC	Winter Harbor	9	$25	$22	72	NA	NA	6,190
Hampden CC	Hampden	9	$10	$10	72	64.0	106	5,434
Hermon Meadows GC	Bangor	18	$17	$16	72	66.7	110	5,895
Hillcrest GC	Millinocket	9	$14	$12	66	63.2	104	4,954
Houlton Community GC	Houlton	9	$20	$18	72	68.7	117	6,080
Island CC	Deer Isle	9	$12	$10	62	58.8	97	3,865
Johnson W. Parks GC	Pittsfield	9	$18	$16	70	68.4	114	5,776
Katahdin CC	Milo	9	$10	$10	72	64.7	102	6,006
Kebo Valley GC	Bar Harbor	18	$36	$36	70	69.0	129	5,925
Kenduskeag Valley GC	Kenduskeag	9	$10	$9	68	63.8	108	5,124
Kennebec Heights CC	Farmingdale	18	$22	$20	70	67.1	123	5,525
Lake Kezar CC	Lovell	9	$20	$18	72	68.0	119	5,850
Lakeview GC	Burnham	9	$13	$13	72	68.0	114	5,900
Lakewood GC	Madison	18	$14	$14	70	68.5	114	5,729
Lucerne Hills GC	E. Holden	9	$15	$12	72	67.4	119	5,760
Maple Lane CC	Livermore Falls	9	$15	$15	70	NA	NA	5,146
Mars Hill CC	Mars Hill	9	$17	$17	72	68.8	120	5,940
Mingo Springs GC	Rangeley	18	$24	$24	72	66.3	109	5,923
Moose River GC	Moose River	9	$10	$10	62	NA	NA	3,952
Mt. Kineo GC	Mt. Kineo	9	$13	$13	72	NA	NA	6,022
Naples Golf and CC	Naples	9	$22	$22	72	69.5	115	6,554
Natanis GC-Arrowhead/Indian	Vassalboro	18	$20	$20	73	66.8	112	5,923
Natanis GC-Indian/Tomahawk	Vassalboro	18	$20	$20	72	68.4	120	6,170
Natanis - Tomahawk/Arrwhd	Vassalboro	18	$20	$20	73	66.0	109	5,803
Naval Air St. Brunswick GC	Brunswick	9	$17	$15	70	68.4	115	6,199
Northeast Harbor GC	NorthE. Harbor	18	$30	$30	69	66.7	118	5,278
Northport GC	Northport	9	$17	$17	72	68.0	112	6,094
Norway CC	Norway	9	$18	$18	70	68.0	113	6,200
Oakdale CC	Mexico	9	$18	$12	72	68.8	119	6,366
Old Orchard Beach CC	Old Orchard Beach	9	$22	$20	72	67.1	112	6,016
Orchard View GC	Newport	9	$15	$13	60	NA	NA	4,480
Palmyra GC	Palmyra	18	$18	$18	72	69.0	118	6,367
Paris Hill CC	Paris	9	$13	$13	66	62.1	109	4,637
Penobscott Valley CC	Orono	18	$45	$45	72	69.6	121	6,301
Pine Hill GC	Brewer	9	$13	$11	72	66.0	99	5,868
Pine Ridge GC	Waterville	9	$6	$6	54	64.3	116	5,147
Piscataquis CC	Guilford	9	$15	$12	70	64.6	109	5,488
Pleasant Hill CC	Scarborough	9	$12	$10	68	62.3	115	4,786
Point Sebago GC	Casco	18	$42	$42	72	70.2	129	6,474
Poland Spring CC	Poland Spring	18	$20	$20	71	67.2	117	5,854
Portage Hills CC	Portage	9	$18	$18	72	69.5	113	6,420
Presque Isle CC	Presque Isle	18	$20	$20	72	69.2	112	6,393

Maine (Continued)

Course	Town	Holes	Weekend	Weekday	Par	Rating	Slope	Distance
Prospect Hill GC	Auburn	18	$16	$16	71	69.9	110	5,846
Province Lake CC	E. Wakefield	18	$25	$25	71	68.8	114	5,887
River Meadow GC	Westbrook	9	$12	$10	70	66.9	117	5,498
Riverside Municipal GC-18	Portland	18	$19	$16	72	69.2	117	6,400
Riverside Municipal GC-9	Portland	9	$19	$16	72	70.4	114	6,290
Rockland GC	Rockland	18	$25	$25	70	67.2	109	5,941
Sable Oaks GC	S. Portland	18	$29	$23	70	70.2	129	6,056
Salmon Falls GC	Hollis	9	$20	$20	72	67.6	119	5,756
Samoset Resort GC	Rockport	18	$70	$70	70	68.4	122	6,021
Sandy River GC	Farmington Falls	9	$10	$10	54	NA	NA	2,672
Sanford CC	Sanford	9	$23	$18	72	70.8	122	6,592
Shore Acres GC	Sebasco Estates	9	$14	$14	66	NA	NA	4,218
South Portland Muni GC	S. Portland	9	$8	$7	66	NA	NA	4,142
Spring Brook GC	Leeds	18	$18	$18	71	68.7	120	6,163
Squaw Mt Village GC	Greenville	9	$15	$15	68	NA	NA	4,926
St. Croix CC	Calais	9	$20	$20	64	NA	102	5,470
Sugarloaf GC	Carrabassett Valley	18	$75	$75	72	70.8	137	6,456
Summit GC	Poland	13	$15	$15	72	67.2	118	5,726
Todd Valley GC	Charlestown	9	$12	$12	66	61.1	93	4,672
Turner Highlands	Turner	9	$18	$18	72	69.2	121	5,960
Twin Falls GC	Westbrook	9	$12	$12	66	68.3	112	4,880
Va-Jo-Wa GC	Island Falls	18	$21	$21	72	68.9	117	5,860
Val Halla GC	Cumberland Center	18	$22	$17	72	69.6	122	6,201
Waterville CC	Oakland	18	$38	$38	70	68.1	121	6,108
Wawenock CC	Walpole	9	$20	$20	70	70.0	NA	6,112
Webhannet GC	Kennebunk Beach	18	$30	$30	71	NA	117	6,248
Westerly Winds GC	Westbrook	9	$7	$6	54	NA	NA	1,660
Western View GC	Augusta	9	$15	$15	70	64.5	107	5,430
West Newfield GC	W. Newfield	9	$10	$10	60	54.1	86	2,990
White Birches GC	Ellsworth	9	$15	$15	68	68.2	109	4,788
Willowdale GC	Scarborough	18	$21	$21	70	67.9	110	5,980
Wilson Lake CC	Wilton	9	$18	$18	70	68.8	117	6,044
Woodland Terrace GC	E. Holden	9	$11	$11	60	53.0	NA	3,110

Massachusetts

Course	Town	Holes	Weekend	Weekday	Par	Rating	Slope	Distance
Agawam CC	Feeding Hills	18	$21	$15	71	69.1	117	6,129
Amesbury Golf and CC	Amesbury	9	$23	$23	70	70.5	125	6,089
Amherst GC	Amherst	18	$20	$20	70	68.9	117	6,083
Apple CC	Chelmsford	9	$22	$18	68	65.3	114	5,004
Ashfield Community GC	Ashfield	9	$14	$10	66	NA	NA	3,458
Atlantic CC	Plymouth	18	$33	$28	72	69.0	119	5,840
Ballymeade CC	N. Falmouth	18	$65	$50	72	70.1	130	6,055
Bas Ridge GC	Hinsdale	9	$12	$10	70	NA	110	5,108
Bass River GC	S. Yarmouth	18	$30	$30	72	67.7	117	5,702

QUICK GUIDE TO COURSES

Massachusetts (Continued)

Course	Town	Holes	Weekend	Weekday	Par	Rating	Slope	Distance
Bayberry Hills GC	S. Yarmouth	18	$30	$30	72	68.5	125	6,067
Bay Path GC	E. Brookfield	9	$18	$15	72	69.5	NA	6,030
Bay Pointe CC	Wareham	18	$30	$28	70	67.6	118	5,720
Beaver Brook CC	Haydenville	9	$15	$12	72	68.1	110	5,992
Bedrock GC	Rutland	9	$22	$15	72	69.8	122	6,186
Berlin CC	Berlin	9	$15	$15	66	62.9	108	4,466
Beverly Golf and Tennis Club	Beverly	18	$32	$28	70	70.1	123	5,965
Blissful Meadows GC	Uxbridge	18	$28	$22	72	68.4	120	6,022
Blue Rock GC	S. Yarmouth	18	$26	$22	54	NA	NA	2,923
Bradford CC	Bradford	18	$30	$25	70	70.3	134	6,005
Braintree Municipal GC	Braintree	18	$25	$20	72	70.4	116	6,423
Brookmeadow CC	Canton	18	$27	$22	72	69.2	118	6,292
Butternut Farm GC	Stow	18	$29	$23	70	69.9	125	6,205
Candlewood GC	Ipswich	9	$15	$15	66	NA	NA	4,685
Cape Ann GC	Essex	9	$24	$22	70	67.3	110	5,866
Cape Cod CC	N. Falmouth	18	$32	$26	71	67.7	118	6,018
Captains GC	Brewster	18	$40	$40	72	69.8	123	6,176
Cedar Glen GC	Saugus	9	$20	$19	70	66.7	NA	6,170
Cedar Hill GC	Stoughton	9	$17	$12	66	60.4	92	4,310
Chatham Seaside Links	Chatham	9	$22	$22	68	66.4	107	4,980
Chemawa CC	N. Attleborough	9	$21	$16	70	67.2	113	5,244
Chequessett Yacht & CC	Wellfleet	9	$34	$34	70	65.1	110	5,169
Cherry Hill GC	N. Amherst	9	$15	$13	70	65.7	101	5,815
Chicopee Municipal GC	Chicopee	18	$15	$14	72	70.4	120	6,365
Clearview GC	Millbury	9	$15	$13	70	65.9	114	5,448
Colonial Hilton GC	Wakefield	18	$49	$39	70	71.1	129	6,187
Cotuit-Highground GC	Cotuit	9	$10	$10	56	NA	NA	2,580
CC of Billerica	Billerica	18	$26	$24	66	63.9	107	4,965
Cranberry Valley GC	Harwich	18	$40	$40	72	67.1	113	5,644
Cranwell Resort	Lenox	18	$55	$55	70	70.0	125	6,169
Crumpin-Fox Club	Bernardston	18	$55	$55	72	71.3	136	6,508
Crystal Springs GC	Haverhill	18	$20	$17	72	70.8	114	6,436
Dennis Highlands	S. Dennis	18	$35	$35	71	68.7	115	6,076
Dennis Pines GC	S. Dennis	18	$34	$34	71	71.0	122	6,525
Devens GC	Fort Devens	9	$15	$12	70	67.1	112	5,657
Dunroamin CC	Gilbertville	9	$18	$16	70	68.6	117	5,726
D. W. Fields GC	Brockton	18	$20	$16	70	68.9	116	5,660
East Mountain CC	Westfield	18	$20	$17	71	65.9	101	6,031
Easton CC	S. Easton	18	$25	$23	71	68.0	114	6,060
Edge Hill GC	Ashfield	9	$16	$14	72	NA	NA	6,500
Edgewood GC	Southwick	18	$18	$14	71	67.6	113	6,050
Edgewood GC	Uxbridge	9	$10	$8	64	NA	NA	4,520
Egremont CC	Great Barrington	18	$28	$20	71	66.3	115	5,180
Ellinwood CC	Athol	18	$24	$19	71	67.8	117	5,737
Falmouth CC	Falmouth	18	$30	$25	72	68.8	114	6,227
Far Corner GC	Boxford	27	$30	$27	72	70.9	126	6,189

Massachusetts (Continued)

Course	Town	Holes	Weekend	Weekday	Par	Rating	Slope	Distance
Farm Neck GC	Oak Bluffs	18	$60	$60	72	69.6	126	6,094
Fire Fly CC	Seekonk	18	$20	$19	60	54.4	81	3,083
Forest Park CC	Adams	9	$12	$12	68	63.8	110	5,100
Foxborough CC	Springfield	18	$35	$30	72	70.9	123	6,462
Franconia Municipal GC	Springfield	18	$15	$13	71	67.1	115	6,053
Fresh Pond GC	Cambridge	18	$25	$20	70	68.9	114	5,954
Furnace Brook GC	Quincy	18	$44	$44	70	NA	NA	5,746
Gannon Municipal GC	Lynn	18	$23	$23	70	67.9	113	6,036
Gardner Municipal GC	Gardner	18	$25	$20	71	68.3	120	6,106
Garrison Golf Center	Haverhill	9	$13	$11	54	NA	NA	2,000
GEAA GC	Pittsfield	9	$20	$15	72	69.6	117	6,205
Georgetown CC	Georgetown	9	$27	$25	72	70.5	128	6,105
George Wright GC	Hyde Park	18	$26	$23	70	68.6	123	6,105
Glen Ellen CC	Millis	18	$30	$22	72	69.2	118	6,073
Grand View CC	Leominister	18	$20	$16	72	68.8	113	6,746
Green Harbor GC	Marshfield	18	$26	$25	71	67.3	111	5,808
Green Hill Municipal GC	Worcester	18	$22	$18	72	67.4	106	6,110
Greenock CC	Lee	9	$30	$18	70	67.4	NA	6,027
Green Valley GC	Newburyport	9	$20	$17	70	67.4	108	5,804
Groton CC	Groton	9	$21	$16	70	66.5	116	5,506
Hampden CC	Hampden	18	$29	$24	72	70.1	126	6,350
Harwich Port GC	Harwich Port	9	$21	$21	68	NA	NA	5,076
Heather Hill CC	Plainville	27	$20	$15	70	66.5	115	5,734
Hemlock Ridge GC	Fiskdale	9	$18	$15	72	70.6	117	6,272
Heritage CC	Charlton	18	$25	$19	71	69.7	118	6,375
Heritage Hill CC	Lakeville	18	$21	$19	54	54.7	84	2,575
Hickory Hill GC	Methuen	18	$30	$27	71	67.9	119	6,017
Hickory Ridge CC	S. Amherst	18	$43	$32	72	71.1	128	6,411
Hidden Hollow CC	Rehoboth	9	$15	$12	70	NA	NA	5,810
Highland Links	N. Truro	9	$25	$25	72	64.6	100	5,578
Hillcrest CC	Leicester	9	$25	$20	70	67.1	103	5,466
Hillside CC	Rehoboth	9	$20	$17	60	68.9	121	6,310
Hillview GC	N. Reading	18	$27	$25	69	66.0	106	5,754
Holden Hills CC	Holden	18	$25	$20	71	71.9	125	5,826
Holly Ridge GC	S. Sandwich	18	$20	$20	54	NA	NA	2,952
Holyoke CC	Holyoke	9	$25	$19	72	67.5	118	6,265
Hopedale CC	Hopedale	9	$18	$18	70	68.0	121	6,068
Hyannis GC	Hyannis	18	$40	$32	71	68.2	115	6,002
Indian Meadows GC	Westborough	9	$26	$23	72	69.4	119	6,038
John F. Parker GC	Taunton	9	$20	$16	70	69.7	118	6,130
Juniper Hill GC - Lakeside	Northborough	18	$28	$23	71	69.9	127	6,282
Juniper Hill GC - Riverside	Northborough	18	$28	$23	71	70.4	123	6,306
Kelly Greens	Nahant	9	$20	$18	60	57.0	103	3,784
Kings Way GC	Yarmouthport	18	$45	$45	59	58.9	93	4,100
Lakeview GC	Wenham	9	$18	$17	62	59.3	91	4,080
Lakeville CC	Lakeville	18	$28	$23	72	70.1	118	6,274

QUICK GUIDE TO COURSES

Massachusetts (Continued)

Course	Town	Holes	Weekend	Weekday	Par	Rating	Slope	Distance
Leo J. Martin GC	Weston	18	$20	$17	72	68.8	115	6,140
Little Harbor CC	Wareham	18	$18	$18	56	54.4	79	3,038
Locust Valley CC	Attleborough	18	$18	$14	72	69.3	121	6,148
Lost Brook GC	Norwood	18	$20	$17	54	NA	NA	3,002
Lynnfield Center GC	Lynnfield	9	$22	$21	68	61.5	NA	5,120
Maplegate CC	Bellingham	18	$39	$33	72	69.5	122	5,837
Maplewood GC	Lunenburg	9	$18	$15	70	63.9	106	5,370
Marion GC	Marion	9	$15	$15	68	67.0	116	5,390
Maynard GC	Maynard	9	$28	$22	68	65.8	118	5,389
Meadows GC	Greenfield	9	$15	$12	72	NA	NA	5,740
Merrimack Valley GC	Methuen	18	$23	$19	71	69.0	120	5,938
Miacomet GC	Nantucket	9	$40	$40	74	70.2	113	6,400
Middlebrook CC	Rehoboth	9	$16	$13	67	65.5	108	5,968
Middleton GC	Middleton	18	$24	$24	54	54.0	NA	3,215
Mill Valley CC	Belchertown	9	$15	$12	72	67.0	110	5,879
Millwood Farms Course	Framingham	14	$23	$20	54	63.1	101	4,883
Mink Meadows GC	Vineyard Haven	9	$40	$40	70	68.7	121	6,004
Monoosnock CC	Leominister	9	NA	$24	70	68.6	113	6,107
Mount Hood GC	Melrose	18	$24	$21	69	65.7	107	5,553
Nabnasset Lake CC	Westford	9	$25	$21	70	67.4	118	5,408
New Bedford Municipal GC	New Bedford	18	$18	$15	72	70.0	120	6,410
New England CC	Bellingham	18	$48	$38	71	67.2	125	5,665
New Meadows GC	Topsfield	9	$24	$22	70	64.8	117	5,763
New Seabury GC Blue	Mashpee	18	$60	$60	72	71.7	124	6,508
New Seabury GC Green	Mashpee	18	$40	$40	70	61.6	110	5,105
Newton Commonwealth GC	Chestnut Hill	18	$25	$20	70	66.8	128	5,590
Nichols College GC	Dudley	9	$23	$18	72	71.4	123	6,482
North Adams CC	Clarksburg	9	$13	$13	72	69.4	114	6,050
Northampton CC	Leeds	9	$17	$15	70	67.6	113	6,100
Northfield CC	E. Northfield	9	$22	$18	72	66.2	121	5,664
North Hill CC	Duxbury	9	$21	$18	72	70.8	121	7,002
Norton CC	Norton	18	$43	$26	71	69.9	120	5,754
Norwood CC	Norwood	18	$22	$18	71	65.9	108	5,665
Oak Ridge GC (Feeding Hills)	Feeding Hills	9	$30	$25	70	66.5	116	5,711
Oak Ridge GC (Gill)	Gill	18	$23	$19	72	68.7	117	5,813
Ocean Edge GC	Brewster	18	$46	$28	72	68.7	125	6,127
Olde Barnstable Fairgrnds GC	Marston Mills	18	$37	$35	71	69.1	120	6,150
Olde Salem Greens	Salem	9	$19	$17	70	68.5	116	6,056
Orchards GC	S. Hadley	18	$50	$50	71	69.9	123	6,279
Ould Newbury GC	Newburyport	9	$20	$24	70	69.0	120	6,184
Pakachoag GC	Auburn	9	$12	$11	72	70.0	119	6,510
Paul Harney GC	E. Falmouth	18	$20	$20	59	59.9	91	3,235
Pembroke CC	Pembroke	18	$35	$30	71	71.1	124	6,532
Petersham CC	Petersham	9	$20	$16	70	68.9	116	6,046
Pine Acres GC	Bellingham	9	$15	$15	56	NA	NA	2,292
Pine Crest GC	Holliston	18	$23	$18	66	63.2	103	5,003

Massachusetts (Continued)

Course	Town	Holes	Weekend	Weekday	Par	Rating	Slope	Distance
Pine Grove GC	Northampton	18	$16	$13	72	68.8	111	6,115
Pine Knoll GC	E. Longmeadow	9	$6	$6	54	NA	NA	1,600
Pine Meadows GC	Lexington	9	$25	$22	70	64.5	110	5,350
Pine Oaks GC	S. Easton	9	$23	$20	68	67.0	111	5,824
Pine Ridge CC	Oxford	18	$24	$18	71	69.7	117	5,700
Pine Valley GC	Rehoboth	9	$14	$11	70	NA	NA	6,400
Plymouth CC	Plymouth	18	$40	$40	69	70.0	125	6,164
Ponkapoag GC #1	Canton	18	$20	$17	72	72.0	126	6,726
Ponkapoag GC #2	Canton	18	$20	$17	71	70.3	116	6,332
Pontoosuc Lake CC	Pittsfield	18	$15	$13	70	69.7	NA	6,305
Poquoy Brook GC	Lakeville	18	$32	$32	72	69.9	125	6,286
Presidents GC	Quincy	18	$25	$21	70	64.3	108	5,055
Putterham Meadows	Brookline	18	$26	$23	71	68.3	118	6,003
Quaboag CC	Monson	9	$25	$25	68	67.2	116	5,760
Quail Hollow Golf & CC	Oakham	9	$20	$18	70	66.6	112	5,600
Quashnet Valley CC	Mashpee	18	$43	$30	72	69.1	126	6,073
Rehoboth CC	Rehoboth	18	$24	$19	72	69.5	117	6,295
Ridder GC	Whitman	18	$25	$25	70	67.6	109	5,857
Rochester GC	Rochester	18	$17	$17	69	69.0	107	4,830
Rockland GC	Rockland	18	$20	$18	54	58.0	79	3,055
Rockport GC	Rockport	9	NA	$25	72	65.2	104	5,514
Rolling Green GC	Andover	9	$18	$16	54	NA	NA	3,000
Round Hill CC	E. Sandwich	18	$37	$32	71	66.6	120	5,920
Rowley CC	Rowley	9	$27	$24	72	70.7	127	6,380
Saddle Hill CC	Hopkinton	18	$28	$22	72	69.4	119	6,200
Sagamore Spring GC	Lynnfield	18	$33	$27	70	66.5	114	5,505
Saint Anne CC	Feeding Hills	18	$16	$12	72	69.5	115	6,500
Saint Mark's GC	Southborough	9	$25	$20	70	67.1	117	5,810
Sandy Burr CC	Wayland	18	$32	$29	72	69.9	122	6,229
Scituate CC	Scituate	9	NA	$24	70	69.7	121	5,948
Shaker Farms CC	Westfield	18	$24	$18	72	71.9	125	6,669
Shaker Hills CC	Harvard	18	$50	$45	71	67.3	121	5,914
Siasconset GC	Siasconset	9	$30	$30	70	68.1	113	5,086
Skyline CC	Lanesborough	18	$18	$16	72	70.4	124	5,773
Southampton CC	Southampton	18	$19	$13	72	69.0	114	6,720
South Shore CC	Hingham	18	$33	$29	72	69.9	124	6,197
Southwick CC	Southwick	18	$18	$15	71	68.0	116	6,100
Squirrel Run CC	Plymouth	18	$22	$20	57	53.7	82	2,284
Stone-E-Lea GC	Attleborough	18	$20	$15	71	70.0	112	6,261
Stoneham Oaks GC	Stoneham	9	$18	$16	54	NA	NA	4,500
Stow Acres (North)	Stow	18	$38	$30	72	69.8	127	6,310
Stow Acres (South)	Stow	18	$38	$30	72	70.5	118	6,105
Stowaway GC	Stow	9	$10	$8	72	68.3	NA	5,445
Strawberry Hills CC	Leicester	18	$20	$16	70	68.4	118	5,740
Strawberry Valley GC	Abington	9	$21	$18	70	66.9	108	4,716
Sun Valley CC	Rehoboth	18	$23	$18	71	69.8	116	6,383

QUICK GUIDE TO COURSES

Massachusetts (Continued)

Course	Town	Holes	Weekend	Weekday	Par	Rating	Slope	Distance
Swansea CC	Swansea	18	$27	$22	72	70.6	121	6,355
Taconic GC	Williamstown	18	$80	$80	71	69.5	125	6,185
Tara Hyannis GC	Hyannis	18	$22	$22	54	NA	NA	2,621
Tekoa CC	Westfield	18	$25	$20	71	68.2	116	5,965
Thomas Memorial CC	Turner Falls	9	$20	$16	70	66.0	NA	5,103
Touisset CC	Swansea	9	$17	$15	71	69.1	111	6,203
Trull Brook GC	Tewksbury	18	$35	$32	72	68.2	115	6,003
Twin Springs GC	Bolton	9	$16	$13	68	64.8	113	5,224
Tyngsboro GC	Tyngsboro	9	$22	$18	70	65.2	108	5,149
Unicorn GC	Stoneham	9	$28	$22	70	68.7	109	6,159
Veterans GC	Springfield	18	$15	$13	72	68.7	118	6,115
Wachusett CC	W. Boylston	18	$30	$25	72	71.7	124	6,608
Wading River GC	Norton	18	$14	$12	54	NA	NA	2,421
Wahconah CC	Dalton	18	$55	$45	71	69.9	118	6,187
Wampanoag GC	N. Swansea	9	$16	$14	70	66.7	108	6,225
Waubeeka Golf Links	S. Williamstown	18	$22	$17	72	69.5	124	6,024
Wayland CC	Wayland	18	$35	$26	70	67.3	112	5,229
Wedgewood CC	Brockton	9	$15	$12	72	66.7	113	5,200
Wenham CC	Wenham	18	$28	$25	65	62.3	102	4,429
Westborough CC	Westborough	9	$24	$20	71	69.2	118	6,210
Westminster CC	Westminster	18	$25	$20	71	69.5	123	6,223
Westover GC	Granby	18	$15	$13	72	71.7	123	6,610
Whippernon CC	Russell	9	$16	$14	68	NA	113	5,186
Wilbraham CC	Wilbraham	9	$29	$22	72	69.3	108	6,194
William J. Devine GC	Dorcester	18	$23	$20	72	71.1	113	6,360
Willowdale GC	Mansfield	9	$14	$12	60	NA	NA	3,424
Winchendon CC	Winchendon	18	$20	$16	70	65.8	114	5,317
Woburn CC	Woburn	9	$24	$22	68	69.4	125	5,973
Woodbriar CC	Falmouth	9	$16	$14	54	NA	NA	2,820
Worthington GC	Worthington	9	$22	$18	70	66.8	115	5,629

New Hampshire

Course	Town	Holes	Weekend	Weekday	Par	Rating	Slope	Distance
Amherst CC	Amherst	18	$32	$24	72	68.7	118	6,000
Androscoggin Valley CC	Gorham	18	$24	$20	70	68.9	116	5,499
Angus Lea GC	Hillsborough	9	$19	$19	66	60.8	101	4,270
Applewood Golf Links	Windham	9	$16	$16	54	NA	NA	2,594
Atkinson CC	Atkinson	9	$27	$22	72	NA	NA	6,585
Balsams Panorama GC	Dixville Notch	18	$50	$50	72	70.5	130	6,097
Beaver Meadow GC	Concord	18	$25	$23	72	68.5	118	6,034
Bethlehem CC	Bethlehem	18	$22	$18	70	68.2	114	5,656
Bramber Valley GC	Greenland	9	$18	$18	64	60.8	99	4,228
Bretwood GC - North	Keene	18	$30	$25	72	73.9	128	6,434
Bretwood GC - South	Keene	18	$30	$25	72	70.4	133	6,309
Buckmeadow GC	Amherst	9	$28	$21	66	60.9	100	4,680

New Hampshire (Continued)

Course	Town	Holes	Weekend	Weekday	Par	Rating	Slope	Distance
Campbell's Scottish Highlands	Salem	18	$30	$25	71	66.4	112	5,746
Candia Woods	Candia	18	$30	$23	71	69.4	118	6,307
Carter CC	W. Lebanon	9	$20	$18	72	66.1	116	5,610
Claremont CC	Claremont	9	$22	$18	68	64.7	104	5,419
Colebrook CC	Colebrook	9	$18	$18	72	67.1	105	5,893
CC of New Hampshire	N. Sutton	18	$30	$25	72	69.6	122	6,226
Countryside GC	Dunbarton	9	$20	$18	72	70.5	129	6,002
Den Brae GC	Sanbornton	9	$20	$18	72	67.1	109	5,926
Derryfield CC	Manchester	18	$24	$24	70	68.2	112	6,000
Duston CC	Hopkinton	9	$16	$14	64	59.2	99	4,194
Eagle Mountain Resort	Jackson	9	$24	$18	64	NA	NA	4,252
East Kingston GC	E. Kingston	18	$23	$20	69	68.1	116	5,957
Eastman Golf Links	Grantham	18	$37	$37	71	71.7	133	6,338
Exeter CC	Exeter	9	$22	$20	70	67.8	115	5,800
Farmington CC	Farmington	9	$18	$15	64	61.8	95	4,690
Green Meadow GC North	Hudson	18	$28	$22	72	67.6	109	6,088
Green Meadow GC South	Hudson	18	$28	$22	72	69.3	113	6,182
Hale's Location CC	N. Conway	9	$35	$33	72	66.8	117	5,632
Hanover CC	Hanover	18	$30	$30	69	68.7	118	5,876
Highlands Links Colony GC	Holderness	9	$12	$12	54	56.7	92	3,000
Hoodkroft CC	Derry	9	$24	$22	71	70.1	121	6,466
Hooper GC	Walpole	9	$22	$22	72	69.3	122	6,038
Indian Mound GC	Center Ossipee	18	$28	$28	70	66.5	113	5,360
Intervale CC	Manchester	9	$25	$22	72	68.8	107	6,074
Jack O'Lantern Resort	Woodstock	18	$32	$29	70	67.5	113	5,829
John H. Cain GC	Newport	18	$29	$25	71	68.3	127	6,005
Keene CC	Keene	18	$55	$55	72	69.0	120	5,912
Kingswood GC	Wolfeboro	18	$35	$30	72	68.8	125	5,860
Kona Mansion Inn	Moultonboro	9	$13	$13	54	64.2	111	4,680
Laconia CC	Laconia	18	$60	$60	72	70.7	126	6,253
Lakeview GC	Belmont	18	$20	$20	70	69.0	NA	6,220
Lisbon Village CC	Lisbon	9	$20	$20	72	67.9	126	5,782
Lochmere Golf and CC	Tilton	10	$24	$20	71	68.7	126	6,010
Londonderry CC	Londonderry	18	$22	$20	62	57.2	86	3,740
Loudon CC	Loudon	9	$22	$20	70	69.2	123	5,534
Maplewood Casino & GC	Bethlehem	18	$20	$18	72	67.4	109	6,001
Mojalaki CC	Franklin	9	$20	$15	70	69.4	122	5,970
Monadnock CC	Peterborough	9	$15	$13	58	54.0	76	3,152
Mountain View Golf and CC	Whitefield	9	$20	$20	70	67.3	109	5,874
Mount Washington GC	Bretton Woods	18	$29	$25	71	69.0	120	6,154
Nippo Lake GC	Barrington	9	$20	$18	68	64.5	105	5,172
North Conway GC	N. Conway	18	$35	$28	71	70.3	123	6,281
Oak Hill GC	Meredith	9	$16	$16	68	60.6	90	4,468
Overlook CC	Hollis	18	$35	$28	71	69.0	128	6,051
Passaconaway CC	Litchfield	18	$33	$26	71	70.7	123	6,462
Pease GC	Portsmouth	18	$26	$26	70	67.8	114	5,820

QUICK GUIDE TO COURSES

New Hampshire (Continued)

Course	Town	Holes	Weekend	Weekday	Par	Rating	Slope	Distance
Perry Hollow Golf and CC	Wolfboro	18	$30	$30	71	69.9	129	5,927
Pheasant Ridge CC	Gilford	9	$22	$20	70	67.1	103	6,044
Pine Grove Springs CC	Spofford	9	$20	$15	68	70.8	132	5,980
Pine Valley Golf Links	Pelham	9	$22	$17	70	67.0	119	5,820
Plausawa Valley CC	Pembroke	18	$27	$24	72	70.6	131	6,162
Ponemah Greens	Amherst	9	$23	$21	68	59.7	97	4,042
Portsmouth CC	Exeter	18	$50	$50	72	72.0	122	6,609
Profile GC	Franconia	9	$15	$14	72	70.2	129	6,003
Rochester CC	Rochester	18	$42	$37	72	68.7	123	6,317
Rockingham CC	Newmarket	9	$20	$20	70	65.3	113	6,150
Sagamore-Hampton GC	N. Hampton	18	$24	$24	71	70.5	101	6,489
Shattuck GC	Jaffrey	18	$35	$35	71	71.0	143	6,077
Sky Meadow CC	Nashua	18	$85	$65	72	70.8	128	6,036
Souhegan Woods GC	Amherst	18	$32	$25	72	68.7	117	6,122
Sunningdale GC	Somersworth	9	$22	$20	72	70.4	121	6,660
Sunset Hill Golf Links	Sugar Hill	9	$18	$16	66	58.2	81	3,954
Tory Pines Resort	Fancestown	18	$29	$22	71	67.5	126	5,477
Twin Lake Village GC	New London	9	$19	$16	54	NA	NA	2,424
Waterville Valley GC	Waterville Valley	9	$22	$20	64	NA	NA	4,808
Waukewan GC	Meredith	18	$25	$25	71	67.1	120	5,735
Waumbek Inn & CC	Jefferson	18	$18	$18	71	69.9	107	5,874
Wentworth-By-The-Sea	Portsmouth	18	$75	$75	70	66.7	121	6,100
Wentworth Resort GC	Jackson	18	$35	$25	69	63.9	105	5,305
Whip-Poor-Will GC	Hudson	9	$24	$20	72	67.8	120	5,980
White Mountain CC	Ashland	18	$29	$23	71	68.6	121	5,974
Windham CC	Windham	18	$35	$30	72	69.1	132	6,013
Woodbound Inn GC	Jaffrey	9	$12	$12	54	NA	NA	1,956

Rhode Island

Course	Town	Holes	Weekend	Weekday	Par	Rating	Slope	Distance
Boulder Hills Golf & CC	Richmond	9	$34	$25	71	NA	NA	6,215
Bristol GC	Bristol	9	$10	$8	66	NA	NA	5,030
Country View GC	Harrisville	18	$23	$19	70	67.7	116	5,721
Coventry Pines GC	Coventry	9	$18	$16	70	NA	113	6,340
Cranston CC	Cranston	18	$27	$23	71	71.3	124	6,241
East Greenwich Golf & CC	E. Greenwich	9	$21	$17	70	68.6	NA	6,042
Exeter CC	Exeter	18	$25	$20	72	69.9	118	6,390
Fairlawn GC	Lincoln	9	$14	$12	54	52.2	NA	2,534
Foster CC	Foster	18	$20	$18	72	69.5	114	6,187
Goddard Park GC	Warwick	9	$16	$12	72	NA	NA	6,042
Green Valley CC	Portsmouth	18	$27	$22	71	71.6	120	6,641
Jamestown Golf & CC	Jamestown	9	$16	$15	72	69.7	110	5,998
Laurel Lane GC	W. Kingston	18	$20	$18	71	68.1	113	5,806
Lindhbrook CC	Hope Valley	9	$14	$12	54	NA	NA	2,885

Rhode Island (Continued)

Course	Town	Holes	Weekend	Weekday	Par	Rating	Slope	Distance
Meadow Brook GC	Wyoming	18	$15	$12	71	70.1	118	6,075
Melody Hill GC	Harmony	18	$18	$15	71	69.0	113	6,185
Midville CC	W. Warwick	9	$24	$20	70	68.2	114	5,536
Montaup CC	Portsmouth	18	$42	$42	71	71.4	123	6,236
North Kingstown Municipal GC	N. Kingstown	18	$23	$21	70	68.3	116	5,848
Pocasset CC	Portsmouth	9	$18	$15	70	67.0	110	5,590
Pond View GC	Westerly	9	$20	$20	72	70.0	118	6,324
Richmond CC	Hope Valley	18	$29	$24	71	68.5	114	5,827
Rolling Greens GC	N. Kingstown	9	$22	$18	70	NA	NA	6,144
Seaview CC	Warwick	9	$20	$16	72	66.8	117	5,646
Silver Spring GC	E. Providence	6	$12	$12	69	NA	NA	4,936
Triggs Memorial GC	Providence	18	$25	$21	72	71.7	126	6,394
Washington Village GC	Coventry	9	$18	$15	66	NA	NA	4,846
Winnapaug GC	Westerly	18	$28	$22	72	67.9	111	5,914
Woodland Greens GC	N. Kingstown	9	$20	$18	72	67.1	110	6,046

Vermont

Course	Town	Holes	Weekend	Weekday	Par	Rating	Slope	Distance
Alburg CC	S. Alburg	18	$25	$20	72	69.4	110	6,388
Appletree Bay GC	S. Hero	9	$8	$7	54	NA	NA	2,264
Bakersfield GC	Bakersfield	9	$15	$12	70	69.0	115	5,960
Barre CC	Barre	18	$30	$30	71	69.2	119	5,986
Barton GC	Barton	9	$15	$15	71	66.0	113	5,800
Basin Harbor GC	Vergennes	18	$35	$35	72	70.4	120	6,232
Bellows Falls CC	Bellows Falls	9	$24	$18	70	68.5	111	5,752
Blush Hill CC	Waterbury	9	$20	$16	66	63.0	101	4,730
Bradford GC	Bradford	9	$18	$15	64	60.4	102	4,260
Brattleboro CC	Brattleboro	9	$25	$25	70	69.8	117	6,265
Cedar Knoll CC	Hinesburg	18	$18	$18	72	67.4	117	5,903
Champlain CC	Saint Albans	18	$24	$21	70	69.0	119	5,976
Copley CC	Morrisville	9	$20	$20	70	66.5	106	5,549
Crown Point CC	Springfield	18	$39	$32	72	70.0	119	6,120
Enosberg Falls CC	Enosberg Falls	9	$17	$15	72	NA	117	5,568
Essex CC	Essex Junction	18	$18	$16	72	68.6	114	6,310
Farm Resort GC	Morisville	9	$20	$18	72	67.6	112	5,798
Fox Run GC	Ludlow	9	$27	$25	70	65.6	106	5,124
Gleneagles GC	Manchester Vil.	18	$80	$70	71	69.1	125	6,069
Granddad's Invitational GC	Newark	9	$5	$5	60	NA	NA	4,568
Haystack GC	Wilmington	18	$45	$39	72	69.8	125	6,164
Killington Golf Resort	Killington	18	$39	$39	72	69.6	123	5,876
Kwiniaska GC	Shelburne	18	$22	$22	72	71.2	122	6,796
Lake Morey CC	Fairlee	18	$30	$25	70	68.4	118	5,807
Lake St. Catherine CC	Poultney	9	$30	$25	70	68.8	119	5,906
Marble Island CC	Mallets Bay	9	$16	$12	66	65.6	110	5,086

Vermont (Continued)

Course	Town	Holes	Weekend	Weekday	Par	Rating	Slope	Distance
Montague GC	Randolph	18	$25	$19	70	67.2	117	5,596
Montpelier CC	Montpelier	9	$21	$18	70	66.6	114	5,226
Mountain View CC	Greensboro	9	NA	$21	70	67.3	112	5,592
Mount Anthony CC	Bennington	9	$30	$25	71	69.2	125	5,941
Mount Snow GC	Mount Snow	18	$59	$49	72	70.3	127	6,443
Neshobe CC	Brandon	9	$28	$26	70	66.8	120	5,592
Newport CC	Newport	18	$21	$21	72	69.2	106	6,117
Northfield CC	Northfield	9	$22	$18	70	68.8	115	5,712
Orleans CC	Orleans	18	$20	$20	72	68.5	115	5,938
Proctor Pittsford CC	Pittsford	18	$27	$27	70	67.9	118	5,728
Prospect Bay CC	Bomoseen	9	$20	$17	70	64.0	107	5,010
Quechee Club Resort-Highland	Quechee	18	$60	$60	72	70.4	123	6,342
Quechee Club Resort-Lakeland	Quechee	18	$60	$60	72	69.8	124	6,016
Ralph Myhre GC	Middlebury	18	$28	$28	71	69.6	126	6,014
Richford CC	Richford	9	$34	$30	74	68.2	113	6,006
Rocky Ridge GC	Burlington	18	$20	$20	72	69.1	124	5,933
Rutland CC	Rutland	18	NA	$64	70	67.9	122	5,761
Sitzmark GC	Wilmington	18	$12	$12	54	NA	NA	2,643
Someday Golf Resort	W. Dover	9	$47	$47	72	NA	NA	4,716
St. Johnsbury CC	St. Johnsbury	18	$28	$24	70	68.6	125	5,860
Stamford Valley CC	Stamford	9	$10	$10	72	66.6	104	5,418
Stonehedge CC	N. Claredon	9	$15	$12	54	NA	NA	2,214
Stowe CC	Stowe	18	$45	$45	72	68.5	121	5,851
Stratton Mt. GC (Forest)	Stratton	18	$66	$56	72	69.4	122	6,044
Stratton Mt. GC (Lake)	Stratton	18	$66	$56	72	70.3	123	6,107
Stratton Mt. GC (Mountain)	Stratton	18	$66	$56	72	69.3	123	6,019
Sugarbush GC	Warren	18	$49	$40	72	69.0	122	5,886
Tater Hill Resort	Chester	18	$59	$55	72	71.4	124	6,015
West Bolton GC	W. Bolton	18	$17	$15	69	66.3	109	5,432
White River GC	Rochester	9	$20	$20	66	62.6	101	4,518
Wilcox Cove Cottages and GC	Grand Isle	9	$10	$8	64	NA	NA	3,410
Williston GC	Williston	18	$19	$19	69	66.6	113	5,262
Windsor CC	Windsor	9	$24	$19	68	65.1	105	5,286
Wolf Run CC	Bakersfield	9	$15	$12	70	NA	NA	5,940
Woodstock Inn and Resort	Woodstock	18	$56	$49	69	67.0	117	5,555

Short History of Golf

Golf originates in the 1400s in Scotland. However, the game as we know it today got started in the 1700s. Golfers played on a 5 hole golf course in Leith in the early 1700s. In 1744, these players got together and formed the Honourable Company of Edinburgh Golfers, the first known organized golf club. They also developed the first rules of golf. The rules were written in order to have a basis for an annual tournament for a trophy provided by the town. The *Code of Rules* had 13 articles - many of which have stayed unchanged over the years. In 1754, the Royal and Ancient Golf Club of St. Andrews was formed. This club became the arbiter of the rules over the years. During this period, courses varied from 5 to 22 holes. In 1764, the Royal and Ancient club decreed that the golf course should consist of 18 holes rather than the 22 holes they were previously playing on. In 1860, the first British Championship tournament was held in Prestwick. A year later, this became the British Open.

A record of golf in the United States has been found as early as the 1780s in South Carolina and Georgia. However, right before the war of 1812, golf declined and did not recover until later in the 1800s. In 1887, John Reid asked Robert Lockhart to purchase six clubs and several dozen balls when he went to Scotland. Lockhart bought the equipment from Tom Morris at St. Andrews. In 1888, John Reid built a three hole course in New York. Later the course was moved to another location nearby and expanded to six holes. John Reid and seven other players formed the St. Andrew's Golf Club. In 1892, the course was moved again to a bigger location and membership is expanded to thirty players. After two more moves, the club relocates to Mt. Hope, New York and expands to 18 holes.

By the mid 1890s, clubs began to flourish. In 1894, five clubs formed the Amateur Golf Association of the United States (later called the United States Golf Association) to provide direction for the game in the US. The five clubs were St. Andrew's (Yonkers, NY), Shinnecock Hills (Long Island, NY), Newport (RI), The Country Club (Brookline, MA), and the Chicago Golf Club (IL). In 1895, the first 18 hole golf course (Chicago Golf Club) in the United States was constructed by Charles Macdonald. The first national golf tournaments in the United States, the US Open and the US Amateur, were held in 1895.

By the turn of the century, golf started taking off. New ball and club designs such as rubber cored Haskell balls and mass produced steel shafts made golf easier to play and much less expensive. The sport now became available to the middle class and over a thousand clubs in the US were formed. Golf vacations became the vogue in places such as Poland Springs Maine, Woodstock Vermont, Colorado Springs Colorado, and Cape Cod Massachusetts.

Another turning point in the public's interest in golf occurred in 1913. In the US Open, Francis Ouimet, an amateur who caddied at the The Country Club of Brookline, Massachusetts, beat the two professional champions from Europe, Harry Vardon and Ted Ray. Golf in the US surged after this tournament.

Today, there are over 15,000 golf courses and approximately 25 million golfers in the US. A more detailed timeline of golf follows on the next page.

Golf in the Olympics

Golf was included in the Olympics as a medal sport only two times. The first time golf was included was in the 1900 Paris games. Margaret Abbot, an American, won the women's competition. In 1904 at the St. Louis games, only men competed and George Lyon, a Canadian, won the medal. Golf was considered for the 1920 Belgium Olympics and for the 1996 Atlanta games but both times failed to become an Olympic sport.

Golf Timeline

1353: The first time chole, the precedent to golf, is referenced.
1421: The game of chole is introduced to a Scottish regiment who are helping the French against the English.
1457: Because it interfered with military training against the English, golf is banned by the Scots Parliament.
1502: After the signing of the Treaty of Glasgow, the golf ban is removed.
1552: Golf is recorded as being played at St. Andrews.
1567: The first female golfer is Mary, Queen of Scots.
1618: The feathery ball is introduced.
1659: The first reference to golf in America is a reference to the banning of golf from the streets of Albany, NY.
1724: The first time a golf match reported in a newspaper (Alexander Elphinstone vs. Captain John Porteous).
1744: The first golf club (Honourable Company of Edinburgh Golfers) is formed and plays at Leith links.
1754: St. Andrews has first 18 hole golf course. The first Rules of Golf published by the St. Andrews Golfers.
1786: The first golf club (South Carolina Golf Club) outside of the United Kingdom is formed in Charleston.
1810: Earliest reference to women competing is at Musselburgh.
1826: American hickory is imported and used to make golf shafts.
1836: The Honourable Company of Edinburgh Golfers leave Leith Links and move to Musselburgh.
1848: The gutta-percha ball (guttie) is invented.
1865: Players started to use bags to carry their clubs.
1867: The first golf club for women (the Ladies' Golf Club at St. Andrews) is formed.
1867: The western hemisphere's first golf club, Canada's Royal Montreal Golf Club, is founded.
1880: The gutta-percha ball is dimpled using molds.
1885: At Holylake in Cheshire, the first Amateur Golf Championship is played.
1888: The oldest existing golf club in America (St. Andrews Golf Club) is founded in Yonkers, NY.
1893: A nine hole course is built for wives at Shinnecock Hills. The first golf magazine, Golf, is published.
1894: The first golf club on the Pacific Coast (the Tacoma Golf Club) is founded.
1894: The United States Golf Association is formed.
1894: Spalding makes and sells the first club made in the US.
1895: The United States Open is held. Chicago Golf Club opens the first 18-hole golf course in the US.
1898: Spalding makes and sells the first ball made in the US.
1898: The Haskell ball (the first rubber-cored ball) is designed by Coburn Haskell.
1899: The Western Open later known as the PGA Tour, is played at Glenview G.C.
1916: The PGA of America is founded. Pinehurst, North Carolina opens first miniature golf course.
1920: Dentist William Lowell invents the golf tee.
1921: The size and weight of the ball is limited and specified by the R & A.
1922: The Walker Cup was started for amateurs in the US to compete with amateurs in Britain and Ireland.
1927: Britain and the U.S. play the first Ryder Cup Matches.
1932: The Curtis Cup competition was started for women golfers in the US, Britain, and Ireland
1934: The first time the Masters is played at the Augusta National Club in Georgia.
1939: Royal and Ancient club limits the number of golf clubs to be carried to 14.
1947: St. Louis U.S. Open is the first time golf is televised.
1950: The Women's Professional Golf Association becomes the LPGA.
1951: The USGA and the R & A revise the Rules of Golf. The ball size is still debated but stymie abolished.
1953: Tam O'Shanter World Championship is first nationally televised tournament. The Canada Cup begins.
1963: The casting method is used to make irons.
1966: The Canada Cup becomes the World Cup.
1971: Alan Shepard plays golf on the moon with a 6 iron.
1973: The graphite shaft is invented.
1974: Pinehurst, North Carolina opens the World Golf Hall of Fame.
1980: The PGA Senior Tour begins.
1985: Slope is introduced by the United States Golf Association (USGA) to adjust handicaps.
1990: The R & A adopts the 1.68 inch diameter ball limitation. The Rules of Golf are standardized worldwide.

Golf Course Design and Construction

There are six general types of golf courses: links, prairie, parkland, desert, mountain, and tropical. *Links* courses (also known as seaside courses) are built on sandy soil formed by the ocean and the wind. They usually have undulating hills and dunes, lack trees, and are windy. Judging distances on these courses can be very difficult. *Prairie* courses are similar to links courses. They are open, affected by the wind, and usually found in the midwest.

Parkland courses are built from heavily wooded areas. They are found in the northeast, contain water hazards, and have many elevation changes. *Desert* courses are mainly found out west and in Florida. They have very little variation in the topology, are built on sandy soil, and the rough is usually desert. They are made possible only because of recent improvements in irrigation systems. *Mountain* courses tend to have drastic changes in elevation and lots of water. *Tropical* courses are found in the Caribbean, Mexico, and anyplace with jungles.

Fairways are constructed in a variety of shapes. The most common shapes include:

- *Corridored* fairways use trees to direct the golfer to the green.
- *Dogleg* fairways are crooked, designed to hide the green, and require shot placement.
- *Flat* fairways were the standard type of fairways before earth moving equipment was available.
- *Island* fairways create landing areas surrounded by hazards.
- *Linear* fairways are flat and straight - the flag can be seen from the tee.
- *Mounded* fairways are an evolution of the original dunes found in links courses.
- *Rolling* fairways many difficult downhill lies.
- *Split* fairways allow golfers to choose more than one path to the green. Fairways are usually split by a strand of trees.
- *Tilted* fairways slope to one side.

Greens can be classified by their contours and size. Typical contours include:

- *Bowled* greens have depressions and slopes.
- *Decked* greens have multiple flat areas.
- *Elevated* greens are raised above the fairway.
- *Island* greens are surrounded by water or other hazards.
- *Mounded* greens have convex shapes or crowns.
- *Postage stamp* greens are very small and get a large amount of foot traffic for size of the green.
- *Sloped* greens have very gradual inclines or drastic tilts.
- *Swaled* greens have gentle meandering paths that direct the ball to the edge of the green.
- *Undulating* greens are rolling and very wavy.

Typical grass found in golf courses are described below. Each type of grass has different characteristics which require different hitting and putting strategies.

Grass Type	Where Found	Green Speed
Bent Grass	Cool climates for greens	Very fast
Bermuda Grass	Humid climates, fairways, greens, and rough	Very slow
Bluegrass	Cool climates	Average
Fescue	Sandy soil links courses, greens	Slow
Kikuyu	Mild climates	Average
Poa Annua	Natural US grass for greens	Average
Rye Grass	Cool weather courses, mostly for rough areas	----------
Zoysia	Warm climates - popular in Japan	Very slow

GOLFING

Bunkers are constructed and designed for specific purposes. The following describe the wide variety of bunkers you may find:

- *Carry* bunkers are flat and usually protrude onto the fairways. These are designed to be shot over.
- *Collection* bunkers are typically deep and designed so that balls roll into them. They can be so deep that the only way out of them is to hit the ball sideways or backward.
- *Definition* bunkers can be deep or shallow and define a particular target area such as a green, landing area from the tee, etc.
- *Face* bunkers are part of a green. As golfers approach the green, face bunkers hide the flag and are difficult to maneuver around.
- *Pot* bunkers are small, round, and steep. These are typically found on links courses and are very difficult to escape from.
- *Saving* bunkers are found around greens and are designed to stop the ball from rolling down elevated greens or going out of bounds.
- *Target* bunkers are used to show golfers where to hit the ball to on dogleg fairways.
- *Waste* bunkers are long hazards along the side of the fairway and are designed to protect the ball from rolling into problem areas. Sometimes, waste bunkers have islands built into them.

Bunkers contain four types of sand - coral, limestone, river, and silica. The sand used depends the course location and is usually local rather than imported. *Coral* sand, found in tropical courses, is loose with large particles which cause the ball to sit on top of the sand. *Limestone* is found in inland courses and the ball lie depends on the particular consistency of the sand which can be either very powdery or coarse. *River* sand is hard so that the ball sits up on the sand. *Silica* sand is very white and powdery which creates many buried lies.

Golf courses are described by three parameters - par, course rating, and slope. Each hole also has a handicap parameter. *Par* for each course is calculated on a hole by hole basis and summed for the entire course. Par for each hole is based on the yardage to the green plus an allowance of 2 putting strokes on the green. For example, for a 300 yard hole, a golfer is expected to reach the green in 2 shots and putt twice to get a par 4.

Par	Men's Yardage	Women's Yardage
3	Less than 251	Less than 211
4	251-470	211-400
5	Greater than 471	401-575
6	Not Applicable	Greater than 575

Course rating is the score that a scratch player is expected to have on a particular course and varies for women and men. It is based on yardage and is used to calculate personal handicaps. Course ratings are calculated as the sum of the yardage ratings for each individual hole. For example, a 350 yard hole would be given a 3.9 yardage rating for men and a 4.2 rating for women. The table below provides hole yardage ratings for both men and women used by the US Golf Association. For each 0.1 increase in yardage rating, men's yardage increases 20 yards and women's 18 yards.

Yardage Rating	Men's Yardage	Women's Yardage
2.7	Less than 125	Less than 94
2.8	126-145	95-112
2.9	146-165	113-130
3.0	166-185	131-148
4.0	366-385	311-328
4.5	466-485	401-418
5.0	566-585	491-508
5.5	Greater than 665	Greater than 580

Slope is a measure of how difficult a course is to play and calculated for each tee box on a course. Slope is calculated by taking into account length of course, number and type of hazards (sand traps, water, etc.), narrowness of the fairways, and greens design (size, flatness, etc.). The higher the slope; the more difficult the course. Courses with slopes of 113 are considered average, slopes under 113 easier, slopes around 120 more difficult, and slopes over 130 are very hard. The lowest slope rating is 55 and the highest 155.

Golf course score cards include a *handicap* for each hole. The handicap is a number from 1-18 on an 18 hole course. These numbers are an indication of which holes are the hardest on the course. A handicap 1 hole is the toughest hole while a handicap 18 hole is the easiest.

The better known designers are listed below along with a of a well known and a local course they designed. By far, Cornish and Ross were the most prolific designers in New England.

Architect	Well Known Courses	Local New England Courses
Geoffrey Cornish	Mt. Snow Resort, Mt. Snow, VT	Exeter Country Club, Exeter, RI
George Crumb	Pine Valley, Philadelphia, PA	None
Pete Dye	TPC at Sawgrass, Ponte Vedra, FL	None
George Fazio	Butler National, Chicago, IL	Tumble Brook Country Club, Bloomfield, CT
William Flynn	Cherry Hills, Engelwood, CO	None
Robert Trent Jones	Augusta National GC, Augusta, GA	Haystack Golf Course, Wilmington, VT
Herbert Leeds	Myopia Hunt Club, Hamilton, MA	Kebo Valley Club, Bar Harbor, ME
Charles Blair Macdonald	Yale University, New Haven, CT	None
Alister Mackensie	Cypress Point, Pebble Beach, CA	None
Jack Nicklaus	Muirfield Village, Dublin, OH	None
Donald Ross	Oak Hill, Rochester, NY	Manchester Country Club, Bedford, NH
George C. Thomas	Riviera, Pacific Palisades, CA	None
A. W. Tillinghast	Winged Foot, Mamaroneck, NY	Berkshire Hills Country Club, Pittsfield, MA
Dick Wilson	Shinnecock Hills, Southampton, NY	None
Hugh Wilson	Merion, Ardmore, PA	None

Unusual Golf Courses

There are some very unusual golf courses throughout the world. The Hunting and Equestrian Club in Kuwait is constructed entirely on sand. Greens are built on hard packed sand coated with oil to keep the sand from blowing away and golfers carry artificial turf to hit off the sand fairway. The course with the highest elevation is the Tuctu Club in Peru at 14,335 feet above sea level while the course with the lowest elevation is a 9 hole course in Kallia along the Dead Sea at 1,250 feet below sea level. The coldest course is the High Country Club which is 400 miles inside the arctic circle. The course with the longest hole is the Black Mountain Club in North Carolina with a 745 yard 17th hole. The Oak Ridge Golf Club in Wellesley Island New York has 19 holes - players can discard their worst hole score. Millwood Farms Golf Course in Massachusetts has only 14 holes.

Golf Balls

Golf balls have evolved over the years. In the 1400s, golf balls were constructed of wet goose or chicken feathers stitched in a covering of several pieces of wet leather. As the water dried, the feathers expanded and the leather shrank forming a hard ball. These balls were called *featheries*.

In 1848, featheries were replaced by the gutta-percha, a one piece ball made from Malaysian tree sap. The *gutties*, as they were called, were smooth but became cut and nicked over time. After it was discovered that the nicks made the ball perform better, hand hammered gutties were created which became the precursor of the modern dimpled ball. Spalding was the first American company to manufacture gutties in the United States in 1898.

GOLFING

In 1898, Coburn Haskell invented a wound rubber ball covered with gutta-percha. These balls later revolutionized the game of golf and were referred to as *Haskells*.

Today, there are two basic types of balls: two piece balls and three piece balls. Two piece balls have a solid core center and a cover. Three piece balls have a soft center, a rubber winding, and a cover. Both two and three piece balls are covered with surlyn, balata, or other synthetic materials. Balata is derived from the sap of the bulletwood tree. Because it required cutting down trees to create the balata, in 1979, manufacturers stopped extracting balata from trees and started using synthetic balata. Typical brands by type of ball are shown in the table below.

3 Piece Balata	3 Piece Surlyn	2 Piece Surlyn
Ben Hogan 428 Balata	Dunlop CD	Bridgestone Precept EV
Bridgestone Rextar Pro	Dunlop Maxfli CD	Dunlop Maxfli MD
Dunlop Maxfli HT	Spalding Top-Flite Tour	Nitro 440
Hansberger Ram Tour	Titleist DT	Pinnacle and Pinnacle Gold
Slazenger 420 Interlok	Wilson ProStaff Control	Spalding Top-Flite Magna
Spalding Tour Edition	Wilson Staff TC	Spalding Top-Flite XL
Titleist Tour Balata		Titleist MVC
Wilson Ultra Tour		Wilson Ultra

How balls are constructed and the type of material used creates *backspin*. Three piece balata balls provide more back spin than three piece Surlyn balls which in turn provide more than two piece Surlyn balls. In terms of revolutions per minute, a 5 iron will produce 7,000 revolutions per minute on a three piece balata ball and only 5,500 on a two piece Surlyn ball. Typically, depending on the club, three piece balata balls spin 6-8% more than three piece Surlyn balls and three piece Surlyn balls spin 12-18% more than two piece Surlyn balls.

Golfers can choose balls for a variety of performance characteristics including distance control, spin or accuracy control, or a combination of the two. Distance balls are used to get yardage and reduce the possibilities of hooks and slices. Most of the distance balls are two piece construction with Surlyn, Zylin, or Trylin covers. Typically, these balls are used by higher handicap players.

High spin balls are used by pros or low handicap players to control the ball around the greens. Most of the high spin balls are three piece with soft, thin balata covers although there are some with Surlyn coverings. Since balata covered balls can get damaged easily, they should not be used by the casual golfer.

The combination balls balance distance and spin control. They are used to get lower or higher trajectories or as good overall performance balls. The combination balls can be either two piece with a soft cover or three piece with a hard cover.

A brief comparison between Surlyn and Balata covered balls is summarized below.

Balata	Surlyn
Softer cover	Harder cover
More spin	Less spin
Cuts and marks up easily	Harder to cut and mark up
Easier to backspin, fade, or draw ball	Harder to backspin, fade, or draw ball
Less distance	More distance
More expensive	Less expensive
Shorter life	Longer life

Compression is a measure of how much a ball will deform when hit. The lower the compression, the more the ball will distort and the softer it will feel on impact. Typically, balls have a nominal compression of 100, 90, or 80. A ball with a compression of 80 includes any compression between 80 and 90. Lower compression balls are good for players who cannot swing the club at a high rate of speed and high compression balls are better suited for solid hitters. Casual players should use balls with 90 compression or less.

Compression will change over time. A balata covered wound ball loses compression over a 3-4 year period while a Surlyn covered ball loses compression more slowly. A solid two piece ball actually hardens over time and gains compression.

Cold weather affects a ball's performance. Higher compression balls (100) will feel harder and hurt your hands on mis-hits and Balata covered balls will travel significantly less distance. Two piece balls are preferred for colder weather.

Distance/Little Spin	High Spin	Combination
Bridgestone Precept EV Extra Distance	Ben Hogan 428 Balata	Bridgestone EV Extra Spin
Bridgestone Precept 15	Ben Hogan 428 Balata	Hansberger Laser Lite
Bullet .444	Bullet USA Balata	Hansberger Laser Acra
Hansberger Ram Tour XDC	Hansberger Laser Tour	Hansberger Laser TDX 150
Ben Hogan 428 Distance	Hansberger Ram Tour Pro Balata	Ben Hogan 428 Hi-Spin
Maxfli MD 80, 90, 100	Hansberger Ram Tour Balata LB	Maxfli CD
Maxfli HT Distance	HPG Ram Tour LB	Maxfli HT Hi-Spin
Nitro Golf 440 Nitro	Maxfli HT Balata	Nitro Golf SGP
Slazenger 420p	Maxfli HT Tour Balata	Slazenger 420t Touch-Spin
Slazenger 420i	Maxfli XF	Spalding Top-Flite Magna EX
Spalding Top-Flite Hot XL	Nitro Golf Plus 8	Spalding Top-Flite Tour SD
Spalding Top-Flite XL	Slazenger 420 Interlok	Spalding Top-Flite Magna
Spalding Molitor	Slazenger 420t Touch Spin	Titleist DT
Titleist Pinnacle Distance	Spalding Top-Flite Z-Balata	Titleist HP2
Titleist Pinnacle Gold	Titleist Tour Balata	Titleist Super Pinnacle Plus
Titleist HVC	Titleist Professional	Titleist Pinnacle Performance
Wilson Original Ultra DPS	Wilson Classic Wound Ultra DPS	Wilson Ultra 500 Competition
Wilson Ultra 500 Distance	Wilson Ultra Tour Balata	Wilson P.S. Performance/Spin
Wilson ProStaff Distance	Wilson ProStaff Control	Wilson ProStaff Tour Trajectory

Balls are limited in weight to 1.62 ounces and generally 1.68 inches in diameter. Companies are now experimenting with lighter weight balls which benefit players with slow swing speeds. Some companies (ie, Top Flite Magna) have manufactured oversized balls. These balls reduce the potential for hooks and slices but do not go as far as regular sized balls.

Ball recovery from water is becoming a big business. For example, over 150,000 golf balls are recovered annually just from the 17th hole of Stadium Course at TPC at Sawgrass[1]. The recovery companies charge the golf course approximately $0.10 - $0.14 per ball and the course then charges customers about a dollar each for the same balls.

Do balls retrieved from water still go as far as new balls? Golf Digest conducted tests on balls submerged for 8 days, 3 months, and 6 months using 3 piece balata balls and 2 piece Surlyn balls. They found that balata balls lost approximately 2.5% (8 days) to 6.4% (6 months) of their distance[2]. Two piece Surlyn balls lost 2.3% (8 days) to 3.3% (6 months) of their distance.

Golf Clubs

Club design evolved as ball construction changed. With featheries, club heads were thin and long and made from hardwood such as apple. Shafts were constructed from ash and grips from sheepskin. Irons could not be used because they destroyed the featheries.

---

[1] Golf Digest, September 1996

[2] Golf Digest, September 1996

With the introduction of gutties, wood club heads became shorter and fatter and shafts were constructed of hickory. Because of the harder ball surface, iron headed clubs could now be used with the gutties.

With the introuction of wound rubber balls, club heads were constructed with harder woods such as persimmon. The heads on irons became larger and grooves became the accepted norm.

With the introduction of steel shafts in the 1930s, golf clubs became numbered and manufacturers started making matched sets. Previously, clubs were sold individually with a variety of specifications and each had names rather than numbers. This technology also brought the cost of equipment down so that the common man could afford to play.

Irons	Name
1	Driving Iron
2	Mid-Iron
3	Mid-Mashie
4	Mashie Iron or Jigger
5	Mashie
6	Spade Mashie
7	Mashie Niblick
8	Pitching Niblick
9	Niblick

Woods	Name
1	Driver
2	Brassie
3	Spoon
4	Cleek
5	Baffy

Today, you can buy a variety of golf clubs. For example, you can buy woods with wood heads, regular metal wood heads, titanium heads, steel shafts, and graphite shafts. Some head designs have grooves, others do not. (While the grooves on irons are used to create ball spin, grooves on woods and metal woods are cosmetic only and do not affect the ball in any way.)

Club lengths can also vary from manufacturer to manufacturer and player to player. Most players (tall and short) can use standard length clubs. Because a player is taller does not necessarily mean that they should have longer clubs. Typically, some players choose slightly longer clubs (0.5 to 1.0 inches) when their handicap is low to get a little more distance on their shots.

To measure club length, lay the club head flat to the ground with the shaft standing up. Put a long hard 48 inch ruler along the shaft so that it touches the heel of the club head and the ground. The length of the club is the distance between the ground and the top of the circle on the grip cap. The bulge at the very end of the cap should not be counted. Standard club lengths in inches are shown below. Clubs labeled Ladies Petites are usually one half or one inch shorter than normal ladies' length.

Woods	Men's	Ladies'
1	43.0	42.0
2	42.5	41.5
3	42.0	41.0
4	41.5	40.5
5	41.0	40.0
6	40.5	39.5
7	40.0	39.0
8	39.5	38.5
9	39.0	38.0

Irons	Men's	Ladies'
1	39.5	38.5
2	39.0	38.0
3	38.5	37.5
4	38.0	37.0
5	37.5	36.5
6	37.0	36.0
7	36.5	35.5
8	36.0	35.0
9	35.5	34.5
PW/SW	35.5	34.5

Swingweight measures a golf club's weight distribution and varies between clubs and manufacturers. One way to think about swingweight is that the heavier the head of the club, the higher the swingweight number and the heavier the club feels in your hands. Swingweight numbers range from A-0 (lightest) to G-9 (heaviest) and can be changed by adding/removing weight from the grip, shaft, or head. Swingweight should be consistent from club to club. In the past, most manufacturers used D-1 or D-2 as the standard swingweights for most clubs. Recently, due to innovations in shaft, head, and grip materials, larger swingweight clubs (D-7) such as the Taylor Made's Burner Bubble are being manufactured. Swingweight is measured using a swingweight scale. However, you can measure your clubs' swingweight using the following method. Weigh your club in ounces with a kitchen scale. Next, use your finger to balance your club along the shaft. Mark the shaft at the balance point on the shaft. Next, measure the distance in inches from the balance point to a point 12 inches from the grip end of the club. Multiply this distance by the weight of the club to get a number in units of inch-ounces. Finally, use the table below to determine the swingweight[3].

Inch-Ounces	Irons	Woods
220	B-8	C-0
222	B-9	C-1
224	C-0	C-2
226	C-1	C-3
228	C-2	C-4
230	C-3	C-5
232	C-4	C-6
234	C-5	C-7
236	C-6	C-8
238	C-7	C-9
240	C-8	D-0

Inch-Ounces	Irons	Woods
242	C-9	D-1
244	D-0	D-2
246	D-1	D-3
248	D-2	D-4
250	D-3	D-5
252	D-4	D-6
254	D-5	D-7
256	D-6	D-8
258	D-7	D-9
260	D-8	E-0
260	D-9	E-1

Since clubs with the same number can vary in loft from manufacturer to manufacturer, the same player can potentially hit further with a 6 iron than a 5 iron. Keeping this caveat in mind, the distances an average player can hit the ball are shown below.

Club	*Yards*
1 Wood	205 - 220
2 Wood	195 - 215
3 Wood	185 - 210
4 Wood	175 - 205
5 Wood	165 - 195
Pitching Wedge	95 - 100
Sand Wedge	85 - 90

Club	*Yards*
1 Iron	185 - 190
2 Iron	175 - 180
3 Iron	165 - 170
4 Iron	155 - 160
5 Iron	145 - 155
6 Iron	135 - 145
7 Iron	125 - 140
8 Iron	115 - 130
9 Iron	105 - 115

Building Your Own Clubs

Golf clubs can be easily made by amateurs using only a hacksaw, epoxy, ruler, and two-sided tape. You simply buy the separate components (heads, shafts, and grips), cut the shaft to size with a hacksaw, epoxy the heads to the shafts, and use two-sided tape to attach the grips to the shafts. Of course, the components you buy will have a large effect on how the clubs turn out. Many of the companies that sell components also offer free instructions for making your own clubs. Some of the major component manufacturers include:

The Golfworks, 1800-848-8358
Golfsmith, 1800-848-2582
UT Golf, 1-800-666-6033

Dynacraft, 1-800-321-4833
Pro-Swing, 1-800-451-1995
Original Clubkits, 1-800-359-3739

---

[3] Golf Digest, October 1996

Golf Rules

While most players are familiar with the rules for golf, there are several situations where the average player may have some confusion on what is permissible. The following paragraphs describe some of these situations and the rules associated with them. It is not by any means comprehensive. To get more details on these rules, please refer to the Rules of Golf published by the United States Golf Association.

Ball Lands in Water and is Unplayable: If the ball lands in water and you cannot play the ball, you have several options. First, you can hit the ball from where it was hit previously. Second, you can play the ball from two club lengths away but no closer to the hole. Finally, you can move the ball anywhere back on a line extended from the hole through where your ball entered the water. No matter which choice you make, you take a penalty stroke. If the ball crosses over water, hits the grass on the other side, and then rolls into the water, you cannot play the ball from the other side of the water where the ball rolled in. You must extend an imaginary line from the stick through where the ball originally crossed the water and play the ball from anywhere along that line behind where the ball crossed the water. A penalty stroke is taken.

Ball Lands Out of Bounds or Cannot Be Found: When the ball lands out of bounds or is lost, you are required to go back to where you hit the original ball, hit another one, and take a penalty stroke. You cannot hit the ball from where it went out of bounds or was lost. If you think the ball may have gone out of bounds but you're not sure, you should hit a provisional ball, then go look for your first ball. You should not spend more than 5 minutes looking for your ball. If you do find your ball after the 5 minutes, you cannot play that ball -- you must play the provisional ball.

Ball Lands in Hazard (Sand or Water) and is Playable: If a ball lands in a sand trap or water hazard, there are several rules that you must follow to play the ball. First, you cannot touch the sand or water with your club before hitting the ball. Second, if the ball is buried, you cannot lift it to clean it but you can brush away sand or leaves until you see a portion of the ball. Third, if there are man made objects (wrappers, rake, etc.) around the ball, you can move them. However, you cannot remove natural objects such as leaves, branches, acorns, etc.

Natural Impediments: You cannot bend, break, or move growing vegetation at all. If you do, you incur a 2 stroke penalty. However, you can move loose natural impediments away from the ball such as twigs, leaves, branches, rocks, etc. unless the ball is in a sand trap.

Man Made Impediments: You can move moveable man made impediments such as a hose or a cart marker without any penalties. However, you cannot move or get relief from an out of bounds marker. If an unmoveable man made impediment (drinking fountain, bench, etc.) interferes in any way with your swing or stance, you can drop the ball one club length away (but not nearer the hole) without any penalty.

Ground Under Repair: If the ball lands in this area, you can drop the ball one club length away (but not nearer the hole) without any penalty. If you are sure you lost your ball in the repair area, you can also drop the ball one club length away (but not nearer the hole) without any penalty.

Cannot Play a Ball (Unplayable Lie): You can declare a ball unplayable anywhere on the course except in a water hazard. If you take an unplayable lie, you have three choices. First, you can hit the ball from where it was hit previously. Second, you can play the ball from two club lengths away but no closer to the hole. Finally, you can move the ball anywhere back on a line extended from the hole through your ball backwards. In a sand trap, you have all three options. However, unless you select to hit the ball from where you previously hit it, the other two options require that the ball stay within the sand hazard. No matter which choice you make, an one-stroke penalty is incurred.

Hitting Flag Stick: If you are on the green and hit the flag stick with your putt, you incur a 2 stroke penalty. If you are off the green and hit an attended flag stick, you incur the same 2 stroke penalty.

Calculating Your Handicap

Handicap is a method of allowing players of different capabilities to compete on a level playing field. In a competition, each player subtracts their handicap from their course score. The resulting score can then be compared to all other players. This score should be close to the course par rating.

How do you calculate your handicap? Handicaps are calculated using the best 10 scores of the most recent 20 games. The calculation is as follows. First, calculate the *handicap differential* for each game played:

Handicap Differential = (Your Score - Course Rating) X (113/Slope Rating)

Next, take the average of the 10 lowest handicap differentials and multiply the average by 0.96. The resulting number is your *handicap index*. Does this mean that you should score the course rating plus your handicap index whenever you play golf? The answer is no - typically this will happen only 20 percent of the time.

Short Game Statistics

Almost two thirds (63%) of all golf is played from less than 60 yards away from the green[4]. A breakdown of which clubs are used is shown below. The bottom line is that good putting can improve your score more so than any other stroke. As the old saying goes, "Drive for show and putt for dough".

Long Game		Short Game	
Driver	15%	Putting	43%
Fairway Woods	10%	Chips & Pitches	13%
Medium Irons	4%	Short Irons	7%
Long Irons	3%		
Trouble Shots	5%		

Discount Golf Cards

Discount golf cards allow golfers to try new courses at discounted rates. Some of the national and local golf cards are shown below.

Card	States	Phone
Golf Access	National	800-359-4653
Golf Card International	National	800-321-8269
Golf Digest Golf & Travel Club	National	800-666-8459
Green Card	New England	800-333-7274
Hale Irwin's Golfer's Passport	National	800-775-GOLF
National Golfer's Club	National	544 Wilmore Court, Smyrna, TN
The Golf Card	National	800-321-8269
American Lung Ass. Golf Privilege	Connecticut	203-289-5401
American Lung Ass. Golf Privilege	Maine	207-622-6394
American Lung Ass. Golf Privilege	Massachusetts	508-947-7204
American Lung Ass. Golf Privilege	New Hampshire	800-835-8647
American Lung Ass. Golf Privilege	Rhode Island	401-421-6487
American Lung Ass. Golf Privilege	Vermont	802-863-6817
New Hampshire Golf Links Golf Card	New Hampshire	800-639-1941
Vermont Golf Links Golf Card	Vermont	800-639-1941

---

[4] The Player's Course, Chuck Hogan

Tournament Scoring Systems

Tournaments can be played using a variety of scoring systems. Some of the most frequent ones used are:

Stroke Play or Medal Play: In low gross stroke play, the least number of strokes for the whole game wins. In low net, the handicap is subtracted first. Then, the low score wins.

Match Play: Two players compete and the winner is the one who wins the most holes. The player with the least amount of strokes for a particular hole wins that hole.

Best-Ball: This is a team event where each player subtracts their stroke allowance at each hole. The lowest net score of all team players is written at each hole. The total for the game is the team's best ball score.

Scramble: This is a team event. Each player tees off and then the team selects the ball which is in the best position. All members pick up their ball and play from that spot. This is repeated for all shots.

Foursomes: Two players play one ball. Players take turns, each hitting alternative shots. One player tees off at the odd numbered holes and the other at the even numbered holes.

Chapman (2 man teams): Each player hits their tee shot. Each player takes a second shot using their partner's ball. Now, they select the best ball. The player who did not hit the best ball plays. Players alternate shots until the hole is completed.

Pinehurst (2 man teams): Pinehurst is similar to Chapman. The difference is that after each player hits a drive, the best drive is chosen and players alternate from there.

Hero-Bum (4 man teams): This is a team competition where the best and worst scores are counted and summed for each hole. This can be played net or gross. Lowest team score wins.

Tournaments

A few of the more well known international and national tournaments include the following:

- The British Open has been held annually since 1860. The first Open was played at Prestwick, a 12 hole course, with 8 professional players. The following year, amateurs were allowed to play.
- The Masters is held annually since 1934 and is played at the Augusta National Club in Georgia. Players are invited to compete in this tournament.
- US Open held annually since 1894. One of the most important events in promoting US golf was the Open at the Brookline Country Club in Massachusetts where Francis Ouimet beat Vardon.
- The Ryder Cup, begun in 1927, is a biennial men's national team competition that includes members from all over Europe and the US. US players qualify based on major tournament championships. European players qualify on money won on PGA tournaments.
- The Walker Cup was started in 1922 and now held in odd numbered years. This is an amateur team competition for men from the United States, England, Scotland, and Ireland.
- The Curtis Cup (started in 1932 and held in even numbered years) is an amateur competition for women, from the United States, England, Scotland, and Ireland.
- The World Cup (professional) has been held annually since 1953.
- The World Amateur Team Championship is held biennially since 1958.
- PGA Championship has been held annually since 1916.
- US Amateur and the US Women's Amateur has been held annually since 1895.
- US Women's Open has been held annually since 1946.
- The LPGA Championship has been held annually since 1955.

Golfing Records and Facts

Some of the best documented golfing records are presented below:

- There are over 40,000 holes in one made in the United States each year. The odds of making a hole in one has been calculated to be 11,000 to 1 for the average player. The odds for a PGA Tour player improves substantially to 750 to 1.
- Thirty players are recorded by Golf Digest as having aced every par 3 at a particular course (Grand Slammers).
- Robert Mitera holds the record for the longest men's hole in one of 447 yards at the Miracle Hills Golf Course in Omaha on October 7, 1965. The longest women's straight hole in one was 393 yards by Marie Robie at Furnace Brook Golf Course in Wollaston, Massachusetts on September 4, 1949.
- The youngest person to make a hole in one was Tommy Moore (6 years and month old) at the 145 yard hole in Woodbrier Golf Course in Martinsburg, West Virginia on March 8, 1968.
- The most hole in ones record (59) is held by amateur Norman Manley from Long Beach, California.
- Kevin Murray has the record for the longest double eagle - 647 yards at the Guam Navy Club on January 3, 1982.
- The best 18 hole score (59) on the PGA Tour was made by Al Geiberger in the Danny Thomas Memphis Classic in 1977.
- The best 18 hole score (62) on the LPGA Tour was made by Vicky Fergon in the San Jose Classic in 1984.
- The best 18 hole score (61) on the Senior PGA Tour was made by Bud Allin in the FHP Health Care Classic in 1995.
- The fewest putts on an 18 hole LPGA Tour round was 17 made by Joan Joyce in 1982 at the Lady Michelob tournament.
- The fewest putts on an 18 hole PGA Tour round was 18 made by Jim McGovern in 1992 at the Federal Express Saint Jude Classic.
- Surprisingly, an average PGA Tour player only hits twelve greens (66%) and less than ten (50%) fairways per round. (A player hits a green when he reaches the green on 1 hit for a par 3 hole, 2 hits for a par 4 hole, and 3 hits for a par 5 hole. A fairway is hit when the ball lands in the fairway on the tee shot.) Remember this statistic when you are having a bad golf day.

Publicly Traded Golf Companies

If you can't make money on the golf course, you might want to try your luck on the stock exchange. There are many golf companies that you can invest your money with in the stock market. Some of these companies are shown below with their associated stock symbols.

AGT Sports (AGTP)	Golf Enterprises (GLFE)
Aldila (ALDA)	Griptec (GTEC)
Arnold Palmer Golf Company (APGC)	Golf Training Systems (GTSX)
Ashworth (ASHW)	Golf Ventures (GVIM)
Brassie Golf (PUTT)	Las Vegas Discount Golf (LVDG)
Bullet Golf (PARR)	National Golf Properties (TEE)
CoastCast (PAR)	Royal Grip (GRIP)
Cutter & Buck (CBUK)	St. Andrews Golf (SAGC)
Carlyle Golf (CRLG)	Snake Eyes (SNKE)
Callaway Golf (ELY)	Sport Haley (SPOR)
Family Golf Centers (FGCI)	Senior Tour Development (SRTR)
Fila Golf (FGLF)	S2 Golf (GOLF)
GlenGate (GLNN)	

Golf Sites on the Internet

Internet golf sites have been developed by manufacturers, retailers, magazines, golf organizations, and celebrities. The following list shows several of the internet addresses for these sites.

Major Manufacturers

Alien Sport: aliensport.com
Callaway Golf: www.callawaygolf.com
Cleveland Golf: www.clevelandgolf.com
Cobra: www.cobragolf.com
Cubic Balance Golf: www.cubicbalance.com
Daiwa Golf: www.daiwa.com/golf/
Dynacraft: www.dynacraftgolf.com
Goldsmith: www.golfsmith.com
Killer Bee: www.killerbee.com
Lynx Golf: www.lynxgolf.com

Mizuno: www.mizunogolf.com
Odyssey Golf: www.odysseygolf.com
Ping: www.pinggolf.com
Powerbilt Golf: powerbiltgolf.com
Ram Golf: www.ramgolf.com
Taylor Made: www.taylormadegolf.com
Titleist: www.titleist.com
Tommy Armour Golf: www.tommyarmour.com
Top-Flite: www.topflite.com
Wilson: www.wilsonsports.com

Golf Celebrities

Crenshaw: www.bencrenshaw.com
Couples: ce.ecn.purdue.edu/~tayloran/
Daly: www.gripitanddripit.com
Floyd: www.rayfloyd.com
Langer: www.geocities.com/Paris/3298/

Norman: www.golfonline.com/greatwhiteshark/index.html
Palmer: www.sandhills.org/plantation/palmer.htm
Penick: www.sport.net/golf/harvey.html
Snead: www.ici.net/cust_pages/ddemelo/SSnead.html
Woods: www.calweb.com/~jamiecap/tiger/woods.html

Golf Magazines and Periodicals

Divot: golf.com/divot
Fairway Bunker: www.fairwaysgolf.com
Golf Digest: golf.com/golfdigest/
Golf Magazine: www.GOLFonline.com
Golf Shop Operations: golf.com/gso/

Double Eagle: www.doubleeagle-golfmag.com
GolfWatch Weekly: www.best.com/~net53/golfwatch/
GolfWorld: golf.com/golfworld/
Links Online: www.golfweb.com/linksonline/
The Total Golfer: www.totalgolfer.com

Golf Organizations

PGA: www.pga.com
LPGA: www.lpga.com
USGA: www.usga.org
National Golf Foundation: www.ngf.org

American Society Golf Course Architects: www.golfdesign.org
Professional Clubmakers Society: www.proclubmakers.org
National Left Handed Golfers: www.dca.net/golf/index.html
Club Manager Association: www.bus.msu.edu/broad/shb/ha/cmaa

News and Information Related

CBS Sports: www.cbs.com/sports/golf/
ESPN: espnet.sportszone.com/pga/
GolfWeb: www.golfweb.com/ga97/index.html
NBC Golf: golf.com

PGA Tour: www.pgatour.com
USA Today: www.usatoday.com/sports/golf/sg.htm
Golf Yellow Pages: www.yellowpagesgolf.com

There are also golf news groups and a mailing list you can subscribe to. The news groups are rec.sport.golf and pdx.golf. The mailing list is called Golf-L and can be subscribed at listserv@UBVM.CC.Buffalo.edu.

Golf Collecting

Collecting old golf equipment such as clubs, balls, books, sports cards, etc. is another way to enjoy golf. If you decide to collect golf paraphernalia, you might get started by contacting the following golf collectible shops:

>   Morton Olman
>   325 West 5th Street
>   Cincinnati, OH 45202
>   513-241-7797
>
>   Golf's Golden Years
>   2929 North Western Avenue
>   Chicago, IL 60618
>   708-934-4108
>
>   Richard Donovan
>   P.O. Box 7070
>   305 Massachusetts Avenue
>   Endicott, NY 13760
>   607-786-0883
>
>   George and Susan Lewis
>   P.O. Box 291
>   Mamaroneck, NY 10543
>   914-698-4579

Featheries are not easy to find. However, if you run across one, you should look for the names of the early makers of featheries: Allan Robertson, James Gourlay, Willie Dunn, Tom Morris, and Thomas Stewart. For gutties, look for Allan Robertson, James Gourlay, Willie Dunn, and Robert Forgan.

National Golf Associations and Societies

There are many national golf associations. Most of the associations are for professionals (architects, course superintendents, manufacturers, etc.) but there are others for non-professionals such as golf collectors. A comprehensive list of national associations are shown below. Local golf associations can be found in each state's section of this book.

- Amateur Golfers Association of America, 42143 A. Alvarado, Temecula, CA 92590 714-695-1201
- American Association of Real Golfers, 1522 NW 26th Place, Cape Coral, FL 33909, 813-283-3393
- American Golf Association, 1034 W. Arrow Highway, San Dimas, CA 91773, 818-967-9225
- American Golf Sponsors, 4 Sawgrass Village, St 140F, Ponte Vedra Beach, FL 32082, 904-285-4222
- American Junior Golf Association, 2415 Steeplechase Lane, Roswell, GA 30076 404-998-4653
- American Modified Golf Association, PO Box 5287, Albany, GA 31706, 912-883-5017
- American Society of Golf Course Architects, 221 North LaSalle St, Chicago, IL 60601, 312-372-7090
- Association of Disabled American Golfers, 7700 E. Arapahoe Road, Suite 350, Englewood, CO 80112, 303-220-0921
- Association of Golf Merchandisers, 16743 East Palisades, Fountain Hills, AZ 85268, 602-837-0708
- Business and Charity Golf Link, 4450 California Avenue, Bakersfield, CA 93309, 805-322-5601
- Club Managers Association of America, 1733 King Street, Alexandria, VA 22313, 703-739-9500
- Executive Women's Golf League, 1 Marlwood Lane, Palm Beach Gardens, FL 33418, 407-694-2820
- Fairways Association, 1560-1 Newbury Road, #211, Newbury Park, CA 91319
- Futures Golf Tour, 2003 US 27 South, Sebring, FL 33870 813-385-3320
- Golf Coaches Associations of America, PO Box 215, Raymore, MO 64083, 800-356-9794
- Golf Club Collectors Association, 640 East Liberty Street, Girard, OH 44420
- Golf Collectors Society, PO Box 20546, Dayton, OH 45420, 913-649-4618
- Golf Course Builders Association of America, 920 Airport Road, Suite 210, Chapel Hill, NC 27514, 919-942-8922
- Golf Course Superintendents Association of America, 1421 Research Park Drive, Lawrence, KS 66046, 913-841-2240
- Golf Manufacturers and Distributors Ass., PO Box 37324, Cincinnati, OH 45222, 513-631-4400

GOLFING

- Golf Range and Recreation Association of America, 211 West 92nd Street, #58, New York, NY 10025, 212-865-8676
- Golf Writers Association of America, PO Box 328054, Farmington Hills, MI 48332, 313-442-1481
- Hole-In-One Association, 8350 N. Central Expressway, #730, Dallas, TX 75206, 800-527-6944
- Hook a Kid on Golf, 2611 Old Okeechobee Road, West Palm Beach, FL 33409, 407-684-1141
- Indoor Golf Association of America, 2665 Ariane Drive, #208, San Diego, CA 92117, 619-273-0373
- International Association of Golf Administrators, 6550 York Avenue South, Suite 405, Edina, MN 55435, 612-927-4643
- Junior Golf Council, PO Box 452, Winter Park, FL 32790, 407-351-GOLF
- The Junior Tour, 6905 Telegraph Road, Bloomfield Hills, MI 48301, 313-642-6120
- Ladies' Professional Golf Association, 2570 Volusia Avenue, Suite B, Daytona Beach, FL 32114
- LPGA Junior Girls Golf Club, 2570 Volusia Ave, Suite B, Daytona Beach, FL 32114, 904-254-8800
- Miniature Golf Association of America, PO Box 32353, Jacksonville, FL 32237, 904-781-4653
- Minority Golf Association of America, 38 Jessup Avenue, Quogue, NY 11959, 516-653-6008
- National Advertising Golf Association, 5520 Park Avenue, Trumbull, CT 06611, 203-373-7000
- National Amputee Golf Association, PO Box 1228, Amherst, NH 03031 603-673-1135
- National Association of Left Handed Golfers, PO Box 801223, Houston, TX 77280, 713-464-8683
- National Golf, 1625 I Street NW, Washington, DC 20006, 202-625-2080
- National Advertising Golf Association, 5520 Park Avenue, Trumbull, CT 06611, 203-373-7000
- National Golf Cart Manufacturers Association, 2 Ravinia Drive, Atlanta, GA 30346, 404-394-7200
- National Golf Coaches Association, Wake Forest University, PO Box 7346, Winston-Salem, NC 27107, 919-759-5751
- National Golf Course Owners Association, 14 Exchange Street, Charleston, SC 29401, 803-577-5239
- National Golf Foundation, 1150 South US Highway One, Jupiter, FL 33477 800-733-6006
- National Golf Reporters Association Scorecard, 1180 Spring Centre South Boulevard, #301, Altamonte Springs, FL 32714, 407-869-8448
- National Golf Salesmen Association, PO Box 6134, Scottsdale, AZ 85261, 602-860-6348
- National Hole-In-One Association, 730 Campbell Centre, Dallas, TX 75206, 800-527-6944
- PGA Tour, 112 TPC Boulevard, Ponte Vedra Beach, FL 32082 904-285-3700
- Nike Tour, 112 TPC Boulevard, Ponte Vedra Beach, FL 32082 904-285-3700
- Professional Association of Golf Officials, 1735 Market Street, Philadelphia, PA 19103, 215-979-3200
- Professional Clubmakers' Society, 70 Persimmon Ridge Drive, Louisville, KY 40245, 502-241-2816
- Professional Golf Association, Golf House, Far Hills, NJ 07931 908-234-2300
- Professional Golf Club Repairmen's Association, 2053 Harvard Avenue, Dunedin, FL 34698, 813-733-4348
- Professional Golfers' Association Hall of Fame, 100 Avenue of Champions, Palm Beach Gardens, FL 33410, 407-624-8400
- Professional Golfer Club Repairmen's Association, 2053 Harvard Avenue, Dunedin, FL 34698, 813-733-4348
- Professional Putters Association, PO Box 35237, Fayetteville, NC 28303, 919-485-7131
- Senior PGA Tour, 112 TPC Boulevard, Ponte Vedra Beach, FL 32082 904-285-3700
- Tournament Sponsors Association, 604 Country Club Drive, Stockbridge, GA 30281, 404-474-0258
- United States Golf Association, Golf House, Liberty Corner, Far Hills, NJ 07931 908-234-2300
- United States Golfers' Association of America, 100 Avenue of the Champions, Palm Beach Gardens, FL 33418 407-624-8400
- United States Putting Association, 27-A Big Spring Road, Clear Spring, MD 21722, 301-791-9332
- US Blind Golfers Association, 160 Lago Vista Boulevard, Casselberry, FL 32707, 407-332-0700
- US Golf Federation, 6320 Canoga Avenue, #1600, Woodland Hills, CA 91367, 818-595-1099
- US Golf Teachers Association, 2010 Harbortown Dr., Suite G, Fort Pierce, FL 34948, 407-464-3272
- Women's Public Links Golf Association, 3647 Poe Street, San Diego, CA 92107, 619-222-9166
- Worldwide Golf Marketers Association, PO Box 950492, Lake Mary, FL 32795, 407-321-6322
- Women's Trans National, PO Box 5682, Midland, TX 79704, 915-683-7745

Golf Museums

Most of the golf museums are located outside of New England. The exception is the Ouimet museum in Weston, Massachusetts.

- American Golf Hall of Fame, Foxburg Country Club, Harvey Rd, Foxburg, PA 16036, 412-659-3196
- Golf Association Golf House, Liberty Corner Road, Far Hills, NJ, 07931, 908-234-2300
- Golf Museum and Library, James River Country Club, 1500 Country Club Road, Newport News, VA, 23606, 804-595-3327
- Jude E. Poynter Golf Museum, College of the Desert, 43-500 Monterey Avenue, Palm Desert, CA, 92260, 619-341-0994
- Miller Golf Library & Museum, 1 Industry Hills Parkway, City of Industry, CA 91744, 818-854-2354
- Ouimet Museum and Golf House, 190 Park Road, Weston, MA, 02193, 617-891-6400
- PGA World Golf Hall of Fame, PGA Boulevard, Box 1908, Pinehurst, NC 28374, 919-259-6651
- World Golf Hall of Fame, St. Augustine, St. John's County, FL

Glossary of Selected Golf Terms

If you want to sound like you know what you are talking about on the golf course, learn the following golf terms.

Ace: A hole made in one stroke on a par 3 hole.
Airball: Swinging and missing the ball completely.
Albatross: A British term for making a hole 3 strokes under par. Also known as a Double Eagle.
Apron: The grassy area surrounding the putting surface of the green.
Back door: The rear part of the hole.
Banana ball: A ball that curves to the right in the shape of a banana when sliced.
Beach: Sand hazard.
Bend one: To hook or slice a ball.
Bite: The ball stopping quickly rather than rolling because of backspin.
Blade: A type of putter.
Blast: Taking a large amount of sand when hitting out of a sand trap.
Blind hole: Putting green cannot be seen by player as he approaches.
Borrow: To play ball to one side of the hole to compensate for the slope of the green.
Bowker: A horrible shot that hits something (tree, rock, spectator) and goes back into play.
Bunt: To hit a short shot intentionally.
Cross handed grip: A grip where left hand is below the right for a right-handed player.
Dead ball: When there is no doubt ball will be sunk on the next shot.
Deuce: A hole made in two shots.
Dogleg: A bend in the fairway.
Drain: To hole a putt.
Draw shot: A controlled shot that curves (hooks) from left to right.
Dub: A shot that is completely missed or badly hit.
Duffer: A beginning or unskilled golfer.
Dunk: To hit ball into water hazard.
Explosion shot: A shot out of a sand trap that takes along a lot of sand.
Fade: A shot where the ball turns slightly from left to right the air at the very end.
Fan: Missing the ball completely when swinging.
Fat shot: The club hits the ground well behind the ball.
Flash trap: A small sand bunker that is shallow.
Flier: A ball hit without spin that goes greater distance than normal.
Flub: A badly hit shot usually caused by hitting the ground well before the ball.

GOLFING

Fringe: The grassy area surrounding the putting surface of the green.
Frog hair: The grassy area surrounding the putting surface of the green.
Grand Slam: The four major championships: British Open, PGA Championship, U.S. Open, and Masters.
Hacker: A beginning or unskilled golfer.
Hanging lie: A ball lieing on a downhill slope.
Hole high: A ball even with the hole but off to the side.
Honor: The privilege of hitting first from the tee given to the winner of the last hole.
Hook: A shot that curves to the left of the target.
Jungle: Heavy rough.
Lag: To intentionally putt the ball short.
Mallet: A wide-headed putter.
Match play: A competition that is won by the number of holes won rather than strokes.
Medal play: A competition that is won by the number of strokes used to complete the round.
Mulligan: A shot allowed to be replayed in a friendly match.
Nineteenth hole: The clubhouse bar.
Overclubbing: Using a club that gives more distance than needed.
Pitch: A short shot with a high arc and landing with backspin.
Pitch and run: Short shot hit with lower arc and landing with less backspin so that it runs after it lands.
Pot bunker: A small, deep sand trap.
Pull: A ball that goes to the left of the target with little curve.
Punch: A low shot made by hitting the club down into the ball with a short swing usually used for shooting into the wind.
Push: A ball that goes to the right of the target with little curving.
Qualifying school: Where golfers attempt to qualify for the PGA and LPGA tours.
Rough: Long grass areas next to fairways or greens.
Rub of the green: When ball is deflected by something that it shouldn't have - bad luck.
Run: The distance the ball rolls on the ground or when it lands.
Sandy: Making a par after landing in a bunker.
Scratch player: A player who has a zero handicap.
Shank: A shot hit by the hosel of the club.
Shotgun start: When players start at different holes at the same time in a tournament.
Sidehill lie: A ball lieing either above or below your feet.
Skulling: Hitting the ball at or above the center.
Sky: To hit beneath the ball sending it much higher than desired.
Slice: A ball that curves right.
Snake: A long putt traveling over several breaks in the green.
Snipe: A hooked ball that drops quickly.
Sole: The bottom of the club head.
Spray: Hitting the ball way off the target line.
Stimpmetre: Green speeds are measured with a stimpmetre.
Stony: To hit ball close to the flagstick.
Stroke play: A competition that is won by the number of strokes used to complete the round.
Stymie: When a ball is in the line of a player's putt or when a tree is in the way of a shot.
Swale: Depression or dip in the fairway or green.
Sweet spot: The center of the face of the club - the perfect place to hit the ball.
Texas wedge: Using the putter from off the green.
Thread: To shoot the ball through a narrow area.
Tiger tee: Slang for the back tee.
Top: Hitting the ball above the center making it roll or hop.
Underclubbing: Using a higher lofted club than needed for the distance.
Waggle: Shaking the club head before swinging at the ball.
Whiff: Swinging and missing the ball completely.
Whins: British term for very heavy rough.
Wormburner: A ball that flies just over the ground but still gets distance.

NEW ENGLAND GOLF COURSES

Public Courses	608	Private Courses	215
Total Courses	823	Percent Public Courses	74%
18 Hole Public Courses	322	9 Hole Public Courses	286
Total Golfers	1,341,000	Total Rounds of Golf	26,366,100
Percent Female Golfers	18.0%	Percent Senior Golfers	23.6%
Rounds Per Course	32,311	Rounds Per Golfer	19.7
Golfers Per Course	1,629	Courses Per 100 Square Miles	1.24
Average Weekend Fee	$25.26	Average Weekday Fee	$22.45
Average Weekend Fee w/Power Cart	$36.08	Average Weekday Fee w/Power Cart	$33.12
Average Slope	115.4	Average Yardage	5,557

New England has 823 golf courses - 215 are private and 608 are open to the public. Slightly more than 10 percent of the population of New England plays golf which translates into more than 1.3 million golfers playing over 26 million rounds of golf every year[1] (19.7 rounds per golfer). Almost one quarter of the golfers are senior citizens and 18 percent are women.

The public can play on three quarters of all golf courses. Most of the private courses are located in Connecticut, Massachusetts, and Rhode Island. Approximately one half of all the public courses are 18 holes - Connecticut has the largest percentage of 18 hole courses of all the New England states.

State	Public Courses	Percent Public	Percent 18 Holes
Connecticut	100	58%	63%
Maine	110	92%	37%
Massachusetts	223	68%	58%
New Hampshire	85	91%	53%
Rhode Island	29	60%	45%
Vermont	61	94%	54%
Total	608	74%	53%

Slightly more than 5 percent of all golfers and golf courses in the United States are found in New England. Overall, New England has golfer and golf course densities similar to the US averages. There are 1,629 golfers per course and 32,311 rounds of golf are played annually per golf course in New England.

Massachusetts is the most active golfing state. Massachusetts has the largest percentage of golfers and golf courses in New England and almost half of all golf rounds are played on Massachusetts courses.

An average golfer in Rhode Island and Vermont plays more rounds of golf than golfers in the other New England states. Maine and Vermont appear to have less crowded golf courses -- they have the least number of golfers per course and the least number of golf rounds per course.

State	Courses	Percent	Golfers	Percent	Rounds	Percent
Massachusetts	326	39.6%	593,000	44.2%	11,089,100	42.1%
Connecticut	172	20.9%	398,000	29.7%	8,039,600	30.5%
Maine	119	14.5%	92,000	6.9%	1,913,600	7.3%
New Hampshire	93	11.3%	110,000	8.2%	1,727,000	6.6%
Vermont	65	7.9%	42,000	3.1%	978,600	3.7%
Rhode Island	48	5.8%	106,000	7.9%	2,618,200	9.9%
New England	823	100%	1,341,000	100%	26,366,100	100%
United States	14,000		24,563,000		499,000,000	

---

[1] The Complete Golfer's Almanac 1995

NEW ENGLAND

Greens Fees

On weekends, the average greens fees to play a round of 18 holes on New England public courses is $25.26 ($30.50 for 18 hole and $19.24 for 9 hole courses). (These costs include courses where power cart fees are part of the greens fees.) Golfers can save $2.81 by playing during the week when the average greens fee is $22.45 ($27.19 for 18 hole and $17.13 for 9 hole courses).

Vermont and New Hampshire are the most expensive states to play golf in New England. Maine and Rhode Island with a large percentage of 9 hole courses are the least expensive states to play in New England.

State	Weekend Greens Fee	Weekday Greens Fee
Vermont	$30.66	$27.97
New Hampshire	$28.13	$24.94
Massachusetts	$26.15	$22.71
Connecticut	$24.12	$20.87
Rhode Island	$22.03	$19.10
Maine	$20.29	$19.28
New England	**$25.26**	**$22.45**

The most expensive courses in New England are the 18 hole Sky Meadow Country Club in Nashua, Massachusetts ($85) and the 9 hole Someday Golf Resort in West Dover, Vermont ($47). The least expensive courses are the 9 hole Granddad's Invitational Golf Course in Newark, Vermont ($5) and the 18 hole Connecticut Golf Land in Vernon, Connecticut ($6).

Power cart rentals will cost an average of $19.73 for two players in New England. On weekends, a round of golf with a power cart will cost each golfer an average of $36.08.

Slope and Yardage

The average slope rating of all public New England courses from the white tees is 115.4 (117.7 for 18 hole and 112.0 for 9 hole courses). The courses with the highest slope rating from the white tees are the 18 hole Shattuck Golf Course in Jaffrey, New Hampshire (143) and the 9 hole Countryside Golf Club in Dunbarton, New Hampshire (132). The easiest 18 and 9 hole courses are the Rockland Golf Course in Massachusetts (78) and the Monadnock Country Club in Peterborough, New Hampshire (76), respectively. Connecticut courses, on average, have higher slope ratings than other states' courses.

The average yardage of all public courses from the white tees is 5,834 yards for 18 hole and 5,245 yards for 9 hole courses. On average, Rhode Island has the longest courses and Connecticut the shortest courses. The courses with the longest yardage from the white tees are the 18 hole Sugarloaf Golf Club in Carrabassett Valley (6,850) and the 9 North Hill Country Club in Duxbury, Massachusetts (7,002). The shortest 18 and 9 hole courses are the Connecticut Golf Land in Vernon, Connecticut (980) and the Westerly Winds Golf Course in Westbrook, Maine (1,600), respectively.

State	Slope	Yards
Connecticut	116.7	5,449
Vermont	116.2	5,531
Massachusetts	115.3	5,588
Rhode Island	115.9	5,711
New Hampshire	115.4	5,562
Maine	113.8	5,563
New England	**115.6**	**5,537**

CONNECTICUT GOLF COURSES

Public Courses	100	Private Courses	72
Total Courses	172	Percent Public Courses	58%
18 Hole Public Courses	63	9 Hole Public Courses	37
Total Golfers	398,000	Total Rounds of Golf	8,039,600
Percent Female Golfers	17.1%	Percent Senior Golfers	22.2%
Rounds Per Course	46,742	Rounds Per Golfer	20.2
Golfers Per Course	2,314	Courses Per 100 Square Miles	3.44
Average Weekend Fee	$24.12	Average Weekday Fee	$20.87
Average Weekend Fee w/Power Cart	$34.85	Average Weekday Fee w/Power Cart	$31.42
Average Slope	116.7	Average Yardage	5,449

Connecticut has 172 golf courses but only 100 courses are open to the public. A large percentage (12%) of the Connecticut population plays golf which translates into 398,000 golfers playing over 8 million rounds of golf every year[1] (20.2 rounds per golfer). Almost one quarter of the golfers are senior citizens and 17 percent are women.

Connecticut is one of the most crowded states to play golf in New England. There are 2,314 golfers per golf course and, annually, 46,742 rounds of golf are played per golf course.

The proportion of 18 hole golf courses is higher in Connecticut than any other New England state. Courses with 18 holes or more comprise almost two thirds of all the public golf courses.

Greens Fees

Connecticut is average in greens fees versus the other states in New England. On weekends, the average greens fees to play a round of 18 holes on public courses is $24.12 ($26.59 on 18 hole courses and $19.92 on 9 hole courses). (These costs include courses where power cart fees are part of the greens fees.) Golfers can save $3.25 by playing during the week when the average greens fee is $20.87 ($23.16 for 18 hole courses and $16.97 for 9 hole courses).

The courses with the most expensive greens fees are the 18 hole Silver Spring Country Club in Ridgefield ($50) and the 9 hole Quarry Ridge in Portland ($36). The least expensive courses are the 9 hole Highland Greens Golf Course in Prospect and the Twin Lakes Golf Course in North Branford ($10) and the 18 hole Connecticut Golf Land in Vernon ($6).

A power cart rental for two players in Connecticut will cost an average of $19.15. On weekends, a round of golf with a power cart will cost each golfer an average of $34.85.

Slope and Yardage

Connecticut courses are, on average, harder to play than the other New England states' courses. The average slope rating of all public courses from the white tees is 116.7 (117.2 for 18 hole and 115.3 for 9 hole courses). The courses with the highest slope rating from the white tees are the 18 hole Lyman Orchards Golf Club - Player in Middlefield (131) and the 9 hole Rolling Greens Golf Club in Rocky Hill (131). The easiest 18 and 9 hole courses are the Portland Golf Course West (79) and the Lisbon Country Club (102), respectively.

Connecticut courses are shorter on average than other states. The average yardage of all public courses from the white tees is 5,449 (5,747 yards for 18 hole and 4,942 yards for 9 hole courses). The courses with the longest yardage from the white tees are the 18 hole Fairchild Wheeler Golf Course (Black) in Fairfield

---

[1] The Complete Golfer's Almanac 1995

CONNECTICUT

(6,402) and the 9 hole Woodhaven Country Club in Bethany (6,384). The shortest 18 and 9 hole courses are the Connecticut Golf Land in Vernon (980) and the Twin Lakes Golf Course in North Branford (1,702), respectively.

Public Courses Rated in Top 10 by Golf Digest

Rank	Course
1	Richter Park Golf Club
2	Portland Golf Course
3	Pine Valley Country Club
4	Tallwood Country Club
5	Crestbrook Park Golf Course

Rank	Course
6	Stanley Golf Course
7	Shennecossett Municipal Golf Course
8	Lyman Orchards Golf Club
9	H. Smith Richardson Golf Course
10	Timberlin Golf Club

Oldest Golf Courses

Club	Year
Greenwich Country Club (private)	1892
Woodstock Golf Course	1896
Shennecossett Golf Club	1898
New Haven Country Club (private)	1898
Country Club of Waterbury (private)	1898

Club	Year
Highland Golf Club (private)	1900
Pequabuck Golf Club of Bristol	1902
Wee Burn Country Club	1902
Pine Orchard Yacht and Country	1903

Private Golf Courses

Course	Town
Aspetuck Valley Country Club	Weston
Birchwood Country Club	Westport
Black Hall Club	Old Lyme
Burning Tree Country Club	Greenwich
Chippanee Golf Club	Bristol
Clinton Country Club	Clinton
Connecticut Golf Club	Easton
Country Club of Darien	Darien
Country Club of Fairfield	Fairfield
Country Club of Farmington	Fairfield
Country Club of New Canaan	New Canaan
Country Club of Waterbury	Waterbury
Ellington Ridge Country Club	Ellington
Fairview Country Club	Greenwich
Farmington Woods Golf Course	Avon
Farms Country Club	Wallingford
Glastonbury Hills Country Club	South Glastonbury
Golf Club of Avon	Avon
Greenwich Country Club	Greenwich
Greenwoods Country Club	Winsted
Harry Brownson Country Club	Huntington
Hartford Golf Club	West Hartford
Heritage Village Course	Southbury
Highfield Club	Middlebury
Highland Golf Club	Shelton
Hop Meadow Country Club	Simsbury
Innis Arden Golf Club	Old Greenwich
Lake Waramaug Country Club	New Preston
Litchfield Country Club	Litchfield
Madison Country Club	Madison
Milbrook Club	Greenwich
Mill River Country Club	Stratford
New Haven Country Club	Hamden
New London Country Club	Waterford
Newtown Country Club	Newtown
Norfolk Country Club	Norfolk

Course	Town
Oak Lane Country Club	Woodbridge
Old Lyme Country Club	Old Lyme
Oronoque Village Country Club	Stratford
Patterson Club	Fairfield
Pautipaug Country Club	Baltic
Pine Orchard Yacht and CC	Branford
Quinnatisset Country Club	Thompson
Race Brook Country Club	Orange
Redding Country Club	West Redding
Ridgewood Country Club	Danbury
Rock Ridge Country Club	Newtown
Rockrimmon Country Club	Stamford
Rolling Hills Country Club	Wilton
Round Hill Club	Greenwich
Sharon Country Club	Sharon
Shore Haven Golf Club	East Norwalk
Shuttle Meadow Country Club	Kensington
Silvermine Golf Club	Norwalk
Stanwich Club	Greenwich
Stonington Country Club	Stonington
Suffield Country Club	Suffield
Tamarack Country Club	Greenwich
Torrington Country Club	Torrington
Tower Ridge Country Club	Simsbury
TPC at River Highlands	Cromwell
Tumble Brook Country Club	Bloomfield
Vineyard Valley Golf Club	Pomfret
Wallingford Country Club	Wallingford
Wampanoag Country Club	West Hartford
Washington Golf Club	Washington Depot
Watertown Golf Club	Watertown
Wee Burn Country Club	Darien
Wethersfield Country Club	Wethersfield
Woodbridge Country Club	Woodbridge
Woodway Country Club	Darien
Yale Golf Course	New Haven

Golf Schools and Instruction

- Ben Jackson's New England Golf Academy, PO Box 432, Mystic 06355, 800-790-6342
- Connecticut Golf Academy, 460 Hillstown Road, Manchester, 203-646-6773
- Golf Digest Instruction School, 5520 Park Avenue, Box 395, Trumbull, 06611, 203-373-7128
- Western Hills Golf Teaching, 78 Kendle Road, Jewett City, 203-376-4325

Retailers

- Carimbo Sport, 177 Post Road West, Westport, 06880, 203-226-3361
- Class Act Custom Golf, 97 Center Street, Shelton, 06484, 203-924-5534
- Connecticut Pro Golf Discount, 437 Westport Avenue, Norwalk, 203-846-4864
- Custom Golf of Connecticut, 2802 Summer Street, Stamford, 06905, 203-323-7888
- Crestbrook Park Pro Shop, 834 Northfield Road, Watertown, 203-945-3054
- Darien Golf Center, 233 Post Road, Darien, 203-655-2788
- David McGoldrick Pro Shop, 2390 Easton Turnpike, Fairfield, 203-372-6265
- De Mane Golf Inc., 35 Chapel Street, Greenwich, 06831, 203-531-9126
- East Hartford Golf Center, 55 Hillside Avenue, East Hartford, 203-291-0660
- Fore Golf, 38 Ward Street, Middletown, 06457, 860-347-5353
- Fore Your Swing, 19 Edgewood Drive, Greenwich, 06831, 203-869-1600
- Golf Bum, 464 Boston Post Road, Orange, 203-799-0042
- Golf Country, 464 Foxon Road, North Branford, 203-484-2531
- Golf Day, 55 Boston Post Road, Orange, 203-891-8899
- Golf Day, 3135 Berlin Turnpike, Newington, 203-667-8434
- Golfers Warehouse, 196 Boston Post Road, Orange, 203-799-3606
- Golfers Warehouse, 216 Murphy Road, Hartford, 203-522-6829
- Golfers Warehouse, 65 Albany Turnpike, Canton, 203-693-6286
- Golf Supply, 21 Tolland Turnpike, Manchester, 203-646-7454
- Golf USA, 573 Bank Street, New London, 203-442-6502
- Grantmore Golf Center, 3060 Berlin Turnpike, Newington, 203-666-4653
- Great Golf Pro Shop, 1580 Post Road, Fairfield, 06430, 203-254-1223
- Las Vegas Discount Golf, 909 Post Road, Fairfield, 203-254-8337
- Mickey Homa Pro Shop, 2425 Morehouse Highway, Fairfield, 203-255-6094
- Mulligan Shop, 3936 Whitney Avenue, Hamden, 06518, 203-248-4762
- Nevada Bob's, 35 Lake Avenue, Danbury, 203-797-9691
- Nevada Bob's, 520 Hartford Turnpike, Vernon, 203-872-0228
- New England Golf Supply, 405 Queen Street, Southington, 203-628-8544
- New England Golf Supply, 1041 Orange Avenue, West Haven, 203-932-2512
- New England Golf Supply, 21 Tolland Turnpike, Manchester, 203-646-7454
- On Par Golf Shop, 40 Plaza Court, Groton, 203-448-2396
- Paul McGuire Golf Shop, 175 Shelton Road, Monroe, 203-268-5811
- Play it Again Sports, 15 South Main Street, West Hartford, 06107, 860-523-4692
- Play it Again Sports, 1153 Tolland Turnpike, Manchester, 06040, 860-646-3732
- Pro Golf Discount, 437 Westport Avenue, Norwalk, 203-846-4864
- Pro Golf Discount, Park Road, Waterbury, 203-755-6828
- Red Tees Only, 719 Post Road East, Westport, 06880, 203-222-0671
- Rob's Golf Shop, 855 Wilbur Cross Highway, Berlin, 203-828-6118
- Tee to Green Golf, 142 Kings Highway, Groton, 203-448-3114

CONNECTICUT

Golf Associations and Touring Clubs

- Connecticut Golf Association, Golf House, 35 Cold Spring Road, Suite 212, Rocky Hill, 06067
- Connecticut PGA, 35 Cold Spring Road, Suite 212, Avon, 06001, 203-678-0380
- Connecticut Women's Golf Association, 27 Hunter Road, Rocky Hill, 06067, 203-257-4653
- Executive Women's Golf League, Fairfield, 203-363-7045
- Executive Women's Golf League, Middlefield, 203-889-8358
- Southern NE Women's Golf Association, 5 Ranch Drive, Trumbull, 06611, 203-268-2519
- USGA, Northeast Region, 186 Prospect Street, Willimantic, 06226, 908-234-2300

Driving Ranges and Practice Areas

Name	Address	Town	Phone
Belmont's Ridgefield Golf	824 Ethan Allen Highway	Ridgefield	203-431-8989
Bethany Airport Golf	Route 63	Bethany	203-393-0485
Bristol Driving Range	West Street	Bristol	203-621-4447
Brown's Driving Range	1849 Poquonock Avenue	Windsor	203-688-1745
Burlington Golf Center	522 Spielman Highway	Burlington	203-675-7320
Connecticut Golf Academy	460 Hillstown Avenue	Manchester	203-646-6773
Connecticut Golf Center	562 Danbury Road	New Milford	203-354-0012
Danbury Golf Center	94 Mill Plain Road	Danbury	203-743-2190
Dantes	160 Old Hebron Road	Colchester	203-537-4653
East Hartford Golf Center	55 Hillside Street	East Hartford	203-291-0660
East Lyme Driving Range	298 Flanders Road	Niantic	203-739-1183
Fore Golf	38 Ward Street	Middletown	860-347-5353
Fore Your Swing	50 Holly Hill Lane	Greenwich	203-869-1600
Golf Country	Route 80	Branford	203-484-2531
Golf Links at Landmark	6 Landmark Square	Stamford	203-326-4920
Golf Training Center	145 Main Street	Norwalk	203-847-8008
Grantmore Golf Center	199 Deming Street	Newington	203-666-4653
Great Golf Learning Center	10 Eastview Drive	Farmington	203-676-0151
Great Golf Learning Center	1580 Post Road	Fairfield	203-254-0385
Malerba Golf Driving Range	650 New London Turnpike	Norwich	203-889-5770
Mar Lea Mini Golf	244 Boston Turnpike	Bolton	203-649-7023
Milford Driving Range	Oronoque Road	Milford	203-878-6735
Nippy's Field	Norwich Avenue	Norwich	203-886-0865
Pleasant Valley Golf Center	452 South Street	Somers	203-749-5868
Practice Tee	12 South Main Street	East Windsor	203-623-9422
Prospect Golf Driving Range	144 Waterbury Road	Prospect	203-758-4121
Sullivan's Total Practice Center	685 Hale Street	Suffield	203-668-5700
The Only Game In Town	275 Valley Service Road	North Haven	203-234-7166
Torza Driving Range	211 Sullivan Avenue	South Windsor	203-289-5646
Tunxis Fore Driving Range	1024 Farmington Avenue	Farmington	203-674-8924
Western Hills Golf	Park Road	Waterbury	203-596-7424
Woodbury Golf & Driving Range	787 Main Street South	Woodbury	203-263-0357

Year-Round Courses

Course	Town	Holes
Alling Memorial GC	New Haven	18
Banner Lodge CC	Moodus	18
Cedar Knob GC	Somers	18
East Gaynor Brennan GC	Stamford	18
Fairchild Wheeler - Black	Fairfield	18
Fairchild Wheeler - Red	Fairfield	18
Goodwin GC - Goodwin	Hartford	18
Goodwin GC - North	Hartford	9
H. Smith Richardson GC	Fairfield	18
Hunter Memorial GC	Meriden	18

Course	Town	Holes
Indian Springs GC	Middlefield	9
Lisbon CC	Lisbon	9
Meadowbrook CC	Hamden	9
Orange Hills CC	Orange	18
Pequabuck GC of Bristol	Pequabuck	18
Shennecossett GC	Groton	18
Short Beach GC	Stratford	9
Sleeping Giant GC	Hamden	9
Trumbull GC	Groton	18
Woodhaven CC	Bethany	9

Courses By Town

Course	Town	Holes
Bel Compo GC	Avon	18
Woodhaven CC	Bethany	9
Sunset Hill GC	Brookfield	18
Canaan CC	Canaan	9
Canton Public GC	Canton	9
Chanticlair GC	Colchester	9
Skungamaug River GC	Coventry	18
Twin Hills CC	Coventry	18
Richter Park GC	Danbury	18
Brooklyn Hill CC	Danielson	9
Hillside Links	Deep River	9
Copper Hill CC	East Granby	9
East Hartford GC	East Hartford	18
Cedar Ridge GC	East Lyme	18
Ellington Golf Center	Ellington	9
Grassmere CC	Enfield	9
Fairchild Wheeler - Black	Fairfield	18
Fairchild Wheeler - Red	Fairfield	18
H. Smith Richardson GC	Fairfield	18
South Pine Creek Park	Fairfield	9
Tunxis Plantation - Green	Farmington	18
Tunxis Plantation - Red	Farmington	9
Tunxis Plantation - White	Farmington	18
Westwoods GC	Farmington	18
Minnechaug GC	Glastonbury	9
Bruce Memorial GC	Greenwich	18
Shennecossett GC	Groton	18
Trumbull GC	Groton	18
Laurel View CC	Hamden	18
Meadowbrook CC	Hamden	9
Sleeping Giant GC	Hamden	9
Goodwin GC - Goodwin	Hartford	18
Goodwin GC - North	Hartford	9
Keney Park GC	Hartford	18
Rockledge CC	Hartford	18
Blackledge CC - A/G	Hebron	18
Blackledge CC - G/L	Hebron	18
Blackledge CC - L/A	Hebron	18
Tallwood CC	Hebron	18
Timberlin GC	Kensington	18
Hotchkiss School GC	Lakeville	9
Lisbon CC	Lisbon	9
Stonybrook GC	Litchfield	9
Manchester CC	Manchester	18
Hunter Memorial GC	Meriden	18
Indian Springs GC	Middlefield	9
Lyman Orchards - Jones	Middlefield	18
Lyman Orchards - Player	Middlefield	18
Miner Hills GC	Middletown	9
Mill Stone CC	Milford	9

Course	Town	Holes
Whitney Farms GC	Monroe	18
Banner Lodge CC	Moodus	18
Hop Brook CC	Naugatuck	9
Stanley Municipal - Blue/Red	New Britain	18
Stanley Municipal - White	New Britain	9
Alling Memorial GC	New Haven	18
Candlewood Valley CC	New Milford	18
Indian Hill CC	Newington	18
Twin Lakes GC	North Branford	9
Oak Hills GC	Norwalk	18
Norwich GC	Norwich	18
Fenwick GC	Old Saybrook	9
Grassy Hill CC	Orange	18
Orange Hills CC	Orange	18
Elmridge GC	Pawcatuck	18
Pequabuck GC of Bristol	Pequabuck	18
Portland GC	Portland	18
Portland GC West	Portland	18
Quarry Ridge	Portland	9
Highland Greens GC	Prospect	9
Putnam CC	Putnam	9
Ridgefield GC	Ridgefield	18
Silver Spring CC	Ridgefield	18
Rolling Greens GC	Rocky Hill	9
Cedar Knob GC	Somers	18
Gainfield Farms GC	Southbury	9
Patton Brook CC	Southington	18
Pine Valley GC	Southington	18
Southington CC	Southington	18
East Gaynor Brennan GC	Stamford	18
Sterling Farms GC	Stamford	18
Pequot GC	Stonington	18
Short Beach GC	Stratford	9
Airways GC	Suffield	18
Raceway GC	Thompson	18
Eastwood CC	Torrington	9
Tashua Knolls GC	Trumbull	18
Connecticut Golf Land	Vernon	18
Pilgrim's Harbor GC	Wallingford	9
East Mountain GC	Waterbury	18
Western Hills GC	Waterbury	18
Crestbrook Park GC	Watertown	18
Buena Vista GC	West Hartford	9
Simsbury Farms GC	West Simsbury	18
Westport Longshore GC	Westport	18
Willimantic CC	Willimantic	18
Millbrook GC	Windsor	18
Farmingbury Hill CC	Wolcott	9
Harrisville GC	Woodstock	9
Woodstock GC	Woodstock	9

CONNECTICUT

Easiest Courses

Course	Town	Holes	Slope
Portland GC West	Portland	18	79
Westwoods GC	Farmington	18	85
Patton Brook CC	Southington	18	93
Sunset Hill GC	Brookfield	18	100
Lisbon CC	Lisbon	9	102
Airways GC	Suffield	18	103
Woodstock GC	Woodstock	9	104
Goodwin GC - Goodwin	Hartford	18	108
Pequot GC	Stonington	18	108
Hop Brook CC	Naugatuck	9	109
Grassmere CC	Enfield	9	111
Hotchkiss School GC	Lakeville	9	111
Minnechaug GC	Glastonbury	9	111

Hardest Courses

Course	Town	Holes	Slope
Fairchild Wheeler - Black	Fairfield	18	124
H. Smith Richardson GC	Fairfield	18	124
Indian Hill CC	Newington	18	124
Laurel View CC	Hamden	18	124
Lyman Orchards - Jones	Middlefield	18	124
Bel Compo GC	Avon	18	125
Crestbrook Park GC	Watertown	18	125
Silver Spring CC	Ridgefield	18	125
Richter Park GC	Danbury	18	126
Pilgrim's Harbor GC	Wallingford	9	127
Whitney Farms GC	Monroe	18	127
Lyman Orchards - Player	Middlefield	18	131
Rolling Greens GC	Rocky Hill	9	131

Least Expensive Courses

Course	Town	Holes	Fee
Connecticut Golf Land	Vernon	18	$6
Highland Greens GC	Prospect	9	$10
Twin Lakes GC	North Branford	9	$10
Ellington Golf Center	Ellington	9	$12
Hillside Links	Deep River	9	$12
Mill Stone CC	Milford	9	$12
Short Beach GC	Stratford	9	$13
Fenwick GC	Old Saybrook	9	$14
Meadowbrook CC	Hamden	9	$14
Trumbull GC	Groton	18	$15
Lisbon CC	Lisbon	9	$16
Woodstock GC	Woodstock	9	$16
Brooklyn Hill CC	Danielson	9	$17
Cedar Ridge GC	East Lyme	18	$17

Most Expensive Courses

Course	Town	Holes	Fee
East Gaynor Brennan GC	Stamford	18	$30
Indian Hill CC	Newington	18	$30
Oak Hills GC	Norwalk	18	$30
Orange Hills CC	Orange	18	$30
Stonybrook GC	Litchfield	9	$30
Pequabuck GC of Bristol	Pequabuck	18	$31
Manchester CC	Manchester	18	$32
Sterling Farms GC	Stamford	18	$33
Quarry Ridge	Portland	9	$36
Grassy Hill CC	Orange	18	$40
Whitney Farms GC	Monroe	18	$42
Richter Park GC	Danbury	18	$44
Lyman Orchards - Jones	Middlefield	18	$49
Lyman Orchards - Player	Middlefield	18	$49
Silver Spring CC	Ridgefield	18	$50

Shortest Courses

Course	Town	Holes	Distance
Connecticut Golf Land	Vernon	18	980
Twin Lakes GC	North Branford	9	1,702
Ellington Golf Center	Ellington	9	1,716
Hillside Links	Deep River	9	1,864
South Pine Creek Park	Fairfield	9	2,146
Short Beach GC	Stratford	9	2,540
Trumbull GC	Groton	18	2,660
Gainfield Farms GC	Southbury	9	2,768
Highland Greens GC	Prospect	9	2,796
Cedar Ridge GC	East Lyme	18	2,958
Miner Hills GC	Middletown	9	3,400
Portland GC West	Portland	18	3,620
Buena Vista GC	West Hartford	9	3,664
Patton Brook CC	Southington	18	4,056
Westwoods GC	Farmington	18	4,407
Woodstock GC	Woodstock	9	4,500

Longest Courses

Course	Town	Holes	Distance
Hunter Memorial GC	Meriden	18	6,243
Western Hills GC	Waterbury	18	6,246
Rolling Greens GC	Rocky Hill	9	6,258
Whitney Farms GC	Monroe	18	6,262
Lyman Orchards - Player	Middlefield	18	6,269
Candlewood Valley CC	New Milford	18	6,295
Cedar Knob GC	Somers	18	6,298
Bel Compo GC	Avon	18	6,304
H. Smith Richardson GC	Fairfield	18	6,323
Richter Park GC	Danbury	18	6,325
Timberlin GC	Kensington	18	6,342
Crestbrook Park GC	Watertown	18	6,367
Laurel View CC	Hamden	18	6,372
Fairchild Wheeler - Red	Fairfield	18	6,382
Woodhaven CC	Bethany	9	6,384
Fairchild Wheeler - Black	Fairfield	18	6,402

Brooklyn Hill Country Club
Danielson, Connecticut

Woodhaven Country Club
Bethany, Connecticut

Connecticut

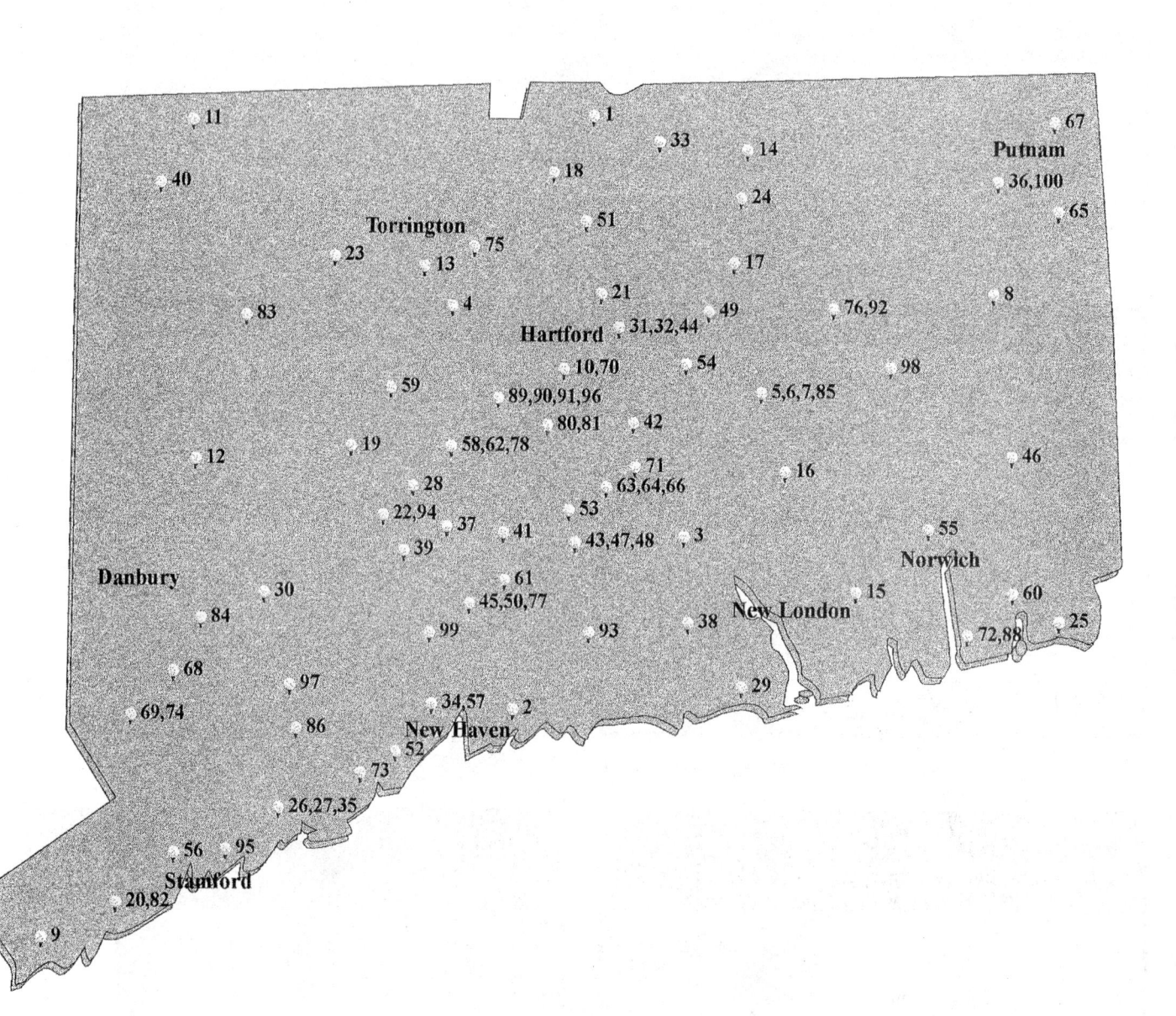

CONNECTICUT

1 Airways Golf Course
1070 South Grand Street, Suffield, CT 06078
203-668-4973

Weekend Fee	$20	*Weekday Fee*	$19
Power Cart Fee	$20	*Pull Carts*	Yes
Putting Green	Yes	*Driving Range*	No
Season	Mar 15 - Nov 15	*Credit Cards*	No
Pro	Wayne Leale	*Tee Times*	7 days
Comments	Flat, easy to walk, lots of water		
Directions	Hartford, I-91N, exit 40, Rt 20W, East Granby, 4th light right on East St		

Tee	Holes	Par	Rating	Slope	Yards
Red	18	71	65.0	103	5,154
White	18	71	65.0	103	5,493
Blue	18	71	66.0	106	5,845

2 Alling Memorial Golf Club
35 Eastern Street, New Haven, CT 06513
203-787-8014

Weekend Fee	$25	*Weekday Fee*	$24
Power Cart Fee	$20	*Pull Carts*	Yes
Putting Green	Yes	*Driving Range*	No
Season	Year-round	*Credit Cards*	No
Pro	John Olowski	*Tee Times*	3 days
Comments	Open, rolling hills, small greens		
Directions	I-91, exit 8, Rt 80E, right 2nd light, Eastern St		

Tee	Holes	Par	Rating	Slope	Yards
Red	18	72	68.0	121	5,070
White	18	72	68.0	119	5,884
Blue	18	72	69.5	123	6,241

3 Banner Lodge Country Club
100 Moodus Road, Moodus, CT 06469
203-873-9075

Weekend Fee	$23	*Weekday Fee*	$20
Power Cart Fee	$20	*Pull Carts*	Yes
Putting Green	Yes	*Driving Range*	No
Season	Year-round	*Credit Cards*	No
Pro	Tom Vece	*Tee Times*	7 days
Comments	Small greens, tree lined		
Directions	Rt 9, exit 7, Rt 154N, 1st light right, Rt 82, over bridge, left Rt 149, 0.5 mi Moodus Rd		

Tee	Holes	Par	Rating	Slope	Yards
Red	18	72	NA	118	5,800
White	18	72	68.9	118	5,950
Blue	NA	NA	NA	NA	NA

4 Bel Compo Golf Club
65 Nod Road, Avon, CT 06001
203-678-1358

Weekend Fee	$28	*Weekday Fee*	$23
Power Cart Fee	$24	*Pull Carts*	Yes
Putting Green	Yes	*Driving Range*	Yes
Season	Apr 1 - Nov 30	*Credit Cards*	No
Pro	Skip Rotondo	*Tee Times*	2 days
Comments	18th has a 2 tiered bunkered green		
Directions	I-84, exit 39, Rt 10N, 5 mi, on left after cross Rt 44		

Tee	Holes	Par	Rating	Slope	Yards
Red	18	72	71.6	112	5,452
White	18	72	70.1	125	6,304
Blue	18	72	73.4	131	7,028

5 Blackledge CC - Anderson/Gilead
180 West Street, Hebron, CT 06248
203-228-0250

Weekend Fee	$27	*Weekday Fee*	$25
Power Cart Fee	$20	*Pull Carts*	Yes
Putting Green	Yes	*Driving Range*	Yes
Season	Mar 15 - Dec 15	*Credit Cards*	No
Pro	Kevin Higgins	*Tee Times*	5 days
Comments	27 holes in total, scenic		
Directions	Rt 2E, exit 12, left, left 3rd stop sign West St		

Tee	Holes	Par	Rating	Slope	Yards
Red	18	72	71.2	116	5,518
White	18	72	69.6	118	6,173
Blue	18	72	72.3	123	6,853

6 Blackledge CC - Gilead/Links
180 West Street, Hebron, CT 06248
203-228-0250

Weekend Fee	$27	*Weekday Fee*	$25
Power Cart Fee	$20	*Pull Carts*	Yes
Putting Green	Yes	*Driving Range*	Yes
Season	Mar 15 - Dec 15	*Credit Cards*	No
Pro	Kevin Higgins	*Tee Times*	5 days
Comments	27 holes in total		
Directions	Rt 2E, exit 12, left, left 3rd stop sign West St		

Tee	Holes	Par	Rating	Slope	Yards
Red	18	72	NA	NA	NA
White	18	72	NA	NA	6,015
Blue	18	72	NA	NA	NA

7 Blackledge CC - Links/Anderson
180 West Street, Hebron, CT 06248
203-228-0250

Weekend Fee	$27	*Weekday Fee*	$25
Power Cart Fee	$20	*Pull Carts*	Yes
Putting Green	Yes	*Driving Range*	Yes
Season	Mar 15 - Dec 15	*Credit Cards*	No
Pro	Kevin Higgins	*Tee Times*	5 days
Comments	Tree lined, watered fairways		
Directions	Rt 2E, exit 12, left, left 3rd stop sign West St		

Tee	Holes	Par	Rating	Slope	Yards
Red	18	72	NA	NA	NA
White	18	72	NA	NA	6,058
Blue	18	72	NA	NA	NA

10 Buena Vista Golf Course
37 Buena Vista Road, West Hartford, CT 06107
203-521-7359

Weekend Fee	$20	*Weekday Fee*	$18
Power Cart Fee	$20	*Pull Carts*	Yes
Putting Green	Yes	*Driving Range*	No
Season	Apr 1 - Nov 25	*Credit Cards*	No
Pro	Rich Crowe	*Tee Times*	No
Comments	Good beginner's course, slow greens		
Directions	I-84, exit 43, left to Park Rd, left on Buena Vista Rd after 3 lights		

Tee	Holes	Par	Rating	Slope	Yards
Red	9	62	NA	NA	3,408
White	9	64	NA	NA	3,664
Blue	NA	NA	NA	NA	NA

8 Brooklyn Hill Country Club
170 South Street, Danielson, CT 06234
203-779-2400

Weekend Fee	$17	*Weekday Fee*	$15
Power Cart Fee	$18	*Pull Carts*	Yes
Putting Green	Yes	*Driving Range*	Yes
Season	Mar 1 - Dec 1	*Credit Cards*	No
Pro	Ray Carignan	*Tee Times*	No
Comments	Wooded, very picturesque, narrow fairways		
Directions	I-395, exit 91, Rt 6W, follow signs to Brooklyn, left across from Markley Motors, left on South St		

Tee	Holes	Par	Rating	Slope	Yards
Red	9	70	NA	NA	5,488
White	9	70	NA	NA	5,760
Blue	NA	NA	NA	NA	NA

11 Canaan Country Club
74 South Canaan Road, Canaan, CT 06018
203-824-7683

Weekend Fee	$20	*Weekday Fee*	$20
Power Cart Fee	$20	*Pull Carts*	Yes
Putting Green	Yes	*Driving Range*	No
Season	Apr - Dec	*Credit Cards*	No
Pro	Paul Julian	*Tee Times*	No
Comments	Flat, easy walker, picturesque		
Directions	Rt 7N, Canaan, left across from hospital, watch for sign		

Tee	Holes	Par	Rating	Slope	Yards
Red	9	70	67.0	113	5,586
White	9	70	67.0	113	5,586
Blue	NA	NA	NA	NA	NA

9 Bruce Memorial Golf Course
1300 King Street, Greenwich, CT 06831
203-531-6944

Weekend Fee	$28	*Weekday Fee*	$28
Power Cart Fee	$23	*Pull Carts*	Yes
Putting Green	Yes	*Driving Range*	Yes
Season	Apr 1 - Dec 1	*Credit Cards*	No
Pro	Joe Felder	*Tee Times*	No
Comments	Public play w/resident only, Jones design		
Directions	Merritt Pkwy south, exit 27, 3.5 mi, right on Rt 120A (King St)		

Tee	Holes	Par	Rating	Slope	Yards
Red	18	73	72.0	115	5,710
White	18	72	69.3	120	6,093
Blue	18	71	71.1	124	6,492

12 Candlewood Valley Country Club
401 Danbury Road, New Milford, CT 06776
203-354-9359

Weekend Fee	$27	*Weekday Fee*	$22
Power Cart Fee	$22	*Pull Carts*	Yes
Putting Green	Yes	*Driving Range*	Yes
Season	Apr 1 - Dec 20	*Credit Cards*	Yes
Pro	John Farrell	*Tee Times*	3 days
Comments	Scenic nature preserve, flat, large greens		
Directions	I-84N, right Rt 7, 4 mi		

Tee	Holes	Par	Rating	Slope	Yards
Red	18	72	71.5	126	5,403
White	18	72	70.3	120	6,295
Blue	NA	NA	NA	NA	NA

13 Canton Public Golf Course
110 Albany Turnpike, Canton, CT 06019
203-693-8305

Weekend Fee	$23	*Weekday Fee*	$20
Power Cart Fee	$24	*Pull Carts*	Yes
Putting Green	Yes	*Driving Range*	No
Season	Apr 1 - Dec 1	*Credit Cards*	No
Pro	Walter Lowell	*Tee Times*	7 days
Comments	Wide fairways, undulating greens		
Directions	Hartford, Rt 44W, 12 mi		

Tee	Holes	Par	Rating	Slope	Yards
Red	9	72	67.0	117	5,138
White	9	72	68.0	116	5,798
Blue	9	72	68.0	123	6,136

14 Cedar Knob Golf Course
Billings Road, Somers, CT 06071
203-749-3550

Weekend Fee	$22	*Weekday Fee*	$20
Power Cart Fee	$20	*Pull Carts*	Yes
Putting Green	Yes	*Driving Range*	No
Season	Year-round	*Credit Cards*	No
Pro	John Holst	*Tee Times*	3 days
Comments	Cornish design, large greens, many traps		
Directions	I-91N, exit 47E, Rt 190E, right Rt 83, 1 mi, right Billings Rd		

Tee	Holes	Par	Rating	Slope	Yards
Red	18	74	73.8	126	5,784
White	18	72	70.3	116	6,298
Blue	18	72	72.3	118	6,734

15 Cedar Ridge Golf Course
18 Drabic Road, East Lyme, CT 06333
203-691-4568

Weekend Fee	$17	*Weekday Fee*	$13
Power Cart Fee	No carts	*Pull Carts*	Yes
Putting Green	Yes	*Driving Range*	No
Season	Mar - Nov	*Credit Cards*	No
Pro	None	*Tee Times*	7 days
Comments	Rated best par 3 in CT, water hazards		
Directions	I-95, exit 74, left Rt 161N, 1 mi, Drabic Rd		

Tee	Holes	Par	Rating	Slope	Yards
Red	18	54	NA	NA	2,958
White	18	54	NA	NA	2,958
Blue	NA	NA	NA	NA	NA

16 Chanticlair Golf Course
228 Old Hebron Road, Colchester, CT 06415
203-537-3223

Weekend Fee	$18	*Weekday Fee*	$16
Power Cart Fee	$18	*Pull Carts*	Yes
Putting Green	Yes	*Driving Range*	Yes
Season	Apr 1 - Nov 15	*Credit Cards*	Yes
Pro	None	*Tee Times*	5 days
Comments	Elevated island green, easy to walk		
Directions	Rt 2E, exit 17, left, left Old Hebron Rd		

Tee	Holes	Par	Rating	Slope	Yards
Red	9	72	69.8	117	5,844
White	9	70	69.8	117	5,983
Blue	NA	NA	NA	NA	NA

17 Connecticut Golf Land
95 Hartford Turnpike, Route 83, Vernon, CT 06066
203-643-2654

Weekend Fee	$6	*Weekday Fee*	$6
Power Cart Fee	No carts	*Pull Carts*	Yes
Putting Green	Yes	*Driving Range*	No
Season	Apr 1 - Nov 30	*Credit Cards*	No
Pro	None	*Tee Times*	No
Comments	Lit at night, part of larger recreation center		
Directions	Off I-84, near Rt 83 and Rt 30		

Tee	Holes	Par	Rating	Slope	Yards
Red	18	54	NA	NA	980
White	18	54	NA	NA	980
Blue	NA	NA	NA	NA	NA

18 Copper Hill Country Club
145 Newgate Road, East Granby, CT 06026
203-653-6191

Weekend Fee	$22	*Weekday Fee*	$18
Power Cart Fee	$18	*Pull Carts*	Yes
Putting Green	Yes	*Driving Range*	No
Season	Mar 15 - Nov 20	*Credit Cards*	Yes
Pro	Vic Svenberg	*Tee Times*	7 days
Comments	Scenic, country setting, sand traps each hole		
Directions	I-91, exit 40, Rt 20W, right Newgate Rd		

Tee	Holes	Par	Rating	Slope	Yards
Red	9	72	73.0	NA	4,790
White	9	72	69.0	116	5,772
Blue	9	72	69.0	116	6,022

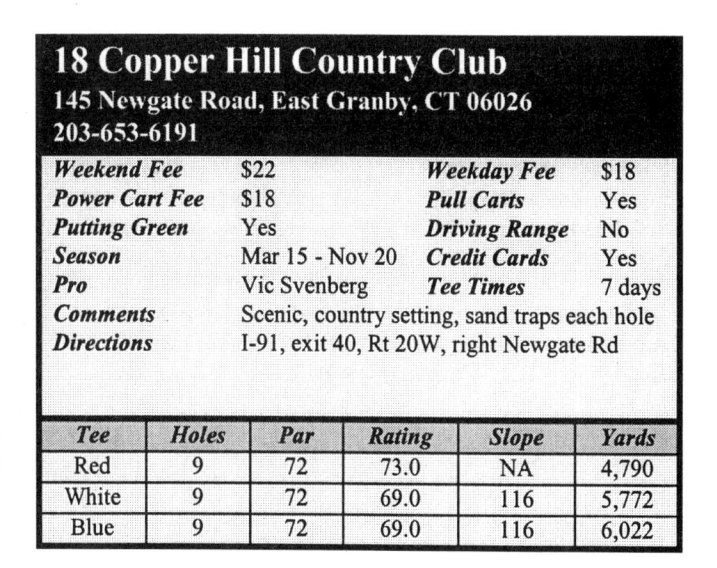

CONNECTICUT

19 Crestbrook Park Golf Course
834 Northfield Road, Watertown, CT 06795
203-945-5249

Weekend Fee	$23	Weekday Fee	$21
Power Cart Fee	$21	Pull Carts	Yes
Putting Green	Yes	Driving Range	Yes
Season	Apr 1 - Dec 15	Credit Cards	No
Pro	Ken Gemmell	Tee Times	2 days
Comments	Undulating greens, long course		
Directions	Rt 8, exit 37, 1 mi west Buckingham Rd, right Northfield Rd		

Tee	Holes	Par	Rating	Slope	Yards
Red	18	75	73.8	128	5,718
White	18	71	71.1	125	6,367
Blue	18	71	73.2	132	6,906

22 East Mountain Golf Course
171 East Mountain Road, Waterbury, CT 06708
203-753-1425

Weekend Fee	$20	Weekday Fee	$18
Power Cart Fee	$18	Pull Carts	Yes
Putting Green	Yes	Driving Range	No
Season	Apr 1 - Dec 30	Credit Cards	No
Pro	None	Tee Times	2 days
Comments	Senior program, reduced fees for residents		
Directions	I-84, exit 23, Rt 69S, 3 mi, right East Mountain Rd		

Tee	Holes	Par	Rating	Slope	Yards
Red	18	68	67.0	111	5,211
White	18	67	67.0	113	5,701
Blue	18	67	67.0	118	5,817

20 East Gaynor Brennan Golf Course
451 Stillwater Road, Stamford, CT 06902
203-324-4185

Weekend Fee	$30	Weekday Fee	$25
Power Cart Fee	$22	Pull Carts	Yes
Putting Green	Yes	Driving Range	No
Season	Year-round	Credit Cards	Yes
Pro	C. Pugliese	Tee Times	7 days
Comments	A little hilly, good sloped greens		
Directions	I-95, exit 6, north West Ave, left at end to West Broad St, 0.5 mi		

Tee	Holes	Par	Rating	Slope	Yards
Red	18	73	67.8	124	5,596
White	18	71	71.0	122	5,868
Blue	NA	NA	NA	NA	NA

23 Eastwood Country Club
1301 Torringford West Street, Torrington, CT 06790
203-489-2630

Weekend Fee	$21	Weekday Fee	$19
Power Cart Fee	$24	Pull Carts	Yes
Putting Green	Yes	Driving Range	No
Season	Mar 15 - Dec 15	Credit Cards	Yes
Pro	Bill Fox	Tee Times	No
Comments	Some narrow fairways, ponds, hilly		
Directions	Rt 8, exit 45, east, left at 4 way stop, 0.5 mi		

Tee	Holes	Par	Rating	Slope	Yards
Red	9	72	65.0	111	4,718
White	9	72	67.0	113	5,866
Blue	NA	NA	NA	NA	NA

21 East Hartford Golf Course
130 Long Hill Street, East Hartford, CT 06108
203-528-5082

Weekend Fee	$23	Weekday Fee	$21
Power Cart Fee	$20	Pull Carts	Yes
Putting Green	Yes	Driving Range	No
Season	Apr 1 - Dec 1	Credit Cards	No
Pro	Richard Thivia	Tee Times	7 days
Comments	Water on several holes, flat, wide fairways		
Directions	I-84, exit 60, Rt 44N to East Hartford, 0.5 mi, right Longhill St		

Tee	Holes	Par	Rating	Slope	Yards
Red	18	72	68.1	112	5,072
White	18	71	68.6	114	6,076
Blue	NA	NA	NA	NA	NA

24 Ellington Golf Center
Route 83, 125 West Road, Ellington, CT 06029
203-872-9574

Weekend Fee	$12	Weekday Fee	$12
Power Cart Fee	No carts	Pull Carts	Yes
Putting Green	Yes	Driving Range	No
Season	Apr - Nov	Credit Cards	No
Pro	None	Tee Times	No
Comments	Fees include clubs and balls		
Directions	I-84N, exit 64, Rt 83N to Ellington		

Tee	Holes	Par	Rating	Slope	Yards
Red	NA	NA	NA	NA	NA
White	18	71	69.5	117	6,082
Blue	NA	NA	NA	NA	NA

25 Elmridge Golf Course
Elmridge Road, Pawcatuck, CT 06379
203-599-2248

Weekend Fee	$29	*Weekday Fee*	$26
Power Cart Fee	$22	*Pull Carts*	Yes
Putting Green	Yes	*Driving Range*	Yes
Season	Mar 15 - Dec	*Credit Cards*	Yes
Pro	Tom Jones	*Tee Times*	5 days
Comments	Hilly, semi-private, undulating greens		
Directions	I-95N, exit 92, right, Rt 2, 0.5 mi right on Elmridge Rd		

Tee	Holes	Par	Rating	Slope	Yards
Red	18	71	70.4	113	5,463
White	18	71	69.5	117	6,200
Blue	18	71	71.2	121	6,520

26 Fairchild Wheeler GC - Black
2390 East Turnpike, Fairfield, CT 06430
203-372-6265

Weekend Fee	$23	*Weekday Fee*	$18
Power Cart Fee	$22	*Pull Carts*	Yes
Putting Green	Yes	*Driving Range*	Yes
Season	Year-round	*Credit Cards*	No
Pro	D. McGoldrick	*Tee Times*	No
Comments	Lower resident fees, near Foxwoods Casino		
Directions	Merritt Pkwy, exit 46, East Turnpike, 1 mi		

Tee	Holes	Par	Rating	Slope	Yards
Red	18	73	71.9	114	5,764
White	18	71	71.0	124	6,402
Blue	NA	NA	NA	NA	NA

27 Fairchild Wheeler GC - Red
2390 East Turnpike, Fairfield, CT 06430
203-372-6265

Weekend Fee	$23	*Weekday Fee*	$18
Power Cart Fee	$22	*Pull Carts*	Yes
Putting Green	Yes	*Driving Range*	Yes
Season	Year-round	*Credit Cards*	No
Pro	D. McGoldrick	*Tee Times*	No
Comments	Lower fees for residents		
Directions	Merritt Pkwy, exit 46, East Turnpike, 1 mi		

Tee	Holes	Par	Rating	Slope	Yards
Red	18	74	71.9	114	5,800
White	18	72	70.0	124	6,382
Blue	NA	NA	NA	NA	NA

28 Farmingbury Hill Country Club
141 East Street, Wolcott, CT 06716
203-879-9380

Weekend Fee	$19	*Weekday Fee*	$19
Power Cart Fee	$22	*Pull Carts*	Yes
Putting Green	Yes	*Driving Range*	No
Season	Apr - Nov	*Credit Cards*	No
Pro	Craig Kealey	*Tee Times*	No
Comments	Double tees, small greens, narrow fairways		
Directions	I-84, W. of Hartford Rt 322N exit, right at top of hill		

Tee	Holes	Par	Rating	Slope	Yards
Red	9	74	68.7	120	5,366
White	9	72	68.7	117	6,078
Blue	NA	NA	NA	NA	NA

29 Fenwick Golf Course
580 Maple Avenue, Old Saybrook, CT 06475
203-388-2516

Weekend Fee	$14	*Weekday Fee*	$14
Power Cart Fee	No carts	*Pull Carts*	Yes
Putting Green	Yes	*Driving Range*	No
Season	Apr - Dec	*Credit Cards*	No
Pro	None	*Tee Times*	1 day
Comments	Call ahead for information		
Directions	I-95N, exit 66, left Rt 166, right Boston Post Rd, right Great Hammock, turns to Maple		

Tee	Holes	Par	Rating	Slope	Yards
Red	NA	NA	NA	NA	NA
White	9	70	NA	NA	5,722
Blue	NA	NA	NA	NA	NA

30 Gainfield Farms Golf Course
255 Old Field Road, Southbury, CT 06488
203-262-1100

Weekend Fee	$22	*Weekday Fee*	$20
Power Cart Fee	$20	*Pull Carts*	Yes
Putting Green	Yes	*Driving Range*	No
Season	Mar 15 - Nov 20	*Credit Cards*	No
Pro	Bert Boyce	*Tee Times*	5 days
Comments	Irrigated, picturesque, rolling, open		
Directions	I-84E, exit 14, left, right 1st light, left at light Oldfield Rd		

Tee	Holes	Par	Rating	Slope	Yards
Red	9	54	NA	NA	2,406
White	9	56	NA	NA	2,768
Blue	NA	NA	NA	NA	NA

CONNECTICUT

31 Goodwin Golf Course - Goodwin
1192 Maple Avenue, Hartford, CT 06114
203-956-3601

Weekend Fee	$21	Weekday Fee	$18
Power Cart Fee	$20	Pull Carts	Yes
Putting Green	Yes	Driving Range	Yes
Season	Year-round	Credit Cards	Yes
Pro	Kevin Tierney	Tee Times	7 days
Comments	Tree lined and narrow, some elevated greens		
Directions	I-91N, exit 27, left, left at stop sign, 1 mi, left on Maple Ave		

Tee	Holes	Par	Rating	Slope	Yards
Red	18	70	69.6	109	5,343
White	18	70	66.7	108	5,638
Blue	18	70	67.8	110	5,929

32 Goodwin Golf Course - North
1192 Maple Avenue, Hartford, CT 06114
203-956-3601

Weekend Fee	$19	Weekday Fee	$16
Power Cart Fee	$19	Pull Carts	Yes
Putting Green	Yes	Driving Range	Yes
Season	Year-round	Credit Cards	Yes
Pro	Kevin Tierney	Tee Times	7 days
Comments	Flat and open		
Directions	I-91N, exit 27, left, left at stop sign, 1 mi, left on Maple Ave		

Tee	Holes	Par	Rating	Slope	Yards
Red	9	70	NA	NA	5,088
White	9	70	NA	NA	5,088
Blue	NA	NA	NA	NA	NA

33 Grassmere Country Club
130 Town Farm Road, Enfield, CT 06082
203-749-7740

Weekend Fee	$22	Weekday Fee	$20
Power Cart Fee	$18	Pull Carts	Yes
Putting Green	Yes	Driving Range	No
Season	Mar 15 - Nov 1	Credit Cards	No
Pro	None	Tee Times	7 days
Comments	Irrigated, good for walking, tight fairways		
Directions	I-91N, exit 46, right, right 3rd light Post Office Rd, 1 mi		

Tee	Holes	Par	Rating	Slope	Yards
Red	9	70	71.0	113	5,346
White	9	70	69.1	111	6,130
Blue	NA	NA	NA	NA	NA

34 Grassy Hill Country Club
441 Clark Lane, Orange, CT 06477
203-795-1422

Weekend Fee	$40	Weekday Fee	$33
Power Cart Fee	Included	Pull Carts	Yes
Putting Green	Yes	Driving Range	Yes
Season	Mar - Dec	Credit Cards	Yes
Pro	Mark Mayette	Tee Times	4 days
Comments	610 yard hole, double tiered greens		
Directions	Merritt Pkwy, exit 56, Rt 121E, 1.5 mi		

Tee	Holes	Par	Rating	Slope	Yards
Red	18	71	71.1	118	5,209
White	18	70	69.4	119	5,849
Blue	18	70	70.5	122	6,118

35 H. Smith Richardson Golf Course
2425 Moorehouse Highway, Fairfield, CT 06430
203-255-6094

Weekend Fee	$27	Weekday Fee	$22
Power Cart Fee	$19	Pull Carts	Yes
Putting Green	Yes	Driving Range	Yes
Season	Year-round	Credit Cards	No
Pro	Michael Homa	Tee Times	Yes
Comments	Narrow fairways, view Long Island Sound		
Directions	Merritt Pkwy N, exit 45, under Merritt Pkwy, 1st right, 2nd left		

Tee	Holes	Par	Rating	Slope	Yards
Red	18	72	72.8	129	5,764
White	18	72	70.2	124	6,323
Blue	18	72	71.0	127	6,676

36 Harrisville Golf Course
125 Harrisville Road, Woodstock, CT 06281
203-928-6098

Weekend Fee	$18	Weekday Fee	$14
Power Cart Fee	$18	Pull Carts	Yes
Putting Green	Yes	Driving Range	No
Season	Apr 1 - Oct 30	Credit Cards	No
Pro	Gene Testa	Tee Times	7 days
Comments	610 par 5 hole, open fairways		
Directions	I-395, exit 97, Rt 44W, Rt 169N, Woodstock, 2nd right		

Tee	Holes	Par	Rating	Slope	Yards
Red	9	70	NA	NA	5,628
White	9	70	NA	NA	5,928
Blue	NA	NA	NA	NA	NA

37 Highland Greens Golf Course
122 Cooke Road, Prospect, CT 06712
203-758-4022

Weekend Fee	$10	Weekday Fee	$8
Power Cart Fee	No carts	Pull Carts	Yes
Putting Green	No	Driving Range	No
Season	Apr 1 - Nov 15	Credit Cards	No
Pro	None	Tee Times	No
Comments	Lit at night, most greens have bunkers		
Directions	I-84E, exit 23, Rt 69S, Prospect, left Rt 68, 2 mi, right		

Tee	Holes	Par	Rating	Slope	Yards
Red	9	54	NA	NA	2,644
White	9	54	NA	NA	2,796
Blue	NA	NA	NA	NA	NA

38 Hillside Links
Hillside Terrace, Deep River, CT 06417
860-526-9986

Weekend Fee	$12	Weekday Fee	$10
Power Cart Fee	No carts	Pull Carts	Yes
Putting Green	Yes	Driving Range	No
Season	Apr 1 - Nov 1	Credit Cards	No
Pro	Don Carlson	Tee Times	No
Comments	Short practice course		
Directions	I-95, exit 5, left, Rt 80, 1st right		

Tee	Holes	Par	Rating	Slope	Yards
Red	9	54	NA	NA	1,864
White	9	54	NA	NA	1,864
Blue	NA	NA	NA	NA	NA

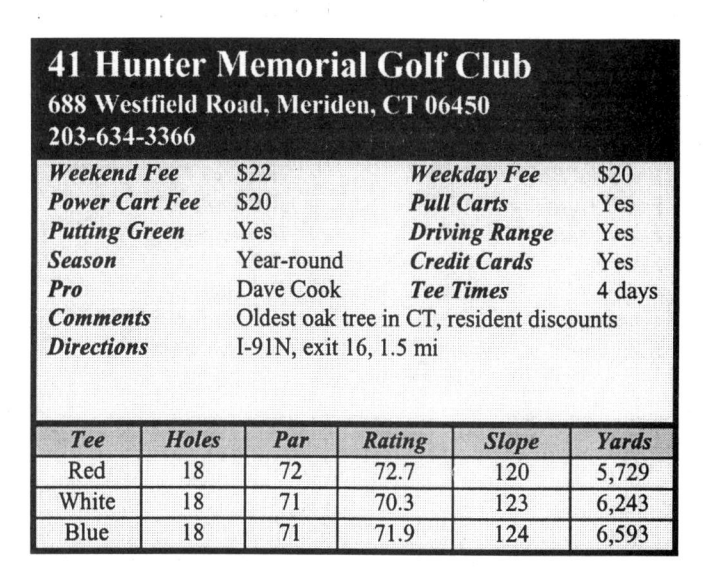

39 Hop Brook Country Club
615 North Church Street, Naugatuck, CT 06770
203-729-8013

Weekend Fee	$20	Weekday Fee	$17
Power Cart Fee	$17	Pull Carts	Yes
Putting Green	Yes	Driving Range	No
Season	Mar - Dec	Credit Cards	No
Pro	Ed Hogan	Tee Times	2 days
Comments	Level course, residents get a discount		
Directions	Rt 8, exit 26, Rt 63N		

Tee	Holes	Par	Rating	Slope	Yards
Red	9	72	67.8	109	4,898
White	9	72	67.8	109	5,774
Blue	NA	NA	NA	NA	NA

40 Hotchkiss School Golf Course
Inter Laken Road, Route 112, Lakeville, CT 06039
203-435-9033

Weekend Fee	$25	Weekday Fee	$15
Power Cart Fee	$18	Pull Carts	Yes
Putting Green	Yes	Driving Range	No
Season	Apr 15 - Oct 15	Credit Cards	No
Pro	Joe Rueger	Tee Times	No
Comments	Wooded and hilly, located at prep school		
Directions	Rt 7, Rt 44W, Rt 122, 0.2 mi		

Tee	Holes	Par	Rating	Slope	Yards
Red	9	76	NA	NA	6,008
White	9	70	69.2	111	6,008
Blue	NA	NA	NA	NA	NA

41 Hunter Memorial Golf Club
688 Westfield Road, Meriden, CT 06450
203-634-3366

Weekend Fee	$22	Weekday Fee	$20
Power Cart Fee	$20	Pull Carts	Yes
Putting Green	Yes	Driving Range	Yes
Season	Year-round	Credit Cards	Yes
Pro	Dave Cook	Tee Times	4 days
Comments	Oldest oak tree in CT, resident discounts		
Directions	I-91N, exit 16, 1.5 mi		

Tee	Holes	Par	Rating	Slope	Yards
Red	18	72	72.7	120	5,729
White	18	71	70.3	123	6,243
Blue	18	71	71.9	124	6,593

42 Indian Hill Country Club
111 Golf Street, Newington, CT 06111
203-666-5447

Weekend Fee	$30	Weekday Fee	$30
Power Cart Fee	$24	Pull Carts	Yes
Putting Green	Yes	Driving Range	No
Season	Year-round	Credit Cards	Yes
Pro	Jim Beadus	Tee Times	4 days
Comments	Narrow, undulating greens, 6 water holes		
Directions	I-91, exit 18, Rt 66E, 2 mi, right Rt 147, 1.5 mi		

Tee	Holes	Par	Rating	Slope	Yards
Red	18	74	71.3	123	5,532
White	18	72	69.6	121	6,120
Blue	18	72	71.6	124	6,443

CONNECTICUT

43 Indian Springs Golf Club
124 Mack Road, Middlefield, CT 06455
203-349-8109

Weekend Fee	$24	Weekday Fee	$20
Power Cart Fee	$22	Pull Carts	Yes
Putting Green	Yes	Driving Range	Yes
Season	Year-round	Credit Cards	No
Pro	Rich Broderick	Tee Times	7 days
Comments	Small greens, play position golf		
Directions	I-91, exit 18, Rt 66E, 2 mi, right Rt 147, 1.5 mi		

Tee	Holes	Par	Rating	Slope	Yards
Red	9	72	73.2	126	5,600
White	9	72	68.9	116	6,000
Blue	NA	NA	NA	NA	NA

44 Keney Park Golf Course
280 Tower Avenue, Hartford, CT 06120
203-525-3656

Weekend Fee	$20	Weekday Fee	$18
Power Cart Fee	$20	Pull Carts	Yes
Putting Green	Yes	Driving Range	No
Season	Apr 1 - Nov 30	Credit Cards	Yes
Pro	Robert Powell	Tee Times	7 days
Comments	One hole over a ravine to elevated green		
Directions	I-91N, exit 34, left, right 1st light, left into Keney Park		

Tee	Holes	Par	Rating	Slope	Yards
Red	18	70	67.7	108	4,917
White	18	70	67.7	116	5,678
Blue	18	70	68.2	118	5,969

45 Laurel View Country Club
310 West Shepherd Avenue, Hamden, CT 06518
203-288-1819

Weekend Fee	$23	Weekday Fee	$20
Power Cart Fee	$20	Pull Carts	Yes
Putting Green	Yes	Driving Range	Yes
Season	Apr 1 - Dec 1	Credit Cards	No
Pro	Jon Wilson	Tee Times	3 days
Comments	Tough course, Ben Hogan Open qualifier		
Directions	Merritt Pkwy, Wilbur Cross Pkwy Rt 15, exit 60, right Dixwell Ave, follow signs		

Tee	Holes	Par	Rating	Slope	Yards
Red	18	73	71.8	130	5,558
White	18	72	70.8	124	6,372
Blue	18	72	72.7	130	6,899

46 Lisbon Country Club
78 Kendall Road, Lisbon, CT 06351
203-376-4325

Weekend Fee	$16	Weekday Fee	$14
Power Cart Fee	$16	Pull Carts	Yes
Putting Green	Yes	Driving Range	No
Season	Year-round	Credit Cards	No
Pro	Cathy Williams	Tee Times	No
Comments	Family owned, 6 water holes, elevated tees		
Directions	I-395N, exit 83A, left, left Kendall Rd		

Tee	Holes	Par	Rating	Slope	Yards
Red	9	66	65.5	102	4,700
White	9	66	65.5	102	4,700
Blue	NA	NA	NA	NA	NA

47 Lyman Orchards Golf Club - Jones
Route 157, Middlefield, CT 06455
203-349-8055

Weekend Fee	$49	Weekday Fee	$42
Power Cart Fee	Included	Pull Carts	No
Putting Green	Yes	Driving Range	Yes
Season	Apr 1 - Dec 1	Credit Cards	Yes
Pro	Dick Bierkan	Tee Times	6 days
Comments	47 bunkers, undulating greens, RT Jones		
Directions	I-91, exit 15, Rt 68E, left Rt 157		

Tee	Holes	Par	Rating	Slope	Yards
Red	18	72	73.5	122	5,812
White	18	72	70.0	124	6,200
Blue	18	72	73.5	129	7,011

48 Lyman Orchards Golf Club - Player
Route 157, Middlefield, CT 06455
203-349-8055

Weekend Fee	$49	Weekday Fee	$42
Power Cart Fee	Included	Pull Carts	No
Putting Green	Yes	Driving Range	Yes
Season	Apr 1 - Dec 1	Credit Cards	Yes
Pro	Dick Bierkan	Tee Times	6 days
Comments	Narrow fairways, blind shots, Gary Player		
Directions	I-91, exit 15, Rt 68E, left Rt 157		

Tee	Holes	Par	Rating	Slope	Yards
Red	18	71	63.7	116	4,667
White	18	71	71.2	131	6,269
Blue	18	71	73.0	135	6,660

49 Manchester Country Club
305 South Main Street, Manchester, CT 06040
203-646-0226

Weekend Fee	$32	*Weekday Fee*	$28
Power Cart Fee	$22	*Pull Carts*	Yes
Putting Green	Yes	*Driving Range*	No
Season	Mar 15 - Nov 1	*Credit Cards*	Yes
Pro	Ralph DeNicolo	*Tee Times*	2 days
Comments	Built 1917, 50 sand traps, 6 water holes		
Directions	I-84, exit 3, Rt 384E, left 0.2 mi, South Main St		

Tee	Holes	Par	Rating	Slope	Yards
Red	18	73	72.1	120	5,602
White	18	72	69.8	120	6,167
Blue	NA	NA	NA	NA	NA

50 Meadowbrook Country Club
2761 Dixwell Avenue, Hamden, CT 06514
203-281-4847

Weekend Fee	$14	*Weekday Fee*	$12
Power Cart Fee	$20	*Pull Carts*	Yes
Putting Green	Yes	*Driving Range*	Yes
Season	Year-round	*Credit Cards*	No
Pro	None	*Tee Times*	No
Comments	Open, flat, many sand traps		
Directions	Wilbur Cross Pkwy, exit 60, north on Dixwell Ave, 1 mi		

Tee	Holes	Par	Rating	Slope	Yards
Red	9	70	NA	NA	5,442
White	9	70	NA	NA	5,442
Blue	NA	NA	NA	NA	NA

51 Millbrook Golf Course
147 Pigeon Hill Road, Windsor, CT 06095
203-688-2575

Weekend Fee	$24	*Weekday Fee*	$21
Power Cart Fee	$21	*Pull Carts*	Yes
Putting Green	Yes	*Driving Range*	No
Season	Apr 1 - Oct 31	*Credit Cards*	No
Pro	None	*Tee Times*	5 days
Comments	Pond and brooks, hilly, wooded		
Directions	I-91N, exit 38, left, 1 mi		

Tee	Holes	Par	Rating	Slope	Yards
Red	18	73	71.5	125	5,301
White	18	71	69.5	121	6,074
Blue	18	71	69.8	119	6,173

52 Mill Stone Country Club
348 Hebert Street, Milford, CT 06460
203-874-5900

Weekend Fee	$12	*Weekday Fee*	$10
Power Cart Fee	$12	*Pull Carts*	Yes
Putting Green	Yes	*Driving Range*	No
Season	Apr - Dec	*Credit Cards*	No
Pro	Alex Wolinsky	*Tee Times*	No
Comments	Flat, easy to walk, narrow fairways		
Directions	Merritt Pkwy, exit 55, Wheeler Farm Rd, left Herbert St		

Tee	Holes	Par	Rating	Slope	Yards
Red	9	72	NA	NA	5,820
White	9	72	NA	NA	5,820
Blue	NA	NA	NA	NA	NA

53 Miner Hills Golf Club
247 Miner Street, Middletown, CT 06457
203-635-0051

Weekend Fee	$18	*Weekday Fee*	$14
Power Cart Fee	$10	*Pull Carts*	Yes
Putting Green	Yes	*Driving Range*	No
Season	Apr - Nov	*Credit Cards*	No
Pro	None	*Tee Times*	7 days
Comments	Good practice course, tree lined		
Directions	I-91, exit 20, east, Miner St parallel to I-91		

Tee	Holes	Par	Rating	Slope	Yards
Red	9	60	NA	NA	2,870
White	9	60	NA	NA	3,390
Blue	9	60	NA	NA	3,580

54 Minnechaug Golf Course
16 Fairway Crossing, Glastonbury, CT 06033
203-643-9914

Weekend Fee	$24	*Weekday Fee*	$222
Power Cart Fee	$22	*Pull Carts*	Yes
Putting Green	Yes	*Driving Range*	No
Season	Apr 1 - Nov 1	*Credit Cards*	Yes
Pro	Hal Carlson	*Tee Times*	4 days
Comments	Island green, tight course, small greens		
Directions	I-84E, Rt 384E, exit 3, left, Rt 83, 3 mi		

Tee	Holes	Par	Rating	Slope	Yards
Red	9	72	63.5	104	4,558
White	9	70	67.0	111	5,386
Blue	9	70	67.0	111	5,594

CONNECTICUT

55 Norwich Golf Course
685 New London Turnpike, Norwich, CT 06360
203-889-6973

Weekend Fee	$27	*Weekday Fee*	$24
Power Cart Fee	$20	*Pull Carts*	Yes
Putting Green	Yes	*Driving Range*	No
Season	Apr 1 - Nov 1	*Credit Cards*	No
Pro	John Paesani	*Tee Times*	3 days
Comments	Very hilly, greens elevated		
Directions	I-395, exit 80E, Rt 82E, right 5th light, 1 mi		

Tee	Holes	Par	Rating	Slope	Yards
Red	18	74	70.8	120	5,255
White	18	71	68.1	117	5,927
Blue	18	71	69.4	119	6,231

56 Oak Hills Golf Course
165 Fillow Street, Norwalk, CT 06850
203-853-8400

Weekend Fee	$30	*Weekday Fee*	$26
Power Cart Fee	$22	*Pull Carts*	Yes
Putting Green	Yes	*Driving Range*	No
Season	Apr 1 - Dec 1	*Credit Cards*	Yes
Pro	Vincent Grillo	*Tee Times*	7 days
Comments	Hilly, scenic, water on 6 holes		
Directions	I-95, exit 13, right, left 2nd light Richards Ave, right Fillow St at end		

Tee	Holes	Par	Rating	Slope	Yards
Red	18	72	69.2	119	5,221
White	18	71	68.0	120	5,920
Blue	18	71	70.5	125	6,407

57 Orange Hills Country Club
489 Racebrook Road, Orange, CT 06477
203-795-4161

Weekend Fee	$30	*Weekday Fee*	$22
Power Cart Fee	$25	*Pull Carts*	Yes
Putting Green	Yes	*Driving Range*	No
Season	Year-round	*Credit Cards*	Yes
Pro	Art Decko	*Tee Times*	4 days
Comments	Some water, carved from woods, Cornish		
Directions	I-95S, exit 42, right on Rt 1, left Rt 114		

Tee	Holes	Par	Rating	Slope	Yards
Red	18	74	71.5	120	5,729
White	18	71	69.8	119	6,084
Blue	18	71	71.2	122	6,389

58 Patton Brook Country Club
201 Pattonwood Drive, Southington, CT 06489
203-793-6000

Weekend Fee	$18	*Weekday Fee*	$14
Power Cart Fee	$20	*Pull Carts*	Yes
Putting Green	Yes	*Driving Range*	No
Season	Apr 1 - Oct 30	*Credit Cards*	Yes
Pro	None	*Tee Times*	3 days
Comments	Small and fast greens, many hazards		
Directions	I-84E, exit 32, left, left at Bickford's on Laning St, follow signs to course		

Tee	Holes	Par	Rating	Slope	Yards
Red	18	60	59.1	92	3,640
White	18	60	58.5	93	4,056
Blue	18	60	60.6	97	4,433

59 Pequabuck Golf Club of Bristol
School Street, Pequabuck, CT 06781
203-583-7307

Weekend Fee	$31	*Weekday Fee*	$31
Power Cart Fee	$20	*Pull Carts*	Yes
Putting Green	Yes	*Driving Range*	Yes
Season	Year-round	*Credit Cards*	No
Pro	Chris Tremblay	*Tee Times*	No
Comments	Tight back 9, small greens, tree lined, 1902		
Directions	Rt 6, Bushnel Rd, 0.3 mi, left School St		

Tee	Holes	Par	Rating	Slope	Yards
Red	18	72	71.0	117	5,388
White	18	69	67.6	119	5,692
Blue	18	69	69.1	122	6,015

60 Pequot Golf Club
127 Wheeler Road, Stonington, CT 06378
203-535-1898

Weekend Fee	$25	*Weekday Fee*	$20
Power Cart Fee	$22	*Pull Carts*	Yes
Putting Green	Yes	*Driving Range*	No
Season	Feb 15 - Dec 2	*Credit Cards*	No
Pro	Larry Thornhill	*Tee Times*	7 days
Comments	Small greens, accuracy, semi-private		
Directions	I-95, exit 91, follow signs, near Foxwoods Casino (7 minutes)		

Tee	Holes	Par	Rating	Slope	Yards
Red	18	71	69.4	112	5,246
White	18	70	67.2	108	5,903
Blue	NA	NA	NA	NA	NA

61 Pilgrim's Harbor Golf Club
Harrison Road, Wallingford, CT 06492
203-269-6023

Weekend Fee	$29	*Weekday Fee*		$22
Power Cart Fee	$22	*Pull Carts*		Yes
Putting Green	Yes	*Driving Range*		No
Season	Mar 1 - Dec 1	*Credit Cards*		No
Pro	Ward Weischet	*Tee Times*		3 days
Comments	Hard, multiple tees, semi-private, RT Jones
Directions	I-91N, exit 14, right, Woodhouse Rd (Rt 150), 1st right Harrison Rd

Tee	Holes	Par	Rating	Slope	Yards
Red	9	72	NA	NA	5,126
White	9	72	72.6	127	5,898
Blue	9	72	NA	NA	6,684

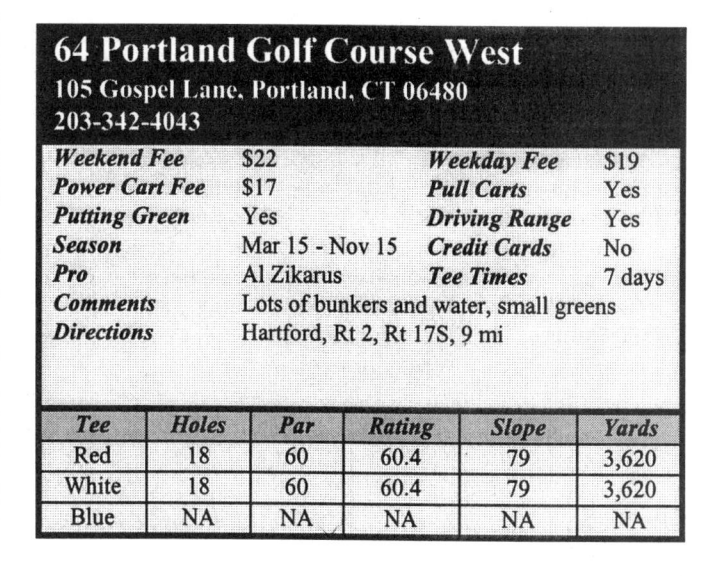

62 Pine Valley Golf Course
300 Welch Road, Southington, CT 06489
203-628-0879

Weekend Fee	$26	*Weekday Fee*		$22
Power Cart Fee	$23	*Pull Carts*		Yes
Putting Green	Yes	*Driving Range*		No
Season	Mar 15 - Dec 1	*Credit Cards*		Yes
Pro	J. McConachie	*Tee Times*		7 days
Comments	Hilly front 9, level back 9, accuracy needed
Directions	I-84, exit 31, Rt 229N, left Welch Rd

Tee	Holes	Par	Rating	Slope	Yards
Red	18	73	72.0	122	5,522
White	18	71	69.5	121	6,039
Blue	18	71	70.3	122	6,325

63 Portland Golf Course
169 Bartlett Street, Portland, CT 06480
203-342-2833

Weekend Fee	$27	*Weekday Fee*		$23
Power Cart Fee	$21	*Pull Carts*		Yes
Putting Green	Yes	*Driving Range*		No
Season	Mar 15 - Dec 31	*Credit Cards*		No
Pro	Mark Sloan	*Tee Times*		7 days
Comments	Some blind shots, well maintained, Cornish
Directions	Hartford, Rt 2, Rt 17N, 2nd right

Tee	Holes	Par	Rating	Slope	Yards
Red	18	71	68.6	118	5,039
White	18	71	68.5	121	5,802
Blue	18	71	70.8	124	6,213

64 Portland Golf Course West
105 Gospel Lane, Portland, CT 06480
203-342-4043

Weekend Fee	$22	*Weekday Fee*		$19
Power Cart Fee	$17	*Pull Carts*		Yes
Putting Green	Yes	*Driving Range*		Yes
Season	Mar 15 - Nov 15	*Credit Cards*		No
Pro	Al Zikarus	*Tee Times*		7 days
Comments	Lots of bunkers and water, small greens
Directions	Hartford, Rt 2, Rt 17S, 9 mi

Tee	Holes	Par	Rating	Slope	Yards
Red	18	60	60.4	79	3,620
White	18	60	60.4	79	3,620
Blue	NA	NA	NA	NA	NA

65 Putnam Country Club
136 Chase Road, Putnam, CT 06260
203-928-7748

Weekend Fee	$22	*Weekday Fee*		$18
Power Cart Fee	$20	*Pull Carts*		Yes
Putting Green	Yes	*Driving Range*		Yes
Season	Apr 1 - Dec 1	*Credit Cards*		Yes
Pro	Brian Morrow	*Tee Times*		4 days
Comments	Expanding to 18, cut through woods
Directions	I-395, exit 97, Rt 44E, right 3 mi past fire station, E. Putnam Rd, right 2nd stop sign

Tee	Holes	Par	Rating	Slope	Yards
Red	9	72	NA	NA	5,350
White	9	72	69.6	112	6,140
Blue	9	72	70.6	115	6,358

66 Quarry Ridge
9 Rose Hill Road, Portland, CT 06480
203-342-6113

Weekend Fee	$36	*Weekday Fee*		$32
Power Cart Fee	Included	*Pull Carts*		No
Putting Green	Yes	*Driving Range*		No
Season	Apr 1 - Dec 1	*Credit Cards*		No
Pro	Joe Kelly	*Tee Times*		7 days
Comments	Carved from rock, side hill lies, boulders
Directions	Hartford, Rt 2, Rt 17N, 2nd right, up hill

Tee	Holes	Par	Rating	Slope	Yards
Red	9	72	NA	NA	4,704
White	9	72	69.3	115	5,608
Blue	9	72	71.5	118	6,210

CONNECTICUT

67 Raceway Golf Club
205 East Thompson Road, Thompson, CT 06277
203-923-9593

Weekend Fee	$22	*Weekday Fee*	$18
Power Cart Fee	$20	*Pull Carts*	Yes
Putting Green	Yes	*Driving Range*	Yes
Season	Apr 1 - Nov 30	*Credit Cards*	No
Pro	Tracey Kelley	*Tee Times*	5 days
Comments	Easy to walk, 6 water holes, 3 state view		
Directions	I-395, exit 99, left, left at 4 way stop, follow signs		

Tee	Holes	Par	Rating	Slope	Yards
Red	18	71	71.3	117	5,437
White	18	71	68.6	116	5,916
Blue	18	71	70.1	121	6,412

70 Rockledge Country Club
289 South Main Street, Hartford, CT 06107
203-521-3156

Weekend Fee	$26 w/member	*Weekday Fee*	$22
Power Cart Fee	$18	*Pull Carts*	Yes
Putting Green	Yes	*Driving Range*	Yes
Season	Apr 1 - Dec 31	*Credit Cards*	No
Pro	Richard Crowe	*Tee Times*	1 day
Comments	Tommy Armour was pro here in past		
Directions	I-84, exit 41, South Main St north, 0.3 mi		

Tee	Holes	Par	Rating	Slope	Yards
Red	18	74	71.5	118	5,608
White	18	72	68.6	119	6,010
Blue	18	72	70.4	123	6,326

68 Richter Park Golf Course
100 Aunt Hack Road, Danbury, CT 06810
203-792-2550

Weekend Fee	$44	*Weekday Fee*	$44
Power Cart Fee	$22	*Pull Carts*	Yes
Putting Green	Yes	*Driving Range*	No
Season	Mar 15 - Nov 1	*Credit Cards*	Yes
Pro	Bob Rogers	*Tee Times*	3 days
Comments	Open tree lined fairways, water on 16 holes		
Directions	I-84E, exit 2, left, right 2nd light Rt 6, left Aunt Hack Rd		

Tee	Holes	Par	Rating	Slope	Yards
Red	18	72	70.3	117	5,502
White	18	72	71.1	126	6,325
Blue	18	72	73.0	130	6,740

71 Rolling Greens Golf Club
600 Cold Spring Road, Rocky Hill, CT 06067
203-257-9775

Weekend Fee	$25	*Weekday Fee*	$20
Power Cart Fee	$13	*Pull Carts*	Yes
Putting Green	Yes	*Driving Range*	No
Season	Apr 1 - Nov 1	*Credit Cards*	Yes
Pro	Joe De Candia	*Tee Times*	3 days
Comments	Tough, well rated 9 holer, 4 ponds		
Directions	I-91N, exit 23, left, 0.3 mi, left Rt 3, right Cold Spring Rd		

Tee	Holes	Par	Rating	Slope	Yards
Red	9	72	71.5	125	5,270
White	9	70	72.0	131	6,258
Blue	NA	NA	NA	NA	NA

69 Ridgefield Golf Club
545 Ridgebury Road, Ridgefield, CT 06877
203-748-7008

Weekend Fee	$27	*Weekday Fee*	$27
Power Cart Fee	$21	*Pull Carts*	Yes
Putting Green	Yes	*Driving Range*	Yes
Season	Apr 1 - Dec 1	*Credit Cards*	No
Pro	Vince Adams	*Tee Times*	2 days
Comments	Tough back 9, rated in best by Golf Digest		
Directions	I-84, exit 1, Saw Mill Rd south, 2.5 mi		

Tee	Holes	Par	Rating	Slope	Yards
Red	18	71	70.7	120	5,295
White	18	70	68.1	119	5,919
Blue	18	70	70.0	122	6,380

72 Shennecossett Golf Club
Plant Street, Groton, CT 06340
203-445-0262

Weekend Fee	$28	*Weekday Fee*	$24
Power Cart Fee	$20	*Pull Carts*	Yes
Putting Green	Yes	*Driving Range*	No
Season	Year-round	*Credit Cards*	No
Pro	Phil Jones	*Tee Times*	4 days
Comments	Links style, Ross design, wide, traps, 1898		
Directions	I-95S, exit 87, Rt 349S, right 2nd light, 1st left, left on Plant St		

Tee	Holes	Par	Rating	Slope	Yards
Red	18	76	73.2	121	5,796
White	18	72	69.5	118	6,142
Blue	18	72	71.1	122	6,491

73 Short Beach Golf Course
1 Dorne Drive, Stratford, CT 06497
203-381-2070

Weekend Fee	$13	*Weekday Fee*	$11
Power Cart Fee	No carts	*Pull Carts*	Yes
Putting Green	Yes	*Driving Range*	No
Season	Year-round	*Credit Cards*	No
Pro	Herb Wry	*Tee Times*	No
Comments	Practice bunker, Cornish design, executive		
Directions	I-95N, exit 30, right, right at end, 0.5 mi, left		

Tee	Holes	Par	Rating	Slope	Yards
Red	9	54	NA	NA	2,540
White	9	54	NA	NA	2,540
Blue	NA	NA	NA	NA	NA

74 Silver Spring Country Club
439 Silver Spring Road, Ridgefield, CT 06877
203-438-0100

Weekend Fee	$50	*Weekday Fee*	$35
Power Cart Fee	$26	*Pull Carts*	Yes
Putting Green	Yes	*Driving Range*	Yes
Season	Apr 1 - Nov 1	*Credit Cards*	Yes
Pro	Stan Garrett	*Tee Times*	No
Comments	Narrow, trees, undulating greens, semi-pri		
Directions	Danbury, Rt 7S, right Branchville Rd, left Main St, left Wilton Rd, right Silver Spring Rd		

Tee	Holes	Par	Rating	Slope	Yards
Red	18	71	72.7	120	5,657
White	18	71	70.3	125	6,142
Blue	18	71	71.4	127	6,493

75 Simsbury Farms Golf Course
100 Old Farms Road, West Simsbury, CT 06070
203-658-6246

Weekend Fee	$26	*Weekday Fee*	$22
Power Cart Fee	$22	*Pull Carts*	Yes
Putting Green	Yes	*Driving Range*	Yes
Season	Apr 1 - Nov 1	*Credit Cards*	No
Pro	Dick Casavant	*Tee Times*	2 days
Comments	Narrow, tree lined fairways, well maintained		
Directions	I-84, exit 39, west on Farmington Ave, Rt 10N, Simsbury, left Strattonbrook Rd, 4 mi		

Tee	Holes	Par	Rating	Slope	Yards
Red	18	72	70.1	117	5,519
White	18	72	68.3	118	6,104
Blue	18	72	69.8	120	6,421

76 Skungamaug River Golf Club
104 Folly Lane, Coventry, CT 06238
203-742-9348

Weekend Fee	$25	*Weekday Fee*	$22
Power Cart Fee	$20	*Pull Carts*	Yes
Putting Green	Yes	*Driving Range*	Yes
Season	Mar 15 - Dec 15	*Credit Cards*	Yes
Pro	Bob Doty	*Tee Times*	7 days
Comments	Undulating greens, wooded, narrow fairways		
Directions	I-84, exit 68, Rt 195S, right 1st light Goose Lane, 2.5 mi		

Tee	Holes	Par	Rating	Slope	Yards
Red	18	71	64.7	113	4,427
White	18	70	68.6	118	5,624
Blue	18	70	69.4	120	5,785

77 Sleeping Giant Golf Course
3931 Whitney Avenue, Hamden, CT 06518
203-281-9456

Weekend Fee	$18	*Weekday Fee*	$15
Power Cart Fee	$16	*Pull Carts*	Yes
Putting Green	Yes	*Driving Range*	No
Season	Year-round	*Credit Cards*	No
Pro	Lee Carter	*Tee Times*	No
Comments	Easy to walk, view of Sleeping Giant Mt		
Directions	I-91, exit 10, right Whitney Ave, 3 mi		

Tee	Holes	Par	Rating	Slope	Yards
Red	9	72	NA	NA	5,200
White	9	70	NA	NA	5,641
Blue	NA	NA	NA	NA	NA

78 Southington Country Club
Savage Street, Southington, CT 06489
203-628-7032

Weekend Fee	$24	*Weekday Fee*	$21
Power Cart Fee	$22	*Pull Carts*	Yes
Putting Green	Yes	*Driving Range*	No
Season	Apr 1 - Nov 1	*Credit Cards*	No
Pro	Walt Richter	*Tee Times*	7 days
Comments	Greens in good condition, hilly front 9		
Directions	I-84, exit Queen St, Rt 10S, left Rt 120, right 1st light, 1.5 mi		

Tee	Holes	Par	Rating	Slope	Yards
Red	18	73	69.8	119	5,103
White	18	71	67.0	113	5,675
Blue	NA	NA	NA	NA	NA

CONNECTICUT

79 South Pine Creek Park
Old Dam Road, Fairfield, CT 06430
203-256-3173

Weekend Fee	$18	Weekday Fee	$16
Power Cart Fee	No carts	Pull Carts	Yes
Putting Green	Yes	Driving Range	No
Season	Apr 1 - Nov 1	Credit Cards	No
Pro	None	Tee Times	No
Comments	Good practice course, fees less for residents		
Directions	I-95, exit 19 to Rt 1N, right South Pine Creek, left Old Dam Rd		

Tee	Holes	Par	Rating	Slope	Yards
Red	9	54	NA	NA	2,146
White	9	54	NA	NA	2,146
Blue	NA	NA	NA	NA	NA

80 Stanley Municipal GC - Blue/Red
245 Hartford Road, New Britain, CT 06053
203-827-8144

Weekend Fee	$23	Weekday Fee	$19
Power Cart Fee	$21	Pull Carts	Yes
Putting Green	Yes	Driving Range	No
Season	Apr 1 - Dec 15	Credit Cards	No
Pro	Ted Pisk	Tee Times	3 days
Comments	3 ponds, elevated greens		
Directions	I-84, exit 39A, Rt 9A south, exit 30, right		

Tee	Holes	Par	Rating	Slope	Yards
Red	18	73	72.0	122	5,700
White	18	72	68.9	119	6,067
Blue	18	72	70.5	122	6,500

81 Stanley Municipal GC - White
245 Hartford Road, New Britain, CT 06053
203-827-8144

Weekend Fee	$23	Weekday Fee	$19
Power Cart Fee	$21	Pull Carts	Yes
Putting Green	Yes	Driving Range	No
Season	Apr 1 - Dec 15	Credit Cards	No
Pro	Ted Pisk	Tee Times	3 days
Comments	Flat, no water		
Directions	I-84, exit 39A, Rt 9A south, exit 30, right		

Tee	Holes	Par	Rating	Slope	Yards
Red	9	72	71.4	NA	5,238
White	9	70	68.4	NA	5,612
Blue	9	70	69.6	NA	6,064

82 Sterling Farms Golf Club
1349 Newfield Avenue, Stamford, CT 06905
203-461-9090

Weekend Fee	$33	Weekday Fee	$28
Power Cart Fee	$20	Pull Carts	Yes
Putting Green	Yes	Driving Range	Yes
Season	Mar 15 - Dec 15	Credit Cards	No
Pro	Angela Aulenti	Tee Times	No
Comments	Open fairways, bunkers at greens		
Directions	Merritt Pkwy, exit 35, right High Ridge Rd, left Vine St, left at end		

Tee	Holes	Par	Rating	Slope	Yards
Red	18	73	72.6	121	5,557
White	18	72	69.7	123	6,082
Blue	18	72	71.1	127	6,401

83 Stonybrook Golf Course
263 Milton Road, Litchfield, CT 06759
203-567-9977

Weekend Fee	$30	Weekday Fee	$24
Power Cart Fee	$24	Pull Carts	Yes
Putting Green	Yes	Driving Range	No
Season	Apr 1 - Dec 1	Credit Cards	Yes
Pro	Rich Bredice	Tee Times	7 days
Comments	Undulating, very hilly, small greens		
Directions	Rt 8, exit Litchfield, Rt 118, left Rt 202, right 4th light, 1.5 mi		

Tee	Holes	Par	Rating	Slope	Yards
Red	9	72	68.0	121	5,166
White	9	70	68.6	122	5,548
Blue	9	70	69.2	124	5,804

84 Sunset Hill Golf Club
13 Sunset Hill Road, Brookfield, CT 06804
203-740-7800

Weekend Fee	$21	Weekday Fee	$17
Power Cart Fee	$11	Pull Carts	Yes
Putting Green	Yes	Driving Range	No
Season	Mar 15 - Dec 1	Credit Cards	No
Pro	Terry Read	Tee Times	No
Comments	Hilly, good greens, greens fees cover all day		
Directions	I-84E, exit 9, Rt 25N, 2.5 mi, left Sunset Hill Rd		

Tee	Holes	Par	Rating	Slope	Yards
Red	18	70	66.3	100	4,236
White	18	69	62.6	100	4,720
Blue	NA	NA	NA	NA	NA

85 Tallwood Country Club
91 North Street, Hebron, CT 06248
203-646-1151

Weekend Fee	$27	*Weekday Fee*	$25
Power Cart Fee	$20	*Pull Carts*	Yes
Putting Green	Yes	*Driving Range*	Yes
Season	Mar 1 - Dec 20	*Credit Cards*	No
Pro	J. Nowobilski	*Tee Times*	7 days
Comments	Flat, scenic, water on back 9, large greens		
Directions	Hartford, I-84E, I-384, exit 5, Rt 85S, 6 mi		

Tee	Holes	Par	Rating	Slope	Yards
Red	18	72	70.8	114	5,430
White	18	72	69.0	117	6,126
Blue	18	72	70.2	119	6,366

86 Tashua Knolls Golf Club
40 Tashua Knolls Lane, Trumbull, CT 06611
203-261-5989

Weekend Fee	$24	*Weekday Fee*	$20
Power Cart Fee	$20	*Pull Carts*	Yes
Putting Green	Yes	*Driving Range*	Yes
Season	Apr 1 - Dec 31	*Credit Cards*	No
Pro	Walter Bogues	*Tee Times*	1 day
Comments	Good mix of doglegs, water, hills		
Directions	Merritt Pkwy, exit 49, Rt 25N, thru light at end, 2nd left		

Tee	Holes	Par	Rating	Slope	Yards
Red	18	72	71.3	112	5,454
White	18	72	69.3	122	6,119
Blue	18	72	71.1	125	6,540

87 Timberlin Golf Club
330 Southington Road, Kensington, CT 06037
203-828-3228

Weekend Fee	$25	*Weekday Fee*	$21
Power Cart Fee	$20	*Pull Carts*	Yes
Putting Green	Yes	*Driving Range*	Yes
Season	Apr 1 - Dec 15	*Credit Cards*	No
Pro	Lindsey Hansen	*Tee Times*	2 days
Comments	Lot of water, rolling terrain		
Directions	I-84, Rt 72E, Rt 71S, 5 mi, right Southington Rd		

Tee	Holes	Par	Rating	Slope	Yards
Red	18	72	70.5	109	5,477
White	18	72	70.0	123	6,342
Blue	18	72	71.9	127	6,733

88 Trumbull Golf Course
119 High Rock Road, Groton, CT 06340
203-445-7991

Weekend Fee	$15	*Weekday Fee*	$13
Power Cart Fee	$18	*Pull Carts*	Yes
Putting Green	Yes	*Driving Range*	Yes
Season	Year-round	*Credit Cards*	No
Pro	Art De Wolf	*Tee Times*	No
Comments	No hills, easy to walk, 3 water holes		
Directions	I-95W, exit 87, signs to Groton, right before airport		

Tee	Holes	Par	Rating	Slope	Yards
Red	18	54	NA	NA	2,660
White	18	54	NA	NA	2,660
Blue	NA	NA	NA	NA	NA

89 Tunxis Plantation CC - Green
87 Town Farm Road, Farmington, CT 06032
203-677-1367

Weekend Fee	$28	*Weekday Fee*	$24
Power Cart Fee	$24	*Pull Carts*	Yes
Putting Green	Yes	*Driving Range*	Yes
Season	Apr 1 - Nov 30	*Credit Cards*	Yes
Pro	Lou Pandolfi	*Tee Times*	4 days
Comments	Narrow, wooded, course has 45 holes		
Directions	I-84, exit 39, west over river, 1st right Town Farm Rd		

Tee	Holes	Par	Rating	Slope	Yards
Red	18	72	71.0	115	4,903
White	18	72	68.1	117	5,958
Blue	18	72	70.0	120	6,424

90 Tunxis Plantation CC - Red
87 Town Farm Road, Farmington, CT 06032
203-677-1367

Weekend Fee	$28	*Weekday Fee*	$24
Power Cart Fee	$24	*Pull Carts*	Yes
Putting Green	Yes	*Driving Range*	Yes
Season	Apr 1 - Nov 30	*Credit Cards*	Yes
Pro	Lou Pandolfi	*Tee Times*	4 days
Comments	Course has 45 holes		
Directions	I-84, exit 39, west over river, 1st right Town Farm Rd		

Tee	Holes	Par	Rating	Slope	Yards
Red	9	72	NA	116	5,580
White	9	72	68.8	119	6,152
Blue	9	72	70.8	123	6,594

CONNECTICUT

91 Tunxis Plantation CC - White
87 Town Farm Road, Farmington, CT 06032
203-677-1367

Weekend Fee	$28	*Weekday Fee*	$24
Power Cart Fee	$24	*Pull Carts*	Yes
Putting Green	Yes	*Driving Range*	Yes
Season	Apr 1 - Nov 30	*Credit Cards*	Yes
Pro	Lou Pandolfi	*Tee Times*	4 days
Comments	Flat, open, 5 island greens, 45 holes		
Directions	I-84, exit 39, west over river, 1st right Town Farm Rd		

Tee	Holes	Par	Rating	Slope	Yards
Red	18	72	71.5	116	5,744
White	18	72	69.2	117	6,241
Blue	18	72	71.0	121	6,638

94 Western Hills Golf Course
600 Park Road, Waterbury, CT 06708
203-756-1211

Weekend Fee	$20	*Weekday Fee*	$18
Power Cart Fee	$18	*Pull Carts*	Yes
Putting Green	Yes	*Driving Range*	No
Season	Mar 15 - Dec 31	*Credit Cards*	No
Pro	Tom Bracken	*Tee Times*	2 days
Comments	Hilly, variety of lies, 1 water hole		
Directions	I-84W, exit 17, Rt 63N, right 3rd light Park Rd, 0.3 mi, left on Clough Rd		

Tee	Holes	Par	Rating	Slope	Yards
Red	18	72	NA	122	5,393
White	18	72	69.6	122	6,246
Blue	18	72	71.1	125	6,427

92 Twin Hills Country Club
199 Bread and Route 31, Coventry, CT 06238
203-742-9705

Weekend Fee	$26	*Weekday Fee*	$24
Power Cart Fee	$20	*Pull Carts*	Yes
Putting Green	Yes	*Driving Range*	No
Season	Apr 1 - Dec 1	*Credit Cards*	No
Pro	None	*Tee Times*	No
Comments	Large greens, wooded fairways but wide		
Directions	I-84, exit 67, Rt 31S, 5 mi		

Tee	Holes	Par	Rating	Slope	Yards
Red	18	71	69.5	116	5,249
White	18	71	68.6	116	5,954
Blue	18	71	69.7	118	6,257

95 Westport Longshore Golf Club
260 South Compo Road, Westport, CT 06880
203-227-1374

Weekend Fee	$26	*Weekday Fee*	$22
Power Cart Fee	$11	*Pull Carts*	Yes
Putting Green	Yes	*Driving Range*	No
Season	Mar 15 - Nov 15	*Credit Cards*	No
Pro	Jim Tennant	*Tee Times*	3 days
Comments	Flat, bunkered greens, semi-private		
Directions	I-95, exit 18, Rt 1, left 2nd light, Green Farms Rd, left at light		

Tee	Holes	Par	Rating	Slope	Yards
Red	18	73	70.0	119	5,227
White	18	69	66.7	113	5,676
Blue	18	69	67.4	115	5,845

93 Twin Lakes Golf Course
241 Twin Lakes Road, North Branford, CT 06471
203-488-8778

Weekend Fee	$10	*Weekday Fee*	$9
Power Cart Fee	No carts	*Pull Carts*	Yes
Putting Green	Yes	*Driving Range*	No
Season	Apr 1 - Nov 1	*Credit Cards*	No
Pro	Brian DeNardi	*Tee Times*	No
Comments	Small greens, narrow fairways		
Directions	I-91N, exit 8, Rt 80E, approximately 5 mi, right Twin Lakes Rd		

Tee	Holes	Par	Rating	Slope	Yards
Red	9	68	NA	NA	1,702
White	9	54	NA	NA	1,702
Blue	NA	NA	NA	NA	NA

96 Westwoods Golf Course
7 Westwoods Drive, Farmington, CT 06032
203-677-9192

Weekend Fee	$21	*Weekday Fee*	$17
Power Cart Fee	$20	*Pull Carts*	Yes
Putting Green	Yes	*Driving Range*	Yes
Season	Apr 1 - Dec 1	*Credit Cards*	No
Pro	Jim Tennant	*Tee Times*	7 days
Comments	Irrigated, flat, some water, open fairways		
Directions	I-84, Bristol exit, Rt 6W, right 5th light Rt 117, 0.5 mi		

Tee	Holes	Par	Rating	Slope	Yards
Red	18	61	58.6	85	3,547
White	18	61	59.5	85	4,407
Blue	NA	NA	NA	NA	NA

97 Whitney Farms Golf Course
175 Shelton Road, Monroe, CT 06468
203-268-0707

Weekend Fee	$42	*Weekday Fee*	$37
Power Cart Fee	Included	*Pull Carts*	No
Putting Green	Yes	*Driving Range*	Yes
Season	Mar 1 - Dec 15	*Credit Cards*	Yes
Pro	Paul McGuire	*Tee Times*	7 days
Comments	Undulating greens, homes along front 9		
Directions	Merritt Pkwy, exit 49N, right 1st stop sign Rt 111, 4 mi, right Rt 110, 1 mi		

Tee	Holes	Par	Rating	Slope	Yards
Red	18	73	72.9	124	5,832
White	18	72	70.9	127	6,262
Blue	18	72	72.4	130	6,628

98 Willimantic Country Club
184 Club Road, Willimantic, CT 06280
203-456-1971

Weekend Fee	$35 w/member	*Weekday Fee*	$35
Power Cart Fee	$12	*Pull Carts*	Yes
Putting Green	Yes	*Driving Range*	No
Season	Apr 1 - Dec 20	*Credit Cards*	Yes
Pro	John Boucher	*Tee Times*	5 days
Comments	Small greens, watered fairways		
Directions	I-384E, Rt 6E, at end take left, Rt 66, 0.3 mi		

Tee	Holes	Par	Rating	Slope	Yards
Red	18	74	68.6	113	5,106
White	18	71	69.2	119	6,003
Blue	18	71	70.5	121	6,271

99 Woodhaven Country Club
275 Miller Road, Bethany, CT 06524
203-393-3230

Weekend Fee	$27	*Weekday Fee*	$22
Power Cart Fee	$24	*Pull Carts*	Yes
Putting Green	Yes	*Driving Range*	Yes
Season	Year-round	*Credit Cards*	No
Pro	None	*Tee Times*	7 days
Comments	Tree lined, large greens, many sand traps		
Directions	Rt 15, Rt 63N, left Rt 67, 2.5 mi, follow signs		

Tee	Holes	Par	Rating	Slope	Yards
Red	9	74	73.0	125	5,718
White	9	72	70.6	123	6,384
Blue	9	72	72.7	128	6,774

100 Woodstock Golf Course
Roseland Park Road, Woodstock, CT 06281
203-928-4130

Weekend Fee	$16	*Weekday Fee*	$13
Power Cart Fee	$17	*Pull Carts*	Yes
Putting Green	Yes	*Driving Range*	Yes
Season	Apr 1 - Nov 25	*Credit Cards*	No
Pro	Butch Allard	*Tee Times*	No
Comments	Small greens, narrow fairways, built 1896		
Directions	I-395, exit 97, Rt 171W, 3 mi, 1st right after Woodstock Fair, right Roseland Park Rd		

Tee	Holes	Par	Rating	Slope	Yards
Red	9	72	63.4	104	3,556
White	9	66	63.4	104	4,500
Blue	NA	NA	NA	NA	NA

MAINE

*Sugarloaf Golf Course
Kingfield, Maine*

*Point Sebago Golf Course
Casco, Maine*

MAINE GOLF COURSES

Public Courses	*110*	*Private Courses*	*9*
Total Courses	*133*	*Percent Public Courses*	*92%*
18 Hole Public Courses	*39*	*9 Hole Public Courses*	*71*
Total Golfers	*92,000*	*Total Rounds of Golf*	*1,913,600*
Percent Female Golfers	*22.6%*	*Percent Senior Golfers*	*29.7%*
Rounds Per Course	*16,081*	*Rounds Per Golfer*	*20.8*
Golfers Per Course	*773*	*Courses Per 100 Square Miles*	*0.36*
Average Weekend Fee	*$20.29*	*Average Weekday Fee*	*$19.28*
Average Weekend Fee w/Power Cart	*$30.37*	*Average Weekday Fee w/Power Cart*	*$29.35*
Average Slope	*113.8*	*Average Yardage*	*5,562*

Maine has 119 golf courses - almost all of the golf courses are open to the public. Only 7 percent of the population plays golf which translates into 92,000 golfers playing 2 million rounds of golf every year[1] (20.8 rounds per golfer). Surprisingly, almost 30 percent of the golfers are senior citizens. Twenty-three percent of all golfers are women.

Maine's golf courses are the least crowded in New England. There are only 773 golfers per course and only 16,081 golf rounds are played annually per golf course.

Maine has a large percentage of 9 hole golf courses. Only 36% of the public courses are 18 holes.

Greens Fees

Maine is the least expensive state to play golf. On weekends, the average greens fees to play a round of 18 holes on public courses is $20.29 ($28.10 for 18 hole and $16.00 for 9 hole courses). (These costs include courses where power cart fees are part of the greens fees.) Golfers save very little ($1.01) by playing during the week when the average greens fee is $19.28 ($27.33 for 18 hole and $14.86 for 9 hole courses).

The most expensive greens fees are for the 18 hole Sugarloaf Golf Club in Carrabassett Valley ($79). The most expensive 9 hole course is the Bridgton Highlands Country Club ($35). The least expensive courses are the 9 hole Pine Ridge Golf Course in Waterville ($6) and the 18 hole Prospect Hill Golf Course in Auburn ($16).

A power cart rental for two players will cost $17.79 in Maine. On weekends, a round of golf with a power cart will cost each golfer an average of $30.37.

Slope and Yardage

Maine has the easiest golf courses in New England probably due to the high number of 9 hole courses. The average slope rating of all public courses from the white tees is 113.8 (118.3 for 18 hole and 110.7 for 9 hole courses). The courses with the highest slope rating from the white tees are the 18 hole Sugarloaf Golf Club in Carrabassett Valley (137) and the 9 hole Bangor Municipal Golf Course (128). The easiest 18 and 9 hole courses are the Natanis Golf Course (Tomahawk/Arrowhead) in Vassalboro (109) and Great Cove Golf Course in Jonesboro (84), respectively.

Maine courses are average in terms of distance from the white tees. The average yardage of all public courses from the white tees is 5,562 (6,040 yards for 18 hole and 5,300 yards for 9 hole courses). The courses with the longest yardage from the white tees are the 18 hole Sugarloaf Golf Club in Carrabassett Valley (6,456) and the 9 Bucksport Golf Club (6,704). The shortest 18 and 9 hole courses are the

---

[1] The Complete Golfer's Almanac 1995

MAINE

Northeast Harbor Golf Course (5,278) and the Westerly Winds Golf Course in Westbrook (1,660), respectively.

Public Courses Rated in Top 10 by Golf Digest

Rank	Course
1	Sugarloaf Golf Club
2	Samoset Resort Golf Course
3	Waterville Country Club
4	Kebo Valley Golf Club
5	Penobscott Valley Country Club

Rank	Course
6	Val Halla Golf Course
7	Brunswick Golf Club
8	Sable Oaks Golf Club
9	Biddeford Saco Golf Club
10	Natanis Golf Club

Oldest Golf Courses

Club	Year
Poland Spring Country Club	1896
Kebo Valley Golf Course	1898
Summit Golf Course	1899
Paris Hill Country Club	1899

Golf Schools and Instruction

- Golfer's Edge, 6 Deacon Road, Yarmouth, 04096, 207-846-9910
- Guaranteed Performance School of Golf, Bethel Inn and Country, Bethel, 04217, 207-824-2175
- J's Fore Season Golf, 1037 Forest Avenue, Portland, 207-797-8835
- Long Shot Golf Center, 305 Bath Road, Brunswick, 04011, 207-725-6377
- Samoset Resort Golf School, Rockport, 04856, 207-594-2511
- Sonny's Training Center, Cove Hill Road, Winterport, 04496, 800-430-5242
- Sugarloaf Golf School, Sugarloaf Inn, Route 27, Box 5000, Kingfield, 04947, 207-237-2000
- XL Indoor Golf, 1620 Outer Hammond Road, Hermon, 04401, 207-848-5850

Golf Associations and Touring Clubs

- Maine Golf Association, PO Box 419, Auburn, 04212, 207-795-6742
- Women's Maine State Golf Association, 33 Scrimshaw Lane, Saco, 04072, 207-282-1467
- Southern Maine Women's Golf Association, PO Box 15, York, 03909, 207-363-2252

Private Golf Courses

Course	Town
Augusta Country Club	Manchester
Blue Hill Country Club	Blue Hill
Cape Neddick Country Club	Cape Neddick
Falmouth Country Club	Falmouth
Martindale Country Club	Auburn
Portland Country Club	Falmouth
Prouts Black Country Club	Scarborough
Purpoodock Club	Cape Elizabeth
Woodlands Club	Falmouth

Retailers

- Golf Connection, 11 Portland N. Business Park, Falmouth, 04105, 207-878-3851
- Golf Day, 200 Gorham Road, South Portland, 207-761-2900
- Golf Day, Freeport Crossing Outlet Center, Freeport, 207-865-2202
- Golfer's Edge, 6 Deacon Road, Yarmouth, 207-846-9910
- Goldsmith's Sporting Goods, 667 Hogan Road, Bangor, 207-947-1168
- Long Shot Golf Center, 305 Bath Road, Brunswick, 04011, 207-725-2986
- Maine Golf, 29 Western Avenue, South Portland, 207-774-1877
- Nevada Bob's, Dansk Square, Route 1, Kittery, 207-439-5546
- Nevada Bob's, 198 Maine Mall, Portland, 207-871-9344
- Play it Again Sports, 270 State Street, Brewer, 04412, 207-989-8350
- Pro Golf Discount, 849 Stillwater Avenue, Bangor, 207-942-0717
- The Golf Connection, 35 Foden Road, South Portland, 207-871-7139

Driving Ranges and Practice Areas

Name	Address	Town	Phone
Cascade Golf Range	Portland Road	Saco	207-282-3524
College Street Driving Range	601 College Street	Lewiston	207-786-7818
Fore Season Golf	1037 Forest Avenue	Portland	207-797-8835
Lazy R Golf Driving Range	Waterville Road	Norridgewock	207-634-4037
Long Shot Golf Center	305 Bath Road	Brunswick	207-725-6377
Mountain View Golf Range	Route 109	Sanford	207-324-4012
Outlook Driving Range	Route 4	South Berwick	207-384-4456
Pine Acres Golf Center	550 Alfred Street	Biddeford	207-284-6489
Portland City Driving Range	1158 Riverside Street	Portland	207-797-3524
Sonny's Driving Range	Cove Road	Winterport	207-223-5242
Tee 'N Tee Golfland	Route 302	Westbrook	207-797-6753
Tee Shots	Route 9	Wells	207-646-2727
Westerly Winds Fun Center	771 Cumberland Street	Westbrook	207-854-9463
XL Indoor Golf	1620 Outer Hammond Road	Hermon	207-848-5850

Least Expensive Courses

Course	Town	Holes	Fee
Pine Ridge GC	Waterville	9	$6
Westerly Winds GC	Westbrook	9	$7
South Portland Municipal	South Portland	9	$8
Carmel Valley GC	Carmel	9	$10
Great Cove GC	Jonesboro	9	$10
Green Acres Inn and CC	Canton	9	$10
Greens at Eaglebrook	Scarborough	9	$10
Hampden CC	Hampden	9	$10
Katahdin CC	Milo	9	$10
Kenduskeag Valley GC	Kenduskeag	9	$10
Moose River GC	Moose River	9	$10
Sandy River GC	Farmington Falls	9	$10
West Newfield GC	West Newfield	9	$10

Most Expensive Courses

Course	Town	Holes	Fee
Sable Oaks Golf Club	South Portland	18	$29
Biddeford and Saco Country	Saco	18	$30
Waterville CC	Oakland	18	$38
Northeast Harbor Golf	Northeast Harbor	18	$30
Webhannet Golf Club	Kennebunk Beach	18	$30
Bethel Inn and CC	Bethel	18	$35
Bridgton Highlands CC	Bridgton	9	$35
Cape Arundel Golf Club	Kennebunkport	18	$40
Kebo Valley GC	Bar Harbor	18	$40
Point Sebago GC	Casco	18	$42
Penobscott Valley CC	Orono	18	$45
Samoset Resort GC	Rockport	18	$75
Sugarloaf GC	Carrabassett Valley	18	$79

Year-Round Courses

Course	Town	Holes
Greens at Eaglebrook	Scarborough	9

MAINE

Courses By Town

Course	Town	Holes
Prospect Hill GC	Auburn	18
Western View GC	Augusta	9
Bangor Municipal GC - 18	Bangor	18
Bangor Municipal GC - 9	Bangor	9
Hermon Meadows GC	Bangor	18
Kebo Valley GC	Bar Harbor	18
Bath CC	Bath	18
Bethel Inn and CC	Bethel	18
Dutch Elm GC	Biddeford	18
Boothbay Region CC	Boothbay	9
Pine Hill GC	Brewer	9
Bridgton Highlands CC	Bridgton	9
Country View GC	Brooks	9
Brunswick GC	Brunswick	18
Naval Air Station GC	Brunswick	9
Bucksport GC	Bucksport	9
Lakeview GC	Burnham	9
St. Croix CC	Calais	9
Goose River GC	Camden	9
Green Acres Inn and CC	Canton	9
Caribou CC	Caribou	18
Carmel Valley GC	Carmel	9
Sugarloaf GC	Carrabassett Valley	18
Point Sebago GC	Casco	18
Castine GC	Castine	9
Todd Valley GC	Charlestown	9
Great Chebeague GC	Chebeague Island	9
Val Halla GC	Cumberland Center	18
Island CC	Deer Isle	9
Dexter Municipal GC	Dexter	9
Foxcroft GC	Dover-Foxcroft	9
Lucerne Hills GC	East Holden	9
Woodland Terrace GC	East Holden	9
Fairlawn GC	East Poland	18
White Birches GC	Ellsworth	9
Green Meadow GC	Farmingdale	18
Kennebec Heights CC	Farmingdale	18
Sandy River GC	Farmington Falls	9
Aroostook Valley CC	Fort Fairfield	18
Fort Kent GC	Fort Kent	9
Freeport CC	Freeport	9
Gorham CC	Gorham	18
Squaw Mt. Village GC	Greenville	9
Piscataquis CC	Guilford	9
Hampden CC	Hampden	9
Salmon Falls GC	Hollis	18
Houlton Community GC	Houlton	9
Va-Jo-Wa GC	Island Falls	18
Great Cove GC	Jonesboro	9
Kenduskeag Valley GC	Kenduskeag	9
Webhannet GC	Kennebunk Beach	18
Cape Arundel GC	Kennebunkport	18
Spring Brook GC	Leeds	18
Apple Valley GC	Lewiston	9
Maple Lane CC	Livermore Falls	9
Lake Kezar CC	Lovell	9
Birch Point GC	Madawaska	9
Lakewood GC	Madison	18
Mars Hill CC	Mars Hill	9
Oakdale CC	Mexico	9
Hillcrest GC	Millinocket	9
Katahdin CC	Milo	9
Cobbossee Colony GC	Monmouth	9
Moose River GC	Moose River	9
Mt. Kineo GC	Mt. Kineo	9
Naples Golf and CC	Naples	9
Orchard View GC	Newport	9
Northeast Harbor GC	Northeast Harbor	18
Northport GC	Northport	9
Norway CC	Norway	9
Waterville CC	Oakland	18
Old Orchard Beach CC	Old Orchard	9
Penobscott Valley CC	Orono	18
Palmyra GC	Palmyra	18
Paris Hill CC	Paris	9
Province Lake CC	Parsonsfield	18
Johnson W. Parks GC	Pittsfield	9
Summit GC	Poland	13
Poland Spring CC	Poland Spring	18
Portage Hills CC	Portage	9
Riverside Municipal GC -	Portland	18
Riverside Municipal GC - 9	Portland	9
Presque Isle CC	Presque Isle	18
Mingo Springs GC	Rangeley	18
Frye Island GC	Raymond	9
Rockland GC	Rockland	18
Samoset Resort GC	Rockport	18
Biddeford and Saco CC	Saco	18
Sanford CC	Sanford	9
Greens at Eaglebrook	Scarborough	9
Pleasant Hill CC	Scarborough	9
Willowdale GC	Scarborough	18
Shore Acres GC	Sebasco Estates	9
Sable Oaks GC	South Portland	18
South Portland Muni GC	South Portland	9
Causeway GC	South West	9
Bar Harbor GC	Trenton	18
Turner Highlands	Turner	9
Natanis GC - A/I	Vassalboro	18
Natanis GC - I/T	Vassalboro	18
Natanis GC - T/A	Vassalboro	18
Wawenock CC	Walpole	9
Pine Ridge GC	Waterville	9
Green Valley GC	West Enfield	9
West Newfield GC	West Newfield	9
River Meadow GC	Westbrook	9
Twin Falls GC	Westbrook	9
Westerly Winds GC	Westbrook	9
Wilson Lake CC	Wilton	9
Grindstone Neck GC	Winter Harbor	9

Easiest Courses

Course	Town	Holes	Slope
Great Cove GC	Jonesboro	9	84
West Newfield GC	West Newfield	9	86
Todd Valley GC	Charlestown	9	93
Causeway GC	South West Harbor	9	95
Island CC	Deer Isle	9	97
Pine Hill GC	Brewer	9	99
Green Valley GC	West Enfield	9	101
Cobbossee Colony GC	Monmouth	9	102
Katahdin CC	Milo	9	102
St. Croix CC	Calais	9	102

Hardest Courses

Course	Town	Holes	Slope
Bath CC	Bath	18	123
Brunswick GC	Brunswick	18	123
Green Meadow GC	Farmingdale	18	123
Kennebec Heights CC	Farmingdale	18	123
Bethel Inn and CC	Bethel	18	124
Bangor Municipal GC - 9	Bangor	9	128
Kebo Valley GC	Bar Harbor	18	129
Point Sebago GC	Casco	18	129
Sable Oaks GC	South Portland	18	129
Sugarloaf GC	Carrabassett	18	137

Shortest Courses

Course	Town	Holes	Distance
Westerly Winds GC	Westbrook	9	1,660
Carmel Valley GC	Carmel	9	2,416
Sandy River GC	Farmington Falls	9	2,672
West Newfield GC	West Newfield	9	2,990
Woodland Terrace GC	East Holden	9	3,110
Great Cove GC	Jonesboro	9	3,388
Green Acres Inn and CC	Canton	9	3,600
Island CC	Deer Isle	9	3,865
Moose River GC	Moose River	9	3,952
South Portland Mun.	South Portland	9	4,142
Shore Acres GC	Sebasco Estates	9	4,218
Great Chebeague GC	Chebeague Island	9	4,468
Orchard View GC	Newport	9	4,480
Causeway GC	South West Harbor	9	4,604
Paris Hill CC	Paris	9	4,637
Todd Valley GC	Charlestown	9	4,672
Cobbossee Colony GC	Monmouth	9	4,702
Pleasant Hill CC	Scarborough	9	4,786
White Birches GC	Ellsworth	9	4,788
Twin Falls GC	Westbrook	9	4,880
Squaw Mountain	Greenville	9	4,926
Hillcrest GC	Millinocket	9	4,954

Longest Courses

Course	Town	Holes	Distance
Fort Kent GC	Fort Kent	9	6,224
Webhannet GC	Kennebunk	18	6,248
Foxcroft GC	Dover-Foxcroft	9	6,250
Brunswick GC	Brunswick	18	6,251
Riverside Muni. GC - 9	Portland	9	6,290
Fairlawn GC	East Poland	18	6,300
Penobscott Valley CC	Orono	18	6,301
Caribou CC	Caribou	18	6,320
Bethel Inn and CC	Bethel	18	6,330
Gorham CC	Gorham	18	6,334
Bangor Mun. GC - 18	Bangor	18	6,345
Oakdale CC	Mexico	9	6,366
Palmyra GC	Newport	18	6,367
Presque Isle CC	Presque Isle	18	6,393
Riverside Municipal	Portland	18	6,400
Portage Hills CC	Portage	9	6,420
Bar Harbor GC	Trenton	18	6,437
Sugarloaf GC	Carrabassett	18	6,456
Point Sebago GC	Casco	18	6474
Naples Golf and CC	Naples	9	6,554
Sanford CC	Sanford	9	6,592
Bucksport GC	Bucksport	9	6,704

Maine

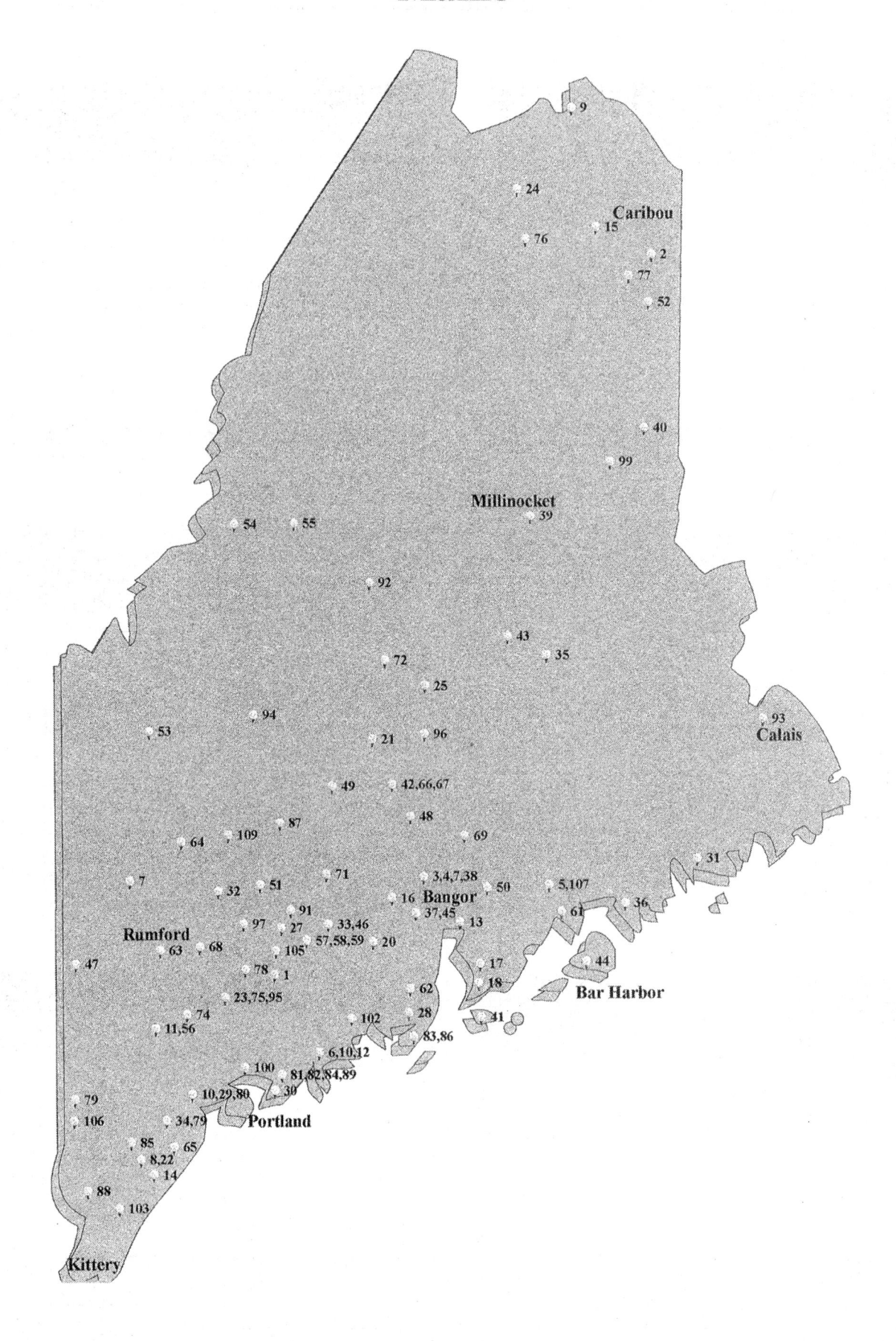

MAINE

1 Apple Valley Golf Club
Pinewoods Road, Lewiston, ME 04240
207-784-9773

Weekend Fee	$16	*Weekday Fee*	$16
Power Cart Fee	$16	*Pull Carts*	Yes
Putting Green	Yes	*Driving Range*	No
Season	Apr 1 - Nov 15	*Credit Cards*	Yes
Pro	Bill Gilroy	*Tee Times*	No
Comments	Fast greens, 4 water holes, tight fairways		
Directions	I-95, exit 13, right Dyer Rd, left Pinewoods Rd, 2 mi		

Tee	Holes	Par	Rating	Slope	Yards
Red	9	72	66.8	109	4,612
White	9	70	64.3	108	5,037
Blue	NA	NA	NA	NA	NA

2 Aroostook Valley Country Club
Russell Road, Fort Fairfield, ME 04742
207-476-6501

Weekend Fee	$22	*Weekday Fee*	$22
Power Cart Fee	$20	*Pull Carts*	Yes
Putting Green	Yes	*Driving Range*	Yes
Season	May 1 - Oct 15	*Credit Cards*	Yes
Pro	Steven Leitch	*Tee Times*	2 days
Comments	Part of course in Canada, hilly		
Directions	I-95, last exit, right Rt 1, over bridge, 1st right		

Tee	Holes	Par	Rating	Slope	Yards
Red	18	72	71.5	112	5,400
White	18	72	69.9	113	5,977
Blue	18	72	72.2	119	6,700

3 Bangor Municipal Golf Course - 18
278 Webster Avenue, Bangor, ME 04401
207-941-0232

Weekend Fee	$19	*Weekday Fee*	$18
Power Cart Fee	$17	*Pull Carts*	Yes
Putting Green	Yes	*Driving Range*	Yes
Season	Apr 15 - Nov 15	*Credit Cards*	No
Pro	Austin Kelly	*Tee Times*	No
Comments	Rated in top 50 in US by Golf Digest		
Directions	I-95N, exit 46, right Norway Rd at stop sign, right stop sign		

Tee	Holes	Par	Rating	Slope	Yards
Red	18	71	66.7	109	5,173
White	18	71	67.9	112	6,345
Blue	NA	NA	NA	NA	NA

4 Bangor Municipal Golf Course - 9
278 Webster Avenue, Bangor, ME 04401
207-941-0232

Weekend Fee	$19	*Weekday Fee*	$18
Power Cart Fee	$17	*Pull Carts*	Yes
Putting Green	Yes	*Driving Range*	Yes
Season	Apr 15 - Oct 31	*Credit Cards*	No
Pro	Brian Enman	*Tee Times*	No
Comments	Great course, Cornish design		
Directions	I-95N, exit 46, right Norway Rd at stop sign, right stop sign		

Tee	Holes	Par	Rating	Slope	Yards
Red	9	72	NA	NA	4,946
White	9	72	69.6	128	6,006
Blue	NA	NA	NA	NA	NA

5 Bar Harbor Golf Course
Route 3 and 204, Trenton, ME 04605
207-667-7505

Weekend Fee	$24	*Weekday Fee*	$24
Power Cart Fee	$22	*Pull Carts*	Yes
Putting Green	Yes	*Driving Range*	No
Season	Apr 15 - Nov 1	*Credit Cards*	Yes
Pro	T. Beauregard	*Tee Times*	No
Comments	Fast and large greens, #18 over 600 yds		
Directions	Rt 3, towards Bar Harbor, at intersection of Rt 3 and Rt 204		

Tee	Holes	Par	Rating	Slope	Yards
Red	18	73	70.4	115	5,428
White	18	71	70.2	122	6,437
Blue	18	71	71.1	122	6,667

6 Bath Country Club
Whiskeag Road, Bath, ME 04530
207-442-8411

Weekend Fee	$25	*Weekday Fee*	$25
Power Cart Fee	$18	*Pull Carts*	Yes
Putting Green	Yes	*Driving Range*	No
Season	May 1 - Nov 1	*Credit Cards*	Yes
Pro	Chris Angis	*Tee Times*	2 days
Comments	Tree lined, tight fairways, Cornish design		
Directions	Rt 1, exit New Meadows Rd, right E. Brunswick Rd		

Tee	Holes	Par	Rating	Slope	Yards
Red	18	70	67.0	115	4,708
White	18	70	67.8	123	5,748
Blue	18	70	70.2	128	6,216

MAINE

7 Bethel Inn and Country Club
1 Broad Street, Bethel, ME 04217
207-824-6276

Weekend Fee	$35	*Weekday Fee*	$26
Power Cart Fee	$28	*Pull Carts*	Yes
Putting Green	Yes	*Driving Range*	Yes
Season	May 1 - Nov 1	*Credit Cards*	Yes
Pro	Phil Grear	*Tee Times*	3 days
Comments	Great views, long fairways, 8 water holes		
Directions	I-95, exit 11, RT 26N, 55 mi, Bethel, left at top of Main St		

Tee	Holes	Par	Rating	Slope	Yards
Red	18	72	69.7	111	5,280
White	18	72	69.6	124	6,330
Blue	18	72	71.3	131	6,663

8 Biddeford and Saco Country Club
101 Old Orchard Road, Saco, ME 04005
207-282-9892

Weekend Fee	$30	*Weekday Fee*	$30
Power Cart Fee	$22	*Pull Carts*	Yes
Putting Green	Yes	*Driving Range*	Yes
Season	Apr 15 - Nov 15	*Credit Cards*	Yes
Pro	Tim Pooler	*Tee Times*	7 days
Comments	Well maintained, Donald Ross design		
Directions	I-95, exit 5, 2 mi to Halfway, right Old Orchard Rd		

Tee	Holes	Par	Rating	Slope	Yards
Red	18	71	71.0	115	5,470
White	18	71	68.2	119	5,835
Blue	18	71	69.5	122	6,192

9 Birch Point Golf Club
Birch Point Road, RR 1, Madawaska, ME 04756
207-895-6957

Weekend Fee	$15	*Weekday Fee*	$15
Power Cart Fee	$15	*Pull Carts*	Yes
Putting Green	Yes	*Driving Range*	Yes
Season	Apr 1 - Oct 1	*Credit Cards*	No
Pro	Larry Toonerde	*Tee Times*	No
Comments	Semi-private, small undulating greens		
Directions	Rt 1N, Madawaska, left Beauliew Rd, Birch Point Rd		

Tee	Holes	Par	Rating	Slope	Yards
Red	9	72	NA	105	5,800
White	9	70	NA	105	5,900
Blue	NA	NA	NA	NA	NA

10 Boothbay Region Country Club
Country Club Road, Boothbay, ME 04537
207-633-6085

Weekend Fee	$22	*Weekday Fee*	$22
Power Cart Fee	$20	*Pull Carts*	Yes
Putting Green	Yes	*Driving Range*	No
Season	May - Oct	*Credit Cards*	Yes
Pro	None	*Tee Times*	5 days
Comments	Small domed greens, water on some holes		
Directions	I-95, Rt 1, Rt 27, 10 mi, left at Texaco, Country Club Rd		

Tee	Holes	Par	Rating	Slope	Yards
Red	9	70	65.4	115	5,380
White	9	70	66.1	118	5,630
Blue	9	70	66.1	118	5,800

11 Bridgton Highlands Country Club
Lower Ridge Road, Bridgton, ME 04009
207-647-3491

Weekend Fee	$35	*Weekday Fee*	$30
Power Cart Fee	$20	*Pull Carts*	Yes
Putting Green	Yes	*Driving Range*	No
Season	Apr 15 - Nov 15	*Credit Cards*	No
Pro	Gordon Tenney	*Tee Times*	1 day
Comments	Irrigated, built in 1930s, expanding to 18		
Directions	Rt 302 in Bridgton, Highland Rd, 2 mi		

Tee	Holes	Par	Rating	Slope	Yards
Red	9	74	71.8	125	5,396
White	9	72	68.1	116	5,940
Blue	9	72	68.1	116	6,064

12 Brunswick Golf Club
River Road, Brunswick, ME 04011
207-725-8224

Weekend Fee	$30	*Weekday Fee*	$30
Power Cart Fee	$20	*Pull Carts*	Yes
Putting Green	Yes	*Driving Range*	No
Season	Apr 1 - Nov 15	*Credit Cards*	No
Pro	Mal Strange	*Tee Times*	No
Comments	Regulation championship course		
Directions	I-295, Brunswick, left 2nd light, River Rd		

Tee	Holes	Par	Rating	Slope	Yards
Red	18	72	NA	NA	5,772
White	18	72	70.0	123	6,251
Blue	18	72	NA	NA	6,609

13 Bucksport Golf Club
Duck Cove Road, Bucksport, ME 04416
207-469-7612

Weekend Fee	$18	*Weekday Fee*	$17
Power Cart Fee	$18	*Pull Carts*	Yes
Putting Green	Yes	*Driving Range*	Yes
Season	Apr 1 - Oct 31	*Credit Cards*	Yes
Pro	Wayne Hand	*Tee Times*	No
Comments	2 sets of tees, large bunkered greens, long		
Directions	Rt 3 to Belfast, Rt 1N, 3 mi from Bucksport		

Tee	Holes	Par	Rating	Slope	Yards
Red	9	72	72.2	115	5,578
White	9	72	70.6	117	6,704
Blue	9	72	70.6	117	6,796

16 Carmel Valley Golf Club
Main Road, Route 2, Carmel, ME 04419
207-848-2217

Weekend Fee	$10	*Weekday Fee*	$10
Power Cart Fee	No carts	*Pull Carts*	Yes
Putting Green	Yes	*Driving Range*	No
Season	Apr 1 - Nov	*Credit Cards*	Yes
Pro	Ted Johns	*Tee Times*	No
Comments	Executive course, fees are for all day golf		
Directions	I-95N, exit 39, Rt 7N, Rt 2W, look for signs		

Tee	Holes	Par	Rating	Slope	Yards
Red	9	54	55.7	NA	2,415
White	9	54	55.7	NA	2,415
Blue	NA	NA	NA	NA	NA

14 Cape Arundel Golf Club
1447 Old River Road, Kennebunkport, ME 04046
207-967-3494

Weekend Fee	$35	*Weekday Fee*	$35
Power Cart Fee	$20	*Pull Carts*	Yes
Putting Green	Yes	*Driving Range*	No
Season	Apr 15 - Nov 10	*Credit Cards*	Yes
Pro	Ken Raynor	*Tee Times*	1 day
Comments	Semi-private, small greens, unavailable 11-2		
Directions	I-95, Biddeford exit, left, sharp right 1st light, 5 mi, left light, log Cabin Rd, 4 mi, right		

Tee	Holes	Par	Rating	Slope	Yards
Red	18	70	68.6	106	5,134
White	18	69	67.0	117	5,869
Blue	NA	NA	NA	NA	NA

17 Castine Golf Club
Battle Avenue, Castine, ME 04421
207-326-8844

Weekend Fee	$20	*Weekday Fee*	$20
Power Cart Fee	$20	*Pull Carts*	Yes
Putting Green	Yes	*Driving Range*	Yes
Season	May 15 - Oct 15	*Credit Cards*	No
Pro	Tom Roberts	*Tee Times*	No
Comments	Small, sloped, elevated greens, hilly		
Directions	Rt 1 thru Bucksport, right Rt 175, Rt 166		

Tee	Holes	Par	Rating	Slope	Yards
Red	9	72	71.4	122	5,228
White	9	70	68.1	116	5,954
Blue	NA	NA	NA	NA	NA

15 Caribou Country Club
New Sweden Road, Caribou, ME 04736
207-493-3933

Weekend Fee	$15	*Weekday Fee*	$15
Power Cart Fee	$15	*Pull Carts*	Yes
Putting Green	Yes	*Driving Range*	Yes
Season	May 1 - Oct 15	*Credit Cards*	Yes
Pro	Jeff Jose	*Tee Times*	No
Comments	Log cabin club house, hilly fairways		
Directions	Rt 61N, course 1.5 mi from Caribou		

Tee	Holes	Par	Rating	Slope	Yards
Red	9	72	70.4	116	5,580
White	9	72	68.8	116	6,320
Blue	NA	NA	NA	NA	NA

18 Causeway Golf Club
Fernald Point Road, Southwest Harbor, ME 04676
207-244-3780

Weekend Fee	$24	*Weekday Fee*	$24
Power Cart Fee	No carts	*Pull Carts*	Yes
Putting Green	Yes	*Driving Range*	No
Season	May - Oct	*Credit Cards*	No
Pro	None	*Tee Times*	No
Comments	Views of harbor, hilly, undulating greens		
Directions	I-95, Rt 1A Ellsworth center, Rt 3S, Rt 102S follow signs		

Tee	Holes	Par	Rating	Slope	Yards
Red	9	64	64.8	102	4,170
White	9	64	60.8	95	4,604
Blue	NA	NA	NA	NA	NA

MAINE

19 Cobbossee Colony Golf Club
885 Cobbosseecontee Road, Monmouth, ME 04259
207-268-4182

Weekend Fee	$11	*Weekday Fee*	$10	
Power Cart Fee	$11	*Pull Carts*	Yes	
Putting Green	Yes	*Driving Range*	No	
Season	Apr 1 - Nov 1	*Credit Cards*	No	
Pro	None	*Tee Times*	No	
Comments	Small greens, resort course built in 1930s			
Directions	I-295, Gardiner exit, left, Rt 126, 4 mi, right Hallowell-Litchfield Rd, 1.5 mi			

Tee	Holes	Par	Rating	Slope	Yards
Red	9	72	63.2	103	4,600
White	9	68	62.0	102	4,702
Blue	NA	NA	NA	NA	NA

20 Country View Golf Course
Route 7 Box 56, Brooks, ME 04921
207-722-3161

Weekend Fee	$16	*Weekday Fee*	$16	
Power Cart Fee	$16	*Pull Carts*	Yes	
Putting Green	Yes	*Driving Range*	No	
Season	Apr 1 - Nov 1	*Credit Cards*	No	
Pro	None	*Tee Times*	No	
Comments	Well maintained			
Directions	Rt 1, Rt 137N, right Rt 7, 1 mi north of Brooks			

Tee	Holes	Par	Rating	Slope	Yards
Red	9	72	68.1	105	4,960
White	9	72	66.4	115	5,770
Blue	NA	NA	NA	NA	NA

21 Dexter Municipal Golf Course
Sunrise Avenue, Dexter, ME 04930
207-924-6477

Weekend Fee	$15	*Weekday Fee*	$13	
Power Cart Fee	$19	*Pull Carts*	Yes	
Putting Green	Yes	*Driving Range*	Yes	
Season	Apr 15 - Oct 15	*Credit Cards*	No	
Pro	Steve Hodgkins	*Tee Times*	No	
Comments	5 holes with ponds, hilly fairways			
Directions	I-95, exit 39, Rt 7 Dexter, 14 mi, left Liberty St, left at end			

Tee	Holes	Par	Rating	Slope	Yards
Red	9	70	NA	NA	4,784
White	9	70	65.7	115	5,172
Blue	NA	NA	NA	NA	NA

22 Dutch Elm Golf Course
Brimstone Road, Biddeford, ME 04005
207-282-9850

Weekend Fee	$27	*Weekday Fee*	$25	
Power Cart Fee	$20	*Pull Carts*	Yes	
Putting Green	Yes	*Driving Range*	No	
Season	Apr 15 - Nov 15	*Credit Cards*	Yes	
Pro	Norm Hevey	*Tee Times*	3 days	
Comments	Irrigated, scenic, undulating greens, wooded			
Directions	I-95, exit 4, right, Rt 111, 1 mi, left at Sunoco, 1 mi, right at stop sign			

Tee	Holes	Par	Rating	Slope	Yards
Red	18	73	70.1	115	5,384
White	18	72	67.4	115	5,882
Blue	18	72	68.9	119	6,230

23 Fairlawn Golf Club
Route 1 Box 622, East Poland, ME 04230
207-998-4277

Weekend Fee	$17	*Weekday Fee*	$15	
Power Cart Fee	$12	*Pull Carts*	Yes	
Putting Green	Yes	*Driving Range*	Yes	
Season	Apr 1 - Nov 1	*Credit Cards*	No	
Pro	David Bartasuis	*Tee Times*	No	
Comments	Rent condos overlooking 18th green			
Directions	I-95, exit 12, right, 1st right, left at end, Lewiston Jct Rd, right at stop sign			

Tee	Holes	Par	Rating	Slope	Yards
Red	18	74	70.1	121	5,379
White	18	72	69.3	119	6,300
Blue	NA	NA	NA	NA	NA

24 Fort Kent Golf Course
St. John Road, Fort Kent, ME 04743
207-924-6477

Weekend Fee	$18	*Weekday Fee*	$18	
Power Cart Fee	$15	*Pull Carts*	Yes	
Putting Green	Yes	*Driving Range*	Yes	
Season	May 1 - Oct 31	*Credit Cards*	No	
Pro	None	*Tee Times*	No	
Comments	Undulating and elevated greens			
Directions	Rt 161, Fort Kent, 3 mi, follow signs			

Tee	Holes	Par	Rating	Slope	Yards
Red	9	72	72.3	115	5,900
White	9	70	69.0	111	6,224
Blue	9	70	70.1	113	6,490

25 Foxcroft Golf Club
24 Foxcroft Center Road, Dover-Foxcroft, ME 04426
207-564-8887

Weekend Fee	$20	*Weekday Fee*	$20
Power Cart Fee	$16	*Pull Carts*	Yes
Putting Green	Yes	*Driving Range*	No
Season	May 1 - Oct 31	*Credit Cards*	No
Pro	Lou Thibeault	*Tee Times*	No
Comments	Easy course		
Directions	Rt 16E through Dover-Foxcroft, left Foxcroft Center Rd		

Tee	Holes	Par	Rating	Slope	Yards
Red	9	72	NA	107	6,250
White	9	72	NA	107	6,250
Blue	NA	NA	NA	NA	NA

26 Freeport Country Club
2 Old County Road Extension, Freeport, ME 04032
207-865-4922

Weekend Fee	$16	*Weekday Fee*	$13
Power Cart Fee	$18	*Pull Carts*	Yes
Putting Green	Yes	*Driving Range*	No
Season	Apr 1 - Nov 1	*Credit Cards*	Yes
Pro	Gary Rees	*Tee Times*	7 days
Comments	Links style, open fairways, small greens		
Directions	I-95N, exit 17, Rt 1, 1 mi, left Old County Rd		

Tee	Holes	Par	Rating	Slope	Yards
Red	9	72	72.4	114	5,164
White	9	72	68.2	113	5,884
Blue	NA	NA	NA	NA	NA

27 Frye Island Golf Course
115 Cape Road Extension, Raymond, ME 04071
207-655-3551

Weekend Fee	$20	*Weekday Fee*	$15
Power Cart Fee	$16	*Pull Carts*	Yes
Putting Green	Yes	*Driving Range*	No
Season	May 1 - Nov 1	*Credit Cards*	No
Pro	Mary Dresser	*Tee Times*	No
Comments	Water, tree lined, narrow		
Directions	Exit 8, Westbrook, 2 mi, Rt 302, 20 mi, Raymond Cape Rd, Frye Island ferry, follow signs		

Tee	Holes	Par	Rating	Slope	Yards
Red	9	72	66.9	109	5,302
White	9	72	68.7	113	6,046
Blue	9	72	71.6	123	6,510

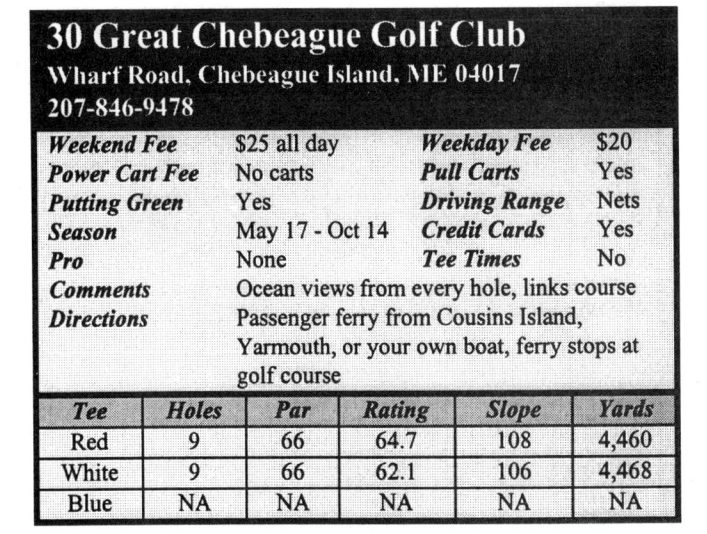

28 Goose River Golf Club
50 Park Street, Camden, ME 04843
207-236-8488

Weekend Fee	$20	*Weekday Fee*	$20
Power Cart Fee	$20	*Pull Carts*	Yes
Putting Green	Yes	*Driving Range*	No
Season	Apr 1 - Nov 1	*Credit Cards*	No
Pro	Chris Christie	*Tee Times*	3 days
Comments	Semi-private, 18 different tees, hilly		
Directions	I-95N, Rt 1N, to Camden, follow signs		

Tee	Holes	Par	Rating	Slope	Yards
Red	9	72	67.8	115	5,208
White	9	70	68.7	115	6,098
Blue	NA	NA	NA	NA	NA

29 Gorham Country Club
134 McLellan Road, Gorham, ME 04038
207-839-3490

Weekend Fee	$22	*Weekday Fee*	$22
Power Cart Fee	$20	*Pull Carts*	Yes
Putting Green	Yes	*Driving Range*	Yes
Season	Apr 15 - Nov 15	*Credit Cards*	No
Pro	Mark Fogg	*Tee Times*	7 days
Comments	On protected game preserve, very wooded		
Directions	I-95, exit 7, Rt 114, Gorham, right McLellan Rd		

Tee	Holes	Par	Rating	Slope	Yards
Red	18	73	72.7	119	5,868
White	18	71	68.3	116	6,334
Blue	18	71	70.1	120	6,552

30 Great Chebeague Golf Club
Wharf Road, Chebeague Island, ME 04017
207-846-9478

Weekend Fee	$25 all day	*Weekday Fee*	$20
Power Cart Fee	No carts	*Pull Carts*	Yes
Putting Green	Yes	*Driving Range*	Nets
Season	May 17 - Oct 14	*Credit Cards*	Yes
Pro	None	*Tee Times*	No
Comments	Ocean views from every hole, links course		
Directions	Passenger ferry from Cousins Island, Yarmouth, or your own boat, ferry stops at golf course		

Tee	Holes	Par	Rating	Slope	Yards
Red	9	66	64.7	108	4,460
White	9	66	62.1	106	4,468
Blue	NA	NA	NA	NA	NA

MAINE

31 Great Cove Golf Course
Rogue Bluffs Road, Jonesboro, ME 04648
207-434-2981

Weekend Fee	$10	Weekday Fee	$10
Power Cart Fee	$10	Pull Carts	Yes
Putting Green	Yes	Driving Range	Yes
Season	May - Oct	Credit Cards	No
Pro	Leon Sinford	Tee Times	No
Comments	Short, easy course		
Directions	Jonesboro, Rt 1, 3 mi		

Tee	Holes	Par	Rating	Slope	Yards
Red	9	60	NA	NA	3,388
White	9	60	NA	84	3,388
Blue	NA	NA	NA	NA	NA

32 Green Acres Inn and Country Club
Green Acre Road, Route 140, Canton, ME 04221
207-597-2333

Weekend Fee	$10	Weekday Fee	$10
Power Cart Fee	Yes	Pull Carts	Yes
Putting Green	Yes	Driving Range	No
Season	Jun - Oct	Credit Cards	No
Pro	None	Tee Times	No
Comments	Resort course, on Lake Anaasigundicook		
Directions	I-95, Rt 4 exit, Rt 108 to Canton, Rt 140		

Tee	Holes	Par	Rating	Slope	Yards
Red	9	62	NA	NA	3,600
White	9	62	NA	NA	3,600
Blue	NA	NA	NA	NA	NA

33 Green Meadow Golf Club
Meadow Hill Drive, Farmingdale, ME 04344
207-623-9831

Weekend Fee	$20	Weekday Fee	$20
Power Cart Fee	Yes	Pull Carts	Yes
Putting Green	Yes	Driving Range	Yes
Season	Apr 1 - Snow	Credit Cards	No
Pro	Bob Mathews	Tee Times	Yes
Comments	Back 9 designed by Cornish and Silva		
Directions	I-95, Augusta exit, Rt 202, Rt 201S		

Tee	Holes	Par	Rating	Slope	Yards
Red	18	70	67.1	123	5,525
White	18	70	67.1	123	5,525
Blue	NA	NA	NA	NA	NA

34 Greens at Eaglebrook
304 Gorham Road, Scarborough, ME 04074
207-839-6795

Weekend Fee	$10	Weekday Fee	$10
Power Cart Fee	$11	Pull Carts	Yes
Putting Green	Yes	Driving Range	No
Season	Apr 1 - Nov 1	Credit Cards	No
Pro	Nancy Harris	Tee Times	No
Comments	3 ponds, undulating greens w/deep bunkers		
Directions	I-95W, Rt 114, 0.3 mi		

Tee	Holes	Par	Rating	Slope	Yards
Red	9	70	69.0	109	5,144
White	9	70	66.8	106	5,768
Blue	NA	NA	NA	NA	NA

35 Green Valley Golf Course
Route 2, West Enfield, ME 04493
207-732-3006

Weekend Fee	$11	Weekday Fee	$11
Power Cart Fee	$15	Pull Carts	Yes
Putting Green	Yes	Driving Range	No
Season	May - Nov	Credit Cards	No
Pro	James Plourde	Tee Times	7 days
Comments	Well maintained, sloped, fast greens		
Directions	I-95, Howland exit, Rt 2 to Lincoln, on Rt 2		

Tee	Holes	Par	Rating	Slope	Yards
Red	9	72	63.0	101	5,248
White	9	72	63.0	101	5,248
Blue	NA	NA	NA	NA	NA

36 Grindstone Neck Golf Course
Grindstone Avenue, Rt 86, Winter Harbor, ME 04693
207-963-7760

Weekend Fee	$25	Weekday Fee	$22
Power Cart Fee	$18	Pull Carts	Yes
Putting Green	Yes	Driving Range	No
Season	Jun 1 - Oct 18	Credit Cards	Yes
Pro	Oscar Young	Tee Times	No
Comments	On Frenchman's Bay, water every hole		
Directions	Rt 1N, Rt 86, 6 mi		

Tee	Holes	Par	Rating	Slope	Yards
Red	9	72	NA	NA	5,030
White	9	72	NA	NA	6,190
Blue	NA	NA	NA	NA	NA

37 Hampden Country Club
Thomas Road, Hampden, ME 04444
207-862-9999

Weekend Fee	$10	Weekday Fee	$10
Power Cart Fee	$10	Pull Carts	Yes
Putting Green	Yes	Driving Range	No
Season	Apr 20 - Oct 20	Credit Cards	No
Pro	Sunny Reynolds	Tee Times	7 days
Comments	Open, easy to walk, wooded		
Directions	I-95, exit 43, Rt 69E, 1.5 mi, Rt 9E, 2 mi		

Tee	Holes	Par	Rating	Slope	Yards
Red	9	72	64.0	112	5,100
White	9	72	64.0	106	5,434
Blue	NA	NA	NA	NA	NA

40 Houlton Community Golf Course
Nickerson Lake Road, Houlton, ME 04730
207-532-2662

Weekend Fee	$20	Weekday Fee	$18
Power Cart Fee	$20	Pull Carts	Yes
Putting Green	Yes	Driving Range	No
Season	Apr 1 - Nov 1	Credit Cards	No
Pro	Babe Caron	Tee Times	7 days
Comments	Small undulating greens, bunkered fairways		
Directions	I-95, Smyra exit, right, right at Tyler's Store, left Nickerson Lake Rd		

Tee	Holes	Par	Rating	Slope	Yards
Red	9	76	73.6	109	5,540
White	9	72	68.7	117	6,080
Blue	NA	NA	NA	NA	NA

38 Hermon Meadows Golf Course
Billings Road, Route 2 Box 6160, Bangor, ME 04401
207-848-3741

Weekend Fee	$18	Weekday Fee	$18
Power Cart Fee	$18	Pull Carts	Yes
Putting Green	Yes	Driving Range	No
Season	May 1 - Nov 1	Credit Cards	Yes
Pro	None	Tee Times	No
Comments	Hilly, wooded, small greens		
Directions	Union St, 4 mi past Bangor airport, left Billings Rd, 2 mi		

Tee	Holes	Par	Rating	Slope	Yards
Red	18	72	70.2	119	5,315
White	18	72	66.7	110	5,895
Blue	18	72	68.0	114	6,329

41 Island Country Club
Route 15A, Deer Isle, ME 04683
207-348-2379

Weekend Fee	$12	Weekday Fee	$10
Power Cart Fee	No carts	Pull Carts	Yes
Putting Green	Yes	Driving Range	No
Season	May 28 - Oct 1	Credit Cards	No
Pro	None	Tee Times	No
Comments	Fees are for all day		
Directions	Rt 1, Rt 15S, go to Deer Island (West Side), follow signs		

Tee	Holes	Par	Rating	Slope	Yards
Red	9	64	62.1	92	3,624
White	9	62	58.8	97	3,865
Blue	NA	NA	NA	NA	NA

39 Hillcrest Golf Course
Westwood Avenue, Millinocket, ME 04462
207-723-8410

Weekend Fee	$14	Weekday Fee	$12
Power Cart Fee	No carts	Pull Carts	Yes
Putting Green	Yes	Driving Range	No
Season	May 1 - Oct 31	Credit Cards	No
Pro	None	Tee Times	No
Comments	Narrow, tight, tree lined		
Directions	I-95, Medway exit, left, Rt 157, 12 mi, right 1st light, left 3rd stop sign, left stop sign		

Tee	Holes	Par	Rating	Slope	Yards
Red	9	72	63.9	97	4,944
White	9	66	63.2	104	4,954
Blue	NA	NA	NA	NA	NA

42 Johnson W. Parks Golf Course
94 Hartland Avenue, Pittsfield, ME 04967
207-487-5545

Weekend Fee	$18	Weekday Fee	$16
Power Cart Fee	$18	Pull Carts	Yes
Putting Green	Yes	Driving Range	No
Season	Apr 1 - Oct 31	Credit Cards	No
Pro	D. McAllister	Tee Times	7 days
Comments	Narrow fairways with tall pines, fast greens		
Directions	I-95, exit 38 (Sommerset Ave), left at Hartland Ave		

Tee	Holes	Par	Rating	Slope	Yards
Red	9	70	68.9	111	4,972
White	9	70	68.4	114	5,776
Blue	NA	NA	NA	NA	NA

MAINE

43 Katahdin Country Club
70 Park Street, Milo, ME 04463
207-943-2868

Weekend Fee	$10	*Weekday Fee*	$10
Power Cart Fee	$14	*Pull Carts*	Yes
Putting Green	Yes	*Driving Range*	No
Season	Apr 15 - Nov 31	*Credit Cards*	No
Pro	None	*Tee Times*	No
Comments	Open fairways, no water		
Directions	I-95N, LaGrange-Milo exit, follow signs		

Tee	Holes	Par	Rating	Slope	Yards
Red	9	72	64.7	102	6,006
White	9	72	64.7	102	6,006
Blue	NA	NA	NA	NA	NA

44 Kebo Valley Golf Course
Eagle Lake Road, Bar Harbor, ME 04609
207-288-3000

Weekend Fee	$40	*Weekday Fee*	$40
Power Cart Fee	$28	*Pull Carts*	Yes
Putting Green	Yes	*Driving Range*	No
Season	Apr 1 - Oct 31	*Credit Cards*	Yes
Pro	Greg Baker	*Tee Times*	2 days
Comments	Rated in top 50, built 1888, 8th oldest in US		
Directions	I-95, Bangor exit, Rt 1 (Ellsworth), Rt 3 to Bar Harbor, follow signs		

Tee	Holes	Par	Rating	Slope	Yards
Red	18	72	72.0	121	5,440
White	18	70	69.0	129	5,925
Blue	NA	NA	NA	NA	NA

45 Kenduskeag Valley Golf Course
Higginsville Road, Kenduskeag, ME 04450
207-884-7330

Weekend Fee	$10	*Weekday Fee*	$9
Power Cart Fee	$10	*Pull Carts*	Yes
Putting Green	Yes	*Driving Range*	No
Season	Apr 1 - Oct 31	*Credit Cards*	No
Pro	None	*Tee Times*	No
Comments	Wooded with small greens		
Directions	I-95, Bangor-Broadway exit, Rt 15N, 11 mi, 1st left after Kenduskeag		

Tee	Holes	Par	Rating	Slope	Yards
Red	9	68	NA	NA	4,850
White	9	68	63.8	108	5,124
Blue	NA	NA	NA	NA	NA

46 Kennebec Heights Country Club
Green Meadow Drive, Farmingdale, ME 04344
207-582-2000

Weekend Fee	$22	*Weekday Fee*	$20
Power Cart Fee	$20	*Pull Carts*	Yes
Putting Green	Yes	*Driving Range*	No
Season	Apr 1 - Oct 31	*Credit Cards*	Yes
Pro	Robert Mathews	*Tee Times*	7 days
Comments	3 ponds, mainly flat, few elevated greens		
Directions	I-95N, exit 27, Rt 201N, look for signs		

Tee	Holes	Par	Rating	Slope	Yards
Red	18	70	67.1	117	4,820
White	18	70	67.1	123	5,525
Blue	18	70	69.0	129	6,003

47 Lake Kezar Country Club
Route 5, Lovell, ME 04051
207-925-2462

Weekend Fee	$20	*Weekday Fee*	$18
Power Cart Fee	$20	*Pull Carts*	Yes
Putting Green	Yes	*Driving Range*	Yes
Season	May 1 - Oct 31	*Credit Cards*	No
Pro	Randy Greason	*Tee Times*	7 days
Comments	Scenic, building another 9 in 1996		
Directions	I-95, Rt 302, right Knights Hill Rd, Lovell Village, Rt 5N, 2 mi		

Tee	Holes	Par	Rating	Slope	Yards
Red	9	72	66.8	107	4,956
White	9	72	68.0	119	5,850
Blue	NA	NA	NA	NA	NA

48 Lakeview Golf Club
Prairie Road, Burnham, ME 04922
207-948-5414

Weekend Fee	$15	*Weekday Fee*	$13
Power Cart Fee	No carts	*Pull Carts*	Yes
Putting Green	Yes	*Driving Range*	No
Season	Apr 15 - Oct 30	*Credit Cards*	No
Pro	None	*Tee Times*	1 day
Comments	Level course, next to Lake Winnercook		
Directions	Rt 137N, 22 mi, Rt 139 to Unity, watch for signs		

Tee	Holes	Par	Rating	Slope	Yards
Red	9	72	69.9	114	5,396
White	9	72	68.0	114	5,900
Blue	9	72	68.0	114	6,032

MAINE

49 Lakewood Golf Course
Route 201 Lakewood Center, Madison, ME 04976
207-474-5955

Weekend Fee	$18	Weekday Fee	$18
Power Cart Fee	$16	Pull Carts	Yes
Putting Green	Yes	Driving Range	No
Season	May - Nov	Credit Cards	No
Pro	Burt Dumis	Tee Times	No
Comments	13 holes w/water, undulating greens		
Directions	I-95, exit 36 (Rt 201), 5 mi towards Bingham		

Tee	Holes	Par	Rating	Slope	Yards
Red	18	70	66.3	110	5,226
White	18	70	68.5	114	5,729
Blue	NA	NA	NA	NA	NA

50 Lucerne Hills Golf Club
Route 1A, East Holden, ME 04429
207-843-6282

Weekend Fee	$15	Weekday Fee	$12
Power Cart Fee	$16	Pull Carts	Yes
Putting Green	Yes	Driving Range	Yes
Season	Apr 1 - Nov 15	Credit Cards	Yes
Pro	Roger Tracy	Tee Times	Month
Comments	Open, scenic, Donald Ross design		
Directions	Located 7 mi south of I-395 in Brewer on Bar Harbor Rd		

Tee	Holes	Par	Rating	Slope	Yards
Red	9	72	NA	NA	4,560
White	9	72	67.4	119	5,760
Blue	9	72	70.6	119	6,410

51 Maple Lane Country Club
River Road, Livermore Falls, ME 04254
207-897-4453

Weekend Fee	$15	Weekday Fee	$15
Power Cart Fee	$16	Pull Carts	Yes
Putting Green	Yes	Driving Range	No
Season	Apr - Nov	Credit Cards	No
Pro	None	Tee Times	No
Comments	Short course		
Directions	I-95, Rt 4 towards Livermore, right Rt 108, follow signs		

Tee	Holes	Par	Rating	Slope	Yards
Red	9	70	NA	NA	5,146
White	9	70	NA	NA	5,146
Blue	NA	NA	NA	NA	NA

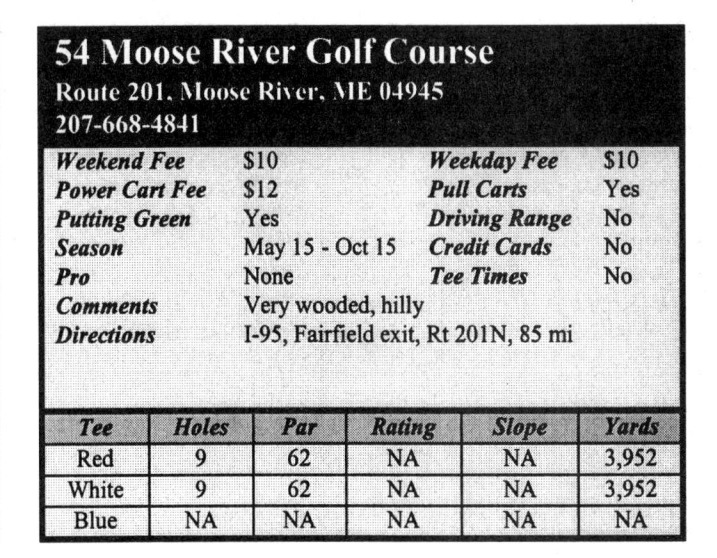

52 Mars Hill Country Club
York Road, Mars Hill, ME 04758
207-425-4802

Weekend Fee	$17	Weekday Fee	$17
Power Cart Fee	$14	Pull Carts	Yes
Putting Green	Yes	Driving Range	Yes
Season	May 1 - Oct 1	Credit Cards	Yes
Pro	None	Tee Times	No
Comments	Scenic, at base of Mars Hill Mountain		
Directions	I-95N, exit 62, Rt 1N, 1 mi past Rt 1A, right E. Ridge Rd, 1 mi, east on Bell Hill Rd		

Tee	Holes	Par	Rating	Slope	Yards
Red	9	72	68.8	120	5,940
White	9	72	68.8	120	5,940
Blue	NA	NA	NA	NA	NA

53 Mingo Springs Golf Course
Procter Road and Route 4, Rangeley, ME 04970
207-864-5021

Weekend Fee	$24	Weekday Fee	$24
Power Cart Fee	$24	Pull Carts	Yes
Putting Green	Yes	Driving Range	No
Season	May 26 - Oct 15	Credit Cards	No
Pro	Si Pillsbury	Tee Times	No
Comments	Very scenic, elevated tees and greens		
Directions	I-95, exit 12 (Auburn), Rt 4 towards Rangeley, follow signs		

Tee	Holes	Par	Rating	Slope	Yards
Red	18	72	67.4	110	5,334
White	18	72	66.3	109	5,923
Blue	NA	NA	NA	NA	NA

54 Moose River Golf Course
Route 201, Moose River, ME 04945
207-668-4841

Weekend Fee	$10	Weekday Fee	$10
Power Cart Fee	$12	Pull Carts	Yes
Putting Green	Yes	Driving Range	No
Season	May 15 - Oct 15	Credit Cards	No
Pro	None	Tee Times	No
Comments	Very wooded, hilly		
Directions	I-95, Fairfield exit, Rt 201N, 85 mi		

Tee	Holes	Par	Rating	Slope	Yards
Red	9	62	NA	NA	3,952
White	9	62	NA	NA	3,952
Blue	NA	NA	NA	NA	NA

MAINE

55 Mt. Kineo Golf Course
Mt. Kineo on Moosehead Lake, Mt. Kineo, ME 04478
207-534-2221

Weekend Fee	$13	Weekday Fee	$13
Power Cart Fee	$20	Pull Carts	Yes
Putting Green	Yes	Driving Range	No
Season	Jun 1 - Oct 15	Credit Cards	No
Pro	None	Tee Times	No
Comments	On island		
Directions	At Kineo, take shuttle boat to island		

Tee	Holes	Par	Rating	Slope	Yards
Red	9	72	NA	NA	6,022
White	9	72	NA	NA	6,022
Blue	NA	NA	NA	NA	NA

56 Naples Golf and Country Club
Old Route 114, Naples, ME 04055
207-693-6424

Weekend Fee	$24	Weekday Fee	$22
Power Cart Fee	$20	Pull Carts	Yes
Putting Green	Yes	Driving Range	No
Season	Apr 15 - Nov 1	Credit Cards	Yes
Pro	Harry Andrews	Tee Times	No
Comments	Few elevated tees and greens, 3 water holes		
Directions	Rt 302W to Naples center, left on Rt 114, look for signs		

Tee	Holes	Par	Rating	Slope	Yards
Red	9	72	69.3	116	5,216
White	9	72	69.5	115	6,554
Blue	9	72	NA	NA	6,022

57 Natanis GC - Arrowhead/Indian
Webber Pond Road, Vassalboro, ME 04989
207-622-3561

Weekend Fee	$20	Weekday Fee	$20
Power Cart Fee	$18	Pull Carts	Yes
Putting Green	Yes	Driving Range	Yes
Season	Apr 15 - Nov 1	Credit Cards	Yes
Pro	Richard Browne	Tee Times	7 days
Comments	27 holes in total		
Directions	I-95N, Augusta exit, Rt 201N, 10 mi		

Tee	Holes	Par	Rating	Slope	Yards
Red	18	72	68.7	117	5,218
White	18	73	66.8	112	5,923
Blue	18	73	69.0	117	6,223

58 Natanis GC - Indian/Tomahawk
Webber Pond Road, Vassalboro, ME 04989
207-622-3561

Weekend Fee	$20	Weekday Fee	$20
Power Cart Fee	$18	Pull Carts	Yes
Putting Green	Yes	Driving Range	Yes
Season	Apr 15 - Nov 1	Credit Cards	Yes
Pro	Richard Browne	Tee Times	7 days
Comments	27 holes in total		
Directions	I-95N, Augusta exit, Rt 201N, 10 mi		

Tee	Holes	Par	Rating	Slope	Yards
Red	18	72	71.6	122	5,376
White	18	72	68.4	120	6,170
Blue	18	72	71.8	126	6,627

59 Natanis GC Tomahawk/Arrow head
Webber Pond Road, Vassalboro, ME 04989
207-622-3561

Weekend Fee	$20	Weekday Fee	$20
Power Cart Fee	$18	Pull Carts	Yes
Putting Green	Yes	Driving Range	Yes
Season	Apr 15 - Nov 1	Credit Cards	Yes
Pro	Richard Browne	Tee Times	7 days
Comments	27 holes in total		
Directions	I-95N, Augusta exit, Rt 201N, 10 mi		

Tee	Holes	Par	Rating	Slope	Yards
Red	18	72	70.7	116	4,974
White	18	73	66.0	109	5,803
Blue	18	73	68.1	114	6,290

60 Naval Air Station Brunswick GC
551 Fitch Avenue, Brunswick, ME 04011
207-921-2155

Weekend Fee	$17	Weekday Fee	$15
Power Cart Fee	$16	Pull Carts	Yes
Putting Green	Yes	Driving Range	Yes
Season	Apr 15 - Nov 15	Credit Cards	Yes
Pro	Terry Russell	Tee Times	No
Comments	Fast & small greens, tree lined, double tees		
Directions	Rt 1S, 0.5 mi past Cook's Corner		

Tee	Holes	Par	Rating	Slope	Yards
Red	9	70	71.4	116	5,594
White	9	70	68.4	115	6,199
Blue	NA	NA	NA	NA	NA

61 Northeast Harbor Golf Course
Sargent Drive, Northeast Harbor, ME 04662
207-276-5335

Weekend Fee	$40	*Weekday Fee*	$40
Power Cart Fee	$24	*Pull Carts*	Yes
Putting Green	Yes	*Driving Range*	No
Season	May 15 - Oct 15	*Credit Cards*	No
Pro	Rob Gardner	*Tee Times*	7 days
Comments	Combination of hilly and level holes		
Directions	I-95, Bangor exit, Rt 1A to Ellsworth, Rt 3 to Arcadia Park, Rt 102, Rt 198, right Sargent		

Tee	Holes	Par	Rating	Slope	Yards
Red	18	71	67.3	116	4,540
White	18	69	66.7	118	5,278
Blue	18	69	67.8	120	5,430

62 Northport Golf Club
Route 1, Northport, ME 04849
207-338-2270

Weekend Fee	$20	*Weekday Fee*	$20
Power Cart Fee	$20	*Pull Carts*	Yes
Putting Green	Yes	*Driving Range*	No
Season	Apr 15 - Oct 15	*Credit Cards*	No
Pro	Paul Dailey	*Tee Times*	No
Comments	Links style, open fairways		
Directions	South of Belfast, Rt 1S, left Bayside Ave		

Tee	Holes	Par	Rating	Slope	Yards
Red	9	74	70.4	110	5,396
White	9	72	68.0	112	6,094
Blue	NA	NA	NA	NA	NA

63 Norway Country Club
Lake Road, Norway, ME 04268
207-743-9840

Weekend Fee	$18	*Weekday Fee*	$18
Power Cart Fee	$15	*Pull Carts*	Yes
Putting Green	Yes	*Driving Range*	No
Season	Apr - Nov	*Credit Cards*	No
Pro	Dave Mazzeo	*Tee Times*	No
Comments	Sloped greens, narrow fairways		
Directions	I-95, exit 11 N. Portland, Rt 26N, 1 mi after lake		

Tee	Holes	Par	Rating	Slope	Yards
Red	9	72	67.2	109	5,600
White	9	70	68.0	113	6,200
Blue	NA	NA	NA	NA	NA

64 Oakdale Country Club
Country Club Road, Mexico, ME 04257
207-364-3951

Weekend Fee	$18	*Weekday Fee*	$12
Power Cart Fee	$24	*Pull Carts*	Yes
Putting Green	Yes	*Driving Range*	No
Season	May 1 - Nov 1	*Credit Cards*	No
Pro	Don Roberts	*Tee Times*	3 days
Comments	6 water holes, undulating greens		
Directions	Rumford, Rt 2E, 1 mi		

Tee	Holes	Par	Rating	Slope	Yards
Red	9	74	70.1	125	5,950
White	9	72	68.8	119	6,366
Blue	NA	NA	NA	NA	NA

65 Old Orchard Beach Country Club
49 Ross Road, Old Orchard Beach, ME 04064
207-934-4513

Weekend Fee	$22	*Weekday Fee*	$20
Power Cart Fee	$18	*Pull Carts*	Yes
Putting Green	Yes	*Driving Range*	No
Season	Apr 1 - Nov 1	*Credit Cards*	Yes
Pro	Gene McNabb	*Tee Times*	No
Comments	Open, view Mt Washington, sloped greens		
Directions	Portland, Rt 1N, 18 mi, Cascade Rd exit		

Tee	Holes	Par	Rating	Slope	Yards
Red	9	72	68.2	113	5,724
White	9	72	67.1	112	6,016
Blue	NA	NA	NA	NA	NA

66 Orchard View Golf Club
Old Corinna Road, Newport, ME 04953
207-368-5600

Weekend Fee	$15	*Weekday Fee*	$13
Power Cart Fee	$15	*Pull Carts*	Yes
Putting Green	Yes	*Driving Range*	No
Season	Apr - Nov	*Credit Cards*	No
Pro	None	*Tee Times*	No
Comments	Night play, lights installed, 3 ponds		
Directions	I-95, exit 39, towards Norway, left Rt 7, right Corinna Rd after orchard		

Tee	Holes	Par	Rating	Slope	Yards
Red	9	60	NA	NA	4,480
White	9	60	NA	NA	4,480
Blue	NA	NA	NA	NA	NA

MAINE

67 Palmyra Golf Course
Rural Route 1, Box 407, Palmyra, ME 04965
207-938-4947

Weekend Fee	$18	Weekday Fee	$18
Power Cart Fee	$18	Pull Carts	Yes
Putting Green	Yes	Driving Range	Yes
Season	Apr 1- Nov 1	Credit Cards	Yes
Pro	Celia Clark	Tee Times	No
Comments	4 holes with water hazards		
Directions	I-95, exit 39, Rt 2W, 4 mi on right		

Tee	Holes	Par	Rating	Slope	Yards
Red	18	72	69.9	118	5,464
White	18	72	69.0	118	6,367
Blue	18	72	70.1	120	6,617

70 Pine Hill Golf Club
Brewer Lake Road, Brewer, ME 04412
207-989-3824

Weekend Fee	$14	Weekday Fee	$12
Power Cart Fee	$15	Pull Carts	Yes
Putting Green	Yes	Driving Range	Yes
Season	Apr 1 - Oct 31	Credit Cards	No
Pro	Mark Hall	Tee Times	No
Comments	Level course, scenic, bunkers, small greens		
Directions	I-395, left at RT 15, 3 mi, left at Brewer Lake Rd		

Tee	Holes	Par	Rating	Slope	Yards
Red	9	72	67.0	100	5,160
White	9	72	66.0	99	5,868
Blue	NA	NA	NA	NA	NA

68 Paris Hill Country Club
355 Paris Hill Road, Paris, ME 04271
207-743-2371

Weekend Fee	$15	Weekday Fee	$15
Power Cart Fee	$16	Pull Carts	Yes
Putting Green	Yes	Driving Range	No
Season	Apr 1 - Oct 31	Credit Cards	No
Pro	H. LaMontagne	Tee Times	No
Comments	Golf school, built in 1899, small greens		
Directions	Rt 26N, through South Paris, right after post office		

Tee	Holes	Par	Rating	Slope	Yards
Red	9	66	63.6	108	4,610
White	9	66	62.1	109	4,637
Blue	NA	NA	NA	NA	NA

71 Pine Ridge Golf Course
West River Road, Waterville, ME 04901
207-873-0474

Weekend Fee	$6	Weekday Fee	$6
Power Cart Fee	No carts	Pull Carts	Yes
Putting Green	Yes	Driving Range	No
Season	Apr - Nov	Credit Cards	No
Pro	None	Tee Times	No
Comments	Well maintained, undulating greens		
Directions	I-95, exit 33 Waterville exit, right, right on West River Rd		

Tee	Holes	Par	Rating	Slope	Yards
Red	9	58	65.1	117	5,147
White	9	54	64.3	116	5,147
Blue	NA	NA	NA	NA	NA

69 Penobscott Valley Country Club
366 Main Street, Orono, ME 04473
207-866-2423

Weekend Fee	$45	Weekday Fee	$45
Power Cart Fee	$22	Pull Carts	Yes
Putting Green	Yes	Driving Range	Yes
Season	Apr 15 - Nov 15	Credit Cards	Yes
Pro	Colin Gillies	Tee Times	7 days
Comments	Ross design, accuracy needed, scenic		
Directions	I-95, exit 50 Kelly Rd, right, follow signs		

Tee	Holes	Par	Rating	Slope	Yards
Red	18	74	73.2	126	5,856
White	18	72	69.6	121	6,301
Blue	18	72	70.3	123	6,445

72 Piscataquis Country Club
Dover Road, Guilford, ME 04443
207-876-3203

Weekend Fee	$15	Weekday Fee	$12
Power Cart Fee	$20	Pull Carts	Yes
Putting Green	Yes	Driving Range	No
Season	Apr 15 - Oct 1	Credit Cards	No
Pro	Robert Dugas	Tee Times	7 days
Comments	Pines between holes, fast & elevated greens		
Directions	Newport exit, Rt 7, Rt 23N, Newport, 25 mi		

Tee	Holes	Par	Rating	Slope	Yards
Red	9	72	67.5	109	4,768
White	9	70	64.6	109	5,488
Blue	NA	NA	NA	NA	NA

MAINE

73 Pleasant Hill Country Club
38 Chamberlain Road, Scarborough, ME 04074
207-883-4425

Weekend Fee	$12	*Weekday Fee*	$10
Power Cart Fee	No carts	*Pull Carts*	Yes
Putting Green	Yes	*Driving Range*	No
Season	Apr 1 - Nov 1	*Credit Cards*	No
Pro	Gene McNabb	*Tee Times*	No
Comments	Well maintained, flat, undulating greens		
Directions	I-95, Rt 1S. Portland exit, left Pleasant Hill, right Chamberlain Rd		

Tee	Holes	Par	Rating	Slope	Yards
Red	9	68	62.3	114	4,786
White	9	68	62.3	115	4,786
Blue	NA	NA	NA	NA	NA

74 Point Sebago Golf Club
RR #1, Box 712B, Casco, ME 04015
207-655-7948

Weekend Fee	$42	*Weekday Fee*	$42
Power Cart Fee	Included	*Pull Carts*	No
Putting Green	Yes	*Driving Range*	Yes
Season	Jun - Nov	*Credit Cards*	Yes
Pro	Greg Martzolf	*Tee Times*	7 days
Comments	Resort, new course		
Directions	Rt 302W towards Casco, look for signs on left		

Tee	Holes	Par	Rating	Slope	Yards
Red	18	72	66.4	120	5,645
White	18	72	70.2	129	6,474
Blue	18	72	73.4	135	7,002

75 Poland Spring Country Club
Route 26, Poland Spring, ME 04274
207-998-6002

Weekend Fee	$20	*Weekday Fee*	$20
Power Cart Fee	$20	*Pull Carts*	Yes
Putting Green	Yes	*Driving Range*	No
Season	May 1 - Nov 1	*Credit Cards*	Yes
Pro	Jim McFadden	*Tee Times*	Month
Comments	Oldest 18 hole resort (1896), Mt views		
Directions	I-95, exit 11, Rt 26, 8 mi		

Tee	Holes	Par	Rating	Slope	Yards
Red	18	74	71.6	117	5,627
White	18	71	67.2	117	5,854
Blue	18	71	68.2	119	6,196

76 Portage Hills Country Club
Route 11, Portage, ME 04768
207-435-8221

Weekend Fee	$18	*Weekday Fee*	$18
Power Cart Fee	$18	*Pull Carts*	Yes
Putting Green	Yes	*Driving Range*	No
Season	May 15 - Sep 15	*Credit Cards*	No
Pro	None	*Tee Times*	No
Comments	Scenic, many holes with sand bunkers		
Directions	I-95, Sherman/Patton exit, Rt 11N, 60 mi		

Tee	Holes	Par	Rating	Slope	Yards
Red	9	72	NA	NA	5,912
White	9	72	69.5	113	6,420
Blue	NA	NA	NA	NA	NA

77 Presque Isle Country Club
35 Parkhurst Siding Road, Presque Isle, ME 04769
207-764-0430

Weekend Fee	$20	*Weekday Fee*	$20
Power Cart Fee	$20	*Pull Carts*	Yes
Putting Green	Yes	*Driving Range*	Yes
Season	May 1 - Oct 31	*Credit Cards*	No
Pro	Ed Phillips	*Tee Times*	No
Comments	Cornish design, picturesque, 6 doglegs		
Directions	Rt 167, Rt 205 to Presque Isle, follow signs		

Tee	Holes	Par	Rating	Slope	Yards
Red	18	73	72.4	119	5,708
White	18	72	69.2	112	6,393
Blue	18	72	71.0	118	6,794

78 Prospect Hill Golf Club
694 South Main Street, Auburn, ME 04210
207-782-9220

Weekend Fee	$16	*Weekday Fee*	$16
Power Cart Fee	$18	*Pull Carts*	Yes
Putting Green	Yes	*Driving Range*	No
Season	Mar 1 - Nov 1	*Credit Cards*	Yes
Pro	R. Vaillancourt	*Tee Times*	No
Comments	Front 9 open, back 9 ponds and tree lined		
Directions	I-95, exit 12, left, follow signs 3.5 mi		

Tee	Holes	Par	Rating	Slope	Yards
Red	18	73	68.7	111	5,227
White	18	71	69.9	110	5,846
Blue	NA	NA	NA	NA	NA

MAINE

79 Province Lake Country Club
Route 153, East Wakefield, ME 03830
207-793-9577

Weekend Fee	$25	*Weekday Fee*	$25
Power Cart Fee	$22	*Pull Carts*	Yes
Putting Green	Yes	*Driving Range*	No
Season	Apr 24 - Nov 1	*Credit Cards*	Yes
Pro	Mike Farina	*Tee Times*	7 days
Comments	2 lakes, 3 creeks		
Directions	I-95, Rt 6 Spaulding TPK, Rt 153N, 12 mi		

Tee	Holes	Par	Rating	Slope	Yards
Red	NA	NA	NA	NA	NA
White	18	71	68.8	114	5,887
Blue	NA	NA	NA	NA	NA

80 River Meadow Golf Course
216 Lincoln Street, Westbrook, ME 04092
207-854-1625

Weekend Fee	$13	*Weekday Fee*	$11
Power Cart Fee	$16	*Pull Carts*	Yes
Putting Green	Yes	*Driving Range*	No
Season	Apr 1 - Nov 15	*Credit Cards*	No
Pro	Dick Dennison	*Tee Times*	No
Comments	Brooks and streams, rolling fairways		
Directions	I-95, exit 8, Rt 25 to Westbrook, right Bridge St, 1st left Lincoln St		

Tee	Holes	Par	Rating	Slope	Yards
Red	9	72	71.0	118	5,220
White	9	70	66.9	117	5,498
Blue	9	70	72.3	119	5,882

81 Riverside Municipal Golf Course-18
1158 Riverside Street, Portland, ME 04013
207-282-0892

Weekend Fee	$20	*Weekday Fee*	$17
Power Cart Fee	$19	*Pull Carts*	Yes
Putting Green	Yes	*Driving Range*	Yes
Season	Apr 15 - Nov 10	*Credit Cards*	Yes
Pro	David Grygiel	*Tee Times*	3 days
Comments	Wide open, bunkered greens		
Directions	I-95, exit 8, right on Riverside St		

Tee	Holes	Par	Rating	Slope	Yards
Red	18	72	70.4	112	5,900
White	18	72	69.2	117	6,400
Blue	NA	NA	NA	NA	NA

82 Riverside Municipal Golf Course - 9
1158 Riverside Street, Portland, ME 04013
207-282-0892

Weekend Fee	$20	*Weekday Fee*	$17
Power Cart Fee	$19	*Pull Carts*	Yes
Putting Green	Yes	*Driving Range*	Yes
Season	Apr 15 - Nov 10	*Credit Cards*	Yes
Pro	David Grygiel	*Tee Times*	3 days
Comments	27 holes in total, bunkered greens		
Directions	I-95, exit 8, right on Riverside St		

Tee	Holes	Par	Rating	Slope	Yards
Red	9	72	69.2	113	5,912
White	9	72	70.4	114	6,290
Blue	NA	NA	NA	NA	NA

83 Rockland Golf Club
606 Old County Road, Rockland, ME 04841
207-594-9322

Weekend Fee	$25	*Weekday Fee*	$25
Power Cart Fee	$20	*Pull Carts*	Yes
Putting Green	Yes	*Driving Range*	No
Season	Apr 1 - Oct 31	*Credit Cards*	Yes
Pro	Peter Hodgkins	*Tee Times*	3 days
Comments	Ocean and lake views, wooded front 9		
Directions	I-95, coastal Rt 1, thru Thomason, left Old County Rd, 3.5 mi		

Tee	Holes	Par	Rating	Slope	Yards
Red	18	73	70.0	114	5,583
White	18	70	67.2	109	5,941
Blue	18	70	68.6	112	6,121

84 Sable Oaks Golf Club
505 Country Club Road, South Portland, ME 04106
207-775-6257

Weekend Fee	$29	*Weekday Fee*	$23
Power Cart Fee	$22	*Pull Carts*	Yes
Putting Green	Yes	*Driving Range*	No
Season	Apr 1 - Nov 1	*Credit Cards*	Yes
Pro	Jim Furlong	*Tee Times*	7 days
Comments	Accuracy needed, rated #2 in state		
Directions	I-95, exit 7, right at light, 4th light left Running Hill Rd, 2nd right		

Tee	Holes	Par	Rating	Slope	Yards
Red	18	72	68.0	118	4,786
White	18	70	70.2	129	6,056
Blue	18	70	71.9	134	6,359

85 Salmon Falls Golf Club
Salmon Falls Road, Hollis, ME 04042
207-929-5233

Weekend Fee	$20	*Weekday Fee*	$20
Power Cart Fee	$20	*Pull Carts*	Yes
Putting Green	Yes	*Driving Range*	Yes
Season	Apr 1 - Oct 1	*Credit Cards*	Yes
Pro	None	*Tee Times*	5 days
Comments	Saco River views, open fairways, wooded		
Directions	I-95, exit 5, Rt 112N, follow signs		

Tee	Holes	Par	Rating	Slope	Yards
Red	9	72	68.6	113	5,164
White	9	72	67.6	119	5,756
Blue	NA	NA	NA	NA	NA

86 Samoset Resort Golf Course
220 Warrenton Street, Rockport, ME 04841
207-594-1431

Weekend Fee	$75	*Weekday Fee*	$75
Power Cart Fee	$30	*Pull Carts*	Yes
Putting Green	Yes	*Driving Range*	Yes
Season	Apr 15 - Nov 15	*Credit Cards*	Yes
Pro	Bob O'Brian	*Tee Times*	2 days
Comments	Borders ocean, rated US 5th most scenic		
Directions	I-95, exit 9, Rt 95, exit 22, Rt 1N, Rockport, right Waldo Ave		

Tee	Holes	Par	Rating	Slope	Yards
Red	18	72	70.1	120	5,432
White	18	70	68.4	122	6,021
Blue	18	70	70.3	128	6,515

87 Sandy River Golf Course
George Thomas Road, Farmington Falls, ME 04940
207-778-2492

Weekend Fee	$10	*Weekday Fee*	$10
Power Cart Fee	No carts	*Pull Carts*	Yes
Putting Green	Yes	*Driving Range*	No
Season	Apr 15 - Nov 1	*Credit Cards*	No
Pro	Ethel Bardsley	*Tee Times*	7 days
Comments	Elevated greens and tees, pitch and putt		
Directions	Farmington, Rt 2E, 3.2 mi		

Tee	Holes	Par	Rating	Slope	Yards
Red	9	54	NA	NA	2,240
White	9	54	NA	NA	2,672
Blue	NA	NA	NA	NA	NA

88 Sanford Country Club
Country Club Road, Route 4, Sanford, ME 04073
207-324-5462

Weekend Fee	$23	*Weekday Fee*	$20
Power Cart Fee	$20	*Pull Carts*	Yes
Putting Green	Yes	*Driving Range*	Yes
Season	Apr 15 - Nov 15	*Credit Cards*	Yes
Pro	M. L'Heureux	*Tee Times*	7 days
Comments	Flat, views of mountain range		
Directions	I-95, exit 2, Rt 109N, 10 mi, Rt 4S, 2.5 mi		

Tee	Holes	Par	Rating	Slope	Yards
Red	9	74	73.0	118	5,684
White	9	72	70.8	122	6,592
Blue	NA	NA	NA	NA	NA

89 Shore Acres Golf Club
Route 217, Sebasco Lodge, Sebasco Estates, ME 04565
207-389-1161

Weekend Fee	$14	*Weekday Fee*	$14
Power Cart Fee	No carts	*Pull Carts*	Yes
Putting Green	Yes	*Driving Range*	No
Season	May 12 - Oct 22	*Credit Cards*	No
Pro	None	*Tee Times*	No
Comments	Hotel, guests 1st preference		
Directions	Call ahead		

Tee	Holes	Par	Rating	Slope	Yards
Red	9	66	NA	NA	4,218
White	9	66	NA	NA	4,218
Blue	NA	NA	NA	NA	NA

90 South Portland Municipal GC
21 Nelson Road, South Portland, ME 04106
207-775-0005

Weekend Fee	$8	*Weekday Fee*	$7
Power Cart Fee	No carts	*Pull Carts*	Yes
Putting Green	Yes	*Driving Range*	No
Season	Apr - Nov	*Credit Cards*	No
Pro	Dick Nelson	*Tee Times*	No
Comments	Flat course		
Directions	I-95, exit 3 Wescott Road, 1st left at top of hill		

Tee	Holes	Par	Rating	Slope	Yards
Red	9	66	NA	NA	4,142
White	9	66	NA	NA	4,142
Blue	NA	NA	NA	NA	NA

MAINE

91 Spring Brook Golf Course
Route 202, Leeds, ME 04263
207-946-5900

Weekend Fee	$18	*Weekday Fee*	$18
Power Cart Fee	$18	*Pull Carts*	Yes
Putting Green	Yes	*Driving Range*	Yes
Season	Apr 15 - Nov 1	*Credit Cards*	Yes
Pro	J. Fennessy	*Tee Times*	7 days
Comments	Scottish style, all day play, flat		
Directions	I-95, Lewiston exit, Rt 202E, 14 mi		

Tee	Holes	Par	Rating	Slope	Yards
Red	18	74	70.8	123	4,989
White	18	71	68.7	120	6,163
Blue	18	71	69.8	123	6,408

94 Sugarloaf Golf Club
Route 27, Carrabassett Valley, ME 04947
207-237-2000

Weekend Fee	$79	*Weekday Fee*	$79
Power Cart Fee	Included	*Pull Carts*	No
Putting Green	Yes	*Driving Range*	Yes
Season	May 20 - Oct 15	*Credit Cards*	Yes
Pro	Scott Hoisington	*Tee Times*	Month
Comments	Highly rated, dramatic holes, wildlife		
Directions	Farmington, Rt 27N, 36 mi		

Tee	Holes	Par	Rating	Slope	Yards
Red	18	72	73.7	136	5,376
White	18	72	70.8	137	5,946
Blue	18	72	70.8	137	6,451

92 Squaw Mountain Village GC
Little Squaw Township, Greenville, ME 04441
207-695-3609

Weekend Fee	$15	*Weekday Fee*	$15
Power Cart Fee	No carts	*Pull Carts*	Yes
Putting Green	Yes	*Driving Range*	No
Season	Apr - Nov	*Credit Cards*	No
Pro	None	*Tee Times*	No
Comments	Easy and short course		
Directions	Greenville, Rt 6S, follow signs to Squaw Mt		

Tee	Holes	Par	Rating	Slope	Yards
Red	9	68	NA	NA	4,926
White	9	68	NA	NA	4,926
Blue	NA	NA	NA	NA	NA

95 Summit Golf Course
Summit Spring Road, Poland, ME 04273
207-998-4515

Weekend Fee	$15	*Weekday Fee*	$15
Power Cart Fee	$14	*Pull Carts*	Yes
Putting Green	Yes	*Driving Range*	No
Season	Apr 1 - Oct 31	*Credit Cards*	No
Pro	Wilbur Benoit	*Tee Times*	No
Comments	Views of White Mountains, built 1899		
Directions	Off Rt 26 in Poland Spring		

Tee	Holes	Par	Rating	Slope	Yards
Red	13	72	67.2	118	5,726
White	13	72	67.2	118	5,726
Blue	NA	NA	NA	NA	NA

93 St. Croix Country Club
River Road, Calais, ME 04619
207-454-8875

Weekend Fee	$20	*Weekday Fee*	$20
Power Cart Fee	$16	*Pull Carts*	Yes
Putting Green	Yes	*Driving Range*	No
Season	May 1 - Oct 15	*Credit Cards*	No
Pro	Duane Ellis	*Tee Times*	No
Comments	Views of St. Croix River, open fairways		
Directions	Rt 9, Rt 1N, 1 mi, River Rd		

Tee	Holes	Par	Rating	Slope	Yards
Red	9	68	NA	NA	5,200
White	9	64	NA	102	5,470
Blue	NA	NA	NA	NA	NA

96 Todd Valley Golf Club
Rural Route 1 Box 2140, Charlestown, ME 04422
207-285-7725

Weekend Fee	$12	*Weekday Fee*	$12
Power Cart Fee	$16	*Pull Carts*	Yes
Putting Green	Yes	*Driving Range*	Yes
Season	Apr 1 - Oct 31	*Credit Cards*	No
Pro	Ken Young	*Tee Times*	No
Comments	Links style, 4 ponds, roller coaster 6th green		
Directions	Rt 15W from Bangor, 1st left out of East Corinth, Bacon Rd		

Tee	Holes	Par	Rating	Slope	Yards
Red	9	66	NA	NA	4,042
White	9	66	61.1	93	4,672
Blue	NA	NA	NA	NA	NA

97 Turner Highlands
Route 117, Turner, ME 04282
207-224-7060

Weekend Fee	$18	*Weekday Fee*	$18
Power Cart Fee	$16	*Pull Carts*	Yes
Putting Green	Yes	*Driving Range*	No
Season	May 1 - Nov 1	*Credit Cards*	Yes
Pro	None	*Tee Times*	4 days
Comments	Elevated tees, narrow fairways		
Directions	Alburn, Rt 4N, right Rt 117, 5 mi		

Tee	Holes	Par	Rating	Slope	Yards
Red	9	72	65.2	105	4,462
White	9	72	69.2	121	5,960
Blue	NA	NA	NA	NA	NA

100 Val Halla Golf Course
1 Val Halla Road, Cumberland Center, ME 04021
207-829-2225

Weekend Fee	$25	*Weekday Fee*	$20
Power Cart Fee	$25	*Pull Carts*	Yes
Putting Green	Yes	*Driving Range*	Yes
Season	Apr 15 - Nov 1	*Credit Cards*	Yes
Pro	Terry Adams	*Tee Times*	7 days
Comments	Scenic with brooks and streams		
Directions	From Portland take exit 10, follow signs to Cumberland		

Tee	Holes	Par	Rating	Slope	Yards
Red	18	72	70.4	116	5,437
White	18	72	69.6	122	6,201
Blue	18	72	71.1	126	6,567

98 Twin Falls Golf Course
364 Spring Street, Westbrook, ME 04092
207-854-5397

Weekend Fee	$12	*Weekday Fee*	$12
Power Cart Fee	$16	*Pull Carts*	Yes
Putting Green	Yes	*Driving Range*	No
Season	Apr 1 - Nov 1	*Credit Cards*	No
Pro	Kathy Boullie	*Tee Times*	No
Comments	5 water holes		
Directions	I-95, exit 7, Maine Mall Rd, Spring St		

Tee	Holes	Par	Rating	Slope	Yards
Red	9	66	70.1	114	4,880
White	9	66	68.3	112	4,880
Blue	NA	NA	NA	NA	NA

101 Waterville Country Club
Country Club Road, Oakland, ME 04963
207-465-9861

Weekend Fee	$38	*Weekday Fee*	$38
Power Cart Fee	$20	*Pull Carts*	Yes
Putting Green	Yes	*Driving Range*	Yes
Season	Apr 1 - Nov 1	*Credit Cards*	No
Pro	Steve Pembrook	*Tee Times*	7 days
Comments	Ranked 4th in state, small undulating greens		
Directions	I-95N, exit 33, towards Oakland, 1.5 mi		

Tee	Holes	Par	Rating	Slope	Yards
Red	18	73	71.4	121	5,466
White	18	70	68.1	121	6,108
Blue	18	70	69.6	124	6,412

99 Va-Jo-Wa Golf Club
142A Walker Settlement Road, Island Falls, ME 04747
207-463-2128

Weekend Fee	$21	*Weekday Fee*	$21
Power Cart Fee	$24	*Pull Carts*	Yes
Putting Green	Yes	*Driving Range*	Yes
Season	May 1 - Oct 31	*Credit Cards*	Yes
Pro	Warren Walker	*Tee Times*	Yes
Comments	Only 18 hole course in area, well maintained		
Directions	I-95, exit 59, Rt 2E, 3 mi, turn on Walker Rd		

Tee	Holes	Par	Rating	Slope	Yards
Red	18	72	69.1	119	5,065
White	18	72	68.9	117	5,860
Blue	18	72	70.4	121	6,223

102 Wawenock Country Club
Route 129, Walpole, ME 04573
207-563-3938

Weekend Fee	$20	*Weekday Fee*	$20
Power Cart Fee	$18	*Pull Carts*	Yes
Putting Green	Yes	*Driving Range*	Yes
Season	May - Oct	*Credit Cards*	Yes
Pro	Leon Oliver	*Tee Times*	Yes
Comments	Open, hilly, small greens		
Directions	Rt 1, Rt 129, 7 mi		

Tee	Holes	Par	Rating	Slope	Yards
Red	9	70	NA	NA	NA
White	9	70	70.0	NA	6,112
Blue	NA	NA	NA	NA	NA

MAINE

103 Webhannet Golf Club
Kennebunk Beach, Kennebunk Beach, ME 04043
207-967-3494

Weekend Fee	$30	Weekday Fee	$30
Power Cart Fee	$24	Pull Carts	Yes
Putting Green	Yes	Driving Range	No
Season	Apr 15 - Nov 10	Credit Cards	No
Pro	None	Tee Times	No
Comments	Call ahead for information		
Directions	Rt 1N, right Rt 9E, look for signs		

Tee	Holes	Par	Rating	Slope	Yards
Red	18	NA	NA	NA	NA
White	18	71	NA	117	6,248
Blue	NA	NA	NA	NA	NA

106 West Newfield Golf Course
Libby Road, West Newfield, ME 04095
207-793-2478

Weekend Fee	$14 all day play	Weekday Fee	$10
Power Cart Fee	$10	Pull Carts	Yes
Putting Green	Yes	Driving Range	No
Season	Apr 1 - Nov 1	Credit Cards	No
Pro	Ray Leavitt	Tee Times	No
Comments	Links style, undulating greens		
Directions	I-95, Rt 16, Rt 153 to E. Wakefield, Rt 110E, 1.5 mi, left 1st intersection		

Tee	Holes	Par	Rating	Slope	Yards
Red	9	60	54.1	86	2,990
White	9	60	54.1	86	2,990
Blue	NA	NA	NA	NA	NA

104 Westerly Winds Golf Course
771 Cumberland Street, Westbrook, ME 04092
207-854-9463

Weekend Fee	$7	Weekday Fee	$6
Power Cart Fee	No carts	Pull Carts	Yes
Putting Green	Yes	Driving Range	Yes
Season	Apr 1 - Oct 31	Credit Cards	Yes
Pro	Harry Andrews	Tee Times	No
Comments	Good practice course, small greens		
Directions	I-95, exit 8, right at McDonalds		

Tee	Holes	Par	Rating	Slope	Yards
Red	9	54	NA	NA	1,660
White	9	54	NA	NA	1,660
Blue	NA	NA	NA	NA	NA

107 White Birches Golf Course
Thornsen Road, Ellsworth, ME 04605
207-667-3621

Weekend Fee	$15	Weekday Fee	$15
Power Cart Fee	$18	Pull Carts	Yes
Putting Green	Yes	Driving Range	No
Season	Apr 1 - Oct 31	Credit Cards	Yes
Pro	Shawn Clark	Tee Times	No
Comments	Elevated greens, ponds, doglegs		
Directions	I-95, Rt 1A exit, Rt 1E towards Ellsworth, 1.5 mi		

Tee	Holes	Par	Rating	Slope	Yards
Red	9	68	67.8	106	4,054
White	9	68	68.2	109	4,788
Blue	9	68	70.0	110	5,244

105 Western View Golf Club
Bolton Hill Road, Augusta, ME 04330
207-622-5309

Weekend Fee	$15	Weekday Fee	$15
Power Cart Fee	$15	Pull Carts	Yes
Putting Green	Yes	Driving Range	Yes
Season	Apr - Oct	Credit Cards	Yes
Pro	None	Tee Times	Yes
Comments	Hilly, wooded, tight		
Directions	Bangor, I-95S, exit 30, east on Western Ave, right on Rt 3, right Bolton Hill Rd		

Tee	Holes	Par	Rating	Slope	Yards
Red	9	72	68.0	110	5,260
White	9	70	64.5	107	5,430
Blue	NA	NA	NA	NA	NA

108 Willowdale Golf Club
52 Willowdale Road, Scarborough, ME 04074
207-883-9351

Weekend Fee	$22	Weekday Fee	$22
Power Cart Fee	$20	Pull Carts	Yes
Putting Green	Yes	Driving Range	No
Season	Apr 15 - Nov 1	Credit Cards	Yes
Pro	Pam Rice	Tee Times	3 days
Comments	Open front 9, narrow back 9, scenic		
Directions	Off Rt 1 in Scarborough, minutes from exit 6 of ME Turnpike		

Tee	Holes	Par	Rating	Slope	Yards
Red	18	70	69.4	112	5,344
White	18	70	67.9	110	5,980
Blue	NA	NA	NA	NA	NA

MAINE

109 Wilson Lake Country Club
Weld Road, Wilton, ME 04234
207-645-2016

Weekend Fee	$20	Weekday Fee	$18
Power Cart Fee	$20	Pull Carts	Yes
Putting Green	Yes	Driving Range	No
Season	May - Oct	Credit Cards	No
Pro	Rick Carl	Tee Times	Yes
Comments	Views of Lake Wilson		
Directions	Rt 4, Rt 2, Rt 156, Wilton, Weld Rd		

Tee	Holes	Par	Rating	Slope	Yards
Red	9	NA	NA	NA	NA
White	9	70	68.8	117	6,044
Blue	NA	NA	NA	NA	NA

Limestone Country Club
Sawyer Road, Limestone, ME
207-328-7277

Weekend Fee	$15	Weekday Fee	$15
Power Cart Fee	$15	Pull Carts	Yes
Putting Green	Yes	Driving Range	Yes
Season	Apr 1 - Oct 15	Credit Cards	Yes
Pro	Craig Phair	Tee Times	No
Comments	Elevated greens, old air force course		
Directions	I-95N, Holton, Rt 1N, Caribou, Rt 89E, Limestone, left Sawyer Rd, 2.5 mi		

Tee	Holes	Par	Rating	Slope	Yards
Red	9	72	NA	NA	5,740
White	9	72	70.4	114	6,710
Blue	NA	NA	NA	NA	NA

110 Woodland Terrace Golf Club
1251 Bar Harbor Road, East Holden, ME 04412
207-989-3750

Weekend Fee	$11	Weekday Fee	$11
Power Cart Fee	No carts	Pull Carts	Yes
Putting Green	Yes	Driving Range	No
Season	Apr 1 - Oct 31	Credit Cards	Yes
Pro	None	Tee Times	No
Comments	Resort, well maintained, wooded		
Directions	I-95N, Rt 395 (Bar Harbor), Rt 1A (E. Holden), 0.25 mi		

Tee	Holes	Par	Rating	Slope	Yards
Red	9	60	53.0	NA	3,004
White	9	60	53.0	NA	3,110
Blue	NA	NA	NA	NA	NA

Loons Cove Golf Course
Skowhegan, ME
207-474-9550

Weekend Fee	$	Weekday Fee	$
Power Cart Fee	$	Pull Carts	
Putting Green		Driving Range	
Season		Credit Cards	
Pro		Tee Times	
Comments	No information yet available		
Directions			

Tee	Holes	Par	Rating	Slope	Yards
Red					
White					
Blue					

Information on several courses recently or soon to be opened was obtained too late to include them in the alphabetical listing or location maps in this book.

Capitol City Golf Course
Augusta, ME
207-623-0504

Weekend Fee	$	Weekday Fee	$
Power Cart Fee	$	Pull Carts	
Putting Green		Driving Range	
Season		Credit Cards	
Pro		Tee Times	
Comments	No information yet available		
Directions			

Tee	Holes	Par	Rating	Slope	Yards
Red					
White					
Blue					

Meriland Farms
Wells, ME
207-646-0508

Weekend Fee	$	Weekday Fee	$
Power Cart Fee	$	Pull Carts	
Putting Green		Driving Range	
Season		Credit Cards	
Pro		Tee Times	
Comments	No information yet available		
Directions			

Tee	Holes	Par	Rating	Slope	Yards
Red					
White					
Blue					

MASSACHUSETTS

Stow Acres
Stow, Massachusetts

MASSACHUSETTS GOLF COURSES

Public Courses	223	Private Courses	103
Total Courses	326	Percent Public Courses	68%
18 Hole Public Courses	129	9 Hole Public Courses	94
Total Golfers	593,000	Total Rounds of Golf	11,089,100
Percent Female Golfers	15.7%	Percent Senior Golfers	24.8%
Rounds Per Course	34,016	Rounds Per Golfer	18.7
Golfers Per Course	1,819	Courses Per 100 Square Miles	3.95
Average Weekend Fee	$26.15	Average Weekday Fee	$22.71
Average Weekend Fee w/Power Cart	$36.92	Average Weekday Fee w/Power Cart	$33.35
Average Slope	115.3	Average Yardage	5,588

Massachusetts has more golf courses than any other New England state. There are 326 golf courses in Massachusetts (103 private and 223 public). Sixty-eight percent of the courses are open to the public.

Almost 10 percent of the population of Massachusetts plays golf which translates into 593,000 golfers playing over 11 million rounds of golf every year[1] (18.7 rounds per golfer). Almost one quarter of the golfers are senior citizens and 16 percent are women.

Massachusetts is one the busiest states to play golf. There are 1,819 golfers per golf course and 34,016 rounds of golf are played annually per golf course.

There are many 9 hole golf courses in Massachusetts. Courses with 9 holes comprise 42% of the total public courses.

Greens Fees

Massachusetts is one of the most expensive New England states to play golf. On weekends, the average greens fees to play a round of 18 holes on public courses is $26.15 ($30.18 for 18 hole and $20.25 for 9 hole courses). (These costs include courses where power cart fees are part of the greens fees.) Golfers can save $3.44 by playing during the week when the average greens fee is $22.71 ($26.17 for 18 hole and $17.96 for 9 hole courses).

The courses with the most expensive greens fees are the 18 hole Taconic Golf Club in Williamstown ($80) and the 9 hole Miacomet Golf Club in Nantucket ($40). The least expensive courses are the 9 hole Pine Knoll Golf Course in East Longmeadow ($6) and the 18 hole Wading River Golf Club in Norton ($14).

On average, a power cart rental for two players will cost $20.01 in Massachusetts. On weekends, a round of golf with a power cart will cost each golfer an average of $36.92.

Slope and Yardage

Massachusetts courses tend to be average in terms of average slope ratings. The average slope rating of all public courses from the white tees is 115.3 (116.6 for 18 hole and 113.3 for 9 hole courses). The courses with the highest slope rating from the white tees are the 18 hole Crumpin-Fox Club in Bernardston (136) and the 9 hole Georgetown Country Club (128). The easiest 18 and 9 hole courses are the Little Harbor Country Club (79) and Lakeview Golf Club (91), respectively.

Massachusetts courses are also average in terms of distance from the white tees. The average yardage of all public courses from the white tees is 5,588 yards (5,723 yards for 18 hole and 5,402 yards for 9 hole courses). The courses with the longest yardage from the white tees are the 18 hole Grand View Country

---

[1] The Complete Golfer's Almanac 1995

MASSACHUSETTS

Club in Leominister (6,746) and the 9 hole North Hill Country Club in Duxbury (7,002). The shortest 18 and 9 hole courses are the Squirrel Run Country Club in Plymouth (2,284) and the Pine Knoll Golf Course in East Longmeadow(1,600), respectively.

Public Courses Rated in Top 10 by Golf Digest

Rank	Course
1	New Seabury Country Club (Blue)
2	Captains Golf Course
3	Shaker Hills Golf Course
4	Crumpin-Fox Club
5	Farm Neck Golf Course

Rank	Course
6	Taconic Golf Course
7	Chicopee Golf Course
8	Tara Ferncroft Country Club
9	Wachusett Country Club
10	Maplegate Country Club

Oldest Golf Courses

Club	Year
William J. Devine Golf Course	1890
Highland Links	1892
Siasconset Golf Course	1894
Nantucket Golf Links	1894
Cummaquid Golf Course	1895

Club	Year
Oak Bluffs Country Club	1896
Taconic Golf Course	1896
Woods Hole Golf Course	1898
Bass River Golf Course	1900
Plymouth Country Club	1902

Golf Schools and Instruction

- Bill Pappas Golf School, 55 Middlesex Street, North Chelmsford, 508-251-3933
- Bob DiPadua Golf School at Fire Fly Country Club, Seekonk, 508-336-6622
- Bob Toski Golf School, Golf Learning Center of NE, 19 Leonard Street, Norton, 508-285-4540
- Cape Cod Golf School, Blue Rock Motor Inn & GC, Todd Road, South Yarmouth, 800-237-8887
- Country Club of Billerica, 6 Baldwin Road, Billerica, 508-670-5396
- Crumpin-Fox Golf School, Parmenter Road, Bernardston, 413-648-9101
- Ed McMahon's Golf Clinic, 2 Cedar Street, Woburn, 617-937-5566
- Golf Digest Instruction School, 5520 Park Avenue, Box 395, Trumbull, CT, 800-243-6121
- Longest Drive, 131 Great Western Road, South Dennis, 508-398-5555
- Mazda Golf Clinics for Executive Women, Spring Valley Country Club, Sharon, 800-262-7888
- Ocean Edge Golf Club, Route 6A, Brewster, 508-896-5911
- Ross Coon Golf, 1287 Main Street, Lynnfield, 617-334-3024
- Stowe Acres Golf School, 58 Randall Road, Stowe, 508-568-1100

Golf Associations and Touring Clubs

- Boston Amateur Golf Society (BAGS), 617-891-7274
- Boston Amateur Golf Society, Women's Division, 508-435-1005
- Business and Professional Women's Golf Association, 508-443-1402
- Executive Women's Golf League, Boston area, 617-262-1948
- Executive Women's Golf League, West Springfield, 413-734-4444
- The Greater Boston Amateur Golf Club (The Tour), 617-484-8687
- Interstate Golf Association, 617-566-7723
- Massachusetts Golf Association, 617-891-4300
- New England Women's Golf Association, 617-934-2425
- Par-Tee Golf Association, 508-758-2111
- Players Club, 617-449-3000
- Professional's Golf Association (PGA), New England section, 617-246-4653
- Sporting Women's Invitational Golf (SWING), 617-447-2299
- Women's Golf Association of Massachusetts, 617-334-6047

Private Golf Courses

Course	Town
Acoaxet Club	Westport
Allendale Country Club	North Dartmouth
Andover Country Club	Andover
Bass Rocks Golf Club	Gloucester
Bear Hill Golf Club	Stoneham
Bedford VAMC Hanson GC	Bedford
Bellevue Golf Club	Melrose
Belmont Country Club	Belmont
Berkshire Hills Country Club	Pittsfield
Blandford Club	Blandford
Bluehill Country Club	Canton
Brae Burn Country Club	Newtonville
Brockton Country Club	Brockton
Country Club of Greenfield	Greenfield
Country Club of New Bedford	North Dartmouth
Country Club of Pittsfield	Pittsfield
Country Club of Wilbraham	Wilbraham
Charles River Country Club	Newton Center
Cohasset Country Club	Southbridge
Cohasset Golf Club	Cohasset
Concord Country Club	Concord
Crestview Country Club	Agawam
Crestwood Country Club	Rehoboth
Cummaquid Golf Club	Yarmouth Port
Dedham Country and Polo Club	Dedham
Duxbury Yacht Club	Duxbury
Eastward Ho Country Club	Chatham
Edgartown Golf Club	Edgartown
Elmcrest Country Club	East Longmeadow
Essex Country Club	Manchester
Fall River Country Club	Fall River
Fort Devens Golf Course	Fort Devens
Framingham Country Club	Framingham
Franklin Country Club	Franklin
Halifax Country Club	Halifax
Hatherly Golf Club	North Scituate
Haverhill Country Club	Haverhill
Hawthorne Country Club	North Dartmouth
Highland Country Club	Attleborough
Hyannisport Club	Hyannisport
Indian Ridge Country Club	Andover
International Golf Club	Bolton
Ipswich Country Club	Ipswich
Kernwood Country Club	Salem
Kittansett Club	Marion
Ledgemont Country Club	Seekonk
Lexington Golf Club	Lexington
Longmeadow Country Club	Longmeadow
Longmeadow Golf Club	Lowell
Ludlow Country Club	Ludlow
Marlboro Country Club	Marlboro
Marshfield Country Club	Marshfield

Course	Town
Meadow Brook Golf Club	Reading
Milford Country Club	Milford
Milton-Hoosic Club	Canton
Mt. Pleasant Country Club	Boylston
Mt. Pleasant Golf Club	Lowell
Myopia Hunt Club	South Hamilton
Nashawtuc Country Club	Concord
Needham Golf Club	Needham
Norfolk Golf Club	Westwood
North Andover Country Club	North Andover
North Fields	Haverhill
Oak Hill Country Club	Fitchburg
Oakley Country Club	Watertown
Oyster Harbors Club	Osterville
Pawt Country Club	Seekonk
Pine Brook Country Club	Weston
Pleasant Valley Country Club	Sutton
Reservation Golf Club	Mattapoisett
Ridge Club	South Sandwich
Royal Crest Country Club	Walpole
Salem Country Club	Peabody
Sankaty Head Golf Club	Siasconset
Segregansett Country Club	Taunton
Sharon Country Club	Sharon
Spring Valley Country Club	Sharon
Springfield Country Club	West Springfield
Sterling Country Club	Sterling
Stockbridge Golf Club	Stockbridge
Tara Ferncroft Country Club	Danvers
Tatnuck Country Club	Worcester
Tedesco Country Club	Marblehead
The Country Club	Chestnut Hill
Thomson Country Club	North Reading
Thorny Lea Golf Club	Brockton
Twin Hills Country Club	Longmeadow
Vesper Country Club	Tyngsboro
Walpole Country Club	Walpole
Wampatuck Country Club	Canton
Wellesley Country Club	Wellesley
Weston Golf Club	Weston
White Cliffs Country Club	Pocasset
Whitensville Golf Club	Whitensville
Wianno Club	Osterville
Willow Bend Country Club	Mashpee
Winchester Country Club	Winchester
Winthrop Golf Club	Winthrop
Wollaston Golf Club	Milton
Woodland Golf Course	Auburndale
Woods Hole Golf Club	Falmouth
Worcester Country Club	Worcester
Wyantenuck Country Club	Great Barrington

MASSACHUSETTS

Retailers

- Bill Flynn Golf Shops, 420 West Street, Hyde Park, 617-361-8313
- Boston Links Golf, 150 Federal Street, Boston, 617-261-0284
- Boston Links Golf, 116 Huntington Avenue, Boston, 617-859-1800
- Club House Golf, Stop & Shop Plaza, East Harwich, MA 508-432-3524
- Dana Quigley Golf Enterprises, 90 Wheeler Street, Rehoboth, 508-336-6446
- Del Penna Pro Shop, 1281 West Roxbury Parkway, Chestnut Hill, 617-566-7794
- Edwin Watts Golf, 200 Webster Street, Hanover, 617-871-6961
- Fran Johnson's Nevada Bob's, 1050 Riverdale Street, West Springfield, 413-734-4444
- Golf City, 40 South Main Street, Bridgewater, 508-588-5020
- Golf Country, Route 114, Middleton, 508-774-4476
- Golf Day, 2 Winter Street, Weymouth, 617-331-2600
- Golf Day, 100 Justin Drive, Chelsea, 617-887-2616
- Golf Day, 135 Revere Beach Parkway, Revere, 617-284-4653
- Golf Day, 120 Andover Street, Route 114, Danvers, 508-750-4410
- Golf Day, 164 G. Summer Street, Kingston, 617-582-1701
- Golf Day, 193 Boston Post Road West, Marlborough, 508-460-1414
- Golf Day, 337 State Road, North Dartmouth, 508-994-0600
- Golf Day, 1458 Riverdale Street, West Springfield, 413-737-1666
- Golf Express, 219 Lexington Street, Waltham, 617-893-4177
- Golf For Less, 1654 Falmouth Road, Centerville, 508-771-7888
- Golf Haus, 16 Shaker Road, East Longmeadow, 413-525-6633
- Golf Market, 1070 Iyanough Road, Hyannis, 508-771-4653
- Golf Tech, 360 Bridge Street, Dedham, 617-329-9696
- Golf Unlimited, 15 West Union Street, Ashland, 508-881-4653
- Golfers Warehouse, 171 Riverdale Street, West Springfield, 413-734-1388
- Highland Golf, 485 Highland Avenue, Sale, 508-741-1434
- Joe Leigh's Discount Golf Pro, 63 Prospect Street, South Easton, 508-238-2320
- Kaufman Disc Golf, 240 Park Street, Palmer, 413-283-2422
- Martin Memorial Pro Shop, 1 Park Road, Weston, 617-891-1119
- McGolf Shop, 124 Bridge Street, Dedham, 617-326-3315
- Middleton Golf Club, 105 South Main Street, Middleton, 508-774-4075
- Nevada Bob's, 30 Enterprise Road, Hyannis, 508-775-9300
- Nevada Bob's, 87 Providence Highway, Westwood, 617-461-0750
- Nevada Bob's, 60 Worcester Road, Route 9E, Framingham, 508-872-3364
- Nevada Bob's, 106 Milk Street, Boston, 617-695-1971
- Nevada Bob's, 1344 Washington Street, Hanover, 617-826-4448
- Nevada Bob's, 425 Washington Street, Woburn, 617-932-3900
- Nevada Bob's, 1 Oak Street, Westborough, 508-870-0520
- Nevada Bob's, 35 Commerce Way, Route 6, Seekonk, 508-336-3962
- Nevada Bob's, 56 Davis Straits, Route 28, Falmouth, 508-540-9200
- Nevada Bob's, 299 Market Street, Swansea, 508-379-9886
- New England Golf Supply II, 567 Southbridge Street, Auburn, 508-832-6686
- New England Golf Supply VI, 270 West Main Street, Marlborough, 508-485-1198
- New England Professional Golf, 10 Rainbow Pond Drive, Walpole, 508-668-8655
- Nine IronGolf Shop, 191 Pleasant Street, Brockton, 508-580-1414
- Northeast Golf Sales, 950 Taunton Avenue, Seekonk, 508-336-4058
- Northeast Golf Sales, 634 State Road, North Dartmouth, 508-991-5689
- R & R Golf, 293 Winter Street, Hanover, 617-857-2424
- Sun 'n Air Range, 210 Conant Street, Danvers, 508-774-8180
- The Golf Market, 1070 Ivanough Road, Route 132, Hyannis, 508-771-4653
- The Golf Shop, 109 Bridge Street, Dedham, 617-326-3315
- Wayland Golf, 28 Highland Avenue, Needham, 617-444-6686

- Wayland Golf, 54 Middlesex Turnpike, Burlington, 617-221-0030
- Wayland Golf, 121 Old Sudbury Road, Sudbury, 508-358-4775
- Wayland Golf, 218 Speen Street, Natick, 508-651-0288
- Whirl-A-Way Golf, 500 Merrimack Street, Methuen, 508-688-8356

Easiest Courses

Course	Town	Holes	Slope
Little Harbor CC	Wareham	18	79
Fire Fly CC	Seekonk	18	81
Squirrel Run CC	Plymouth	18	82
Heritage Hill CC	Lakeville	18	84
Rockland GC	Rockland	18	87
Paul Harney GC	East Falmouth	18	91
Lakeview GC	Wenham	9	91
Cedar Hill GC	Stoughton	9	92
Kings Way GC	Yarmouthport	18	93
Highland Links	North Truro	9	100
Cherry Hill GC	N. Amherst	9	101
East Mountain CC	Westfield	18	101
Millwood Farms Course	Framingham	14	101

Hardest Courses

Course	Town	Holes	Slope
Juniper Hill GC - Lakeside	Northboro	18	127
Rowley CC	Rowley	9	127
Stow Acres (North)	Stow	18	127
Georgetown CC	Georgetown	9	128
Hickory Ridge CC	South Amherst	18	128
Newton Commonwealth GC	Chestnut Hill	18	128
Shaker Hills CC	Harvard	18	128
Colonial Hilton GC	Wakefield	18	129
Ballymeade CC	North Falmouth	18	130
Bradford CC	Bradford	18	134
Crumpin-Fox Club	Bernardston	18	136

Least Expensive Courses

Course	Town	Holes	Fee
Pine Knoll GC	East Longmeadow	9	$6
Cotuit-Highground GC	Cotuit	9	$10
Edgewood GC	Uxbridge	9	$10
Stowaway GC	Stow	9	$10
Bas Ridge GC	Hinsdale	9	$12
Forest Park CC	Adams	9	$12
North Adams CC	Clarksburg	9	$13
Pakachoag GC	Auburn	9	$14
Garrison Golf Center	Haverhill	9	$14
Ashfield Community GC	Ashfield	9	$14
Franconia Municipal GC	Springfield	18	$14
Pine Valley GC	Rehoboth	9	$14
Veterans GC	Springfield	18	$14
Wading River GC	Norton	18	$14
Willowdale GC	Mansfield	9	$14
Woodbriar CC	Falmouth	9	$14

Most Expensive Courses

Course	Town	Holes	Fee
Hickory Ridge CC	South Amherst	18	$43
Furnace Brook GC	Quincy	18	$44
New England CC	Bellingham	18	$45
Ocean Edge GC	Brewster	18	$49
Colonial Hilton GC	Wakefield	18	$49
Orchards GC	South Hadley	18	$50
Shaker Hills CC	Harvard	18	$50
Cranwell Resort	Lenox	18	$55
Crumpin-Fox Club	Bernardston	18	$55
Wahconah CC	Dalton	18	$55
Plymouth CC	Plymouth	18	$58
Farm Neck GC	Oak Bluffs	18	$60
New Seabury GC Blue	Mashpee	18	$60
Ballymeade CC	North Falmouth	18	$65
Taconic GC	Williamstown	18	$80

Shortest Courses

Course	Town	Holes	Distan
Pine Knoll GC	East Longmeadow	9	1,600
Garrison Golf Center	Haverhill	9	2,000
Squirrel Run CC	Plymouth	18	2,284
Pine Acres	Bellingham	9	2,292
Wading River GC	Norton	18	2,421
Heritage Hill CC	Lakeville	18	2,575
Cotuit-Highground GC	Cotuit	9	2,580
Tara Hyannis GC	Hyannis	18	2,621
Blue Rock GC	South Yarmouth	18	2,923
Holly Ridge GC	South Sandwich	18	2,952

Longest Courses

Course	Town	Holes	Distance
Pakachoag GC	Auburn	9	6,510
Dennis Pines GC	South Dennis	18	6,525
Pembroke CC	Pembroke	18	6,532
Wachusett CC	West Boylston	18	6,608
Westover GC	Granby	18	6,610
Shaker Farms CC	Westfield	18	6,669
Southampton CC	Southampton	18	6,720
Ponkapoag GC #1	Canton	18	6,726
Grand View CC	Leominister	18	6,746
North Hill CC	Duxbury	9	7,002

MASSACHUSETTS

Driving Ranges and Practice Areas

Name	Address	Town	Phone
Airport Driving Range	South Meadow Road	Plymouth	508-747-4990
Amesbury Sports Park	12 Hunt Road	Amesbury	508-388-5788
Atlantic Golf Centers	754 Newport Avenue	S. Attleboro	508-761-5484
Auburn Golf Range	541 Southbridge Street	Auburn	508-832-0559
Bakers Golf Center	658 South Main Street	Lanesboro	413-443-6102
Bourne's Sports World	Route 28	Bourne	508-759-5500
Brooke's Long Shot	87 Holliston Street	Medway	508-533-2002
Burch Hills Driving Range	2250 Providence Highway	South Walpole	508-668-6674
Caddy Shack	900 State Road	Dartmouth	508-991-7976
Delisio Brothers	Swampscott Road	Salem	508-745-6766
Dixie's Driving Range	530 Turnpike Street	Easton	508-238-6007
East Coast Practice Center	333 SW Cutoff Street	Northboro	508-842-3311
Easthampton Golf	103 Northampton Street	Easthampton	413-529-2300
Fairway	400 Hudson Street	Marlboro	508-624-9999
Fenway Golf Range	112 Allen Street	East Longmeadow	413-525-6495
Fore Seasons Golf Center	258 Park Avenue	Worcester	508-752-6116
Gilchrist Family Golf Range	155 Lafayette Road	Salisbury	508-462-2240
Golf Acres	315 Union Street	Westfield	413-568-1075
Golf Country	Route 114	Middleton	508-774-4476
Golf Dome	Walnut Street	Shrewsbury	508-845-1001
Golf Gallery	175 Main Street	Fitchburg	508-342-1939
Golf Learning Center	19 Leonard Street	Norton	508-285-4500
Golf Tech	275 North Main Street	Middleton	508-777-8888
Groveland Fairways	156 Main Street	Groveland	508-373-2872
Indian Rock Driving Range	575 E. Central Street	Franklin	508-520-0036
In House Golf	Call for address	Northboro	508-489-0434
Ironwood Golf & Batting Cages	115 Cummings Park	Woburn	617-933-6657
Ironwoods Driving Range	150 Nashua Road	Pepperell	508-433-8912
John Smith Sports Center	70 Sumner Street	Milford	508-634-8080
Kimball Farm Driving Range	400 Littleton Road	Westford	508-486-4944
Lakeview Driving Range	1 Whalom Road	Lunenburg	508-345-7070
Lancaster Golf Center	438 Old Turnpike Road	Lancaster	508-537-8922
Learning Center of New England	19 Leonard Street	Norton	508-285-4500
Longest Drive	Route 6	Dennis	508-398-5555
Longhi's Golf Driving Range	309 Southwick Street	Southwick	413-569-0093
Max's Country Golf	383 Middlesex Road	Tyngsboro	508-649-2020
McGolf Driving Range	138 Bridge Street	Dedham	617-326-9616
Meadowcrest Golf Range	Route 9	Leeds	13-586-6603
Millbury Sport Center	Route 20 South	Millbury	508-799-9033
Mill Valley Driving Range	38 Mill Valley Road	Belchertown	413-323-0264
Natick Golf Center	218 Speen Street	Natick	508-651-2406
Paradise Springs Golf	25 Lonergan Road	Middleton	508-750-4653
Precision Golf	30 Chelmsford Street	Chelmsford	508-251-3933
Quaboag Valley Driving Range	Hospital Road	Monson	413-283-4388
River's Edge Driving Range	305 Brigham Street	Hudson	508-562-7079
Ronnies Driving Range	760 Nashua Road	Dracut	508-957-2000
Rotary Driving Range	Turnpike Road	Westboro	508-366-5327
Sandbagger's Practice Range	829 Washington Street	Pembroke	617-826-1234
Sarkisian Farms	Chandler Road	Andover	508-683-3093
Seekonk Driving Range	1977 Fall River Avenue	Seekonk	508-336-8074
South Meadow Golf Center	South Street Rotary	Berlin	508-838-2333
South Shore Practice Range	262 Forbes Road	Braintree	617-380-4838
Spencer Practice Range	500 Main Street	Spencer	508-885-2694
Sportech Indoor Golf	One Lynwood Lane	Westford	508-692-6123
Sports Graphics International	485 Canton Street	Westwood	617-326-9299
Star Land	645 Washington Street	Hanover	617-826-3083
Sterling Chocksett Driving Range	47 Chocksett Road	Sterling	508-422-8228
Stone Meadow Golf	675 Waltham Street	Lexington	617-863-0445
Sun 'n Air Driving Range	210 Conant Street	Danvers	508-774-8180
Swingaway Golf	180 Newbury Turnpike	Danvers	508-777-4774
T's Indoor Driving Range	281 Essex Street	Salem	508-744-7486
T-2 Green Golf Range	225 Groveland Street	Abington	617-857-2424

Driving Ranges and Practice Areas (Continued)

Name	Address	Town	Phone
Wayside Driving Range	890 Boston Post Road	Marlborough	508-480-8891
Western Mass Golf Center	294 Russell Street	Hadley	413-586-2311
Whirlaway Golf Center & Driving Range	500 Merrimack Street	Methuen	508-688-8356
White's Family Sports Center	211 Middle Road	Acushnet	508-998-5666
Wright Brothers' Sports Center	231 Union Street	Holbrook	617-767-3766

Year-Round Courses

Course	Town	Holes
Ballymeade CC	North Falmouth	18
Bass River GC	South Yarmouth	18
Bay Pointe CC	Wareham	18
Blissful Meadows GC	Uxbridge	18
Blue Rock GC	South Yarmouth	18
Cape Cod CC	North Falmouth	18
Chequessett Yacht & CC	Wellfleet	9
D. W. Fields GC	Brockton	18
Dennis Pines GC	South Dennis	18
East Mountain CC	Westfield	18
Easton CC	South Easton	18
Falmouth CC	Falmouth	18
Far Corner GC	Boxford	27
Fire Fly CC	Seekonk	18
George Wright GC	Hyde Park	18
Green Hill Municipal GC	Worcester	18
Harwich Port GC	Harwich Port	9
Heritage Hill CC	Lakeville	18
Holly Ridge GC	South Sandwich	18
Hyannis GC	Hyannis	18
John F. Parker GC	Taunton	9
Lakeview GC	Wenham	9
Lakeville CC	Lakeville	18
Little Harbor CC	Wareham	18
Miacomet GC	Nantucket	9
Middleton GC	Middleton	18
Mink Meadows GC	Vineyard Haven	9
New Bedford Municipal GC	New Bedford	18

Course	Town	Holes
Newton Commonwealth GC	Chestnut Hill	18
North Hill CC	Duxbury	9
Norwood CC	Norwood	18
Ocean Edge GC	Brewster	18
Olde Barnstable Fairgrounds GC	Marston Mills	18
Paul Harney GC	East Falmouth	18
Pine Oaks GC	South Easton	9
Pine Valley GC	Rehoboth	9
Poquoy Brook GC	Lakeville	18
Quashnet Valley CC	Mashpee	18
Rehoboth CC	Rehoboth	18
Rockland GC	Rockland	18
Round Hill CC	East Sandwich	18
Saddle Hill CC	Hopkinton	18
Saint Anne CC	Feeding Hills	18
Southwick CC	Southwick	18
Squirrel Run CC	Plymouth	18
Stone-E-Lea GC	Attleborough	18
Strawberry Hills CC	Leicester	18
Swansea CC	Swansea	18
Tara Hyannis GC	Hyannis	18
Touisset CC	Swansea	9
Wading River GC	Norton	18
Wampanoag GC	North Swansea	9
Wedgewood CC	Brockton	9
Woodbriar CC	Falmouth	9
Clearview GC	Millbury	9

Courses By Town

Course	Town	Holes
Strawberry Valley GC	Abington	9
Forest Park CC	Adams	9
Amesbury Golf and CC	Amesbury	9
Amherst GC	Amherst	18
Rolling Green GC	Andover	9
Ashfield Community GC	Ashfield	9
Edge Hill GC	Ashfield	9
Ellinwood CC	Athol	18
Locust Valley CC	Attleborough	18
Stone-E-Lea GC	Attleborough	18
Pakachoag GC	Auburn	9
Mill Valley CC	Belchertown	14
Maplegate CC	Bellingham	18

Course	Town	Holes
New England CC	Bellingham	18
Pine Acres	Bellingham	9
Berlin CC	Berlin	9
Crumpin-Fox Club	Bernardston	18
Beverly Golf and Tennis Club	Beverly	18
CC of Billerica	Billerica	18
Twin Springs GC	Bolton	9
Far Corner GC	Boxford	27
Bradford CC	Bradford	18
Braintree Municipal GC	Braintree	18
Captains GC	Brewster	18
Ocean Edge GC	Brewster	18
D. W. Fields GC	Brockton	18

MASSACHUSETTS

Courses By Town (Continued)

Course	Town	Holes
Wedgewood CC	Brockton	9
Putterham Meadows	Brookline	18
Fresh Pond GC	Cambridge	18
Brookmeadow CC	Canton	18
Ponkapoag GC #1	Canton	18
Ponkapoag GC #2	Canton	18
Heritage CC	Charlton	18
Chatham Seaside Links	Chatham	9
Apple CC	Chelmsford	9
Newton Commonwealth GC	Chestnut Hill	18
Chicopee Municipal GC	Chicopee	18
North Adams CC	Clarksburg	9
Cotuit-Highground GC	Cotuit	9
Wahconah CC	Dalton	18
William J. Devine GC	Dorcester	18
Nichols College GC	Dudley	9
North Hill CC	Duxbury	9
Bay Path GC	East Brookfield	9
Paul Harney GC	East Falmouth	18
Pine Knoll GC	East Longmeadow	9
Northfield CC	East Northfield	9
Round Hill CC	East Sandwich	18
Cape Ann GC	Essex	9
Falmouth CC	Falmouth	18
Woodbriar CC	Falmouth	9
Agawam CC	Feeding Hills	18
Oak Ridge GC	Feeding Hills	9
Saint Anne CC	Feeding Hills	18
Hemlock Ridge GC	Fiskdale	9
Devens GC	Fort Devens	9
Millwood Farms Course	Framingham	14
Gardner Municipal GC	Gardner	18
South Shore CC	Hingham	18
Bas Ridge GC	Hinsdale	9
Holden Hills CC	Holden	18
Pine Crest GC	Holliston	18
Holyoke CC	Holyoke	9
Hopedale CC	Hopedale	9
Saddle Hill CC	Hopkinton	18
Hyannis GC	Hyannis	18
Tara Hyannis GC	Hyannis	18
George Wright GC	Hyde Park	18
Candlewood GC	Ipswich	9
Heritage Hill CC	Lakeville	18
Lakeville CC	Lakeville	18
Poquoy Brook GC	Lakeville	18
Skyline CC	Lanesborough	18
Greenock CC	Lee	9
Northampton CC	Leeds	9
Hillcrest CC	Leicester	9
Strawberry Hills CC	Leicester	18
Cranwell Resort	Lenox	18
Grand View CC	Leominister	18
Monoosnock CC	Leominister	9
Pine Meadows GC	Lexington	9
Maplewood GC	Lunenburg	9

Course	Town	Holes
Gannon Municipal GC	Lynn	18
Lynnfield Center GC	Lynnfield	9
Sagamore Spring GC	Lynnfield	18
Willowdale GC	Mansfield	9
Marion GC	Marion	9
Green Harbor GC	Marshfield	18
Olde Barnstable	Marston Mills	18
New Seabury GC Blue	Mashpee	18
New Seabury GC Green	Mashpee	18
Quashnet Valley CC	Mashpee	18
Maynard GC	Maynard	9
Mount Hood GC	Melrose	18
Hickory Hill GC	Methuen	18
Merrimack Valley GC	Methuen	18
Middleton GC	Middleton	18
Clearview GC	Millbury	9
Glen Ellen CC	Millis	18
Quaboag CC	Monson	9
Kelly Greens	Nahant	9
Miacomet GC	Nantucket	9
New Bedford Municipal	New Bedford	18
Green Valley GC	Newburyport	9
Ould Newbury GC	Newburyport	9
Cherry Hills GC	North Amherst	9
Chemawa CC	North Attleborough	9
Ballymeade CC	North Falmouth	18
Cape Cod CC	North Falmouth	18
Hillview GC	North Reading	18
Wampanoag GC	North Swansea	9
Highland Links	North Truro	9
Pine Grove GC	Northampton	18
Juniper Hill GC - Lakeside	Northboro	18
Juniper Hill GC -	Northboro	18
Norton CC	Norton	18
Wading River GC	Norton	18
Lost Brook GC	Norwood	18
Norwood CC	Norwood	18
Farm Neck GC	Oak Bluffs	18
Quail Hollow Golf & CC	Oakham	9
Pine Ridge CC	Oxford	18
Pembroke CC	Pembroke	18
Petersham CC	Petersham	9
GEAA GC	Pittsfield	9
Pontoosuc Lake CC	Pittsfield	18
Heather Hill CC	Plainville	27
Atlantic CC	Plymouth	18
Plymouth CC	Plymouth	18
Squirrel Run CC	Plymouth	18
Furnace Brook GC	Quincy	18
Presidents GC	Quincy	18
Hidden Hollow CC	Rehoboth	9
Hillside CC	Rehoboth	9
Middlebrook CC	Rehoboth	9
Pine Valley GC	Rehoboth	9
Rehoboth CC	Rehoboth	18
Sun Valley CC	Rehoboth	18

100

Courses By Town (Continued)

Course	Town	Holes
Rochester GC	Rochester	18
Rockland GC	Rockland	18
Rockport GC	Rockport	9
Rowley CC	Rowley	9
Whippernon CC	Russell	9
Bedrock GC	Rutland	9
Olde Salem Greens	Salem	9
Cedar Glen GC	Saugus	9
Scituate CC	Scituate	9
Fire Fly CC	Seekonk	18
Siasconset GC	Siasconset	9
Hickory Ridge CC	South Amherst	18
Dennis Highlands	South Dennis	18
Dennis Pines GC	South Dennis	18
Easton CC	South Easton	18
Pine Oaks GC	South Easton	9
Orchards GC	South Hadley	18
Holly Ridge GC	South Sandwich	18
Waubeeka Golf Links	South	18
Bass River GC	South Yarmouth	18
Bayberry Hills GC	South Yarmouth	18
Blue Rock GC	South Yarmouth	18
Southampton CC	Southampton	18
Saint Mark's GC	Southborough	9
Edgewood GC	Southwick	18
Southwick CC	Southwick	18
Foxborough CC	Springfield	18
Franconia Municipal GC	Springfield	18
Veterans GC	Springfield	18
Stoneham Oaks GC	Stoneham	9
Unicorn GC	Stoneham	9
Cedar Hill GC	Stoughton	9
Butternut Farm GC	Stow	18
Stow Acres (North)	Stow	18
Stow Acres (South)	Stow	18
Stowaway GC	Stow	9

Course	Town	Holes
Swansea CC	Swansea	18
Touisset CC	Swansea	9
John F. Parker GC	Taunton	9
Trull Brook GC	Tewksbury	18
New Meadows GC	Topsfield	9
Thomas Memorial CC	Turner Falls	9
Tyngsboro GC	Tyngsboro	9
Blissful Meadows GC	Uxbridge	18
Edgewood GC	Uxbridge	9
Mink Meadows GC	Vineyard Haven	9
Colonial Hilton GC	Wakefield	18
Bay Pointe CC	Wareham	18
Little Harbor CC	Wareham	18
Sandy Burr CC	Wayland	18
Wayland CC	Wayland	18
Chequessett Yacht & CC	Wellfleet	9
Lakeview GC	Wenham	9
Wenham CC	Wenham	18
Wachusett CC	West Boylston	18
Indian Meadows GC	Westborough	9
Westborough CC	Westborough	9
East Mountain CC	Westfield	18
Shaker Farms CC	Westfield	18
Tekoa CC	Westfield	18
Nabnasset Lake CC	Westford	9
Westminster CC	Westminster	18
Leo J. Martin GC	Weston	18
Ridder GC	Whitman	18
Wilbraham CC	Wilbraham	9
Taconic GC	Williamstown	18
Winchendon CC	Winchendon	18
Woburn CC	Woburn	9
Green Hill Municipal GC	Worcester	18
Worthington GC	Worthington	9
Kings Way GC	Yarmouthport	18

Eastern Massachusetts

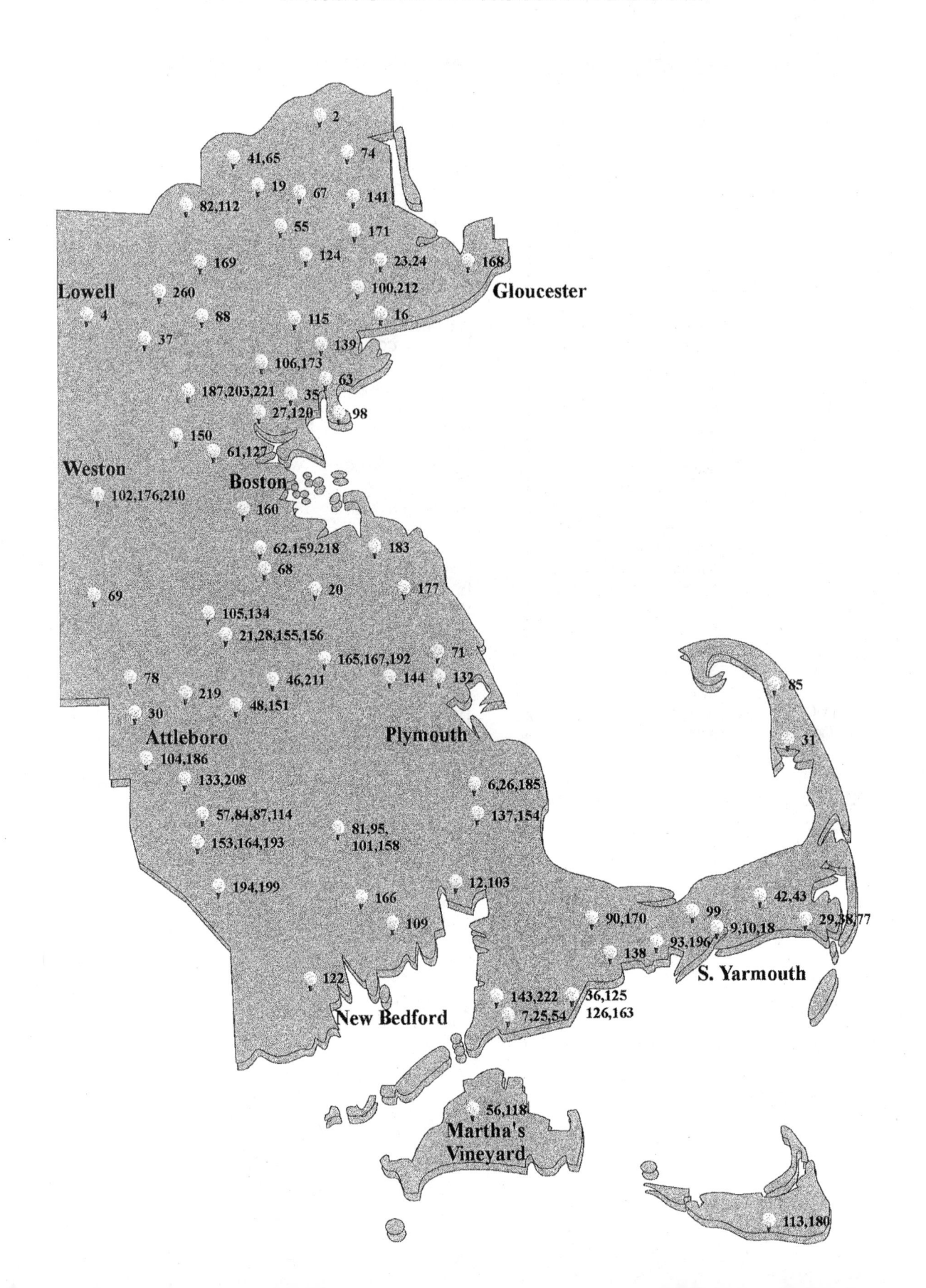

Central Massachusetts

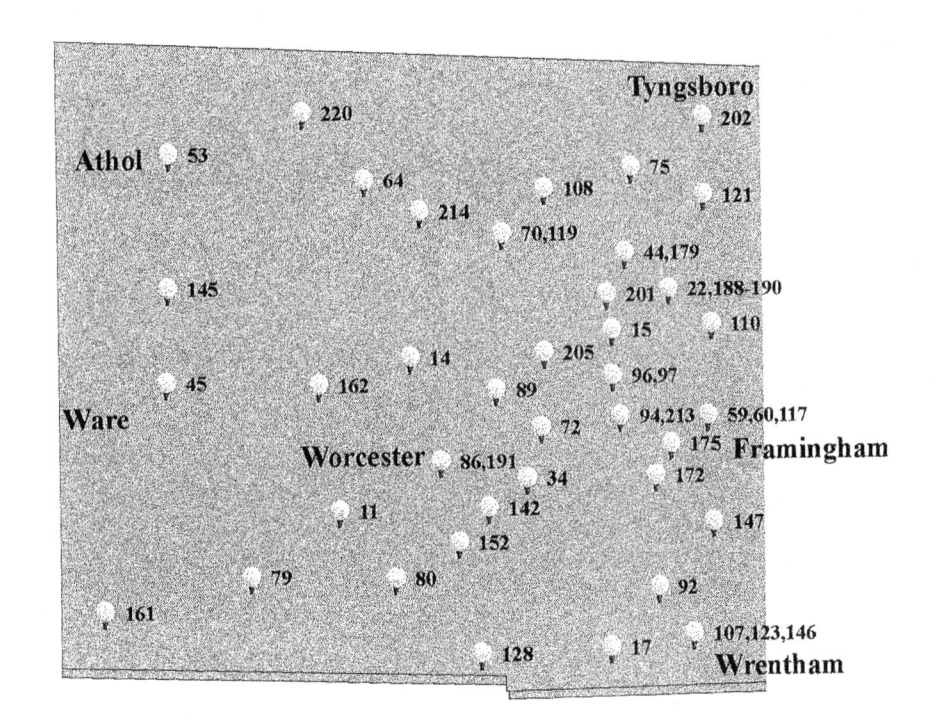

- Tyngsboro
- 220
- Athol 53
- 202
- 64
- 108
- 75
- 214
- 121
- 70,119
- 44,179
- 145
- 201 22,188-190
- 15 110
- 14 205
- 45 162 89 96,97
- Ware 72 94,213 59,60,117
- 175 Framingham
- Worcester 86,191 172
- 34
- 11 142 147
- 152
- 79 80 92
- 161
- 128 17 107,123,146
- Wrentham

Western Massachusetts

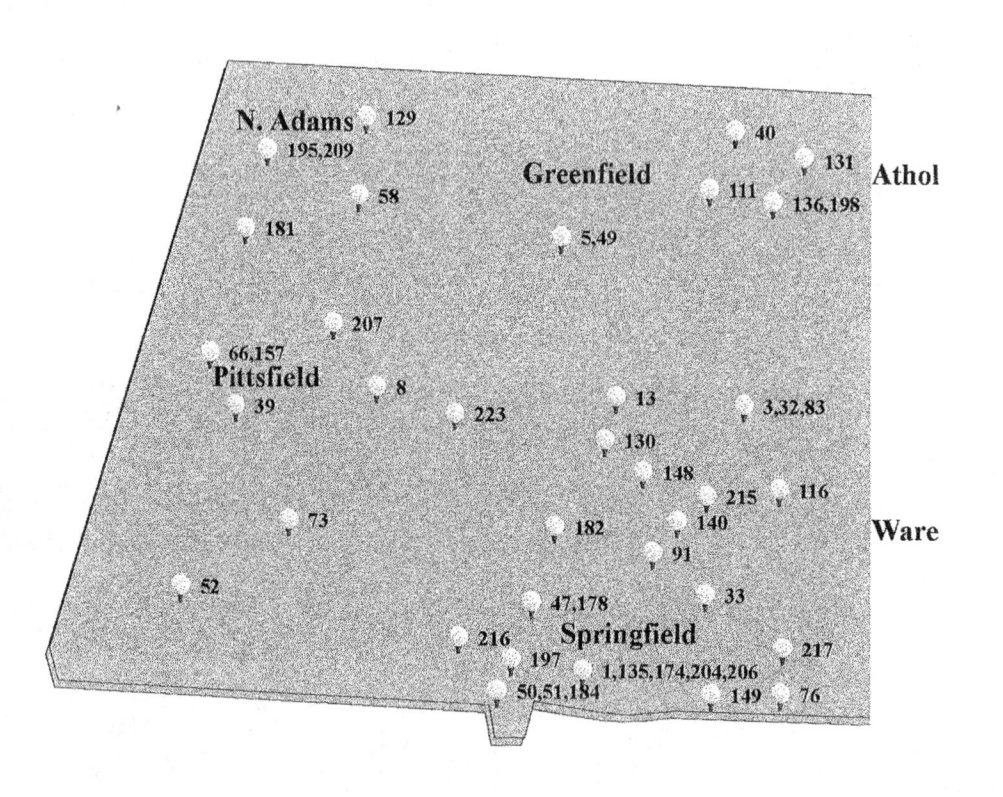

- N. Adams: 129, 195, 209, 58, 181
- Greenfield: 40, 111, 136, 198, 5, 49
- Athol: 131
- Pittsfield: 207, 66, 157, 8, 39, 223, 73, 52
- Ware: 13, 3, 32, 83, 130, 148, 215, 116, 182, 140, 91, 33
- Springfield: 47, 178, 216, 197, 50, 51, 184, 1, 135, 174, 204, 206, 217, 149, 76

1 Agawam Country Club
128 Southwick Street, Feeding Hills, MA 01030
413-786-2194

Weekend Fee	$21	Weekday Fee	$15
Power Cart Fee	$18	Pull Carts	Yes
Putting Green	Yes	Driving Range	No
Season	Apr 15 - Nov 30	Credit Cards	No
Pro	Ronnie Dunn	Tee Times	7 days
Comments	No water, 8 sand traps, narrow fairways		
Directions	I-90, I-91, Rt 57 Agawam to Feeding Hills		

Tee	Holes	Par	Rating	Slope	Yards
Red	18	73	73.0	117	5,300
White	18	71	69.1	117	6,129
Blue	NA	NA	NA	NA	NA

2 Amesbury Golf and Country Club
50 Monroe Street, Amesbury, MA 01913
508-388-5153

Weekend Fee	$23	Weekday Fee	$23
Power Cart Fee	$23	Pull Carts	Yes
Putting Green	Yes	Driving Range	No
Season	Apr 1 - Nov 30	Credit Cards	No
Pro	Butch Mellon	Tee Times	5 days
Comments	Small undulating greens, tree lined		
Directions	I-95N, Rt 110W, right at light (Burger King), right at Monroe St.		

Tee	Holes	Par	Rating	Slope	Yards
Red	9	70	71.9	126	5,400
White	9	70	70.5	125	6,089
Blue	9	70	70.5	125	6,312

3 Amherst Golf Club
365 South Pleasant Street, Amherst, MA 01002
413-256-6894

Weekend Fee	$20	Weekday Fee	$20
Power Cart Fee	$18	Pull Carts	Yes
Putting Green	Yes	Driving Range	No
Season	Apr 1 - Dec 1	Credit Cards	Yes
Pro	Dave Twohig	Tee Times	No
Comments	Small greens, located at Amherst College		
Directions	I-90, Rt 181, Rt 9 (Amherst), right on Rt 116		

Tee	Holes	Par	Rating	Slope	Yards
Red	18	72	71.6	122	5,608
White	18	70	68.9	117	6,083
Blue	NA	NA	NA	NA	NA

4 Apple Country Club
66 Park Road, Chelmsford, MA 01824
508-256-8373

Weekend Fee	$22	Weekday Fee	$18
Power Cart Fee	$20	Pull Carts	Yes
Putting Green	Yes	Driving Range	No
Season	Apr 1 - Nov 30	Credit Cards	Yes
Pro	John Reed	Tee Times	3 days
Comments	Narrow, many water holes, small greens		
Directions	I-495, exit 34, Rt 110W, Rt 27S, 1.7 mi, left on Park Rd		

Tee	Holes	Par	Rating	Slope	Yards
Red	9	68	62.1	109	5,004
White	9	68	65.3	114	5,004
Blue	NA	NA	NA	NA	NA

5 Ashfield Community Golf Course
Norton Hill Road, Ashfield, MA 01330
413-628-4413

Weekend Fee	$14	Weekday Fee	$10
Power Cart Fee	No carts	Pull Carts	Yes
Putting Green	No	Driving Range	No
Season	Apr 1 - Snow	Credit Cards	No
Pro	None	Tee Times	No
Comments	Honor system payment		
Directions	Rt 2, Rt 112 (Ashfield), Rt 112, follow signs		

Tee	Holes	Par	Rating	Slope	Yards
Red	9	66	NA	NA	3,458
White	9	66	NA	NA	3,458
Blue	NA	NA	NA	NA	NA

6 Atlantic Country Club
450 Little Sandy Pond Road, Plymouth, MA 02360
508-888-6644

Weekend Fee	$33	Weekday Fee	$28
Power Cart Fee	$24	Pull Carts	Yes
Putting Green	Yes	Driving Range	Yes
Season	Apr 1 - Snow	Credit Cards	Yes
Pro	None	Tee Times	2 days
Comments	Rolling terrain, on 200 acres, large greens		
Directions	Rt 3, exit 2, right on Long Pond Rd, left Carter Bridge Rd, right Little Sandy Pond Rd, 2.5 mi		

Tee	Holes	Par	Rating	Slope	Yards
Red	18	72	68.3	116	4,918
White	18	72	69.0	119	5,840
Blue	18	72	70.8	127	6,262

MASSACHUSETTS

7 Ballymeade Country Club
125 Falmouth Woods Road, N. Falmouth, MA 02556
508-540-4005

Weekend Fee	$65	Weekday Fee	$50
Power Cart Fee	Included	Pull Carts	No
Putting Green	Yes	Driving Range	Yes
Season	Year-round	Credit Cards	Yes
Pro	Alex Ohlson	Tee Times	7 days
Comments	Ocean views, bent grass greens		
Directions	Bourne bridge, Rt 28S, Rt 151 exit, right off exit		

Tee	Holes	Par	Rating	Slope	Yards
Red	18	70	66.3	112	4,722
White	18	72	70.1	130	6,055
Blue	18	72	71.7	134	6,358

8 Bas Ridge Golf Club
Plunkett Street, Hinsdale, MA 01235
413-655-2605

Weekend Fee	$12	Weekday Fee	$10
Power Cart Fee	$16	Pull Carts	Yes
Putting Green	Yes	Driving Range	Yes
Season	Apr 1 - Nov 1	Credit Cards	No
Pro	Gary Norton	Tee Times	1 day
Comments	Rolling hills but fairly level		
Directions	I-90, Lee exit, left on Rt 8 (Hinsdale), Plunkett St in town center, 0.3 mi		

Tee	Holes	Par	Rating	Slope	Yards
Red	9	70	NA	NA	4,416
White	9	70	NA	110	5,108
Blue	NA	NA	NA	NA	NA

9 Bass River Golf Course
Highbank Road, South Yarmouth, MA 02664
508-398-9079

Weekend Fee	$35	Weekday Fee	$35
Power Cart Fee	$21	Pull Carts	Yes
Putting Green	Yes	Driving Range	No
Season	Year-round	Credit Cards	Yes
Pro	Ron Hewins	Tee Times	4 days
Comments	Small greens, built in 1902, narrow fairways		
Directions	Rt 6E, exit 8, left on Regional Ave, right at 2nd stop sign		

Tee	Holes	Par	Rating	Slope	Yards
Red	18	72	69.3	111	5,343
White	18	72	67.7	117	5,702
Blue	18	72	69.3	122	6,129

10 Bayberry Hills Golf Club
West Yarmouth Road, South Yarmouth, MA 02675
508-394-5597

Weekend Fee	$35	Weekday Fee	$35
Power Cart Fee	$21	Pull Carts	Yes
Putting Green	Yes	Driving Range	Yes
Season	Apr 1 - Nov 30	Credit Cards	Yes
Pro	Ronald Hewins	Tee Times	4 days
Comments	Multiple routes to greens, tree lined		
Directions	Rt 6E, exit 8, right on Old Townhouse Rd (2nd lights), at end of road		

Tee	Holes	Par	Rating	Slope	Yards
Red	18	72	69.2	111	5,275
White	18	72	68.5	125	6,067
Blue	18	72	70.5	125	6,523

11 Bay Path Golf Club
193 North Brookfield Road, E. Brookfield, MA 01515
508-867-3054

Weekend Fee	$18	Weekday Fee	$15
Power Cart Fee	$18	Pull Carts	Yes
Putting Green	No	Driving Range	No
Season	Apr 1 - Nov 30	Credit Cards	No
Pro	None	Tee Times	No
Comments	Very flat course, many sand traps		
Directions	I-90, Sturbridge exit, Rt 20E, Rt 49N, Rt 9W, Rt 67, N. Brookfield Rd		

Tee	Holes	Par	Rating	Slope	Yards
Red	9	74	NA	NA	5,840
White	9	72	69.5	NA	6,030
Blue	NA	NA	NA	NA	NA

12 Bay Pointe Country Club
Onset Avenue, Wareham, MA 02558
508-759-8802

Weekend Fee	$32	Weekday Fee	$30
Power Cart Fee	$25	Pull Carts	Yes
Putting Green	Yes	Driving Range	No
Season	Year-round	Credit Cards	Yes
Pro	R. Gummarson	Tee Times	4 days
Comments	Excellent greens & fairways, 16th all water		
Directions	Rt 24S, I-495S, Onset exit, right on Onset Ave		

Tee	Holes	Par	Rating	Slope	Yards
Red	18	72	71.3	125	5,380
White	18	70	67.6	113	5,720
Blue	18	70	70.3	118	6,201

MASSACHUSETTS

13 Beaver Brook Country Club
191 Main Street, Haydenville, MA 01039
413-268-7229

Weekend Fee	$17	*Weekday Fee*	$13
Power Cart Fee	$18	*Pull Carts*	Yes
Putting Green	Yes	*Driving Range*	No
Season	Apr 15 - Nov 30	*Credit Cards*	No
Pro	None	*Tee Times*	7 days
Comments	Brooks and ponds		
Directions	I-91, exit 19, Rt 9W, 5 mi		

Tee	Holes	Par	Rating	Slope	Yards
Red	9	76	67.7	107	4,960
White	9	72	68.1	110	5,992
Blue	NA	NA	NA	NA	NA

14 Bedrock Golf Club
87 Barre Paxton Road, Rutland, MA 01543
508-886-0202

Weekend Fee	$22	*Weekday Fee*	$15
Power Cart Fee	$22	*Pull Carts*	Yes
Putting Green	Yes	*Driving Range*	No
Season	Apr 15 - Nov 30	*Credit Cards*	No
Pro	Joe Carr	*Tee Times*	7 days
Comments	Small undulating greens, distinct holes		
Directions	I-90, exit 10, Rt 12S, Rt 20W, Rt 56N, Rt 122W, 5 miles		

Tee	Holes	Par	Rating	Slope	Yards
Red	9	72	68.3	126	4,584
White	9	72	69.8	122	6,186
Blue	9	72	71.4	127	6,572

15 Berlin Country Club
25 Carr Road, Berlin, MA 01503
508-838-2733

Weekend Fee	$15	*Weekday Fee*	$15
Power Cart Fee	$20	*Pull Carts*	Yes
Putting Green	No	*Driving Range*	No
Season	Mar - Nov	*Credit Cards*	No
Pro	None	*Tee Times*	No
Comments	Small, challenging greens		
Directions	I-495, Rt 62 exit, west, right on Carter St, left on Randall Rd, right Carr Rd		

Tee	Holes	Par	Rating	Slope	Yards
Red	9	66	62.9	108	4,144
White	9	66	62.9	108	4,466
Blue	NA	NA	NA	NA	NA

16 Beverly Golf and Tennis Club
134 McKay Street, Beverly, MA 01915
508-922-9072

Weekend Fee	$32	*Weekday Fee*	$28
Power Cart Fee	$22	*Pull Carts*	Yes
Putting Green	Yes	*Driving Range*	Yes
Season	Mar 1 - Dec 24	*Credit Cards*	No
Pro	Mike Farrell	*Tee Times*	7 days
Comments	Built in 1910, greens fast and small		
Directions	Rt 128, exit 20S to Cabot St, right on McKay		

Tee	Holes	Par	Rating	Slope	Yards
Red	18	73	NA	NA	5,429
White	18	70	70.1	123	5,965
Blue	NA	70	NA	NA	6,237

17 Blissful Meadows Golf Club
801 Chockalog Road, Uxbridge, MA 01569
508-278-6113

Weekend Fee	$28	*Weekday Fee*	$22
Power Cart Fee	$20	*Pull Carts*	Yes
Putting Green	Yes	*Driving Range*	Yes
Season	Year-round	*Credit Cards*	Yes
Pro	Phil Schustek	*Tee Times*	2 days
Comments	Tight fairways, several ponds		
Directions	I-495S, Rt 109 Milford, Rt 16 Uxbridge, left West St, right to course		

Tee	Holes	Par	Rating	Slope	Yards
Red	18	74	NA	NA	NA
White	18	72	68.4	120	6,022
Blue	18	72	NA	NA	NA

18 Blue Rock Golf Club
48 Todd Road, South Yarmouth, MA 02664
508-398-9295

Weekend Fee	$28	*Weekday Fee*	$25
Power Cart Fee	No carts	*Pull Carts*	Yes
Putting Green	Yes	*Driving Range*	Yes
Season	Year-round	*Credit Cards*	No
Pro	Robert Miller	*Tee Times*	7 days
Comments	Rated best par 3 1985, lodging		
Directions	Rt 6E, exit 8, right, 1st left, right at intersection, left Great Western, right Todd Rd		

Tee	Holes	Par	Rating	Slope	Yards
Red	18	55	NA	NA	2,785
White	18	54	NA	NA	2,923
Blue	NA	NA	NA	NA	NA

MASSACHUSETTS

19 Bradford Country Club
201 Chadwick Road, Bradford, MA 01835
508-372-8587

Weekend Fee	$30	Weekday Fee	$25
Power Cart Fee	$20	Pull Carts	Yes
Putting Green	Yes	Driving Range	No
Season	Apr - Dec 24	Credit Cards	Yes
Pro	Rick Wolshro	Tee Times	5 days
Comments	Narrow fairways, many sand traps		
Directions	I-495, exit 48, Rt 125N, 2.2 mi, right Salem St, 0.9 mi, right Boxford Rd, 1st right		

Tee	Holes	Par	Rating	Slope	Yards
Red	18	70	70.0	113	4,939
White	18	70	70.3	134	6,005
Blue	18	70	72.8	141	6,511

22 Butternut Farm Golf Club
115 Wheeler Road, Stow, MA 01775
508-897-3400

Weekend Fee	$30	Weekday Fee	$24
Power Cart Fee	No carts	Pull Carts	Yes
Putting Green	Yes	Driving Range	No
Season	Apr 1 - Nov 30	Credit Cards	No
Pro	None	Tee Times	5 days
Comments	Scenic, lots of variety, large greens		
Directions	I-495, exit 27, Rt 117E, 5 mi, right Wheeler Rd		

Tee	Holes	Par	Rating	Slope	Yards
Red	18	70	67.0	115	4,729
White	18	70	69.9	125	6,205
Blue	NA	NA	NA	NA	NA

20 Braintree Municipal Golf Course
101 Jefferson Street, Braintree, MA 02184
617-843-9781

Weekend Fee	$26	Weekday Fee	$21
Power Cart Fee	$22	Pull Carts	Yes
Putting Green	Yes	Driving Range	Yes
Season	Apr 1 - Nov 1	Credit Cards	No
Pro	Robert Beach	Tee Times	2 days
Comments	Very busy course, many water hazards		
Directions	Rt 3, Union St, south, left at light after T overpass, right at lights, Rt 37, right Jefferson		

Tee	Holes	Par	Rating	Slope	Yards
Red	18	74	72.1	118	5,751
White	18	72	70.4	116	6,423
Blue	NA	NA	NA	NA	NA

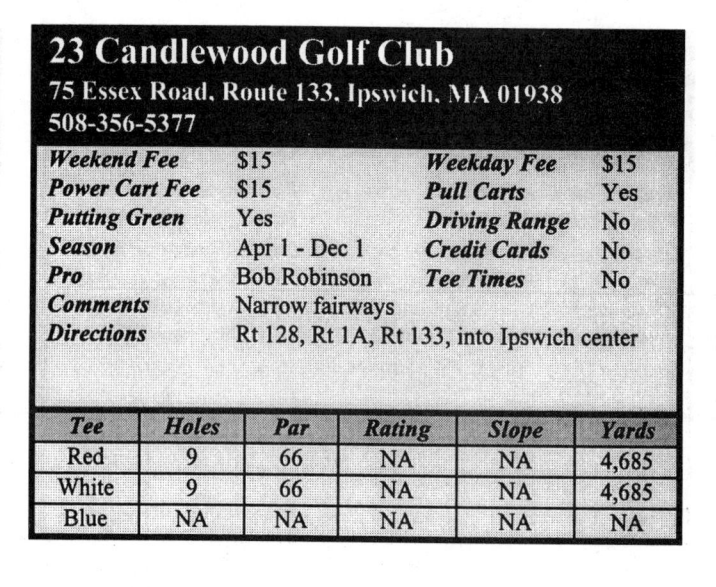

23 Candlewood Golf Club
75 Essex Road, Route 133, Ipswich, MA 01938
508-356-5377

Weekend Fee	$15	Weekday Fee	$15
Power Cart Fee	$15	Pull Carts	Yes
Putting Green	Yes	Driving Range	No
Season	Apr 1 - Dec 1	Credit Cards	No
Pro	Bob Robinson	Tee Times	No
Comments	Narrow fairways		
Directions	Rt 128, Rt 1A, Rt 133, into Ipswich center		

Tee	Holes	Par	Rating	Slope	Yards
Red	9	66	NA	NA	4,685
White	9	66	NA	NA	4,685
Blue	NA	NA	NA	NA	NA

21 Brookmeadow Country Club
100 Everendon Road, Canton, MA 02021
617-828-4444

Weekend Fee	$27	Weekday Fee	$22
Power Cart Fee	$25	Pull Carts	Yes
Putting Green	Yes	Driving Range	Yes
Season	Mar 1 - Nov 30	Credit Cards	Yes
Pro	Joe Videtta	Tee Times	5 days
Comments	Easy to walk, narrow tree lined fairways		
Directions	Rt 128, I-95S, exit Neponset St Canton, 1 mi right before bridge		

Tee	Holes	Par	Rating	Slope	Yards
Red	18	72	71.2	114	5,606
White	18	72	70.1	118	6,292
Blue	18	72	71.7	123	6,659

24 Cape Ann Golf Club
99 John Wise Avenue, Essex, MA 01929
508-768-7544

Weekend Fee	$24	Weekday Fee	$22
Power Cart Fee	$22	Pull Carts	Yes
Putting Green	No	Driving Range	No
Season	Apr 1 - Nov 30	Credit Cards	Yes
Pro	None	Tee Times	No
Comments	Built in 1931, along the water		
Directions	Rt 128N, exit 15, left, left on Rt 133		

Tee	Holes	Par	Rating	Slope	Yards
Red	9	70	NA	NA	4,374
White	9	70	67.3	110	5,866
Blue	9	70	NA	NA	6,018

25 Cape Cod Country Club
Theater Road, North Falmouth, MA 02556
508-563-9842

Weekend Fee	$35	*Weekday Fee*	$28
Power Cart Fee	$22	*Pull Carts*	Yes
Putting Green	Yes	*Driving Range*	No
Season	Year-round	*Credit Cards*	Yes
Pro	Chuck Holmes	*Tee Times*	7 days
Comments	Small greens, built in 1920, hilly		
Directions	Rt 28S, right on Rt 151, 2.3 mi, right on Ranch Rd		

Tee	Holes	Par	Rating	Slope	Yards
Red	18	72	70.6	119	5,348
White	18	71	67.7	118	6,018
Blue	18	71	70.0	122	6,404

26 Captains Golf Club
1000 Freeman's Way, Brewster, MA 02361
508-896-5100

Weekend Fee	$40	*Weekday Fee*	$40
Power Cart Fee	$22	*Pull Carts*	Yes
Putting Green	Yes	*Driving Range*	Yes
Season	Mar 1 - Dec 1	*Credit Cards*	No
Pro	Mike Robichaud	*Tee Times*	2 days
Comments	Rated in top 25 public courses		
Directions	Rt 6, exit 11, right, 1.6 mi take right on Freeman's Way		

Tee	Holes	Par	Rating	Slope	Yards
Red	18	72	70.5	117	5,388
White	18	72	69.8	123	6,176
Blue	18	72	72.7	130	6,794

27 Cedar Glen Golf Club
60 Water Street, Saugus, MA 01906
617-233-3609

Weekend Fee	$20	*Weekday Fee*	$19
Power Cart Fee	$22	*Pull Carts*	Yes
Putting Green	Yes	*Driving Range*	No
Season	Apr 1 - Dec 1	*Credit Cards*	No
Pro	None	*Tee Times*	No
Comments	Built in 1928, flat, easy walker		
Directions	I-95, Walnut Street exit, go east to Water St		

Tee	Holes	Par	Rating	Slope	Yards
Red	9	70	NA	NA	5,930
White	9	70	66.7	107	6,170
Blue	NA	NA	NA	NA	NA

28 Cedar Hill Golf Club
1137 Park Street, Stoughton, MA 02072
617-344-8913

Weekend Fee	$17	*Weekday Fee*	$12
Power Cart Fee	$20	*Pull Carts*	Yes
Putting Green	Yes	*Driving Range*	No
Season	Apr 1 - Nov 30	*Credit Cards*	No
Pro	Jim Devlin	*Tee Times*	No
Comments	Town course, small greens		
Directions	Rt 128, Rt 24 South Stoughton exit, on Rt 27 Park St		

Tee	Holes	Par	Rating	Slope	Yards
Red	9	66	NA	NA	4,310
White	9	66	60.4	92	4,310
Blue	NA	NA	NA	NA	NA

29 Chatham Seaside Links
290 Seaview Road, Chatham, MA 02633
508-945-4774

Weekend Fee	$22	*Weekday Fee*	$22
Power Cart Fee	$21	*Pull Carts*	Yes
Putting Green	Yes	*Driving Range*	No
Season	Apr 1 - Oct 31	*Credit Cards*	Yes
Pro	John Giadino	*Tee Times*	No
Comments	Ocean views, built in 1914		
Directions	Rt 6E, exit 11, Rt 137, Rt 28 to Chatham center, Main St, left on Seaview Rd		

Tee	Holes	Par	Rating	Slope	Yards
Red	9	68	NA	NA	4,800
White	9	68	66.4	107	4,980
Blue	NA	NA	NA	NA	NA

30 Chemawa Country Club
350 Cushman Road, North Attleborough, MA 02760
508-761-8754

Weekend Fee	$23	*Weekday Fee*	$18
Power Cart Fee	$20	*Pull Carts*	Yes
Putting Green	Yes	*Driving Range*	No
Season	Apr 1 - Nov 30	*Credit Cards*	No
Pro	None	*Tee Times*	No
Comments	Wide fairways		
Directions	I-95S, I-295 to Woonsocket, Rt 1S, right at Grossman's, 1st left		

Tee	Holes	Par	Rating	Slope	Yards
Red	9	70	NA	NA	4,804
White	9	70	67.2	113	5,244
Blue	NA	NA	NA	NA	NA

MASSACHUSETTS

31 Chequessett Yacht & Country Club
Chequessett Neck Road, Wellfleet, MA 02667
508-349-3704

Weekend Fee	$34	Weekday Fee	$34
Power Cart Fee	$18	Pull Carts	Yes
Putting Green	No	Driving Range	No
Season	Year-round	Credit Cards	Yes
Pro	None	Tee Times	5 days
Comments	Overlooks harbor, small greens		
Directions	Rt 6, Wellfleet center signs, left Town Piper sign at lights, left East Commercial St, 2 mi		

Tee	Holes	Par	Rating	Slope	Yards
Red	9	74	66.2	113	4,762
White	9	70	65.1	110	5,169
Blue	NA	NA	NA	NA	NA

32 Cherry Hill Golf Club
323 Montague Road, North Amherst, MA 01059
413-256-4071

Weekend Fee	$15	Weekday Fee	$13
Power Cart Fee	$20	Pull Carts	Yes
Putting Green	Yes	Driving Range	No
Season	Apr 1 - Nov 30	Credit Cards	Yes
Pro	None	Tee Times	No
Comments	Wide fairways, hilly, uneven lies		
Directions	I-90, exit 4, 91N, exit 19, Rt 9E, 116N, right at lights, left at next lights		

Tee	Holes	Par	Rating	Slope	Yards
Red	9	70	NA	NA	4,940
White	9	70	65.7	101	5,340
Blue	9	70	NA	NA	5,556

33 Chicopee Municipal Golf Course
1290 Burnett Road, Chicopee, MA 01020
413-592-4156

Weekend Fee	$15	Weekday Fee	$14
Power Cart Fee	$20	Pull Carts	Yes
Putting Green	Yes	Driving Range	No
Season	Apr - Nov	Credit Cards	No
Pro	Mark Jamrog	Tee Times	1 day
Comments	Rated one of best municipals, large greens		
Directions	I-90, exit 6, right at lights, 2 mi		

Tee	Holes	Par	Rating	Slope	Yards
Red	18	73	72.5	115	5,284
White	18	72	70.4	120	6,365
Blue	18	72	73.0	126	7,010

34 Clearview Golf Club
66 Park Hill Avenue, Millbury, MA 01527
508-753-9201

Weekend Fee	$15	Weekday Fee	$13
Power Cart Fee	$18	Pull Carts	Yes
Putting Green	No	Driving Range	No
Season	Apr 5 - Nov 30	Credit Cards	Yes
Pro	Steve Gelineaux	Tee Times	3 days
Comments	Wide fairways, fast and large greens, hilly		
Directions	I-90, Rt 122, Rt 20W		

Tee	Holes	Par	Rating	Slope	Yards
Red	9	70	67.7	112	5,072
White	9	70	65.9	114	5,448
Blue	NA	NA	NA	NA	NA

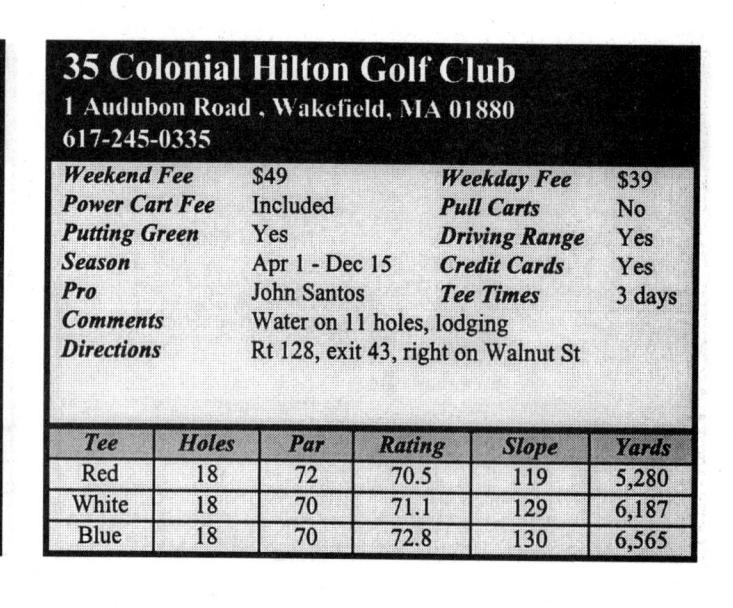

35 Colonial Hilton Golf Club
1 Audubon Road, Wakefield, MA 01880
617-245-0335

Weekend Fee	$49	Weekday Fee	$39
Power Cart Fee	Included	Pull Carts	No
Putting Green	Yes	Driving Range	Yes
Season	Apr 1 - Dec 15	Credit Cards	Yes
Pro	John Santos	Tee Times	3 days
Comments	Water on 11 holes, lodging		
Directions	Rt 128, exit 43, right on Walnut St		

Tee	Holes	Par	Rating	Slope	Yards
Red	18	72	70.5	119	5,280
White	18	70	71.1	129	6,187
Blue	18	70	72.8	130	6,565

36 Cotuit-Highground Golf Club
31 Crocker Neck Road, Cotuit, MA 02365
508-428-9863

Weekend Fee	$10	Weekday Fee	$10
Power Cart Fee	$15	Pull Carts	Yes
Putting Green	Yes	Driving Range	No
Season	Year-round	Credit Cards	No
Pro	None	Tee Times	No
Comments	Tight greens, well watered, semi-private		
Directions	Rt 6, exit 2 (Rt 130S), left on Rt 28, right on Main St in center, right on School St, 2nd left		

Tee	Holes	Par	Rating	Slope	Yards
Red	9	56	NA	NA	2,100
White	9	56	NA	NA	2,580
Blue	NA	NA	NA	NA	NA

37 Country Club of Billerica
Baldwin Road, Billerica, MA 01821
508-667-8061

Weekend Fee	$26	Weekday Fee	$24
Power Cart Fee	$20	Pull Carts	Yes
Putting Green	Yes	Driving Range	Yes
Season	Apr 1 - Nov 15	Credit Cards	Yes
Pro	Barrie Bruce	Tee Times	No
Comments	Short back nine, long front nine		
Directions	Rt 3A N to Billerica center, right before Friendly's, right at end, 3rd left Baldwin		

Tee	Holes	Par	Rating	Slope	Yards
Red	18	66	63.0	99	4,185
White	18	66	63.9	107	4,965
Blue	18	66	65.9	112	5,368

38 Cranberry Valley Golf Club
183 Oak Street, Harwich, MA 02645
508-432-4653

Weekend Fee	$40	Weekday Fee	$40
Power Cart Fee	$20	Pull Carts	Yes
Putting Green	Yes	Driving Range	Yes
Season	May 30 - Sep 9	Credit Cards	No
Pro	Jim Knowles	Tee Times	2 days
Comments	55 sand bunkers, tree lined fairways		
Directions	Rt 6, exit 10, right, 1st left Queen Anne Rd, 3rd light Oak St		

Tee	Holes	Par	Rating	Slope	Yards
Red	18	72	71.5	115	5,518
White	18	72	67.1	113	5,644
Blue	18	72	70.4	125	6,296

39 Cranwell Resort
55 Lee Road, Lenox, MA 01240
413-637-1364

Weekend Fee	$55	Weekday Fee	$55
Power Cart Fee	$24	Pull Carts	Yes
Putting Green	Yes	Driving Range	Yes
Season	Apr - Nov 15	Credit Cards	Yes
Pro	David Strong	Tee Times	7 days
Comments	Lodging, Mt views, small undulating greens		
Directions	I-90, exit 2, Rt 20W Lee Rd		

Tee	Holes	Par	Rating	Slope	Yards
Red	18	73	72.4	129	5,602
White	18	70	70.0	125	6,169
Blue	18	70	70.0	125	6,346

40 Crumpin-Fox Club
Parmenter Road, Bernardston, MA 01337
413-648-9101

Weekend Fee	$55	Weekday Fee	$55
Power Cart Fee	$28	Pull Carts	Yes
Putting Green	Yes	Driving Range	Yes
Season	Apr 15 - Nov 15	Credit Cards	Yes
Pro	Ron Beck	Tee Times	2 days
Comments	Lodging, tough course, rated in top 10 in US		
Directions	I-91, exit 28A, Rt 10N 1 mi, left Parmenter Rd, follow signs		

Tee	Holes	Par	Rating	Slope	Yards
Red	18	72	71.5	131	5,432
White	18	72	71.3	136	6,508
Blue	18	72	73.8	141	7,007

41 Crystal Springs Golf Club
940 North Broadway, Haverhill, MA 01832
508-374-9621

Weekend Fee	$20	Weekday Fee	$17
Power Cart Fee	$20	Pull Carts	Yes
Putting Green	Yes	Driving Range	Yes
Season	Apr 1 - Oct 30	Credit Cards	No
Pro	Ed Thompkins	Tee Times	7 days
Comments	Hilly terrain		
Directions	I-495N, exit 50, Rt 97S, 0.2 mi, left on N. Broadway, 2.5 mi		

Tee	Holes	Par	Rating	Slope	Yards
Red	18	73	72.0	112	5,596
White	18	72	70.8	114	6,436
Blue	18	72	71.1	116	6,706

42 Dennis Highlands Golf Club
825 Old Bass River Road, South Dennis, MA 02368
508-385-8347

Weekend Fee	$40	Weekday Fee	$35
Power Cart Fee	$22	Pull Carts	Yes
Putting Green	Yes	Driving Range	Yes
Season	Mar 15 - Nov 30	Credit Cards	Yes
Pro	Jay Haberl	Tee Times	4 days
Comments	Multi-tiered large greens		
Directions	Rt 6, exit 9, left, left on Access Rd, right on Old Bass River Rd		

Tee	Holes	Par	Rating	Slope	Yards
Red	18	71	67.4	112	4,927
White	18	71	68.7	115	6,076
Blue	18	71	70.4	118	6,464

MASSACHUSETTS

43 Dennis Pines Golf Club
Golf Course Road, Route 134, South Dennis, MA 02660
508-385-8698

Weekend Fee	$40	*Weekday Fee*	$35	
Power Cart Fee	$22	*Pull Carts*	Yes	
Putting Green	Yes	*Driving Range*	Yes	
Season	Year-round	*Credit Cards*	Yes	
Pro	Jay Haberl	*Tee Times*	4 days	
Comments	Tree & water lined, requires accuracy			
Directions	Rt 6, exit 9, left, left on Access Rd, right on Old Bass River Rd			

Tee	Holes	Par	Rating	Slope	Yards
Red	18	71	73.7	122	5,798
White	18	71	71.0	122	6,525
Blue	18	71	71.9	127	7,029

44 Devens Golf Course
Jackson Road, Fort Devens, MA 01433
508-772-3273

Weekend Fee	$18	*Weekday Fee*	$12	
Power Cart Fee	$20	*Pull Carts*	Yes	
Putting Green	Yes	*Driving Range*	Yes	
Season	Apr 1 - Nov 30	*Credit Cards*	No	
Pro	Rod Guilder	*Tee Times*	5 days	
Comments	New course			
Directions	Rt 2, Jackson Rd exit, west			

Tee	Holes	Par	Rating	Slope	Yards
Red	9	70	70.9	118	5,388
White	9	70	67.1	112	5,657
Blue	9	70	67.1	112	5,758

45 Dunroamin Country Club
262 Lower Road, Route 23, Gilbertville, MA 01031
413-477-8880

Weekend Fee	$20	*Weekday Fee*	$20	
Power Cart Fee	$20	*Pull Carts*	Yes	
Putting Green	Yes	*Driving Range*	Yes	
Season	Mar 1 - Dec 1	*Credit Cards*	No	
Pro	None	*Tee Times*	No	
Comments	Doglegs, large greens, hilly			
Directions	I-90, exit 8, Rt 32 into Gilbertville, 6 mi			

Tee	Holes	Par	Rating	Slope	Yards
Red	9	70	66.8	106	4,802
White	9	70	68.6	117	5,726
Blue	NA	NA	NA	NA	NA

46 D. W. Fields Golf Course
31 Oak Street, Brockton, MA 02401
508-580-7855

Weekend Fee	$21	*Weekday Fee*	$17	
Power Cart Fee	$22	*Pull Carts*	Yes	
Putting Green	Yes	*Driving Range*	No	
Season	Year-round	*Credit Cards*	No	
Pro	Jerry Mackedon	*Tee Times*	No	
Comments	Flat, no water, undulating greens			
Directions	Rt 24, Brockton/Stoughton exit, towards Stoughton, right 1st light Oak St			

Tee	Holes	Par	Rating	Slope	Yards
Red	18	70	70.1	111	5,415
White	18	70	68.9	116	5,660
Blue	18	70	68.4	120	5,972

47 East Mountain Country Club
1458 East Mountain Road, Westfield, MA 01085
413-568-1539

Weekend Fee	$20	*Weekday Fee*	$17	
Power Cart Fee	$20	*Pull Carts*	Yes	
Putting Green	Yes	*Driving Range*	Yes	
Season	Year-round	*Credit Cards*	Yes	
Pro	Ted Perez	*Tee Times*	7 days	
Comments	Large greens, shoot over 120 foot gorge			
Directions	I-90, Rt 202N, right on East Mountain Rd			

Tee	Holes	Par	Rating	Slope	Yards
Red	18	71	65.3	101	5,043
White	18	71	65.9	101	6,031
Blue	NA	NA	NA	NA	NA

48 Easton Country Club
265 Purchase Street, South Easton, MA 02375
508-238-2500

Weekend Fee	$25	*Weekday Fee*	$23	
Power Cart Fee	$22	*Pull Carts*	Yes	
Putting Green	Yes	*Driving Range*	Yes	
Season	Year-round	*Credit Cards*	Yes	
Pro	C. Phinney	*Tee Times*	2 days	
Comments	Full facilities, large greens			
Directions	Rt 24S, exit 17B, Rt 123W, Rt 138S, Purchase St exit, right			

Tee	Holes	Par	Rating	Slope	Yards
Red	18	72	70.2	112	5,271
White	18	71	68.0	114	6,060
Blue	18	71	69.3	119	6,328

MASSACHUSETTS

49 Edge Hill Golf Course
Barnes Road, Ashfield, MA 01330
413-625-6018

Weekend Fee	$16	Weekday Fee	$14
Power Cart Fee	$18	Pull Carts	Yes
Putting Green	Yes	Driving Range	Yes
Season	Apr 15 - Nov 15	Credit Cards	No
Pro	None	Tee Times	No
Comments	Elevated tee boxes and greens		
Directions	I-495, Rt 2, I-91S, Rt 112 Ashfield, left Baptist Corner Rd, left Barnes Rd		

Tee	Holes	Par	Rating	Slope	Yards
Red	9	72	NA	NA	5,980
White	9	72	NA	NA	6,500
Blue	9	72	NA	NA	6,820

50 Edgewood Golf Club
161 Sheep Pasture Road, Southwick, MA 01077
413-569-6826

Weekend Fee	$18	Weekday Fee	$14
Power Cart Fee	$20	Pull Carts	Yes
Putting Green	Yes	Driving Range	Yes
Season	Mar 15 - Nov 15	Credit Cards	No
Pro	Michael Grigely	Tee Times	4 days
Comments	Wide fairways, tree lined, many side hill lies		
Directions	I-90, Rt 57 Southwick, through center, left Depot St, right Sheep Pasture Rd		

Tee	Holes	Par	Rating	Slope	Yards
Red	18	71	71.8	109	5,580
White	18	71	67.6	113	6,050
Blue	18	71	69.1	115	6,510

51 Edgewood Golf Club
757 West Hartford Avenue, Uxbridge, MA 01077
508-278-6027

Weekend Fee	$10	Weekday Fee	$8
Power Cart Fee	$14	Pull Carts	Yes
Putting Green	Yes	Driving Range	No
Season	Apr 1 - Dec 1	Credit Cards	No
Pro	None	Tee Times	No
Comments	Slightly hilly, large greens, wide fairways		
Directions	From Worcester, Rt 146S, exit Lackey Dam, right, left at 4 stop, left Charles St, follow signs		

Tee	Holes	Par	Rating	Slope	Yards
Red	9	66	NA	NA	4,010
White	9	64	NA	NA	4,520
Blue	9	64	NA	NA	4,710

52 Egremont Country Club
Route 23, Great Barrington, MA 01230
413-528-4222

Weekend Fee	$28	Weekday Fee	$20
Power Cart Fee	$24	Pull Carts	Yes
Putting Green	Yes	Driving Range	Yes
Season	Apr 1 - Oct 30	Credit Cards	Yes
Pro	Bob Dastoli	Tee Times	1 day
Comments	Many water holes, tight		
Directions	I-90, exit 2, Rt 102 towards Stockbridge, Rt 7S, Rt 23W to Egremont		

Tee	Holes	Par	Rating	Slope	Yards
Red	18	70	NA	NA	4,769
White	18	71	66.3	115	5,180
Blue	18	71	NA	NA	5,578

53 Ellinwood Country Club
1928 Pleasant Street, Athol, MA 01331
508-249-7460

Weekend Fee	$24	Weekday Fee	$19
Power Cart Fee	$22	Pull Carts	Yes
Putting Green	Yes	Driving Range	No
Season	Apr 15 - Nov 1	Credit Cards	No
Pro	No	Tee Times	1 day
Comments	Water on 9 holes, small greens		
Directions	Rt 3, Athol exit, left Pleasant St		

Tee	Holes	Par	Rating	Slope	Yards
Red	18	72	68.7	111	5,047
White	18	71	67.8	117	5,737
Blue	18	71	70.1	122	6,207

54 Falmouth Country Club
630 Carriage Shop Road, Falmouth, MA 02536
508-548-3211

Weekend Fee	$30	Weekday Fee	$25
Power Cart Fee	$20	Pull Carts	Yes
Putting Green	Yes	Driving Range	Yes
Season	Year-round	Credit Cards	Yes
Pro	Kevin Bull	Tee Times	7 days
Comments	Lodging, flat, tree lined		
Directions	Rt 28S to Falmouth, right Rt 151E, right Sandwich Rd, left Carriage Shop Rd		

Tee	Holes	Par	Rating	Slope	Yards
Red	18	72	74.0	125	5,764
White	18	72	68.8	114	6,227
Blue	18	72	70.0	118	6,535

MASSACHUSETTS

55 Far Corner Golf Course
Main Street, Boxford, MA 01885
508-352-8300

Weekend Fee	$30	Weekday Fee	$27
Power Cart Fee	$23	Pull Carts	Yes
Putting Green	Yes	Driving Range	Yes
Season	Year-round	Credit Cards	Yes
Pro	Bob Flynn	Tee Times	2 days
Comments	Championship, 27 holes, stats for 18 holes		
Directions	I-95N, Rt 97W, 1st left Ipswich Rd, right Main St		

Tee	Holes	Par	Rating	Slope	Yards
Red	18	73	68.3	108	5,655
White	18	72	70.9	126	6,189
Blue	18	72	72.9	130	6,719

58 Forest Park Country Club
Forest Park Avenue, Adams, MA 01220
413-743-3311

Weekend Fee	$12	Weekday Fee	$12
Power Cart Fee	$17	Pull Carts	Yes
Putting Green	Yes	Driving Range	No
Season	Mar 15 - Dec 1	Credit Cards	No
Pro	None	Tee Times	No
Comments	On foot of Mount Greylock, small greens		
Directions	I-90 to Adams, Maple Rd at center, 1st left Forest Park Ave		

Tee	Holes	Par	Rating	Slope	Yards
Red	9	68	63.8	110	4,400
White	9	68	63.8	110	5,100
Blue	NA	NA	NA	NA	NA

56 Farm Neck Golf Club
Country Road, Oak Bluffs, MA 02557
508-693-3057

Weekend Fee	$68	Weekday Fee	$68
Power Cart Fee	$22	Pull Carts	Yes
Putting Green	Yes	Driving Range	Yes
Season	May 25 - Oct 11	Credit Cards	Yes
Pro	Mike Zoll	Tee Times	2 days
Comments	65 sand traps, view of Nantucket Sound		
Directions	Call ahead		

Tee	Holes	Par	Rating	Slope	Yards
Red	18	72	68.9	109	5,022
White	18	72	69.6	126	6,094
Blue	18	72	71.8	130	6,709

59 Foxborough Country Club
33 Walnut Street, Springfield, MA 01701
508-543-4661

Weekend Fee	$35	Weekday Fee	$30
Power Cart Fee	$25	Pull Carts	Yes
Putting Green	Yes	Driving Range	Yes
Season	Apr 1 - Nov 30	Credit Cards	Yes
Pro	Bob Day	Tee Times	No
Comments	Well maintained, large, undulating greens		
Directions	I-95S, exit 7B, 1st left		

Tee	Holes	Par	Rating	Slope	Yards
Red	18	73	73.4	122	5,832
White	18	72	70.9	123	6,462
Blue	18	72	72.2	126	6,725

57 Fire Fly Country Club
320 Fall River Avenue, Seekonk, MA 02771
508-336-6622

Weekend Fee	$20	Weekday Fee	$19
Power Cart Fee	$22	Pull Carts	Yes
Putting Green	Yes	Driving Range	Yes
Season	Year-round	Credit Cards	Yes
Pro	Don Wright	Tee Times	5 days
Comments	Great for beginners		
Directions	I-95, I-195E, Seekonk exit, right, left at light, left at light, left at fork, right at Fire Fly		

Tee	Holes	Par	Rating	Slope	Yards
Red	18	60	NA	84	2,786
White	18	60	54.4	81	3,083
Blue	18	60	58.0	87	3,644

60 Franconia Municipal Golf Course
691 Dwight Road, Springfield, MA 01108
413-734-9334

Weekend Fee	$15	Weekday Fee	$13
Power Cart Fee	$19	Pull Carts	Yes
Putting Green	Yes	Driving Range	No
Season	Apr 1 - Nov 1	Credit Cards	No
Pro	Daniel DiRico	Tee Times	No
Comments	Rolling terrain, little water, few traps		
Directions	I-90, Ludlow exit, Rt 21 to E. Longmeadow, right at town, left Dwight Rd		

Tee	Holes	Par	Rating	Slope	Yards
Red	18	70	NA	NA	5,923
White	18	71	67.1	115	6,053
Blue	NA	NA	NA	NA	NA

61 Fresh Pond Golf Club
691 Huron Avenue, Cambridge, MA 02138
617-349-6282

Weekend Fee	$25	*Weekday Fee*	$20
Power Cart Fee	$22	*Pull Carts*	Yes
Putting Green	Yes	*Driving Range*	No
Season	Apr 1 - Dec 15	*Credit Cards*	No
Pro	Bob Carey	*Tee Times*	No
Comments	Tip O'Neill played here ("Tip's Course")		
Directions	Rt 128, Rt 2E, left Huron Avenue		

Tee	Holes	Par	Rating	Slope	Yards
Red	18	70	70.0	113	5,400
White	18	70	68.9	114	5,954
Blue	18	70	70.2	120	6,322

62 Furnace Brook Golf Club
Summit Avenue, Quincy, MA 02170
617-472-8466

Weekend Fee	$44	*Weekday Fee*	$44
Power Cart Fee	Included	*Pull Carts*	No
Putting Green	Yes	*Driving Range*	No
Season	Apr 1 - Nov 30	*Credit Cards*	Yes
Pro	Doug Smith	*Tee Times*	No
Comments	Undulating greens, tree lined fairways		
Directions	I-93, Furnace Brook Pkwy exit, left, right on Reservoir Ave, 0.3 mi		

Tee	Holes	Par	Rating	Slope	Yards
Red	18	70	NA	NA	5,128
White	18	70	NA	NA	5,746
Blue	NA	NA	NA	NA	NA

63 Gannon Municipal Golf Course
42 Great Woods Road, Lynn, MA 01904
617-592-8238

Weekend Fee	$24	*Weekday Fee*	$21
Power Cart Fee	$20	*Pull Carts*	Yes
Putting Green	Yes	*Driving Range*	No
Season	Apr 1 - Nov 30	*Credit Cards*	No
Pro	Mike Foster	*Tee Times*	2 days
Comments	Tight, tree lined fairways, small greens		
Directions	Rt 1, Rt 129, right at rotary Lynnfield St, right at church, left at pillars		

Tee	Holes	Par	Rating	Slope	Yards
Red	18	71	68.8	115	5,215
White	18	70	67.9	113	6,036
Blue	NA	NA	NA	NA	NA

64 Gardner Municipal Golf Course
152 Eaton Road, Gardner, MA 01440
508-632-9703

Weekend Fee	$25	*Weekday Fee*	$20
Power Cart Fee	$20	*Pull Carts*	Yes
Putting Green	Yes	*Driving Range*	Yes
Season	Apr 1 - Nov 15	*Credit Cards*	No
Pro	Mike Eagan	*Tee Times*	Yes
Comments	Small, fast greens		
Directions	Rt 2W, Rt 140N, 5 mi to Gardner center, Green St, Eaton Rd		

Tee	Holes	Par	Rating	Slope	Yards
Red	18	75	72.2	123	5,653
White	18	71	68.3	120	6,106
Blue	18	71	68.9	124	6,200

65 Garrison Golf Center
654 Hilldale Avenue, Haverhill, MA 01832
508-374-9380

Weekend Fee	$14	*Weekday Fee*	$12
Power Cart Fee	No carts	*Pull Carts*	Yes
Putting Green	Yes	*Driving Range*	Yes
Season	Apr - Snow	*Credit Cards*	No
Pro	Ted Murphy	*Tee Times*	No
Comments	Easy par 3		
Directions	I-495N, exit 50, 1 mi, left Hilldale Ave		

Tee	Holes	Par	Rating	Slope	Yards
Red	9	54	NA	NA	2,000
White	9	54	NA	NA	2,000
Blue	NA	NA	NA	NA	NA

66 GEAA Golf Club
303 Crane Avenue, Pittsfield, MA 01201
413-443-5746

Weekend Fee	$20	*Weekday Fee*	$15
Power Cart Fee	$16	*Pull Carts*	Yes
Putting Green	Yes	*Driving Range*	No
Season	Apr 1 - Oct 30	*Credit Cards*	No
Pro	Ed Rossi	*Tee Times*	1 day
Comments	Windy, views of Mt Greylock		
Directions	I-90, Lee exit, Rt 20 through Lee, right on Crane Ave 1/2 mi past Reed School		

Tee	Holes	Par	Rating	Slope	Yards
Red	9	72	70.5	117	5,274
White	9	72	69.6	117	6,205
Blue	NA	NA	NA	NA	NA

MASSACHUSETTS

67 Georgetown Country Club
258 Andover Street, Georgetown, MA 01833
508-352-8777

Weekend Fee	$27	Weekday Fee	$25
Power Cart Fee	$24	Pull Carts	Yes
Putting Green	Yes	Driving Range	Yes
Season	Apr 1 - Dec 15	Credit Cards	Yes
Pro	Dan Cammarata	Tee Times	2 days
Comments	Semi-private, large greens, tree lined		
Directions	I-93, Rt 133E, 11 mi		

Tee	Holes	Par	Rating	Slope	Yards
Red	18	73	70.5	116	6,515
White	18	72	70.5	128	6,105
Blue	18	72	71.9	130	5,040

70 Grand View Country Club
450 Wachusett Street, Leominister, MA 01453
508-537-0614

Weekend Fee	$22	Weekday Fee	$18
Power Cart Fee	$20	Pull Carts	Yes
Putting Green	Yes	Driving Range	No
Season	Apr 1 - Nov 1	Credit Cards	No
Pro	Sammy Mula	Tee Times	2 days
Comments	Large greens, wide, tree lined fairways		
Directions	Rt 2, Rt 12 Leominister, Pleasant St, right Wachusett St		

Tee	Holes	Par	Rating	Slope	Yards
Red	18	74	68.8	113	6,274
White	18	72	68.8	113	6,746
Blue	NA	NA	NA	NA	NA

68 George Wright Golf Club
420 West Street, Hyde Park, MA 02136
617-361-8313

Weekend Fee	$26	Weekday Fee	$23
Power Cart Fee	$23	Pull Carts	Yes
Putting Green	Yes	Driving Range	No
Season	Year-round	Credit Cards	Yes
Pro	Donald Lyons	Tee Times	2 days
Comments	Donald Ross design		
Directions	Jamaica Way, at Forest Hills T stop right Hyde Park Ave, right West St		

Tee	Holes	Par	Rating	Slope	Yards
Red	18	69	70.3	115	5,054
White	18	70	68.6	123	6,105
Blue	18	70	69.5	126	6,357

71 Green Harbor Golf Club
624 Webster Street, Marshfield, MA 02050
617-834-7303

Weekend Fee	$28	Weekday Fee	$26
Power Cart Fee	No carts	Pull Carts	Yes
Putting Green	Yes	Driving Range	No
Season	Mar 15 - Dec 15	Credit Cards	No
Pro	Frik Nelson	Tee Times	2 days
Comments	Flat and open		
Directions	Rt 3, Marshfield exit 12 Rt 139E, 4 mi, right Webster St, 0.3 mi		

Tee	Holes	Par	Rating	Slope	Yards
Red	18	71	69.3	109	5,355
White	18	71	67.3	111	5,808
Blue	18	71	69.1	115	6,211

69 Glen Ellen Country Club
84 Orchard Street, Millis, MA 02054
508-376-2775

Weekend Fee	$30	Weekday Fee	$22
Power Cart Fee	$24	Pull Carts	Yes
Putting Green	Yes	Driving Range	Yes
Season	Apr 1 - Dec 15	Credit Cards	Yes
Pro	Harry Parker	Tee Times	7 days
Comments	Par 5 island green		
Directions	I-495, Rt 109E, left 3rd light, 2 mi, right Goulding St		

Tee	Holes	Par	Rating	Slope	Yards
Red	18	72	69.2	121	5,123
White	18	72	69.2	118	6,073
Blue	18	72	71.6	123	6,552

72 Green Hill Municipal Golf Course
Marsh Avenue, Worcester, MA 01605
508-852-0915

Weekend Fee	$22	Weekday Fee	$18
Power Cart Fee	$20	Pull Carts	Yes
Putting Green	Yes	Driving Range	No
Season	Year-round	Credit Cards	No
Pro	Bruce Dobie	Tee Times	2 days
Comments	Highest point in Worcester, 7 water holes		
Directions	I-495N, Rt 290, exit 20, bear right Lincoln St, right Marsh Ave		

Tee	Holes	Par	Rating	Slope	Yards
Red	18	71	69.9	116	5,547
White	18	72	67.4	106	6,110
Blue	18	72	68.4	112	6,487

73 Greenock Country Club
West Park Street, Lee, MA 01238
413-243-3323

Weekend Fee	$32	*Weekday Fee*	$21
Power Cart Fee	$20	*Pull Carts*	Yes
Putting Green	Yes	*Driving Range*	No
Season	Apr 15 - Oct 15	*Credit Cards*	No
Pro	Tom McDarby	*Tee Times*	No
Comments	Postage sized greens, well rated by MGA		
Directions	I-90, exit 2, right onto West Park St		

Tee	Holes	Par	Rating	Slope	Yards
Red	9	72	NA	NA	5,686
White	9	70	67.4	NA	6,027
Blue	9	70	NA	NA	6,160

74 Green Valley Golf Club
18 Boyd Drive, Newburyport, MA 01950
508-463-8600

Weekend Fee	$20	*Weekday Fee*	$17
Power Cart Fee	$16	*Pull Carts*	Yes
Putting Green	Yes	*Driving Range*	No
Season	Apr 15 - Nov 30	*Credit Cards*	No
Pro	None	*Tee Times*	1 day
Comments	Small greens, tree lined fairways		
Directions	I-95, exit 57, east, left at Friendly's, left at stop sign		

Tee	Holes	Par	Rating	Slope	Yards
Red	9	70	NA	NA	5,262
White	9	70	67.4	108	5,804
Blue	NA	NA	NA	NA	NA

75 Groton Country Club
94 Lovers Lane, Groton, MA 01450
508-448-2564

Weekend Fee	$21	*Weekday Fee*	$16
Power Cart Fee	$21	*Pull Carts*	Yes
Putting Green	Yes	*Driving Range*	Yes
Season	Apr 1 - Nov 30	*Credit Cards*	Yes
Pro	Charlie Elwood	*Tee Times*	1 day
Comments	Tree lined fairways, scenic		
Directions	I-495, exit 32, Rt 119W, 6.5 mi		

Tee	Holes	Par	Rating	Slope	Yards
Red	9	72	NA	NA	4,832
White	9	70	66.5	116	5,506
Blue	9	70	NA	NA	6,312

76 Hampden Country Club
128 Wilbraham Road, Hampden, MA 01036
413-566-8010

Weekend Fee	$29	*Weekday Fee*	$24
Power Cart Fee	$22	*Pull Carts*	Yes
Putting Green	Yes	*Driving Range*	Yes
Season	Apr - Nov	*Credit Cards*	Yes
Pro	G. Balavender	*Tee Times*	2 days
Comments	7 water holes, undulating greens		
Directions	I-91, exit 1, left 2nd light, right Dwight Rd, left Maple, right Rt 83S, left Hampden, 5 mi		

Tee	Holes	Par	Rating	Slope	Yards
Red	18	72	72.3	113	5,283
White	18	72	70.1	126	6,350
Blue	18	72	71.2	127	6,833

77 Harwich Port Golf Club
Forest Street, Harwich Port, MA 02646
508-432-0250

Weekend Fee	$21	*Weekday Fee*	$21
Power Cart Fee	No carts	*Pull Carts*	Yes
Putting Green	No	*Driving Range*	No
Season	Year-round	*Credit Cards*	No
Pro	None	*Tee Times*	No
Comments	Wide and flat fairways, large greens		
Directions	Rt 6, exit 10, Rt 124S, Rt 39S, left Forest St, 1.3 mi		

Tee	Holes	Par	Rating	Slope	Yards
Red	9	68	NA	NA	5,076
White	9	68	NA	NA	5,076
Blue	NA	NA	NA	NA	NA

78 Heather Hill Country Club
149 West Beacon Street, Plainville, MA 02762
508-695-0309

Weekend Fee	$22	*Weekday Fee*	$15
Power Cart Fee	$21	*Pull Carts*	Yes
Putting Green	Yes	*Driving Range*	No
Season	Year-round	*Credit Cards*	No
Pro	Al Shrest	*Tee Times*	7 days
Comments	2 separate courses, statistics on 18 holes		
Directions	I-495, exit 15, Rt 1A S, right Rt 106, West Beacon St in Plainville center		

Tee	Holes	Par	Rating	Slope	Yards
Red	27	70	66.4	103	4,736
White	27	70	66.5	115	5,734
Blue	27	70	67.8	117	6,005

MASSACHUSETTS

79 Hemlock Ridge Golf Club
220 Holland Road, Fiskdale, MA 01518
508-347-9935

Weekend Fee	$20	Weekday Fee	$18
Power Cart Fee	$18	Pull Carts	Yes
Putting Green	Yes	Driving Range	No
Season	Apr 1 - Nov 30	Credit Cards	No
Pro	None	Tee Times	No
Comments	Hilly, tree lined fairways, doglegs		
Directions	I-290, Sturbridge exit, Rt 20W through Sturbridge, left Holland Rd		

Tee	Holes	Par	Rating	Slope	Yards
Red	9	72	69.0	109	5,206
White	9	72	70.6	117	6,272
Blue	NA	NA	NA	NA	NA

80 Heritage Country Club
Sampson Road, Charlton, MA 01507
508-248-5111

Weekend Fee	$25	Weekday Fee	$19
Power Cart Fee	$20	Pull Carts	Yes
Putting Green	Yes	Driving Range	Yes
Season	Apr 1 - Nov 15	Credit Cards	No
Pro	Jack Aldrich	Tee Times	Yes
Comments	Elevated greens and tees		
Directions	I-90, exit 9 Sturbridge, Rt 20E, 3.5 mi		

Tee	Holes	Par	Rating	Slope	Yards
Red	18	72	70.6	114	5,880
White	18	71	69.7	118	6,375
Blue	NA	NA	NA	NA	NA

81 Heritage Hill Country Club
17 Heritage Hill Drive, Lakeville, MA 02347
508-947-7743

Weekend Fee	$23	Weekday Fee	$20
Power Cart Fee	$19	Pull Carts	Yes
Putting Green	Yes	Driving Range	No
Season	Year-round	Credit Cards	Yes
Pro	Bill Raynor	Tee Times	7 days
Comments	Water on few holes, greens have sand traps		
Directions	I-495, Rt 18S, past light in Lakeville center, 0.8 mi right Heritage Rd, right Heritage Hill		

Tee	Holes	Par	Rating	Slope	Yards
Red	18	54	54.7	84	2,155
White	18	54	54.7	84	2,575
Blue	18	54	54.7	84	3,012

82 Hickory Hill Golf Course
200 North Lowell, Methuen, MA 01844
508-686-0822

Weekend Fee	$32	Weekday Fee	$29
Power Cart Fee	$20	Pull Carts	Yes
Putting Green	Yes	Driving Range	Yes
Season	Mar 15 - Nov 15	Credit Cards	No
Pro	Paul Congo	Tee Times	4 days
Comments	Front open and flat, back hilly and wooded		
Directions	I-93, exit 46, right Rt 113W, 1.5 mi		

Tee	Holes	Par	Rating	Slope	Yards
Red	18	74	73.2	127	5,397
White	18	72	67.9	119	6,017
Blue	18	72	69.2	122	6,276

83 Hickory Ridge Country Club
191 West Pomeroy Lane, South Amherst, MA 01002
413-253-9320

Weekend Fee	$43	Weekday Fee	$32
Power Cart Fee	$25	Pull Carts	Yes
Putting Green	Yes	Driving Range	Yes
Season	Apr 1 - Oct 30	Credit Cards	No
Pro	Jim McDonald	Tee Times	1 day
Comments	Last 2 holes rated in top 10 in MA		
Directions	I-91, Rt 9E, Rt 116S, 2.5 mi, right West Pomeroy Lane		

Tee	Holes	Par	Rating	Slope	Yards
Red	18	74	70.3	114	5,340
White	18	72	71.1	128	6,411
Blue	18	72	72.5	129	6,794

84 Hidden Hollow Country Club
30 Pierce Lane, Rehoboth, MA 02769
508-252-9392

Weekend Fee	$15	Weekday Fee	$12
Power Cart Fee	$21	Pull Carts	Yes
Putting Green	No	Driving Range	No
Season	Apr 1 - Nov 30	Credit Cards	No
Pro	None	Tee Times	No
Comments	Narrow, tree lined fairways		
Directions	I-195, exit 2, north, right Davis St, Pleasant St, left Pierce Lane		

Tee	Holes	Par	Rating	Slope	Yards
Red	9	70	NA	NA	5,810
White	9	70	NA	NA	5,810
Blue	NA	NA	NA	NA	NA

85 Highland Links
North Highland Light Road, North Truro, MA 02652
508-487-9201

Weekend Fee	$25	*Weekday Fee*	$25
Power Cart Fee	$21	*Pull Carts*	Yes
Putting Green	Yes	*Driving Range*	No
Season	Apr 7 - Nov 1	*Credit Cards*	No
Pro	Manuel Macara	*Tee Times*	2 days
Comments	Cape's oldest course (1892), ocean views		
Directions	Rt 6 to Truro, after Truro Elementary School		

Tee	Holes	Par	Rating	Slope	Yards
Red	9	72	67.4	107	4,710
White	9	72	64.6	100	5,578
Blue	NA	NA	NA	NA	NA

86 Hillcrest Country Club
325 Pleasant Street, Leicester, MA 01524
508-892-1855

Weekend Fee	$25	*Weekday Fee*	$20
Power Cart Fee	$20	*Pull Carts*	Yes
Putting Green	Yes	*Driving Range*	No
Season	Apr 1 - Nov 1	*Credit Cards*	No
Pro	James Dolan	*Tee Times*	2 days
Comments	Undulating terrain, built 1910		
Directions	I-90, exit 10 Auburn, right Rt 12, 3 mi, right Rt 20, 3 mi, right Rt 56, 4 mi		

Tee	Holes	Par	Rating	Slope	Yards
Red	9	70	67.2	113	5,466
White	9	70	67.1	103	5,466
Blue	NA	NA	NA	NA	NA

87 Hillside Country Club
82 Hillside Avenue, Rehoboth, MA 02769
508-252-9761

Weekend Fee	$20	*Weekday Fee*	$17
Power Cart Fee	$20	*Pull Carts*	Yes
Putting Green	Yes	*Driving Range*	No
Season	Apr 1 - Nov 30	*Credit Cards*	Yes
Pro	None	*Tee Times*	7 days
Comments	Hilly, sloped greens, tree lined		
Directions	Rt 24S, Rt 44W, 1.5 mi past intersection Rt 18 and Rt 44, River St, Hillside Ave		

Tee	Holes	Par	Rating	Slope	Yards
Red	9	66	72.5	116	5,472
White	9	60	68.9	121	6,310
Blue	NA	NA	NA	NA	NA

88 Hillview Golf Course
149 North Street, North Reading, MA 01864
508-664-4435

Weekend Fee	$27	*Weekday Fee*	$25
Power Cart Fee	$22	*Pull Carts*	Yes
Putting Green	Yes	*Driving Range*	Yes
Season	Apr - Dec 24	*Credit Cards*	No
Pro	Brian O'Hearn	*Tee Times*	2 days
Comments	Many trapped greens		
Directions	I-93N, exit 40, east 1.5 mi, left North St		

Tee	Holes	Par	Rating	Slope	Yards
Red	18	70	68.7	108	5,184
White	18	69	66.0	106	5,754
Blue	NA	NA	NA	NA	NA

89 Holden Hills Country Club
1800 Main Street, Holden, MA 01520
508-829-3129

Weekend Fee	$25	*Weekday Fee*	$20
Power Cart Fee	$24	*Pull Carts*	Yes
Putting Green	Yes	*Driving Range*	No
Season	Apr 1 - Dec 1	*Credit Cards*	Yes
Pro	Tim Bishop	*Tee Times*	7 days
Comments	Hilly, wide tree lined fairways		
Directions	I-290, I-190N, exit Holden, left after lights, left at next light, right Main St, Rt 122A N		

Tee	Holes	Par	Rating	Slope	Yards
Red	18	74	NA	NA	5,200
White	18	71	71.9	125	5,826
Blue	NA	NA	NA	NA	NA

90 Holly Ridge Golf Club
121 Country Club Road, South Sandwich, MA 02563
508-428-5577

Weekend Fee	$20	*Weekday Fee*	$20
Power Cart Fee	$17	*Pull Carts*	Yes
Putting Green	Yes	*Driving Range*	Yes
Season	Year-round	*Credit Cards*	Yes
Pro	John Boniface	*Tee Times*	3 days
Comments	Wooded, narrow fairways		
Directions	Rt 3S, Rt 6, exit 2, Rt 130S, left Cotuit Rd, look for signs		

Tee	Holes	Par	Rating	Slope	Yards
Red	18	54	NA	NA	2,349
White	18	54	NA	NA	2,952
Blue	NA	NA	NA	NA	NA

MASSACHUSETTS

91 Holyoke Country Club
Smith Ferry Road, Route 5, Holyoke, MA 01040
413-534-1933

Weekend Fee	$25	Weekday Fee	$19
Power Cart Fee	$20	Pull Carts	Yes
Putting Green	Yes	Driving Range	No
Season	Apr 1 - Nov 30	Credit Cards	No
Pro	Via Wightman	Tee Times	No
Comments	Narrow fairways, water most holes		
Directions	I-91N, exit 17A, left Rt 5 at light, 2.5 mi		

Tee	Holes	Par	Rating	Slope	Yards
Red	9	76	66.3	118	5,360
White	9	72	67.5	118	6,265
Blue	9	72	68.0	118	6,478

94 Indian Meadows Golf Club
275 Turnpike Road, Westborough, MA 01581
508-836-5460

Weekend Fee	$28	Weekday Fee	$24
Power Cart Fee	$23	Pull Carts	Yes
Putting Green	Yes	Driving Range	No
Season	Apr 15 - Dec 1	Credit Cards	Yes
Pro	Art Billingham	Tee Times	4 days
Comments	Water on every hole		
Directions	I-95, Rt 9W, 3 mi		

Tee	Holes	Par	Rating	Slope	Yards
Red	9	72	69.0	NA	4,936
White	9	72	69.4	119	6,038
Blue	9	72	71.7	124	6,530

92 Hopedale Country Club
Mill Street, Hopedale, MA 01747
508-473-9876

Weekend Fee	Members only	Weekday Fee	$18
Power Cart Fee	$18	Pull Carts	Yes
Putting Green	Yes	Driving Range	No
Season	Apr 1 - Nov 1	Credit Cards	No
Pro	None	Tee Times	No
Comments	Semi-private, wide tree lined fairways		
Directions	I-495, Rt 85 Milford, right, right Rt 16 to Hopedale, left Hopedale St, right Green St		

Tee	Holes	Par	Rating	Slope	Yards
Red	9	70	NA	NA	5,438
White	9	70	68	121	6,068
Blue	NA	NA	NA	NA	NA

95 John F. Parker Golf Club
17 Fisher Street, Taunton, MA 02780
508-822-1797

Weekend Fee	$20	Weekday Fee	$16
Power Cart Fee	$16	Pull Carts	Yes
Putting Green	Yes	Driving Range	Yes
Season	Year-round	Credit Cards	No
Pro	None	Tee Times	No
Comments	Elevated tees and greens		
Directions	Rt 24, exit 16A, Rt 138, Rt 44, right N. Walker St, right Fisher St		

Tee	Holes	Par	Rating	Slope	Yards
Red	9	70	NA	NA	6,130
White	9	70	69.7	118	6,130
Blue	NA	NA	NA	NA	NA

93 Hyannis Golf Club
Route 132, Hyannis, MA 02601
508-362-2606

Weekend Fee	$42	Weekday Fee	$35
Power Cart Fee	$26	Pull Carts	Yes
Putting Green	Yes	Driving Range	Yes
Season	Year-round	Credit Cards	Yes
Pro	Mickey Herron	Tee Times	Month
Comments	Cape Cod Open held here, side hill lies		
Directions	Rt 6, exit 6, right Rt 132		

Tee	Holes	Par	Rating	Slope	Yards
Red	18	72	69.0	125	5,149
White	18	71	68.2	115	6,002
Blue	18	71	70.2	121	6,514

96 Juniper Hill Golf Course - Lakeside
202 Brigham Street, Northborough, MA 01532
508-393-2444

Weekend Fee	$30	Weekday Fee	$25
Power Cart Fee	$24	Pull Carts	Yes
Putting Green	Yes	Driving Range	No
Season	Mar 9 - Dec 14	Credit Cards	Yes
Pro	Dudley Darling	Tee Times	7 days
Comments	Water on 5 holes, Carolina style course		
Directions	I-90, I-495N, Rt 9W, Rt 135W, right Brigham St		

Tee	Holes	Par	Rating	Slope	Yards
Red	18	71	65.3	102	4,797
White	18	71	69.9	127	6,282
Blue	NA	NA	NA	NA	NA

97 Juniper Hill Golf Course - Riverside
202 Brigham Street, Northborough, MA 01532
508-393-2444

Weekend Fee	$30	Weekday Fee	$25
Power Cart Fee	$24	Pull Carts	Yes
Putting Green	Yes	Driving Range	No
Season	Mar 15 - Dec 14	Credit Cards	Yes
Pro	Dudley Darling	Tee Times	7 days
Comments	Par 3 island hole, picturesque		
Directions	I-90, I-495N, Rt 9W, Rt 135W, right Brigham St		

Tee	Holes	Par	Rating	Slope	Yards
Red	18	71	70.2	117	5,373
White	18	71	70.4	123	6,306
Blue	NA	NA	NA	NA	NA

98 Kelly Greens
1 Willow Road, Nahant, MA 01908
617-581-0840

Weekend Fee	$20	Weekday Fee	$18
Power Cart Fee	$18	Pull Carts	Yes
Putting Green	Yes	Driving Range	No
Season	Year-round	Credit Cards	Yes
Pro	Bruce Murphy	Tee Times	2 days
Comments	Fees good for unlimited play		
Directions	Rt 1A north to Lynn center, over causeway on Nahant Rd, follow signs		

Tee	Holes	Par	Rating	Slope	Yards
Red	9	60	NA	NA	3,342
White	9	60	57	103	3,784
Blue	NA	NA	NA	NA	NA

99 Kings Way Golf Club
Old Kings Highway, Yarmouthport, MA 02675
508-362-8820

Weekend Fee	$45	Weekday Fee	$45
Power Cart Fee	Included	Pull Carts	No
Putting Green	Yes	Driving Range	No
Season	Mar 15 - Dec 15	Credit Cards	Yes
Pro	Trevor Bateman	Tee Times	3 days
Comments	Narrow fairways, large greens		
Directions	Rt 6, exit 8, north, Rt 6A, right flashing yellow light		

Tee	Holes	Par	Rating	Slope	Yards
Red	18	59	56.7	89	3,039
White	18	59	58.9	93	4,100
Blue	NA	NA	NA	NA	NA

100 Lakeview Golf Club
60 Main Street, Route 1A, Wenham, MA 01984
508-468-6676

Weekend Fee	$18	Weekday Fee	$17
Power Cart Fee	$15	Pull Carts	Yes
Putting Green	Yes	Driving Range	No
Season	Year-round	Credit Cards	No
Pro	Michael Flynn	Tee Times	3 days
Comments	Large tree lined fairways		
Directions	Rt 128N, exit 20N Rt 1A, 2 mi		

Tee	Holes	Par	Rating	Slope	Yards
Red	9	62	NA	NA	3,900
White	9	62	59.3	91	4,080
Blue	NA	NA	NA	NA	NA

101 Lakeville Country Club
44 Clear Pond Road, Lakeville, MA 02346
508-947-6630

Weekend Fee	$28	Weekday Fee	$23
Power Cart Fee	$20	Pull Carts	Yes
Putting Green	Yes	Driving Range	No
Season	Year-round	Credit Cards	Yes
Pro	James Gallivan	Tee Times	7 days
Comments	Island green, large greens		
Directions	Rt 24S, I-495S, exit 4, south, 1 mi, right blinking light, 1 mi		

Tee	Holes	Par	Rating	Slope	Yards
Red	18	74	68.5	123	5,297
White	18	72	70.1	118	6,274
Blue	NA	NA	NA	NA	NA

102 Leo J. Martin Golf Club
85 Park Road, Weston, MA 02193
617-894-4903

Weekend Fee	$20	Weekday Fee	$17
Power Cart Fee	$21	Pull Carts	Yes
Putting Green	Yes	Driving Range	Yes
Season	Apr 1 - Dec 1	Credit Cards	Yes
Pro	Mike Wortis	Tee Times	No
Comments	Easy front 9, challenging back 9		
Directions	I-90, Rt 30 Weston, 1st left Park Rd		

Tee	Holes	Par	Rating	Slope	Yards
Red	18	75	69.7	115	5,250
White	18	72	68.8	115	6,140
Blue	18	72	69.6	120	6,320

MASSACHUSETTS

103 Little Harbor Country Club
Little Harbor Road, Wareham, MA 02571
508-295-2617

Weekend Fee	$18	Weekday Fee	$18
Power Cart Fee	$18	Pull Carts	Yes
Putting Green	Yes	Driving Range	No
Season	Year-round	Credit Cards	Yes
Pro	Jim Jones	Tee Times	3 days
Comments	Very good greens		
Directions	Rt 6, Minot Forest Rd, Great Neck Rd, right Little Harbor Rd		

Tee	Holes	Par	Rating	Slope	Yards
Red	18	56	51.9	72	2,692
White	18	56	54.4	79	3,038
Blue	NA	NA	NA	NA	NA

106 Lynnfield Center Golf Club
195 Summer Street, Lynnfield, MA 01940
617-334-9877

Weekend Fee	$22	Weekday Fee	$21
Power Cart Fee	$18	Pull Carts	Yes
Putting Green	Yes	Driving Range	Yes
Season	Apr 1 - Nov 30	Credit Cards	No
Pro	Bob Ryan	Tee Times	No
Comments	Wide open fairways, large greens		
Directions	Rt 128, exit 41 toward Lynnfield center, 1.2 mi, right Summer St		

Tee	Holes	Par	Rating	Slope	Yards
Red	9	68	NA	NA	4,970
White	9	68	61.5	NA	5,120
Blue	NA	NA	NA	NA	NA

104 Locust Valley Country Club
106 Locust Street, Attleborough, MA 02703
508-222-9790

Weekend Fee	$18 all day play	Weekday Fee	$14
Power Cart Fee	$20	Pull Carts	Yes
Putting Green	Yes	Driving Range	No
Season	Mar 1 - Nov 30	Credit Cards	No
Pro	None	Tee Times	1 day
Comments	Tree lined fairways		
Directions	I-95S, Rt 123A east, Rt 152S, 6 mi, Locust St		

Tee	Holes	Par	Rating	Slope	Yards
Red	18	72	68.0	121	5,070
White	18	72	69.3	121	6,148
Blue	18	72	69.5	123	6,241

107 Maplegate Country Club
160 Maple Street, Bellingham, MA 02019
508-966-4040

Weekend Fee	$39	Weekday Fee	$33
Power Cart Fee	$26	Pull Carts	Yes
Putting Green	Yes	Driving Range	Yes
Season	Apr - Dec	Credit Cards	Yes
Pro	Marc Blades	Tee Times	6 days
Comments	Large landing areas, rolling hills		
Directions	I-495, exit 18, right at exit, 2 mi 1st right, course 12 mi from I-495		

Tee	Holes	Par	Rating	Slope	Yards
Red	18	72	70.2	124	4,852
White	18	72	69.5	122	5,837
Blue	18	72	72.2	128	6,432

105 Lost Brook Golf Club
750 University Avenue, Norwood, MA 02062
617-769-2550

Weekend Fee	$20	Weekday Fee	$17
Power Cart Fee	No carts	Pull Carts	Yes
Putting Green	No	Driving Range	No
Season	Apr 1 - Nov 1	Credit Cards	No
Pro	None	Tee Times	5 days
Comments	Trapped greens, doglegs		
Directions	Rt 128, exit 13, right, follow signs 1.5 mi		

Tee	Holes	Par	Rating	Slope	Yards
Red	18	58	NA	NA	2,468
White	18	54	NA	NA	3,002
Blue	NA	NA	NA	NA	NA

108 Maplewood Golf Club
994 Northfield Road, Lunenburg, MA 01462
508-582-6694

Weekend Fee	$18	Weekday Fee	$15
Power Cart Fee	$18	Pull Carts	Yes
Putting Green	Yes	Driving Range	Yes
Season	Apr 1 - Nov 30	Credit Cards	Yes
Pro	Peter Dupuis	Tee Times	3 days
Comments	Wide tree lined fairways		
Directions	Rt 2, Rt 13 north, left Northfield Rd, 1 mi past Rt 2A		

Tee	Holes	Par	Rating	Slope	Yards
Red	9	72	66.5	105	4,880
White	9	70	63.9	106	5,370
Blue	NA	NA	NA	NA	NA

109 Marion Golf Club
10 South Drive, Marion, MA 02738
508-748-0199

Weekend Fee	$15	Weekday Fee	$15
Power Cart Fee	No carts	Pull Carts	Yes
Putting Green	Yes	Driving Range	No
Season	Mar 15 - Nov 30	Credit Cards	No
Pro	None	Tee Times	No
Comments	Built in 1904		
Directions	I-495S, I-95W, exit 20, Rt 105, Rt 6, 2nd lights Pond Rd, 1 mi		

Tee	Holes	Par	Rating	Slope	Yards
Red	9	78	NA	116	5,390
White	9	68	67	116	5,390
Blue	NA	NA	NA	NA	NA

112 Merrimack Valley Golf Course
210 Howe Street, Methuen, MA 01844
508-685-9717

Weekend Fee	$23	Weekday Fee	$19
Power Cart Fee	$20	Pull Carts	Yes
Putting Green	Yes	Driving Range	No
Season	Apr - Snow	Credit Cards	No
Pro	No	Tee Times	14 day
Comments	Some elevated tees, ponds		
Directions	I-93, Rt 213, Pleasant St exit, left 1st light Howe St, 1 mi		

Tee	Holes	Par	Rating	Slope	Yards
Red	18	72	NA	NA	4,606
White	18	71	69.0	120	5,938
Blue	18	71	NA	NA	6,205

110 Maynard Golf Club
50 Brown Street, Route 27, Maynard, MA 01754
508-897-9885

Weekend Fee	$28	Weekday Fee	$22
Power Cart Fee	$18	Pull Carts	Yes
Putting Green	Yes	Driving Range	No
Season	Apr 1 - Dec 1	Credit Cards	No
Pro	None	Tee Times	No
Comments	Narrow fairways, small greens		
Directions	Rt 2W, Rt 27S Brown St		

Tee	Holes	Par	Rating	Slope	Yards
Red	9	70	67.1	116	5,081
White	9	68	65.8	118	5,389
Blue	NA	NA	NA	NA	NA

113 Miacomet Golf Club
12 Miacomet Road, Nantucket, MA 02554
508-228-9764

Weekend Fee	$40 nonresident	Weekday Fee	$40
Power Cart Fee	$28	Pull Carts	Yes
Putting Green	Yes	Driving Range	Yes
Season	Year-round	Credit Cards	Yes
Pro	None	Tee Times	7 days
Comments	Wide fairways, large greens		
Directions	Main St, Pleasant St, left Atlantic Ave, left Bartlett Rd, left Miacomet Rd		

Tee	Holes	Par	Rating	Slope	Yards
Red	9	76	69.3	111	6,002
White	9	74	70.2	113	6,400
Blue	NA	NA	NA	NA	NA

111 Meadows Golf Course
398 Deerfield Road, Greenfield, MA 01301
413-773-9047

Weekend Fee	$15	Weekday Fee	$12
Power Cart Fee	$12	Pull Carts	Yes
Putting Green	Yes	Driving Range	No
Season	Apr - Snow	Credit Cards	Yes
Pro	None	Tee Times	No
Comments	Open fairways, mountain views		
Directions	Rt 2W, exit Greenfield, left, left at 3rd light Deerfield St		

Tee	Holes	Par	Rating	Slope	Yards
Red	9	72	NA	NA	5,110
White	9	72	NA	NA	5,740
Blue	9	72	NA	NA	5,760

114 Middlebrook Country Club
149 Pleasant Street, Rehoboth, MA 02769
508-252-9395

Weekend Fee	$16	Weekday Fee	$13
Power Cart Fee	$20	Pull Carts	Yes
Putting Green	Yes	Driving Range	No
Season	Mar - Dec	Credit Cards	No
Pro	None	Tee Times	No
Comments	Good for beginners		
Directions	I-95, exit 2, north, right Davis St, left Pleasant St, 1 mi		

Tee	Holes	Par	Rating	Slope	Yards
Red	9	70	NA	NA	5,800
White	9	67	65.5	108	5,968
Blue	NA	NA	NA	NA	NA

MASSACHUSETTS

115 Middleton Golf Course
105 South Main Street, Middleton, MA 01949
508-774-4075

Weekend Fee	$24	*Weekday Fee*	$24
Power Cart Fee	$18	*Pull Carts*	Yes
Putting Green	Yes	*Driving Range*	Yes
Season	Year-round	*Credit Cards*	Yes
Pro	George Lavoie	*Tee Times*	No
Comments	Large greens, 6 water holes		
Directions	Rt 1, Rt 114W, 2.7 mi		

Tee	Holes	Par	Rating	Slope	Yards
Red	18	54	NA	NA	2,800
White	18	54	NA	NA	3,000
Blue	18	54	NA	NA	3,215

116 Mill Valley Country Club
380 Mill Valley Road, Belchertown, MA 01007
413-323-4079

Weekend Fee	$15	*Weekday Fee*	$12
Power Cart Fee	$17	*Pull Carts*	Yes
Putting Green	Yes	*Driving Range*	Yes
Season	Apr 1 - Snow	*Credit Cards*	No
Pro	None	*Tee Times*	2 days
Comments	2 sets of greens, large greens		
Directions	I-90, exit 7, Rt 21 to course		

Tee	Holes	Par	Rating	Slope	Yards
Red	9	72	NA	NA	4,362
White	9	72	67	110	5,879
Blue	NA	NA	NA	NA	NA

117 Millwood Farms Course
175 Millwood Street, Framingham, MA 01701
508-877-1221

Weekend Fee	$23	*Weekday Fee*	$20
Power Cart Fee	$18	*Pull Carts*	Yes
Putting Green	Yes	*Driving Range*	No
Season	Apr 1 - Nov 30	*Credit Cards*	No
Pro	None	*Tee Times*	5 days
Comments	Well manicured greens		
Directions	Rt 9W, Edgell Rd exit, right, left on Belknap Rd after 2 blocks, 3rd right Millwood St		

Tee	Holes	Par	Rating	Slope	Yards
Red	14	54	63.1	102	4,550
White	14	54	62.1	101	4,883
Blue	NA	NA	NA	NA	NA

118 Mink Meadows Golf Club
Franklin Street, Vineyard Haven, MA 02568
508-963-0600

Weekend Fee	$42	*Weekday Fee*	$42
Power Cart Fee	$21	*Pull Carts*	Yes
Putting Green	Yes	*Driving Range*	No
Season	Year-round	*Credit Cards*	No
Pro	Tim Spring	*Tee Times*	2 days
Comments	Ocean views, smaller greens		
Directions	In Vineyard Haven, follow signs or call for directions		

Tee	Holes	Par	Rating	Slope	Yards
Red	9	72	69.5	118	5,204
White	9	70	68.7	121	6,004
Blue	NA	NA	NA	NA	NA

119 Monoosnock Country Club
Monoosnock Avenue, Leominister, MA 01453
508-537-1872

Weekend Fee	Members only	*Weekday Fee*	$24
Power Cart Fee	$22	*Pull Carts*	Yes
Putting Green	Yes	*Driving Range*	Yes
Season	Apr 1 - Nov 30	*Credit Cards*	Yes
Pro	Mike Elliott	*Tee Times*	No
Comments	Semi-private, narrow fairways		
Directions	Rt 2, Rt 13N, right, 1/2 mi		

Tee	Holes	Par	Rating	Slope	Yards
Red	9	70	71.6	115	5,600
White	9	70	68.6	113	6,107
Blue	NA	NA	NA	NA	NA

120 Mount Hood Golf Club
Slayton Road, Melrose, MA 02176
617-665-8139

Weekend Fee	$24	*Weekday Fee*	$22
Power Cart Fee	$21	*Pull Carts*	Yes
Putting Green	Yes	*Driving Range*	No
Season	Apr 1 - Nov 15	*Credit Cards*	No
Pro	Carl Marchia	*Tee Times*	2 days
Comments	Many side hill lies		
Directions	Rt 1N, left Essex St, left Waverly Ave, left Slayton Rd		

Tee	Holes	Par	Rating	Slope	Yards
Red	18	74	65.7	107	5,320
White	18	69	65.7	107	5,553
Blue	NA	NA	NA	NA	NA

121 Nabnasset Lake Country Club
47 Oak Hill Road, Westford, MA 01886
508-692-2560

Weekend Fee	Members only	Weekday Fee	$25
Power Cart Fee	$21	Pull Carts	Yes
Putting Green	Yes	Driving Range	No
Season	Apr 1 - Dec 24	Credit Cards	No
Pro	Tom Thibeault	Tee Times	No
Comments	Semi-private, small greens		
Directions	Rt 3, exit 33, Rt 40W, left Oak Hill Rd, 1 mi		

Tee	Holes	Par	Rating	Slope	Yards
Red	9	71	69.0	119	5,005
White	9	70	67.4	118	5,408
Blue	NA	NA	NA	NA	NA

122 New Bedford Municipal GC
581 Hathaway Road, New Bedford, MA 02740
508-996-9393

Weekend Fee	$18	Weekday Fee	$15
Power Cart Fee	$20	Pull Carts	Yes
Putting Green	Yes	Driving Range	Yes
Season	Year-round	Credit Cards	No
Pro	Jeffrey Lopes	Tee Times	7 days
Comments	Hilly, some undulating greens		
Directions	Rt 128, Rt 24S, Rt 140S, exit Hathaway Rd, bear right		

Tee	Holes	Par	Rating	Slope	Yards
Red	18	74	70.1	111	5,908
White	18	72	70.0	120	6,410
Blue	NA	NA	NA	NA	NA

123 New England Country Club
180 Paine Street, Bellingham, MA 02019
508-883-2300

Weekend Fee	$48	Weekday Fee	$40
Power Cart Fee	Included	Pull Carts	No
Putting Green	Yes	Driving Range	Yes
Season	Apr 1 - Nov 30	Credit Cards	Yes
Pro	Joe Catalano	Tee Times	5 days
Comments	Narrow fairways, large greens		
Directions	I-495, exit 16, west King St, 6 mi, left Wrentham St, right fire station onto Paine St		

Tee	Holes	Par	Rating	Slope	Yards
Red	18	71	68.7	121	4,908
White	18	71	67.2	125	5,665
Blue	18	71	71.1	129	6,409

124 New Meadows Golf Club
30 Wildes Road, Topsfield, MA 01983
508-887-9307

Weekend Fee	$24	Weekday Fee	$20
Power Cart Fee	$20	Pull Carts	Yes
Putting Green	Yes	Driving Range	No
Season	Apr 1 - Nov 30	Credit Cards	No
Pro	None	Tee Times	No
Comments	Large greens, wide fairways		
Directions	I-95, old Rt 1N, past Topsfield fairgrounds, 3 mi		

Tee	Holes	Par	Rating	Slope	Yards
Red	9	70	NA	NA	5,763
White	9	70	64.8	117	5,763
Blue	NA	NA	NA	NA	NA

125 New Seabury Golf Club - Blue
Blue Shore Drive West, Mashpee, MA 02649
508-477-9110

Weekend Fee	$75	Weekday Fee	$75
Power Cart Fee	$30	Pull Carts	Yes
Putting Green	Yes	Driving Range	Yes
Season	May 30 - Sep 9	Credit Cards	Yes
Pro	Mike Pry	Tee Times	1 day
Comments	Resort guests only, ocean views		
Directions	Rt 3, Rt 6E, exit 2 towards New Seabury, follow signs		

Tee	Holes	Par	Rating	Slope	Yards
Red	18	72	73.8	128	5,764
White	18	72	71.7	124	6,508
Blue	18	72	73.8	129	6,909

126 New Seabury Golf Club - Green
Green Shore Drive West, Mashpee, MA 02649
508-477-9110

Weekend Fee	$50	Weekday Fee	$50
Power Cart Fee	$30	Pull Carts	Yes
Putting Green	Yes	Driving Range	Yes
Season	May 30 - Sep 9	Credit Cards	Yes
Pro	Mike Pry	Tee Times	1 day
Comments	Resort guests only, narrow		
Directions	Rt 3, Rt 6E, exit 2 towards New Seabury, follow signs		

Tee	Holes	Par	Rating	Slope	Yards
Red	18	68	66.3	110	5,105
White	18	70	61.6	110	5,105
Blue	18	70	67.0	117	5,986

127 Newton Commonwealth GC
212 Kenrick Street, Chestnut Hill, MA 02158
617-630-1971

Weekend Fee	$25	Weekday Fee	$20
Power Cart Fee	$23	Pull Carts	Yes
Putting Green	Yes	Driving Range	No
Season	Year-round	Credit Cards	Yes
Pro	Bob Travers	Tee Times	7 days
Comments	Narrow fairways, small greens		
Directions	Rt 128, Rt 30E to Boston College, left Lake St, 4th left Kenrick St, 1.5 mi		

Tee	Holes	Par	Rating	Slope	Yards
Red	18	70	65.9	122	4,926
White	18	70	66.8	128	5,590
Blue	NA	NA	NA	NA	NA

130 Northampton Country Club
135 Main Street, Leeds, MA 01053
413-586-1898

Weekend Fee	$17	Weekday Fee	$15
Power Cart Fee	$20	Pull Carts	No
Putting Green	Yes	Driving Range	No
Season	Apr 1 - Nov 1	Credit Cards	Yes
Pro	Ray Millette	Tee Times	1 day
Comments	Small greens, wide fairways		
Directions	I-90, I-91N, Rt 9W to Northampton, left Florence St, left Arch St, left Main St		

Tee	Holes	Par	Rating	Slope	Yards
Red	9	74	67.2	112	5,554
White	9	70	67.6	113	6,100
Blue	NA	NA	NA	NA	NA

128 Nichols College Golf Club
46 Dudley Hill Road, Dudley, MA 01570
508-943-9837

Weekend Fee	$23	Weekday Fee	$18
Power Cart Fee	$16	Pull Carts	Yes
Putting Green	Yes	Driving Range	No
Season	Apr 1 - Nov 1	Credit Cards	No
Pro	None	Tee Times	No
Comments	Very wooded		
Directions	I-395, exit 2, Rt 12W, turns into Rt 197 through Webster, right at fork		

Tee	Holes	Par	Rating	Slope	Yards
Red	9	72	71.3	115	5,696
White	9	72	71.4	123	6,482
Blue	NA	NA	NA	NA	NA

131 Northfield Country Club
31 Holton Street, East Northfield, MA 01360
413-498-2432

Weekend Fee	$22	Weekday Fee	$18
Power Cart Fee	$21	Pull Carts	Yes
Putting Green	Yes	Driving Range	No
Season	Apr 1 - Nov 15	Credit Cards	No
Pro	None	Tee Times	No
Comments	Built in early 1900s, wooded		
Directions	I-91N, Rt 10 exit, Rt 63N, right Holton St, 1 mi		

Tee	Holes	Par	Rating	Slope	Yards
Red	9	72	68.0	121	4,810
White	9	72	66.2	121	5,664
Blue	NA	NA	NA	NA	NA

129 North Adams Country Club
641 River Road, Clarksburg, MA 01247
413-664-9011

Weekend Fee	$13	Weekday Fee	$13
Power Cart Fee	$18	Pull Carts	Yes
Putting Green	Yes	Driving Range	No
Season	May 1 - Nov 1	Credit Cards	No
Pro	None	Tee Times	7 days
Comments	Narrow fairways, small greens		
Directions	Rt 2W, right Rt 8 River Rd, north 3 mi		

Tee	Holes	Par	Rating	Slope	Yards
Red	9	72	67.5	117	5,440
White	9	72	69.4	114	6,050
Blue	NA	NA	NA	NA	NA

132 North Hill Country Club
29 Merry Avenue, Duxbury, MA 02332
617-934-5800

Weekend Fee	$21	Weekday Fee	$18
Power Cart Fee	$24	Pull Carts	Yes
Putting Green	Yes	Driving Range	No
Season	Year-round	Credit Cards	No
Pro	Bob Gunnarson	Tee Times	3 days
Comments	Hilly, views of ocean		
Directions	Rt 3, exit 11, Rt 14E, 2 mi		

Tee	Holes	Par	Rating	Slope	Yards
Red	9	74	NA	NA	5,600
White	9	72	70.8	121	7,002
Blue	NA	NA	NA	NA	NA

133 Norton Country Club
188 Oak Street, Norton, MA 02766
508-285-2400

Weekend Fee	$43 w/cart	*Weekday Fee*	$26
Power Cart Fee	$24	*Pull Carts*	Yes
Putting Green	Yes	*Driving Range*	No
Season	Apr - Oct	*Credit Cards*	Yes
Pro	John Del Bonis	*Tee Times*	3 days
Comments	58 pot bunkers, tree lined		
Directions	I-495, exit 10 Rt 123W, 3 mi, right Oak St		

Tee	Holes	Par	Rating	Slope	Yards
Red	18	71	70.0	124	5,040
White	18	71	69.9	120	5,754
Blue	18	71	72.2	137	6,546

134 Norwood Country Club
400 Providence Highway, Norwood, MA 02062
617-769-5880

Weekend Fee	$22	*Weekday Fee*	$18
Power Cart Fee	$23	*Pull Carts*	Yes
Putting Green	Yes	*Driving Range*	Yes
Season	Year-round	*Credit Cards*	No
Pro	Rick Finlayson	*Tee Times*	7 days
Comments	Good, straight beginner course		
Directions	Rt 128, Rt 1S, exit Norwood Center, Rt 1N, 1/2 mi		

Tee	Holes	Par	Rating	Slope	Yards
Red	18	71	68.7	108	5,575
White	18	71	65.9	108	5,665
Blue	18	71	67.1	112	6,009

135 Oak Ridge GC (Feeding Hills)
850 South Westfield Street, Feeding Hills, MA 01030
413-786-9693

Weekend Fee	$30	*Weekday Fee*	$25
Power Cart Fee	$24	*Pull Carts*	Yes
Putting Green	Yes	*Driving Range*	No
Season	Mar 15 - Dec 1	*Credit Cards*	No
Pro	Jim Modzelesky	*Tee Times*	7 days
Comments	Flowers throughout, large greens		
Directions	I-91, Agawam exit, Rt 57W, left 1st light, 2nd left Oak Ridge sign, 1/4 mi		

Tee	Holes	Par	Rating	Slope	Yards
Red	18	70	70.0	124	5,297
White	18	70	66.5	116	5,711
Blue	18	70	70.0	120	6,390

136 Oak Ridge Golf Club (Gill)
231 West Gill Road, Gill, MA 01376
413-786-9693

Weekend Fee	$23	*Weekday Fee*	$19
Power Cart Fee	$22	*Pull Carts*	Yes
Putting Green	Yes	*Driving Range*	No
Season	Mar 15 - Nov 30	*Credit Cards*	No
Pro	None	*Tee Times*	No
Comments	Undulating fairways, small greens		
Directions	Rt 2 to Gill, right at light, left West Gill Rd, 2 mi		

Tee	Holes	Par	Rating	Slope	Yards
Red	9	72	70.0	117	5,190
White	9	72	68.7	117	5,813
Blue	NA	NA	NA	NA	NA

137 Ocean Edge Golf Club
832 Village Drive, Brewster, MA 02631
508-896-5911

Weekend Fee	$49	*Weekday Fee*	$49
Power Cart Fee	$26	*Pull Carts*	Yes
Putting Green	Yes	*Driving Range*	Yes
Season	Year-round	*Credit Cards*	Yes
Pro	Ron Hallett	*Tee Times*	2 days
Comments	70 pot bunkers, lodging, golf school		
Directions	Rt 6E, exit 11, right on Rt 137 Village Dr, 2.6 mi		

Tee	Holes	Par	Rating	Slope	Yards
Red	18	72	70.6	123	5,168
White	18	72	68.7	125	6,127
Blue	18	72	71.9	129	6,665

138 Olde Barnstable Fairgrounds GC
1460 Route 149, Marston Mills, MA 02648
508-420-1141

Weekend Fee	$39	*Weekday Fee*	$37
Power Cart Fee	$25	*Pull Carts*	Yes
Putting Green	Yes	*Driving Range*	Yes
Season	Year-round	*Credit Cards*	Yes
Pro	Gary Philbrick	*Tee Times*	2 days
Comments	2 MA amateur qualifying tournaments		
Directions	Rt 6E, exit 5 Rt 149S, 1 mi		

Tee	Holes	Par	Rating	Slope	Yards
Red	18	71	69.2	118	5,122
White	18	71	69.1	120	6,113
Blue	18	71	70.7	123	6,479

MASSACHUSETTS

139 Olde Salem Greens
Wilson Street, Salem, MA 01970
508-744-9747

Weekend Fee	$19	Weekday Fee		$17
Power Cart Fee	$22	Pull Carts		Yes
Putting Green	Yes	Driving Range		No
Season	Apr - Snow	Credit Cards		No
Pro	None	Tee Times		2 days
Comments	Small greens and fairways, doglegs			
Directions	Rt 128, Rt 114 Salem, Essex St, Highland Ave, left Wilson St			

Tee	Holes	Par	Rating	Slope	Yards
Red	9	70	NA	112	6,056
White	9	70	68.5	116	6,056
Blue	NA	NA	NA	NA	NA

140 Orchards Golf Club
Silverwood Terrace, South Hadley, MA 01075
413-534-3806

Weekend Fee	$50	Weekday Fee		$50
Power Cart Fee	$22	Pull Carts		Yes
Putting Green	Yes	Driving Range		Yes
Season	Apr 1 - Nov 1	Credit Cards		No
Pro	Bob Bontempo	Tee Times		14 days
Comments	Available M-Th only			
Directions	I-91, Rt 202N, Rt 116N, S. Hadley center, 0.5 mi			

Tee	Holes	Par	Rating	Slope	Yards
Red	18	72	72.9	133	5,611
White	18	71	69.9	123	6,279
Blue	18	71	71.1	125	6,502

141 Ould Newbury Golf Club
Route 1, Newburyport, MA 01951
508-465-9888

Weekend Fee	Members only	Weekday Fee		$24
Power Cart Fee	$21	Pull Carts		Yes
Putting Green	Yes	Driving Range		No
Season	Apr 1 - Nov 30	Credit Cards		Yes
Pro	James Hilton	Tee Times		No
Comments	Semi-private, small, elevated greens			
Directions	I-95, Rt 1N, 15 mi, next to Governor Drummer Academy			

Tee	Holes	Par	Rating	Slope	Yards
Red	9	76	70.8	115	5,434
White	9	70	69.0	120	6,184
Blue	NA	NA	NA	NA	NA

142 Pakachoag Golf Course
20 Upland Street, Auburn, MA 01501
508-755-3291

Weekend Fee	$14	Weekday Fee		$12
Power Cart Fee	No carts	Pull Carts		Yes
Putting Green	Yes	Driving Range		No
Season	Apr - Nov	Credit Cards		No
Pro	None	Tee Times		1 day
Comments	Good for accurate hitters and long drivers			
Directions	I-290, Auburn exit, Rt 20E, left 3rd light, 0.5 mi, left Upland St			

Tee	Holes	Par	Rating	Slope	Yards
Red	9	72	NA	NA	6,510
White	9	72	70	119	6,510
Blue	NA	NA	NA	NA	NA

143 Paul Harney Golf Club
74 Club Valley Drive, East Falmouth, MA 02536
508-563-3454

Weekend Fee	$25	Weekday Fee		$25
Power Cart Fee	$20	Pull Carts		Yes
Putting Green	Yes	Driving Range		No
Season	Year-round	Credit Cards		No
Pro	Mike Harney	Tee Times		No
Comments	Good for beginners, tree lined			
Directions	Rt 28E, Rt 151E, 4.6 mi			

Tee	Holes	Par	Rating	Slope	Yards
Red	18	61	56.7	89	3,070
White	18	59	59.9	91	3,235
Blue	NA	NA	NA	NA	NA

144 Pembroke Country Club
West Elm Street, Pembroke, MA 02359
617-826-5191

Weekend Fee	$35	Weekday Fee		$30
Power Cart Fee	$26	Pull Carts		Yes
Putting Green	Yes	Driving Range		Yes
Season	Mar 1 - Jan 1	Credit Cards		Yes
Pro	Chip Johnson	Tee Times		2 days
Comments	10 ponds, trapped greens, wildlife			
Directions	Rt 3, exit 13, right Rt 53S, right 5th light Broadway, left at island West Elm St			

Tee	Holes	Par	Rating	Slope	Yards
Red	18	75	73.4	120	5,887
White	18	71	71.1	124	6,532
Blue	NA	NA	NA	NA	NA

145 Petersham Country Club
North Main Street, Petersham, MA 01366
508-724-3388

Weekend Fee	$20	Weekday Fee	$16
Power Cart Fee	$20	Pull Carts	Yes
Putting Green	Yes	Driving Range	No
Season	Apr 1 - Nov 1	Credit Cards	No
Pro	Don Cross	Tee Times	2 days
Comments	Donald Ross design, small greens		
Directions	Rt 2, exit 17 Petersham, right on Rt 32, 3 mi		

Tee	Holes	Par	Rating	Slope	Yards
Red	9	72	69.1	114	5,106
White	9	70	68.9	116	6,046
Blue	NA	NA	NA	NA	NA

146 Pine Acres Golf Club
230 Wrentham Road, Bellingham, MA 02019
508-883-2443

Weekend Fee	$15	Weekday Fee	$15
Power Cart Fee	No carts	Pull Carts	Yes
Putting Green	Yes	Driving Range	Yes
Season	Apr 1 - Dec 1	Credit Cards	No
Pro	None	Tee Times	Yes
Comments	New course		
Directions	I-495, King St exit in Franklin, in Bellingham take left at Dean Coop Bank, 0.5 mi		

Tee	Holes	Par	Rating	Slope	Yards
Red	9	56	NA	NA	2,292
White	9	56	NA	NA	2,292
Blue	NA	NA	NA	NA	NA

147 Pine Crest Golf Club
212 Prentice Street, Holliston, MA 01746
508-429-9871

Weekend Fee	$23	Weekday Fee	$18
Power Cart Fee	$20	Pull Carts	Yes
Putting Green	No	Driving Range	Yes
Season	Apr 1 - Dec 1	Credit Cards	No
Pro	Dan Corcoran	Tee Times	7 days
Comments	Tight greens, tree lined fairways		
Directions	I-495, Rt 85 exit to Milford, 3 mi, left at flashing light Chestnut St, signs		

Tee	Holes	Par	Rating	Slope	Yards
Red	18	66	NA	NA	4,307
White	18	66	63.2	103	5,003
Blue	NA	NA	NA	NA	NA

148 Pine Grove Golf Club
254 Wilson Road, Northampton, MA 01060
413-584-4570

Weekend Fee	$16	Weekday Fee	$13
Power Cart Fee	$23	Pull Carts	Yes
Putting Green	Yes	Driving Range	Yes
Season	Apr 1 - Nov 1	Credit Cards	No
Pro	Ed Twohig	Tee Times	4 days
Comments	Rolling hills, narrow fairways, large greens		
Directions	I-91, exit 18, Rt 5N, Rt 9W, left Rt 66W, left Wilson Rd		

Tee	Holes	Par	Rating	Slope	Yards
Red	18	72	67.3	108	4,890
White	18	72	68.8	111	6,115
Blue	NA	NA	NA	NA	NA

149 Pine Knoll Golf Course
400 Porter Road, East Longmeadow, MA 01028
413-525-8320

Weekend Fee	$6	Weekday Fee	$6
Power Cart Fee	No carts	Pull Carts	Yes
Putting Green	Yes	Driving Range	No
Season	Apr 1 - Nov 1	Credit Cards	No
Pro	None	Tee Times	No
Comments	Longest hole is 140 yards		
Directions	I-90, Palmer exit, Rt 20, Stonyhill Rd, 3 mi, left Porter Rd		

Tee	Holes	Par	Rating	Slope	Yards
Red	9	54	NA	NA	1,600
White	9	54	NA	NA	1,600
Blue	NA	NA	NA	NA	NA

150 Pine Meadows Golf Club
255 Cedar Street, Lexington, MA 02173
617-862-5516

Weekend Fee	$25 nonresident	Weekday Fee	$22
Power Cart Fee	$21	Pull Carts	Yes
Putting Green	Yes	Driving Range	No
Season	Apr 1 - Dec 1	Credit Cards	No
Pro	Dick Baker	Tee Times	2 days
Comments	Open fairways, small greens		
Directions	Rt 128, exit 31A, 1 mi, right Hill St at light, right Cedar St		

Tee	Holes	Par	Rating	Slope	Yards
Red	9	70	69.2	117	5,199
White	9	70	64.5	110	5,350
Blue	NA	NA	NA	NA	NA

MASSACHUSETTS

151 Pine Oaks Golf Club
68 Prospect Street, South Easton, MA 02334
508-238-2320

Weekend Fee	$23	*Weekday Fee*	$20
Power Cart Fee	$22	*Pull Carts*	Yes
Putting Green	Yes	*Driving Range*	No
Season	Year-round	*Credit Cards*	No
Pro	Leigh Bader	*Tee Times*	No
Comments	Lots of water, flat, large greens		
Directions	Rt 24, exit 16B, Rt 106W 5 mi, right Prospect St		

Tee	Holes	Par	Rating	Slope	Yards
Red	9	68	67.0	111	5,824
White	9	68	67.0	111	5,824
Blue	NA	NA	NA	NA	NA

152 Pine Ridge Country Club
Pleasant Street, Oxford, MA 01537
508-892-9188

Weekend Fee	$25	*Weekday Fee*	$20
Power Cart Fee	$22	*Pull Carts*	Yes
Putting Green	Yes	*Driving Range*	No
Season	Apr 1 - Dec 1	*Credit Cards*	Yes
Pro	Mark Larrabee	*Tee Times*	4 days
Comments	Hilly		
Directions	I-90, exit 10, Rt 12S, Rt 20W, right at intersection w/Rt 56, 1.2 mi		

Tee	Holes	Par	Rating	Slope	Yards
Red	18	72	69.6	117	5,300
White	18	71	69.7	117	5,700
Blue	18	71	69.7	120	6,200

153 Pine Valley Golf Club
136 Providence Street, Rehoboth, MA 02769
508-336-9815

Weekend Fee	$14	*Weekday Fee*	$11
Power Cart Fee	$20	*Pull Carts*	Yes
Putting Green	Yes	*Driving Range*	No
Season	Year-round	*Credit Cards*	No
Pro	None	*Tee Times*	No
Comments	Several doglegs, open fairways		
Directions	I-95, I-195E, exit 2 Rt 136N, left Davis St, right Providence St		

Tee	Holes	Par	Rating	Slope	Yards
Red	9	70	NA	NA	5,800
White	9	70	NA	NA	6,400
Blue	NA	NA	NA	NA	NA

154 Plymouth Country Club
Plymouth Plantation Highway, Plymouth, MA 02360
508-746-0476

Weekend Fee	$40	*Weekday Fee*	$40
Power Cart Fee	$30	*Pull Carts*	Yes
Putting Green	Yes	*Driving Range*	No
Season	May 1 - Oct 31	*Credit Cards*	Yes
Pro	Tom Hanifan	*Tee Times*	1 day
Comments	Small, elevated greens, built in 1901		
Directions	Rt 3S, exit 4, south 1.3 mi, right Country Club Dr		

Tee	Holes	Par	Rating	Slope	Yards
Red	18	71	68.6	121	5,524
White	18	69	70.0	125	6,164
Blue	NA	NA	NA	NA	NA

155 Ponkapoag Golf Club #1
2167 Washington Street, Canton, MA 02021
617-828-4242

Weekend Fee	$20	*Weekday Fee*	$17
Power Cart Fee	$20	*Pull Carts*	Yes
Putting Green	Yes	*Driving Range*	Yes
Season	Apr 1 - Dec 23	*Credit Cards*	Yes
Pro	Jack Neville	*Tee Times*	No
Comments	Donald Ross design, open fairways		
Directions	Rt 128, exit 2A, 0.8 mi		

Tee	Holes	Par	Rating	Slope	Yards
Red	18	74	70.8	115	6,256
White	18	72	72.0	126	6,726
Blue	NA	NA	NA	NA	NA

156 Ponkapoag Golf Club #2
2167 Washington Street, Canton, MA 02021
617-828-4242

Weekend Fee	$20	*Weekday Fee*	$17
Power Cart Fee	$20	*Pull Carts*	Yes
Putting Green	Yes	*Driving Range*	Yes
Season	Apr - Dec	*Credit Cards*	Yes
Pro	Jack Neville	*Tee Times*	No
Comments	Donald Ross design, tighter than #1		
Directions	Rt 128, exit 2A, 0.8 mi		

Tee	Holes	Par	Rating	Slope	Yards
Red	18	69	68.5	113	5,769
White	18	71	70.3	116	6,332
Blue	NA	NA	NA	NA	NA

157 Pontoosuc Lake Country Club
Kirkwood Drive, Pittsfield, MA 01201
413-445-4217

Weekend Fee	$16	*Weekday Fee*	$14
Power Cart Fee	$19	*Pull Carts*	Yes
Putting Green	Yes	*Driving Range*	No
Season	Apr 15 - Nov 12	*Credit Cards*	No
Pro	Frank Maxon	*Tee Times*	No
Comments	Good views		
Directions	Rt 7, Hancock West, 1.5 mi, right Ridge Ave, left Kirkwood Dr		

Tee	Holes	Par	Rating	Slope	Yards
Red	18	70	NA	NA	5,284
White	18	70	69.7	NA	6,305
Blue	NA	NA	NA	NA	NA

158 Poquoy Brook Golf Club
20 Leonard Street, Lakeville, MA 02347
508-947-5261

Weekend Fee	$35	*Weekday Fee*	$32
Power Cart Fee	$28	*Pull Carts*	Yes
Putting Green	Yes	*Driving Range*	Yes
Season	Year-round	*Credit Cards*	Yes
Pro	Bill Humbertson	*Tee Times*	7 days
Comments	Large undulating greens, water hazards		
Directions	I-495, exit 5, Rt 18S, right at flashing light, 1st left		

Tee	Holes	Par	Rating	Slope	Yards
Red	18	73	71.0	114	5,415
White	18	72	69.9	125	6,286
Blue	18	72	72.4	128	6,762

159 Presidents Golf Course
357 West Squantum Street, Quincy, MA 02171
617-328-3444

Weekend Fee	$25	*Weekday Fee*	$21
Power Cart Fee	$22	*Pull Carts*	Yes
Putting Green	Yes	*Driving Range*	No
Season	Mar 15 - Dec 15	*Credit Cards*	Yes
Pro	Arthur Cicconi	*Tee Times*	2 days
Comments	Hilly, views of Boston		
Directions	I-93, exit 11A, left 1st light West Squantum St		

Tee	Holes	Par	Rating	Slope	Yards
Red	18	70	65.0	110	4,425
White	18	70	64.3	108	5,055
Blue	18	70	66.8	108	5,580

160 Putterham Meadows
1281 West Roxbury Parkway, Brookline, MA 02167
617-730-2078

Weekend Fee	$26	*Weekday Fee*	$23
Power Cart Fee	$25	*Pull Carts*	Yes
Putting Green	Yes	*Driving Range*	No
Season	Apr 1 - Dec 1	*Credit Cards*	Yes
Pro	O. Della Penna	*Tee Times*	2 days
Comments	Tight elevated greens, many brooks		
Directions	Rt 9E, right Hammond St, last exit at rotary turns into Newton St, follow signs		

Tee	Holes	Par	Rating	Slope	Yards
Red	18	72	72.1	121	5,748
White	18	71	68.3	118	6,003
Blue	18	71	70.2	123	6,307

161 Quaboag Country Club
Palmer Road, Monson, MA 01057
413-267-5294

Weekend Fee	$25	*Weekday Fee*	$25
Power Cart Fee	$16	*Pull Carts*	Yes
Putting Green	Yes	*Driving Range*	No
Season	Mar 15 - Nov 15	*Credit Cards*	No
Pro	Tom Sullivan	*Tee Times*	1 day
Comments	Semi-private, tight course, uneven lies		
Directions	I-90, exit 7, right Rt 32S (Main St), 2 mi		

Tee	Holes	Par	Rating	Slope	Yards
Red	9	70	NA	NA	5,220
White	9	68	67.2	116	5,760
Blue	NA	NA	NA	NA	NA

162 Quail Hollow Golf & CC
1822 Old Turnpike Road, Oakham, MA 01068
508-882-5516

Weekend Fee	$20	*Weekday Fee*	$18
Power Cart Fee	$20	*Pull Carts*	Yes
Putting Green	Yes	*Driving Range*	Yes
Season	Apr 1 - Nov 15	*Credit Cards*	Yes
Pro	None	*Tee Times*	2 days
Comments	Elevated undulating greens, view		
Directions	I-290, Rt 122N Old Turnpike Rd, 3.5 mi		

Tee	Holes	Par	Rating	Slope	Yards
Red	9	70	68.8	104	4,800
White	9	70	66.6	112	5,600
Blue	9	70	66.6	116	5,860

163 Quashnet Valley Country Club
309 Old Barnstable Road, Mashpee, MA 02649
508-477-4412

Weekend Fee	$48	Weekday Fee	$30
Power Cart Fee	$25	Pull Carts	Yes
Putting Green	Yes	Driving Range	Yes
Season	Year-round	Credit Cards	Yes
Pro	Bob Chase	Tee Times	7 days
Comments	Well maintained, need accuracy		
Directions	Rt 6E, exit 2, right Rt 130S, 7.2 mi, right Great Neck Rd, 1.6 mi, right		

Tee	Holes	Par	Rating	Slope	Yards
Red	18	72	70.3	119	5,094
White	18	72	69.1	126	6,073
Blue	18	72	71.7	132	6,601

164 Rehoboth Country Club
151 Perryville Road, Rehoboth, MA 02769
508-252-6259

Weekend Fee	$25	Weekday Fee	$20
Power Cart Fee	$20	Pull Carts	Yes
Putting Green	Yes	Driving Range	Yes
Season	Year-round	Credit Cards	No
Pro	Lenny Dingley	Tee Times	3 days
Comments	52 large sand traps, large greens		
Directions	I-90S, Rt 44W, Rt 118E, left Perryville Rd,		

Tee	Holes	Par	Rating	Slope	Yards
Red	18	75	70.4	115	5,450
White	18	72	69.5	117	6,295
Blue	18	72	72.5	125	6,950

165 Ridder Golf Club
300 Oak Street, Whitman, MA 02382
617-447-9003

Weekend Fee	$27	Weekday Fee	$25
Power Cart Fee	$21	Pull Carts	Yes
Putting Green	Yes	Driving Range	Yes
Season	Mar - Dec	Credit Cards	No
Pro	Jeff Butler	Tee Times	2 days
Comments	Open fairways		
Directions	Rt 24N, Rt 27E, Rt 14 Oak St east, 4.5 mi		

Tee	Holes	Par	Rating	Slope	Yards
Red	18	70	NA	NA	5,857
White	18	70	67.6	109	5,857
Blue	NA	NA	NA	NA	NA

166 Rochester Golf Club
Roundsville Road, Rochester, MA 02770
508-763-5155

Weekend Fee	$18	Weekday Fee	$18
Power Cart Fee	$17	Pull Carts	Yes
Putting Green	Yes	Driving Range	No
Season	Apr 1 - Nov 1	Credit Cards	No
Pro	Herb Griffin	Tee Times	No
Comments	Great scenery, tree lined, lots of water		
Directions	I-195, Rochester exit, Rt 105 Roundsville Rd, 2 mi		

Tee	Holes	Par	Rating	Slope	Yards
Red	18	69	58.0	109	4,032
White	18	69	69.0	107	4,830
Blue	18	69	64.0	115	5,200

167 Rockland Golf Course
276 Plain Street, Rockland, MA 02370
617-878-5836

Weekend Fee	$20	Weekday Fee	$18
Power Cart Fee	$21	Pull Carts	Yes
Putting Green	Yes	Driving Range	No
Season	Year-round	Credit Cards	Yes
Pro	C. Lanzetta	Tee Times	3 days
Comments	Longest par 3 course in US		
Directions	Rt 123W, Rt 139N		

Tee	Holes	Par	Rating	Slope	Yards
Red	18	60	58.0	NA	3,055
White	18	54	56.1	87	3,055
Blue	18	54	NA	NA	3,318

168 Rockport Golf Course
Country Club Road, Rockport, MA 01966
508-546-3340

Weekend Fee	Members only	Weekday Fee	$25
Power Cart Fee	$26	Pull Carts	Yes
Putting Green	Yes	Driving Range	No
Season	Apr 1 - Nov 1	Credit Cards	Yes
Pro	Stephen Clayton	Tee Times	1 day
Comments	Semi-private, undulating greens		
Directions	Rt 128N to end, follow signs for Rt 127N, 5 mi, right Country Club Rd		

Tee	Holes	Par	Rating	Slope	Yards
Red	9	74	71.2	116	5,352
White	9	72	65.2	104	5,514
Blue	9	70	68.8	120	5,984

169 Rolling Green Golf Club
311 Lowell Street, Andover, MA 01810
508-475-4066

Weekend Fee	$18	*Weekday Fee*	$16
Power Cart Fee	Yes	*Pull Carts*	Yes
Putting Green	Yes	*Driving Range*	Yes
Season	Apr 1 - Nov 1	*Credit Cards*	Yes
Pro	Joe Russo	*Tee Times*	No
Comments	Semi-private, inexpensive beginner course		
Directions	I-93N, exit Rt 133 Andover, right, on left near exit		

Tee	Holes	Par	Rating	Slope	Yards
Red	9	54	NA	NA	3,000
White	9	54	NA	NA	3,000
Blue	NA	NA	NA	NA	NA

170 Round Hill Country Club
Round Hill Road, East Sandwich, MA 02537
508-888-3384

Weekend Fee	$49	*Weekday Fee*	$40
Power Cart Fee	Included	*Pull Carts*	No
Putting Green	Yes	*Driving Range*	Yes
Season	Year-round	*Credit Cards*	Yes
Pro	John Lyons	*Tee Times*	7 days
Comments	Hilly, tight		
Directions	Rt 6, exit 3, bear right, 1st left Round Hill Rd		

Tee	Holes	Par	Rating	Slope	Yards
Red	18	70	68.1	115	4,842
White	18	71	66.6	120	5,920
Blue	18	71	70.4	124	6,157

171 Rowley Country Club
235 Dodge Road, Rowley, MA 01969
508-948-2731

Weekend Fee	$27	*Weekday Fee*	$24
Power Cart Fee	$22	*Pull Carts*	Yes
Putting Green	Yes	*Driving Range*	Yes
Season	Apr - Snow	*Credit Cards*	Yes
Pro	Dennis Nestle	*Tee Times*	2 days
Comments	Semi-private, tree lined fairways		
Directions	I-95, exit 54, Rt 133E, left Dodge Rd, left at end		

Tee	Holes	Par	Rating	Slope	Yards
Red	9	72	67.5	109	4,940
White	9	72	70.7	127	6,380
Blue	NA	NA	NA	NA	NA

172 Saddle Hill Country Club
204 Saddle Hill Road, Hopkinton, MA 01748
508-435-4630

Weekend Fee	$28	*Weekday Fee*	$22
Power Cart Fee	$22	*Pull Carts*	Yes
Putting Green	Yes	*Driving Range*	Yes
Season	Year-round	*Credit Cards*	Yes
Pro	Steve Gelineau	*Tee Times*	7 days
Comments	Open fairways, well rated		
Directions	I-495, Rt 9W, Flanders Rd east, right Fruit St, right Saddle Hill Rd, 3 mi		

Tee	Holes	Par	Rating	Slope	Yards
Red	18	72	69.0	108	5,619
White	18	72	69.4	119	6,200
Blue	18	72	70.3	128	6,900

173 Sagamore Spring Golf Course
1287 Main Street, Lynnfield, MA 01940
617-334-3151

Weekend Fee	$33	*Weekday Fee*	$27
Power Cart Fee	$22	*Pull Carts*	Yes
Putting Green	No	*Driving Range*	Yes
Season	Mar 1 - Snow	*Credit Cards*	Yes
Pro	Ross Coon	*Tee Times*	4 days
Comments	Wildlife sanctuary, sand traps each green		
Directions	I-95, exit 41 Lynnfield, 3 mi		

Tee	Holes	Par	Rating	Slope	Yards
Red	18	70	66.5	112	4,784
White	18	70	66.5	114	5,505
Blue	18	70	68.6	119	5,936

174 Saint Anne Country Club
781 Shoemaker Lane, Feeding Hills, MA 01030
413-786-2088

Weekend Fee	$16	*Weekday Fee*	$12
Power Cart Fee	$18	*Pull Carts*	Yes
Putting Green	Yes	*Driving Range*	No
Season	Year-round	*Credit Cards*	No
Pro	None	*Tee Times*	7 days
Comments	Back 9 wide open, front more challenging		
Directions	Rt 57, Rt 75S, right 1st light Silver St, right Shoemaker Lane		

Tee	Holes	Par	Rating	Slope	Yards
Red	18	72	70.0	115	5,565
White	18	72	69.5	115	6,412
Blue	18	72	70.8	116	6,608

MASSACHUSETTS

175 Saint Mark's Golf Course
Latisquanma Road, Rt 85, Southborough, MA 01772
508-485-6145

Weekend Fee	$25 after 1 pm	Weekday Fee	$20
Power Cart Fee	No carts	Pull Carts	Yes
Putting Green	Yes	Driving Range	No
Season	Apr 15 - Nov 1	Credit Cards	No
Pro	None	Tee Times	No
Comments	Semi-private, unlimited golf		
Directions	Rt 9W, Rt 85N, 2 mi		

Tee	Holes	Par	Rating	Slope	Yards
Red	9	70	NA	NA	5,810
White	9	70	67.1	117	5,810
Blue	NA	NA	NA	NA	NA

176 Sandy Burr Country Club
103 Cochituate Road, Wayland, MA 01778
508-358-7211

Weekend Fee	$32	Weekday Fee	$29
Power Cart Fee	$24	Pull Carts	Yes
Putting Green	Yes	Driving Range	No
Season	Apr 1 - Nov 15	Credit Cards	No
Pro	Charles Estes	Tee Times	7 days
Comments	Many sand traps, Sandy Burr local beer		
Directions	Rt 128, Rt 20W, left Rt 27S in Wayland center, 1/4 mi		

Tee	Holes	Par	Rating	Slope	Yards
Red	18	72	66.2	110	4,561
White	18	72	69.9	122	6,229
Blue	18	72	70.8	125	6,412

177 Scituate Country Club
91 Old Driftway Road, Scituate, MA 02066
617-545-9768

Weekend Fee	Members only	Weekday Fee	$24
Power Cart Fee	$22	Pull Carts	Yes
Putting Green	No	Driving Range	No
Season	Mar 1 - Nov 1	Credit Cards	No
Pro	John Kan	Tee Times	2 days
Comments	Available on Mondays only		
Directions	Rt 3, exit 13, left, right Rt 123 1st light, Rt 3A, Driftway Rd, 1 mi		

Tee	Holes	Par	Rating	Slope	Yards
Red	9	70	71.6	119	5,492
White	9	70	69.7	121	5,948
Blue	NA	NA	NA	NA	NA

178 Shaker Farms Country Club
Shaker Road, Westfield, MA 01086
413-562-2770

Weekend Fee	$24	Weekday Fee	$18
Power Cart Fee	$24	Pull Carts	Yes
Putting Green	Yes	Driving Range	No
Season	Apr 15 - Oct 31	Credit Cards	Yes
Pro	Thomas Dirio	Tee Times	1 day
Comments	Hilly, tight fairways		
Directions	I-90, exit 3 Westfield, Rt 10/202S, Rt 20W, right Rt 187 at light		

Tee	Holes	Par	Rating	Slope	Yards
Red	18	72	68.4	113	5,212
White	18	72	71.9	125	6,669
Blue	NA	NA	NA	NA	NA

179 Shaker Hills Country Club
Shaker Road, Harvard, MA 01451
508-772-2227

Weekend Fee	$50	Weekday Fee	$45
Power Cart Fee	Included	Pull Carts	No
Putting Green	Yes	Driving Range	Yes
Season	Apr 15 - Nov 15	Credit Cards	Yes
Pro	Joe Keefe	Tee Times	4 days
Comments	Rated #1 public course in 1993, beautiful		
Directions	I-495, exit 30 Rt 2A W, 5 mi, left Shaker Rd		

Tee	Holes	Par	Rating	Slope	Yards
Red	18	71	67.9	116	4,999
White	18	71	67.3	121	5,914
Blue	18	71	69.5	128	6,394

180 Siasconset Golf Club
Milestone Road, Siasconset, MA 02564
508-257-6596

Weekend Fee	$30	Weekday Fee	$30
Power Cart Fee	No carts	Pull Carts	Yes
Putting Green	No	Driving Range	No
Season	Jun 1 - Nov 1	Credit Cards	No
Pro	None	Tee Times	No
Comments	One of 1st 100 clubs in US		
Directions	Main road from Siasconset to Nantucket		

Tee	Holes	Par	Rating	Slope	Yards
Red	9	70	NA	NA	5,086
White	9	70	68.1	113	5,086
Blue	NA	NA	NA	NA	NA

181 Skyline Country Club
405 South Main Street, Lanesborough, MA 01237
413-445-5584

Weekend Fee	$18	Weekday Fee	$16	
Power Cart Fee	$22	Pull Carts	Yes	
Putting Green	Yes	Driving Range	Yes	
Season	Apr 1 - Snow	Credit Cards	No	
Pro	Jim Midus	Tee Times	5 days	
Comments	Hilly, view of Mount Greylock			
Directions	I-90, exit 2, Rt 7N, 20 mi			

Tee	Holes	Par	Rating	Slope	Yards
Red	18	72	68.1	110	4,814
White	18	72	70.4	124	5,773
Blue	18	72	72.3	128	6,197

182 Southampton Country Club
329 College Highway, Southampton, MA 01073
413-527-9815

Weekend Fee	$19	Weekday Fee	$13	
Power Cart Fee	$16	Pull Carts	Yes	
Putting Green	Yes	Driving Range	No	
Season	Apr 1 - Snow	Credit Cards	No	
Pro	John Strycharz	Tee Times	7 days	
Comments	Large undulating greens			
Directions	I-90, exit 3 Westfield, Rt 10N, 4 mi			

Tee	Holes	Par	Rating	Slope	Yards
Red	18	72	NA	NA	6,240
White	18	72	69	114	6,720
Blue	NA	NA	NA	NA	NA

183 South Shore Country Club
274 South Street, Hingham, MA 02043
617-749-8479

Weekend Fee	$33	Weekday Fee	$29	
Power Cart Fee	$21	Pull Carts	Yes	
Putting Green	Yes	Driving Range	No	
Season	Apr - Dec 1	Credit Cards	Yes	
Pro	Joe Keefe	Tee Times	1 day	
Comments	Nice championship course, resident discount			
Directions	Rt 3, exit 14 Rt 228N, 5.4 mi onto Central St, left South St			

Tee	Holes	Par	Rating	Slope	Yards
Red	18	72	69.3	116	5,064
White	18	72	69.9	124	6,197
Blue	18	72	71.0	128	6,444

184 Southwick Country Club
739 College Highway, Southwick, MA 01077
413-569-0136

Weekend Fee	$18	Weekday Fee	$15	
Power Cart Fee	$20	Pull Carts	Yes	
Putting Green	Yes	Driving Range	Yes	
Season	Year-round	Credit Cards	No	
Pro	None	Tee Times	3 days	
Comments	Flat and open			
Directions	I-90, I-90 exit 3 Westfield, right RT 202S, 4 mi			

Tee	Holes	Par	Rating	Slope	Yards
Red	18	71	64.8	102	5,570
White	18	71	64.8	116	6,100
Blue	NA	NA	NA	NA	NA

185 Squirrel Run Country Club
Carver Road, Plymouth, MA 02360
508-746-5001

Weekend Fee	$22	Weekday Fee	$20	
Power Cart Fee	$18	Pull Carts	Yes	
Putting Green	Yes	Driving Range	Yes	
Season	Year-round	Credit Cards	Yes	
Pro	Bruce Murphy	Tee Times	7 days	
Comments	Immaculate tees and greens			
Directions	Rt 3, exit 6, Rt 44W, 1/4 mi			

Tee	Holes	Par	Rating	Slope	Yards
Red	18	57	56.0	83	1,990
White	18	57	53.7	82	2,284
Blue	18	57	55.4	85	2,845

186 Stone-E-Lea Golf Course
1400 County Street, Attleborough, MA 02703
508-222-9735

Weekend Fee	$20	Weekday Fee	$15	
Power Cart Fee	$20	Pull Carts	Yes	
Putting Green	Yes	Driving Range	No	
Season	Year-round	Credit Cards	No	
Pro	Ed Lapierre	Tee Times	No	
Comments	Undulating greens, tree lined fairways			
Directions	I-95, exit 2A, left 1st light Newport Cottage St, 2 mi			

Tee	Holes	Par	Rating	Slope	Yards
Red	18	71	NA	NA	5,832
White	18	71	70.0	112	6,261
Blue	18	71	NA	NA	7,002

MASSACHUSETTS

187 Stoneham Oaks Golf Course
101 Montvale Avenue, Stoneham, MA 02180
617-438-7888

Weekend Fee	$19	*Weekday Fee*	$17
Power Cart Fee	No carts	*Pull Carts*	Yes
Putting Green	Yes	*Driving Range*	No
Season	Apr 1 - Nov 30	*Credit Cards*	No
Pro	Mike Munro	*Tee Times*	No
Comments	Wooded, large, undulating greens		
Directions	I-93, exit 36, course 1 block up on Montvale Ave behind Ice Rink		

Tee	Holes	Par	Rating	Slope	Yards
Red	9	54	NA	NA	3,244
White	9	54	NA	NA	4,500
Blue	NA	NA	NA	NA	NA

188 Stow Acres (North)
58 Randall Road, Stow, MA 01775
508-568-8106

Weekend Fee	$38	*Weekday Fee*	$30
Power Cart Fee	$28	*Pull Carts*	Yes
Putting Green	Yes	*Driving Range*	Yes
Season	Mar 15 - Dec 15	*Credit Cards*	Yes
Pro	Dan Diskin	*Tee Times*	6 days
Comments	Rated top 50, reduced fees after 3 pm		
Directions	Rt 128, Rt 20/117, 15 mi, left Rt 62W Stow center, follow signs		

Tee	Holes	Par	Rating	Slope	Yards
Red	18	72	73.6	130	6,011
White	18	72	69.8	127	6,310
Blue	18	72	72.8	130	6,939

189 Stow Acres (South)
58 Randall Road, Stow, MA 01775
508-568-8106

Weekend Fee	$38	*Weekday Fee*	$30
Power Cart Fee	$24	*Pull Carts*	Yes
Putting Green	Yes	*Driving Range*	Yes
Season	Mar 15 - Dec 15	*Credit Cards*	Yes
Pro	Dan Diskin	*Tee Times*	6 days
Comments	Rated in top 50, reduced fees after 3 pm		
Directions	Rt 128, Rt 20/117, 15 mi, left Rt 62W Stow center, follow signs		

Tee	Holes	Par	Rating	Slope	Yards
Red	18	72	72.5	120	5,642
White	18	72	70.5	118	6,105
Blue	18	72	71.8	120	6,520

190 Stowaway Golf Club
121 White Pond Road, Stow, MA 01775
508-897-4532

Weekend Fee	$10	*Weekday Fee*	$8
Power Cart Fee	No carts	*Pull Carts*	Yes
Putting Green	No	*Driving Range*	No
Season	Apr 1 - Nov 1	*Credit Cards*	No
Pro	Marge Melone	*Tee Times*	No
Comments	Small greens		
Directions	Rt 2W, Rt 62W, past junction Rt 117 1 mi, left White Pond Rd		

Tee	Holes	Par	Rating	Slope	Yards
Red	9	72	68.5	NA	4,374
White	9	72	68.3	NA	5,445
Blue	NA	NA	NA	NA	NA

191 Strawberry Hills Country Club
1430 Main Street, Leicester, MA 01524
508-892-1390

Weekend Fee	$20	*Weekday Fee*	$16
Power Cart Fee	$21	*Pull Carts*	No
Putting Green	Yes	*Driving Range*	No
Season	Year-round	*Credit Cards*	No
Pro	Steve Knowles	*Tee Times*	7 days
Comments	Tree lined, narrow		
Directions	I-90, Rt 9, Main St in Leicester center		

Tee	Holes	Par	Rating	Slope	Yards
Red	18	72	69.9	113	4,820
White	18	70	68.4	118	5,740
Blue	NA	NA	NA	NA	NA

192 Strawberry Valley Golf Club
164 Washington Street, Abington, MA 02351
617-871-5566

Weekend Fee	$21	*Weekday Fee*	$18
Power Cart Fee	$20	*Pull Carts*	Yes
Putting Green	Yes	*Driving Range*	No
Season	Year-round	*Credit Cards*	Yes
Pro	John Oteri	*Tee Times*	2 days
Comments	Good course for beginners, narrow fairways		
Directions	Rt 3, Rt 18S, 7 mi		

Tee	Holes	Par	Rating	Slope	Yards
Red	9	68	NA	NA	4,560
White	9	70	66.9	108	4,716
Blue	NA	NA	NA	NA	NA

193 Sun Valley Country Club
329 Summer Street, Rehoboth, MA 02769
508-336-8686

Weekend Fee	$25	Weekday Fee	$20
Power Cart Fee	$20	Pull Carts	Yes
Putting Green	Yes	Driving Range	Yes
Season	Mar - Dec	Credit Cards	No
Pro	Joan Fitzgerald	Tee Times	No
Comments	Large greens, wide fairways		
Directions	I-95S, I-195E, exit 1, Rt 44, 7 mi, right Taunton Rd, 1 mi		

Tee	Holes	Par	Rating	Slope	Yards
Red	18	73	73.0	114	5,654
White	18	71	69.8	116	6,383
Blue	18	71	71.4	118	6,734

196 Tara Hyannis Golf Club
West End Circle, Hyannis, MA 02601
508-775-7775

Weekend Fee	$23	Weekday Fee	$23
Power Cart Fee	$16	Pull Carts	Yes
Putting Green	Yes	Driving Range	No
Season	Year-round	Credit Cards	Yes
Pro	Fred Ghioto	Tee Times	2 days
Comments	Rated toughest par 3 on Cape		
Directions	Rt 3, Rt 6, exit 6, North St, 1 mi		

Tee	Holes	Par	Rating	Slope	Yards
Red	18	54	NA	NA	2,621
White	18	54	NA	NA	2,621
Blue	NA	NA	NA	NA	NA

194 Swansea Country Club
299 Market Street, Swansea, MA 02777
508-379-9886

Weekend Fee	$27	Weekday Fee	$22
Power Cart Fee	$21	Pull Carts	Yes
Putting Green	Yes	Driving Range	Yes
Season	Year-round	Credit Cards	No
Pro	No	Tee Times	7 days
Comments	Tree lined and water hazards on 7 holes		
Directions	I-195, exit 2, Rt 136S, 1 mi		

Tee	Holes	Par	Rating	Slope	Yards
Red	18	72	69.3	111	5,103
White	18	72	70.6	121	6,355
Blue	18	72	72.6	129	6,809

197 Tekoa Country Club
459 Russell Road, Westfield, MA 01086
413-568-1064

Weekend Fee	$25	Weekday Fee	$20
Power Cart Fee	$23	Pull Carts	Yes
Putting Green	Yes	Driving Range	Yes
Season	Apr 1 - Nov 30	Credit Cards	No
Pro	Tom Longhi	Tee Times	7 days
Comments	Mountain views, large greens		
Directions	I-90, exit 3, Rt 202S, Rt 20W Russell Rd, 2 mi		

Tee	Holes	Par	Rating	Slope	Yards
Red	18	74	75.0	124	5,369
White	18	71	68.2	116	5,965
Blue	18	71	69.6	118	6,275

195 Taconic Golf Club
Meacham Street, Williamstown, MA 01267
413-458-3997

Weekend Fee	$80	Weekday Fee	$80
Power Cart Fee	Included	Pull Carts	No
Putting Green	Yes	Driving Range	Yes
Season	Apr 15 - Nov 15	Credit Cards	Yes
Pro	Rick Pohle	Tee Times	7 days
Comments	Lush fairways, built 1896		
Directions	Pittsfield, Rt 7N, Rt 43W, 5 mi		

Tee	Holes	Par	Rating	Slope	Yards
Red	18	71	69.9	123	5,202
White	18	71	69.5	125	6,185
Blue	18	71	71.7	127	6,640

198 Thomas Memorial Country Club
Country Club Lane, Turner Falls, MA 01376
413-863-8003

Weekend Fee	$20	Weekday Fee	$16
Power Cart Fee	$18	Pull Carts	Yes
Putting Green	Yes	Driving Range	No
Season	Apr 15 - Snow	Credit Cards	No
Pro	None	Tee Times	No
Comments	Small greens, accurate shots a must		
Directions	I-91N, exit 27, Rt 2E, right Ave A, left 3rd St, right at fork, right Griswold St, turns into CC Lane		

Tee	Holes	Par	Rating	Slope	Yards
Red	9	70	68.0	NA	4,634
White	9	70	66.0	NA	5,103
Blue	NA	NA	NA	NA	NA

MASSACHUSETTS

199 Touisset Country Club
221 Pearse Road, Swansea, MA 02777
508-679-9577

Weekend Fee	$18	Weekday Fee	$15
Power Cart Fee	$22	Pull Carts	Yes
Putting Green	Yes	Driving Range	No
Season	Year-round	Credit Cards	Yes
Pro	Les Brigham	Tee Times	No
Comments	4 sets of tees, large greens, tight fairways		
Directions	I-95, Rt 195E, exit 3, Rt 6W, left Maple St, Pearse Rd		

Tee	Holes	Par	Rating	Slope	Yards
Red	9	72	71.1	114	5,456
White	9	70	69.1	111	6,203
Blue	NA	NA	NA	NA	NA

200 Trull Brook Golf Course
170 River Road, Tewksbury, MA 01876
508-851-6731

Weekend Fee	$35	Weekday Fee	$32
Power Cart Fee	$22	Pull Carts	Yes
Putting Green	Yes	Driving Range	No
Season	Mar - Dec	Credit Cards	Yes
Pro	Al Santos	Tee Times	7 days
Comments	Geoffrey Cornish design		
Directions	I-495, Rt 133 exit, toward Lowell, right Mobil Station River Rd		

Tee	Holes	Par	Rating	Slope	Yards
Red	18	72	70.2	118	5,235
White	18	72	68.2	115	6,003
Blue	18	72	NA	NA	6,335

201 Twin Springs Golf Club
295 Wilder Road, Bolton, MA 01740
508-779-5020

Weekend Fee	$16	Weekday Fee	$13
Power Cart Fee	No carts	Pull Carts	Yes
Putting Green	Yes	Driving Range	No
Season	Apr 1 - Nov 30	Credit Cards	Yes
Pro	Robert Keene	Tee Times	No
Comments	Small greens, great views		
Directions	I-495, exit 27, Rt 117W, left Wilder St in Bolton, right at fork, 3 mi		

Tee	Holes	Par	Rating	Slope	Yards
Red	9	70	67.9	114	4,872
White	9	68	64.8	113	5,224
Blue	NA	NA	NA	NA	NA

202 Tyngsboro Golf Club
Pawtucket Boulevard, Tyngsboro, MA 01879
508-649-7334

Weekend Fee	$22	Weekday Fee	$18
Power Cart Fee	$20	Pull Carts	Yes
Putting Green	Yes	Driving Range	No
Season	Apr - Snow	Credit Cards	No
Pro	None	Tee Times	No
Comments	Easy to walk, need accuracy		
Directions	Rt 3, exit 35, Rt 1B east, 2.5 mi		

Tee	Holes	Par	Rating	Slope	Yards
Red	9	70	62.6	97	4,046
White	9	70	65.2	108	5,149
Blue	NA	NA	NA	NA	NA

203 Unicorn Golf Club
460 Williams Street, Stoneham, MA 02180
617-438-9732

Weekend Fee	$30 nonresident	Weekday Fee	$28
Power Cart Fee	$24	Pull Carts	Yes
Putting Green	Yes	Driving Range	No
Season	Apr 1 - Dec 24	Credit Cards	No
Pro	Paul Monroe	Tee Times	No
Comments	Wide, sloping terrain		
Directions	I-93S, Stoneham exit 36, left, 0.9 mi, left at light, left at light Williams St		

Tee	Holes	Par	Rating	Slope	Yards
Red	9	68	72.7	109	5,804
White	9	70	68.7	109	6,154
Blue	9	70	70.8	126	6,448

204 Veterans Golf Club
1059 South Branch Parkway, Springfield, MA 01101
413-783-9611

Weekend Fee	$15	Weekday Fee	$13
Power Cart Fee	$20	Pull Carts	Yes
Putting Green	Yes	Driving Range	No
Season	Apr 1 - Nov 30	Credit Cards	No
Pro	Robert Downes	Tee Times	1 day
Comments	Open front 9, tight back 9		
Directions	I-90, Palmer exit, Rt 20W, 9 mi, left Parker St, 4 mi, South Branch Prkwy		

Tee	Holes	Par	Rating	Slope	Yards
Red	18	72	69.7	112	5,800
White	18	72	68.7	118	6,115
Blue	18	72	69.3	121	6,400

205 Wachusett Country Club
187 Prospect Street, West Boylston, MA 01583
508-835-4453

Weekend Fee	$35	*Weekday Fee*	$25	
Power Cart Fee	$24	*Pull Carts*	Yes	
Putting Green	Yes	*Driving Range*	Yes	
Season	Apr - Dec	*Credit Cards*	Yes	
Pro	Brad Durrin	*Tee Times*	7 days	
Comments	Tree lined fairways			
Directions	I-90, I-290, Rt 190, exit 4 Rt 12N, 2 mi, left Franklin St, left Prospect St			

Tee	Holes	Par	Rating	Slope	Yards
Red	18	73	71.2	120	6,216
White	18	72	71.7	124	6,608
Blue	NA	NA	NA	NA	NA

206 Wading River Golf Club
300 West Main Street, Norton, MA 02766
508-226-1788

Weekend Fee	$14	*Weekday Fee*	$12	
Power Cart Fee	$12	*Pull Carts*	Yes	
Putting Green	Yes	*Driving Range*	No	
Season	Year-round	*Credit Cards*	No	
Pro	None	*Tee Times*	No	
Comments	Good beginner course, large greens			
Directions	I-495, Rt 123W, 4 mi			

Tee	Holes	Par	Rating	Slope	Yards
Red	18	56	NA	NA	1,896
White	18	54	NA	NA	2,421
Blue	NA	NA	NA	NA	NA

207 Wahconah Country Club
15 Orchard Road, Dalton, MA 01226
413-684-2864

Weekend Fee	$55	*Weekday Fee*	$45	
Power Cart Fee	$24	*Pull Carts*	Yes	
Putting Green	Yes	*Driving Range*	Yes	
Season	Apr 15 - Nov 15	*Credit Cards*	Yes	
Pro	Paul Daniels	*Tee Times*	7 days	
Comments	Semi-private, large greens, narrow fairways			
Directions	I-90, exit 2, Rt 7N, Rt 8S, center of Dalton, 0.5 mi			

Tee	Holes	Par	Rating	Slope	Yards
Red	18	73	71.2	113	5,600
White	18	71	69.9	118	6,187
Blue	18	71	71.4	122	6,600

208 Wampanoag Golf Club
168 Old Providence, North Swansea, MA 02777
508-379-9832

Weekend Fee	$16	*Weekday Fee*	$14	
Power Cart Fee	$18	*Pull Carts*	Yes	
Putting Green	No	*Driving Range*	No	
Season	Year-round	*Credit Cards*	No	
Pro	M D'Allesandro	*Tee Times*	No	
Comments	Open fairways, large greens			
Directions	I-95, exit 2, right Rt 6, 3rd left Mason St			

Tee	Holes	Par	Rating	Slope	Yards
Red	9	74	NA	NA	5,000
White	9	70	66.7	108	6,225
Blue	NA	NA	NA	NA	NA

209 Waubeeka Golf Links
137 New Ashford Road, S. Williamstown, MA 01267
413-458-8355

Weekend Fee	$22	*Weekday Fee*	$17	
Power Cart Fee	$20	*Pull Carts*	Yes	
Putting Green	Yes	*Driving Range*	Yes	
Season	Apr 1 - Dec 1	*Credit Cards*	Yes	
Pro	Ed Stawarz	*Tee Times*	7 days	
Comments	Scenic, undulating greens			
Directions	I-90, exit 2, Rt 7N, 20 minutes north of Pittsfield			

Tee	Holes	Par	Rating	Slope	Yards
Red	18	72	70.9	111	5,826
White	18	72	69.5	124	6,024
Blue	18	72	71.2	127	6,296

210 Wayland Country Club
121 Old Sudbury Road, Wayland, MA 01778
508-358-4775

Weekend Fee	$35	*Weekday Fee*	$26	
Power Cart Fee	$22	*Pull Carts*	Yes	
Putting Green	Yes	*Driving Range*	No	
Season	Apr - Dec 1	*Credit Cards*	No	
Pro	John Ronis	*Tee Times*	5 days	
Comments	Flat and open			
Directions	Boston, I-90W, Rt 128N, Rt 20W, right Rt 27N, 1 mi			

Tee	Holes	Par	Rating	Slope	Yards
Red	18	71	70.0	120	4,947
White	18	70	67.3	112	5,229
Blue	18	70	67.9	113	5,838

MASSACHUSETTS

211 Wedgewood Country Club
549 Copeland Street, Brockton, MA 02401
508-583-9525

Weekend Fee	$15	Weekday Fee	$12
Power Cart Fee	$10	Pull Carts	Yes
Putting Green	Yes	Driving Range	No
Season	Year-round	Credit Cards	No
Pro	None	Tee Times	No
Comments	Some elevated greens		
Directions	Rt 24S, Rt 106W, left 2nd light, right Copeland St		

Tee	Holes	Par	Rating	Slope	Yards
Red	9	70	NA	NA	5,280
White	9	72	66.7	113	5,200
Blue	NA	NA	NA	NA	NA

212 Wenham Country Club
96 Main Street, Wenham, MA 01984
508-468-4714

Weekend Fee	$28	Weekday Fee	$25
Power Cart Fee	$24	Pull Carts	Yes
Putting Green	Yes	Driving Range	No
Season	Apr - Nov	Credit Cards	No
Pro	John Thoren	Tee Times	No
Comments	Tight course, small greens		
Directions	Rt 128, exit 20N Rt 1A, 3 mi		

Tee	Holes	Par	Rating	Slope	Yards
Red	18	67	63.8	96	4,528
White	18	65	62.3	102	4,429
Blue	NA	NA	NA	NA	NA

213 Westborough Country Club
121 West Main Street, Westborough, MA 01581
508-366-9947

Weekend Fee	$24	Weekday Fee	$20
Power Cart Fee	$20	Pull Carts	Yes
Putting Green	Yes	Driving Range	No
Season	Apr 1 - Nov 30	Credit Cards	No
Pro	Jack Negoshian	Tee Times	1 day
Comments	Hilly, small greens		
Directions	I-290, I-495N, Rt 9W, Rt 30W, look for signs		

Tee	Holes	Par	Rating	Slope	Yards
Red	9	75	71.4	111	5,662
White	9	71	69.2	118	6,210
Blue	NA	NA	NA	NA	NA

214 Westminster Country Club
51 Ellis Street, Westminster, MA 01473
508-874-5938

Weekend Fee	$25	Weekday Fee	$20
Power Cart Fee	$20	Pull Carts	Yes
Putting Green	Yes	Driving Range	No
Season	Apr 15 - Nov 31	Credit Cards	Yes
Pro	Tom Richardson	Tee Times	2 day
Comments	Front 9 flat, back 9 very hilly		
Directions	Rt 2, exit 25, bear right 2A west through center, left Nichols St, 1 mi		

Tee	Holes	Par	Rating	Slope	Yards
Red	18	71	70.0	115	5,453
White	18	71	69.5	123	6,223
Blue	18	71	70.9	133	6,491

215 Westover Golf Club
New Ludlow Road, Granby, MA 01033
413-547-8610

Weekend Fee	$16	Weekday Fee	$14
Power Cart Fee	$16	Pull Carts	Yes
Putting Green	Yes	Driving Range	Yes
Season	Apr 1 - Dec 15	Credit Cards	No
Pro	Jim Casagrande	Tee Times	2 days
Comments	Great layout, challenging		
Directions	I-90, exit 5, left Memorial Rd, 4 mi, right New Ludlow Rd		

Tee	Holes	Par	Rating	Slope	Yards
Red	18	72	72.0	113	5,580
White	18	72	71.7	123	6,610
Blue	18	72	73.7	131	7,025

216 Whippernon Country Club
490 Westfield Road, Russell, MA 01071
413-862-3606

Weekend Fee	$16	Weekday Fee	$14
Power Cart Fee	$16	Pull Carts	Yes
Putting Green	Yes	Driving Range	No
Season	Apr - Oct	Credit Cards	No
Pro	Steve Benoit	Tee Times	7 days
Comments	Call ahead		
Directions	Rt 20, 6 mi west of Westfield		

Tee	Holes	Par	Rating	Slope	Yards
Red	9	68	NA	NA	NA
White	9	68	NA	113	5,186
Blue	NA	NA	NA	NA	NA

217 Wilbraham Country Club
859 Stony Hill, Wilbraham, MA 01095
413-596-8887

Weekend Fee	$29	*Weekday Fee*	$22
Power Cart Fee	$20	*Pull Carts*	Yes
Putting Green	Yes	*Driving Range*	No
Season	Apr - Dec 1	*Credit Cards*	No
Pro 0	Daril Pacinell	*Tee Times* , ,	No
Comments	Semi-private, small tough greens		
Directions	I-90, exit 7, Rt 21S, 1.5 mi, right Indian Orchard Bridge, left Stony Hill		

Tee	Holes	Par	Rating	Slope	Yards
Red	9	72	69.3	120	5,584
White	9	72	69.3	108	6,194
Blue	9	72	69.3	108	6,515

218 William J. Devine Golf Club
Franklin Park, Dorcester, MA 02121
617-265-4084

Weekend Fee	$24	*Weekday Fee*	$21
Power Cart Fee	$20	*Pull Carts*	Yes
Putting Green	Yes	*Driving Range*	No
Season	Apr - Snow	*Credit Cards*	Yes
Pro	Bill Flynn	*Tee Times*	2 days
Comments	Oldest course in country (1890)		
Directions	Boston, I-93S, exit Columbia Rd, to Blue Hill Ave, look for signs, near Franklin Park Zoo		

Tee	Holes	Par	Rating	Slope	Yards
Red	18	72	70.9	113	5,422
White	18	72	71.1	113	6,360
Blue	18	72	72.1	120	6,601

219 Willowdale Golf Club
54 Willow Street, Mansfield, MA 02048
508-339-3197

Weekend Fee	$14	*Weekday Fee*	$12
Power Cart Fee	No carts	*Pull Carts*	Yes
Putting Green	No	*Driving Range*	No
Season	Apr 1 - Dec 1	*Credit Cards*	No
Pro	None	*Tee Times*	No
Comments	Executive, easy walking course		
Directions	I-495S, Rt 140N, 2 quick rights		

Tee	Holes	Par	Rating	Slope	Yards
Red	9	62	NA	NA	3,424
White	9	60	NA	NA	3,424
Blue	NA	NA	NA	NA	NA

220 Winchendon Country Club
160 Ash Street, Winchendon, MA 01475
508-297-9897

Weekend Fee	$21	*Weekday Fee*	$17
Power Cart Fee	$22	*Pull Carts*	No
Putting Green	Yes	*Driving Range*	No
Season	Apr - Snow	*Credit Cards*	Yes
Pro	None	*Tee Times*	7 days
Comments	Postage sized greens		
Directions	Boston, Rt 2W, Rt 140N, 6 mi, left Rt 12N, 1.5 mi		

Tee	Holes	Par	Rating	Slope	Yards
Red	18	72	68.5	116	5,107
White	18	70	65.8	114	5,317
Blue	NA	NA	NA	NA	NA

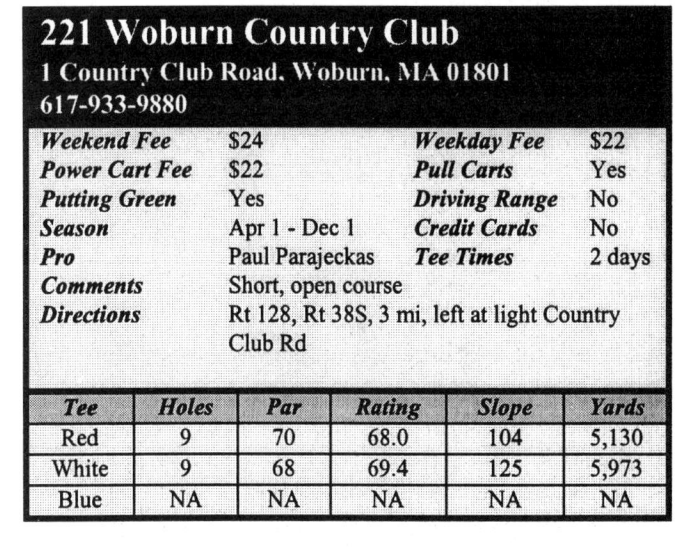

221 Woburn Country Club
1 Country Club Road, Woburn, MA 01801
617-933-9880

Weekend Fee	$24	*Weekday Fee*	$22
Power Cart Fee	$22	*Pull Carts*	Yes
Putting Green	Yes	*Driving Range*	No
Season	Apr 1 - Dec 1	*Credit Cards*	No
Pro	Paul Parajeckas	*Tee Times*	2 days
Comments	Short, open course		
Directions	Rt 128, Rt 38S, 3 mi, left at light Country Club Rd		

Tee	Holes	Par	Rating	Slope	Yards
Red	9	70	68.0	104	5,130
White	9	68	69.4	125	5,973
Blue	NA	NA	NA	NA	NA

222 Woodbriar Country Club
339 Gifford Street, Falmouth, MA 02540
508-540-1600

Weekend Fee	$16	*Weekday Fee*	$14
Power Cart Fee	No carts	*Pull Carts*	Yes
Putting Green	Yes	*Driving Range*	No
Season	Year-round	*Credit Cards*	No
Pro	Ken Collinson	*Tee Times*	No
Comments	Ideal beginners course		
Directions	Rt 28, Brick Kiln exit, left, right 1st light Gifford St, 2.5 mi		

Tee	Holes	Par	Rating	Slope	Yards
Red	9	54	NA	NA	4,400
White	9	54	NA	NA	5,640
Blue	NA	NA	NA	NA	NA

MASSACHUSETTS

223 Worthington Golf Club
Ridge Road, Worthington, MA 01098
413-238-4464

Weekend Fee	$22	Weekday Fee	$18
Power Cart Fee	$18	Pull Carts	Yes
Putting Green	Yes	Driving Range	Yes
Season	May 1 - Oct 31	Credit Cards	No
Pro	Wade Lavige	Tee Times	4 days
Comments	Smallest green in Massachusetts		
Directions	I-91, Northampton, Rt 9N, Rt 143, Buffinton Hill Rd in center, Ridge Rd		

Tee	Holes	Par	Rating	Slope	Yards
Red	9	72	NA	NA	5,100
White	9	70	66.8	115	5,629
Blue	9	70	NA	116	6,200

Townsend Ridge Country Club
Scales Lane, Townsend, MA
508-597-8400

Weekend Fee	$34	Weekday Fee	$27
Power Cart Fee	$11	Pull Carts	Yes
Putting Green	Yes	Driving Range	Yes
Season	Apr - Oct	Credit Cards	Yes
Pro	Neil Gorman	Tee Times	7 days
Comments	Built in 1996		
Directions	I-495, exit 31, Rt 119W, 1st left after Townsend Ford, Scales Lane		

Tee	Holes	Par	Rating	Slope	Yards
Red	18	71	68.4	112	4,927
White	18	70	67.7	118	6,273
Blue	18	70	68.7	120	6,664

Information on several courses recently or soon to be opened was obtained too late to include them in the alphabetical listing or location maps in this book.

Boylston Country Club
Boylston, MA
508-869-6699

Weekend Fee	$	Weekday Fee	$
Power Cart Fee	$	Pull Carts	
Putting Green		Driving Range	
Season		Credit Cards	
Pro		Tee Times	
Comments	No information yet available		
Directions			

Tee	Holes	Par	Rating	Slope	Yards
Red					
White					
Blue					

Stony Brook Golf Course
Holliston, MA
508-458-3151

Weekend Fee	$	Weekday Fee	$
Power Cart Fee	$	Pull Carts	
Putting Green		Driving Range	
Season		Credit Cards	
Pro		Tee Times	
Comments	No information yet available		
Directions			

Tee	Holes	Par	Rating	Slope	Yards
Red	9				
White	9				
Blue	NA				

Kimball Farm Golf Center
Westford, MA
508-486-3891

Weekend Fee	$	Weekday Fee	$
Power Cart Fee	$	Pull Carts	
Putting Green		Driving Range	
Season		Credit Cards	
Pro	Jim Callahan	Tee Times	
Comments	Pitch and putt		
Directions			

Tee	Holes	Par	Rating	Slope	Yards
Red	9				
White	9				
Blue	NA				

Stonemeadow Golf Course
Trapelo Road, Waltham, MA

Weekend Fee	$	Weekday Fee	$
Power Cart Fee	$	Pull Carts	
Putting Green		Driving Range	
Season		Credit Cards	
Pro		Tee Times	
Comments	No information yet available		
Directions			

Tee	Holes	Par	Rating	Slope	Yards
Red	9				
White	9				
Blue	NA				

NEW HAMPSHIRE GOLF COURSES

Public Courses	85	Private Courses	8
Total Courses	93	Percent Public Courses	91%
18 Hole Public Courses	45	9 Hole Public Courses	40
Total Golfers	110,000	Total Rounds of Golf	1,727,000
Percent Female Golfers	29.1%	Percent Senior Golfers	18.4%
Rounds Per Course	18,570	Rounds Per Golfer	15.7
Golfers Per Course	1,183	Courses Per 100 Square Miles	1.00
Average Weekend Fee	$28.13	Average Weekday Fee	$24.94
Average Weekend Fee w/Power Cart	$38.96	Average Weekday Fee w/Power Cart	$35.63
Average Slope	115.3	Average Yardage	5,562

New Hampshire has 93 golf courses. Eighty-five of the courses are open to the public. Almost 10 percent of the population plays golf which translates into 110,000 golfers playing 1.7 million rounds of golf every year[1] (15.7 rounds per golfer). Only 18 percent of the golfers are senior citizens but 29 percent are women.

New Hampshire is one of the least crowded states to golf in. New Hampshire has 1,183 golfers per golf course and 18,570 golf rounds are played per golf course annually.

A large percentage of New Hampshire's public golf courses are 9 hole courses. Only 53% of the courses are 18 holes.

Greens Fees

Other than Vermont, New Hampshire is the most expensive state to play golf in New England. On weekends, the average greens fees to play a round of 18 holes on public courses is $28.13 ($34.62 for 18 hole and $20.83 for 9 hole courses). (These costs include courses where power cart fees are part of the greens fees.) Golfers can save $3.19 by playing during the week when the average greens fee is $24.94 ($30.62 for 18 hole and $18.55 for 9 hole courses).

The courses with the most expensive greens fees are the 18 hole Sky Meadow Country Club in Nashua ($85) and the 9 hole Hale's Location Country Club in North Conway ($35). The least expensive courses are the 9 hole Woodbound Inn Golf Club in Jaffrey ($12) and the 18 hole club Waumbek Inn & Country Club in Jefferson ($18).

A power cart rental for two players will cost $20.24 in New Hampshire. On weekends, a round of golf with a power cart will cost each golfer an average of $38.96.

Slope and Yardage

New Hampshire courses tend to be average in terms of average slope ratings. The average slope rating of all public courses from the white tees is 115.3 (119.6 for 18 hole and 109.8 for 9 hole courses). The courses with the highest slope rating from the white tees are the 18 hole Shattuck Golf Course in Jaffrey (143) and the 9 hole Countryside Golf Club in Dunbarton (132). The easiest 18 and 9 hole courses are the Londonderry Country Club (86) and Monadnock Country Club in Peterborough (76), respectively.

New Hampshire courses are also average in terms of distance from the white tees. The average yardage of all public courses from the white tees is 5,562 (5,976 yards for 18 hole and 5,095 for 9 hole courses). The courses with the longest yardage from the white tees are the 18 hole Portsmouth Country Club in Exeter (6,609) and the 9 hole Sunningdale Golf Club in Somersworth (6,660). The shortest 18 and 9 hole courses

---

[1] The Complete Golfer's Almanac 1995

are the Londonderry Country Club (3,740) and the Woodbound Inn Golf Club in Jaffrey (1,956), respectively.

Public Courses Rated in Top 10 by Golf Digest

Rank	Course
1	Shattuck Golf Course
2	Portsmouth Country Club
3	Sky Meadow Country Club
4	Bretwood Golf Course (North)
5	Balsams Grand Resort

Rank	Course
6	North Conway Country Club
7	Eastman Golf Links
8	Country Club of New Hampshire
9	Concord Country Club
10	Bretwood Golf Course (South)

Oldest Golf Courses

Club	Year
North Conway Golf Club	1895
Beaver Meadow Golf Club	1896
Wentworth-By-The-Sea	1897
Bethlehem Country Club	1898

Club	Year
Hanover Country Club	1899
Keene Country Club	1900
Monadnock Country Club	1901

Golf Schools and Instruction

- Heavy Hitters, 55 Range Road, Windham, 603-898-6793
- The Roland Stafford Golf School at Tory Pines Resort, Francestown, 603-588-2000
- World Cup Golf School, Hudson, 603-598-3838

Golf Associations and Touring Clubs

- Boston Amateur Golf Society (BAGS), 617-639-2780
- Executive Women's Golf League, 603-883-9949
- The Greater Boston Amateur Golf Club (The Tour), 617-484-8687
- InterState Golf Association, 617-566-7723
- New Hampshire Golf Association, 603-228-3089
- New Hampshire Senior Golf Association
- New Hampshire Women's Golf Association, 603-472-5885
- Profile Senior Golfer's Association, 603-668-0783

Retailers

- Auger's Personalized Golf, 1240 Page Street, Manchester, 603-627-1936
- Golf Day, Maple Tree Mall, Manchester, 603-623-0009
- Golf Day, 1 Batchelder Road, Seabrook, 603-474-5858
- Golf & Ski Warehouse, 1680 Greenland Avenue, Greenland, 603-433-8585
- Golf & Ski Warehouse, 294 Plainfield Road, West Lebanon, 603-298-8282
- Golf USA, 1875 South Willow Street, Manchester, 603-626-4653
- Integrity Golf, 18 Plaistow Road, Plaistow, 603-382-8281
- Nevada Bob's, Somerset Plaza, 375 Amherst Street, Nashua, 603-595-8711
- Nevada Bob's, Park Plaza, 125 C South Broadway, Salem, 603-893-3383
- New England Golf Supply, 410 Kelley Road, Salem, 603-893-5080
- Pat's Hi Tec GC, 207 South Willow Street, Manchester, 603-668-2272
- Rick's USA Golf, 1319 White Mountain Highway, Route 16, North Conway, 603-356-6680
- The Golf Shop, 74 Portsmouth Avenue, Exeter, 603-772-4653
- Seacoast Golf Discount Center, 137 Lafayette Road, Hampton Falls, 603-926-7230

Courses By Town

Course	Town	Holes
Amherst CC	Amherst	18
Buckmeadow GC	Amherst	9
Ponemah Greens	Amherst	9
Souhegan Woods GC	Amherst	18
White Mountain CC	Ashland	18
Atkinson CC	Atkinson	9
Nippo Lake GC	Barrington	9
Lakeview GC	Belmont	18
Bethlehem CC	Bethlehem	18
Maplewood Casino & GC	Bethlehem	18
Mount Washington GC	Bretton Woods	18
Candia Woods	Candia	18
Indian Mound GC	Center Ossipee	18
Claremont CC	Claremont	9
Colebrook CC	Colebrook	9
Beaver Meadow GC	Concord	18
Hoodkroft CC	Derry	9
Balsams Panorama GC	Dixville Notch	18
Countryside GC	Dunbarton	9
East Kingston GC	East Kingston	18
Exeter CC	Exeter	9
Portsmouth CC	Exeter	18
Tory Pines Resort	Fancestown	18
Farmington CC	Farmington	9
Profile GC	Franconia	9
Mojalaki CC	Franklin	9
Pheasant Ridge CC	Gilford	9
Androscoggin Valley CC	Gorham	18
Eastman Golf Links	Grantham	18
Bramber Valley GC	Greenland	9
Hanover CC	Hanover	18
Angus Lea GC	Hillsborough	9
Highlands Links Colony GC	Holderness	9
Overlook CC	Hollis	18
Duston CC	Hopkinton	9
Green Meadow GC North	Hudson	18
Green Meadow GC South	Hudson	18
Whip-Poor-Will GC	Hudson	9
Eagle Mountain Resort	Jackson	9
Wentworth Resort GC	Jackson	18
Shattuck GC	Jaffrey	18
Woodbound Inn GC	Jaffrey	9
Waumbek Inn & CC	Jefferson	18

Course	Town	Holes
Bretwood GC - North	Keene	18
Bretwood GC - South	Keene	18
Keene CC	Keene	18
Laconia CC	Laconia	18
Lisbon Village CC	Lisbon	9
Passaconaway CC	Litchfield	18
Londonderry CC	Londonderry	18
Loudon CC	Loudon	9
Derryfield CC	Manchester	18
Intervale CC	Manchester	9
Oak Hill GC	Meredith	9
Waukewan GC	Meredith	18
Kona Mansion Inn	Moultonboro	9
Sky Meadow CC	Nashua	18
Twin Lake Village GC	New London	9
Rockingham CC	Newmarket	9
John H. Cain GC	Newport	18
Hale's Location CC	North Conway	9
North Conway GC	North Conway	18
Sagamore-Hampton GC	North Hampton	18
CC of New Hampshire	North Sutton	18
Pine Valley Golf Links	Pelham	9
Plausawa Valley CC	Pembroke	18
Monadnock CC	Peterborough	9
Pease GC	Portsmouth	18
Wentworth-By-The-Sea	Portsmouth	18
Rochester CC	Rochester	18
Campbell's Scottish	Salem	18
Den Brae GC	Sanbornton	9
Sunningdale GC	Somersworth	9
Pine Grove Springs CC	Spofford	9
Sunset Hill Golf Links	Sugar Hill	9
Lochmere Golf and CC	Tilton	10
Hooper GC	Walpole	9
Waterville Valley GC	Waterville	9
Carter CC	West Lebanon	9
Mountain View Golf and	Whitefield	9
Applewood Golf Links	Windham	9
Windham CC	Windham	18
Perry Hollow Golf and CC	Wolfboro	18
Kingswood GC	Wolfeboro	18
Jack O'Lantern Resort	Woodstock	18

Private Golf Courses

Course	Town
Albenaqui Country Club	Rye Beach
Bald Peak Colony Club	Melvin Village
Cochecho Country Club	Dover
Concord Country Club	Concord

Course	Town
Dublin Lake Golf Club	Dublin
Lake Sunapee Country Club	New London
Manchester Country Club	Bedford
Nashua Country Club	Nashua

NEW HAMPSHIRE

Driving Ranges and Practice Areas

Name	Address	Town	Phone
Bedford Golfland	547 Donald Street	Bedford	603-624-0503
Driving Range	Route 124	Mason	603-878-1324
Fore-U Driving Range	Route 12A	West Lebanon	603-298-9702
Funspot	Rural Route 3	Weirs Beach	603-366-4377
Golf & Ski Warehouse	1680 Greenland Road	Portsmouth	603-430-8573
Greenville Driving Range	Call for address	Greenville	603-878-1324
Littleton Driving Range	Route 302	Littleton	603-444-9998
Mammouth Green Golf Driving Range	135 Route 102	Londonderry	603-437-9669
Northwood Golf Practice Range	Route 4	Northwood	603-942-8605
Palmer Meadows Golf Driving Range	332 Wadleigh Falls Road	New Durham	603-659-4444
Putters	Route 12	Westmoreland	603-352-0277
Sugar Shack Golf Range	Route 175	Campton	603-726-8978
T-Off Driving Range	Route 3A	North Hampton	603-964-8393
Tee Off at Mel's	Charles Bancroft Highway	Litchfield	603-424-2292
Tri City Golf	Somersworth Plaza	Somersworth	603-692-3347
Whirlaway Golf Center	105 Pleasant Street	Salem	603-898-8356
World Cup Driving Range	Steele Road	Hudson	603-598-3838

Easiest Courses

Course	Town	Holes	Slope
Monadnock CC	Peterborough	9	76
Sunset Hill Golf Links	Sugar Hill	9	81
Londonderry CC	Londonderry	18	86
Oak Hill GC	Meredith	9	90
Highlands Links GC	Holderness	9	92
Farmington CC	Farmington	9	95
Ponemah Greens	Amherst	9	97
Bramber Valley GC	Greenland	9	99
Duston CC	Hopkinton	9	99
Buckmeadow GC	Amherst	9	100
Angus Lea GC	Hillsborough	9	101
Sagamore-Hampton GC	N. Hampton	18	101
Pheasant Ridge CC	Gilford	9	103

Hardest Courses

Course	Town	Holes	Slope
Overlook CC	Hollis	18	128
Bretwood GC - North	Keene	18	128
Sky Meadow CC	Nashua	18	128
Countryside GC	Dunbarton	9	129
Perry Hollow G. and CC	Wolfboro	18	129
Profile GC	Franconia	9	129
Balsams Panorama GC	Dixville	18	130
Plausawa Valley CC	Pembroke	18	131
Pine Grove Springs CC	Spofford	9	132
Windham CC	Windham	18	128
Bretwood GC - South	Keene	18	133
Eastman Golf Links	Grantham	18	133
Shattuck GC	Jaffrey	18	143

Least Expensive Courses

Course	Town	Holes	Fee
Highlands Links Colony GC	Holderness	9	$15
Woodbound Inn GC	Jaffrey	9	$12
Kona Mansion Inn	Moultonboro	9	$13
Monadnock CC	Peterborough	9	$15
Pine Grove Springs CC	Spofford	9	$15
Profile GC	Franconia	9	$15
Applewood Golf Links	Windham	9	$16
Duston CC	Hopkinton	9	$16
Oak Hill GC	Meredith	9	$16
Twin Lake Village GC	New London	9	$16
Bramber Valley GC	Greenland	9	$18
Colebrook CC	Colebrook	9	$18
Sunset Hill Golf Links	Sugar Hill	9	$18
Waumbek Inn & CC	Jefferson	18	$18

Most Expensive Courses

Course	Town	Holes	Fee
Hale's Location CC	North	9	$35
Kingswood GC	Wolfeboro	18	$35
Overlook	Hollis	18	$35
Shattuck GC	Jaffrey	18	$35
Wentworth Resort GC	Jackson	18	$35
Windham CC	Windham	18	$35
Eastman Golf Links	Grantham	18	$38
Rochester CC	Rochester	18	$45
North Conway GC	North	18	$46
Portsmouth CC	Exeter	18	$50
Keene CC	Keene	18	$55
Balsams Panorama GC	Dixville	18	$60
Laconia CC	Laconia	18	$65
Wentworth-By-The-Sea	Portsmouth	18	$75
Sky Meadow CC	Nashua	18	$85

Shortest Courses

Course	Town	Holes	Distance
Woodbound Inn GC	Jaffrey	9	1,956
Kona Mansion Inn	Moultonboro	9	2,340
Twin Lake Village GC	New London	9	2,424
Applewood Golf Links	Windham	9	2,594
Highlands Links Colony	Holderness	9	3,000
Monadnock CC	Peterborough	9	3,152
Londonderry CC	Londonderry	18	3,740
Sunset Hill Golf Links	Sugar Hill	9	3,954
Ponemah Greens	Amherst	9	4,042
Duston CC	Hopkinton	9	4,194

Longest Courses

Course	Town	Holes	Distance
Candia Woods	Candia	18	6,307
Bretwood GC - South	Keene	18	6,309
Rochester CC	Rochester	18	6,317
Eastman Golf Links	Grantham	18	6,338
Bretwood GC - North	Keene	18	6,434
Passaconaway CC	Litchfield	18	6,462
Hoodkroft CC	Derry	9	6,466
Atkinson CC	Atkinson	9	6,585
Portsmouth CC	Exeter	18	6,609
Sunningdale GC	Somersworth	9	6,660

Year-Round Courses

Course	Town	Holes
Green Meadow GC North	Hudson	18
Green Meadow GC South	Hudson	18

Bretwood Golf Course
Keene, New Hampshire

New Hampshire

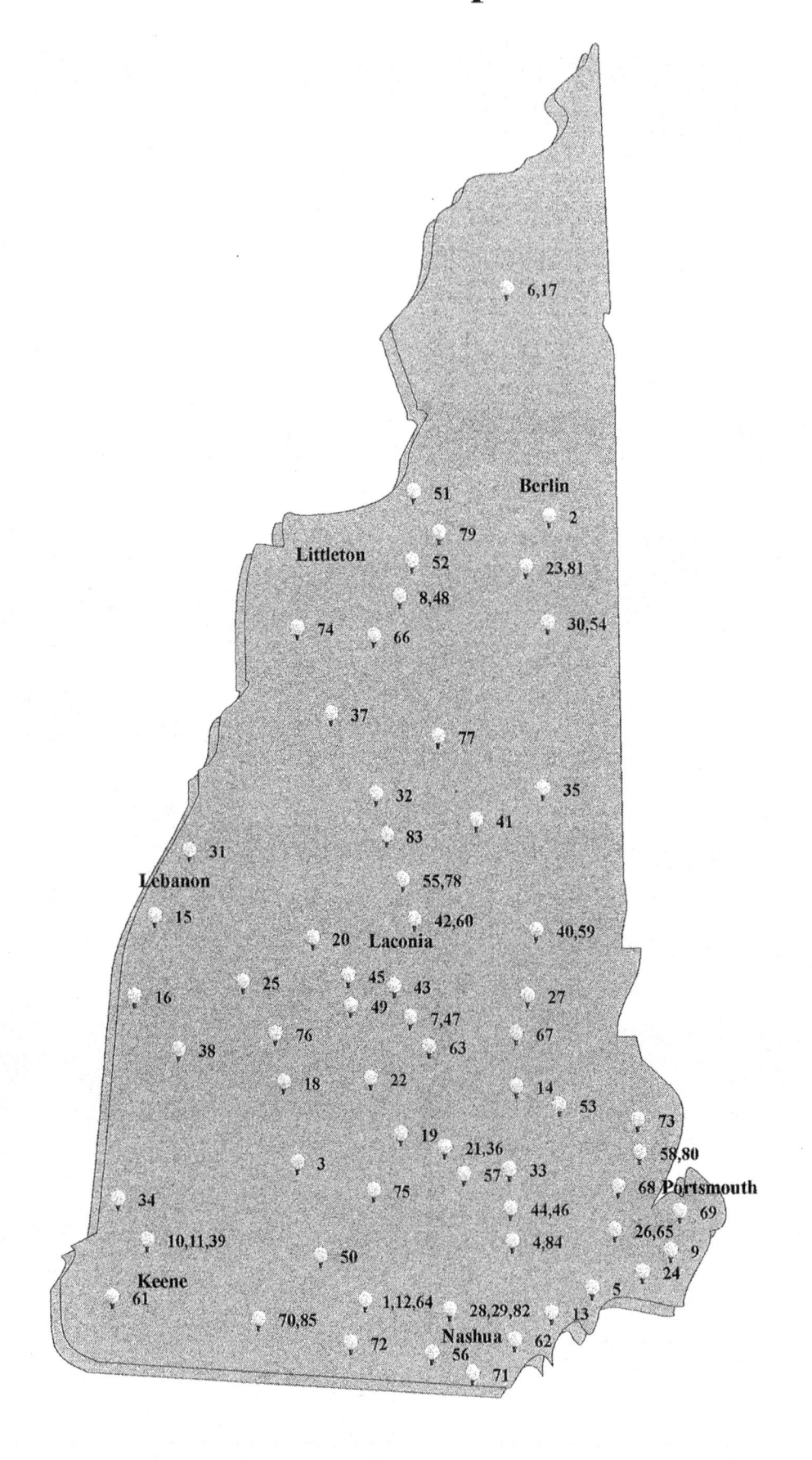

- 6,17
- Berlin
- 51
- 79
- 2
- Littleton
- 52
- 23,81
- 8,48
- 74
- 66
- 30,54
- 37
- 77
- 32
- 35
- 83
- 41
- 31
- Lebanon
- 55,78
- 15
- 42,60
- 40,59
- 20 Laconia
- 16
- 25
- 45 43
- 27
- 49
- 7,47
- 76
- 63
- 67
- 38
- 18
- 22
- 14
- 53
- 73
- 19
- 21,36
- 58,80
- 3
- 57 33
- 75
- 68 Portsmouth
- 34
- 44,46
- 69
- 4,84
- 26,65
- 10,11,39
- 9
- 50
- 24
- Keene
- 5
- 61
- 1,12,64
- 28,29,82
- 70,85
- 13
- 72
- Nashua
- 62
- 56
- 71

NEW HAMPSHIRE

1 Amherst Country Club
76 Ponemah Road, Amherst, NH 03031
603-673-9908

Weekend Fee	$34	Weekday Fee	$26
Power Cart Fee	$23	Pull Carts	Yes
Putting Green	Yes	Driving Range	No
Season	Apr - Nov	Credit Cards	Yes
Pro	Ted Bishop	Tee Times	3 days
Comments	Flat terrain, Souhegan River affects 6 holes		
Directions	Rt 3N, exit 7W, RT 101A west, 7.8 mi, right Rt 122N, 0.4 mi, right		

Tee	Holes	Par	Rating	Slope	Yards
Red	18	74	74.2	126	5,532
White	18	72	68.7	118	6,000
Blue	18	72	71.0	123	6,520

2 Androscoggin Valley Country Club
Route 2, Gorham, NH 03581
603-466-9468

Weekend Fee	$24	Weekday Fee	$20
Power Cart Fee	$25	Pull Carts	No
Putting Green	Yes	Driving Range	Yes
Season	May 15 - Nov 1	Credit Cards	Yes
Pro	Giff Nutbrown	Tee Times	1 day
Comments	Semi-private, flat with mountain scenery		
Directions	I-93, Rt 3, Rt 115E, Rt 2 to Gorham, right at light in center, over bridge		

Tee	Holes	Par	Rating	Slope	Yards
Red	18	70	70.1	118	4,808
White	18	70	68.9	116	5,499
Blue	NA	NA	NA	NA	NA

3 Angus Lea Golf Course
West Main Street, Hillsborough, NH 03244
603-464-5404

Weekend Fee	$19	Weekday Fee	$19
Power Cart Fee	$16	Pull Carts	Yes
Putting Green	Yes	Driving Range	No
Season	Apr - Nov	Credit Cards	No
Pro	Russ Niven	Tee Times	3 days
Comments	Semi-private, wooded and water		
Directions	I-93, I-89, right Rt 9, exit 5 Rt 202, follow signs to Hillsboro		

Tee	Holes	Par	Rating	Slope	Yards
Red	9	66	65.6	97	4,214
White	9	66	60.8	101	4,270
Blue	NA	NA	NA	NA	NA

4 Applewood Golf Links
Range Road, Windham, NH 03087
603-898-6793

Weekend Fee	$16	Weekday Fee	$16
Power Cart Fee	$8	Pull Carts	Yes
Putting Green	Yes	Driving Range	Yes
Season	Apr 1 - Dec 1	Credit Cards	Yes
Pro	Jim Ellis	Tee Times	No
Comments	Good greens		
Directions	I-93N, exit 3, right, 0.2 mi		

Tee	Holes	Par	Rating	Slope	Yards
Red	9	54	NA	NA	2,594
White	9	54	NA	NA	2,594
Blue	NA	NA	NA	NA	NA

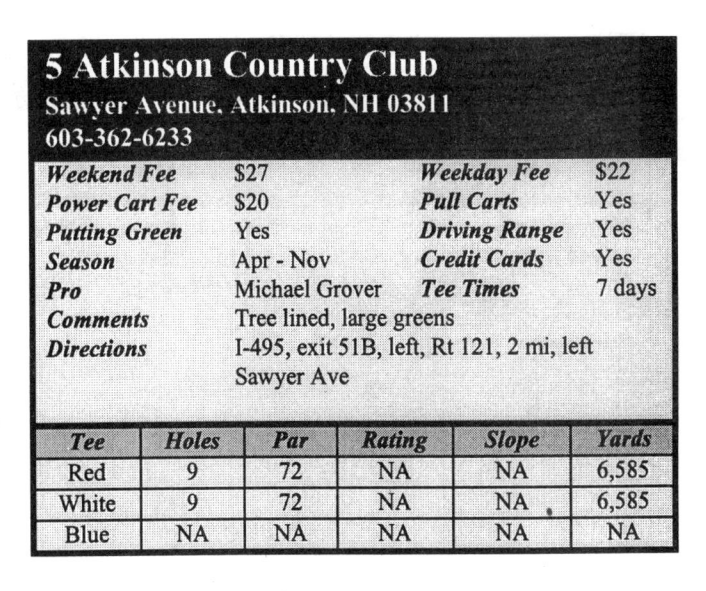

5 Atkinson Country Club
Sawyer Avenue, Atkinson, NH 03811
603-362-6233

Weekend Fee	$27	Weekday Fee	$22
Power Cart Fee	$20	Pull Carts	Yes
Putting Green	Yes	Driving Range	Yes
Season	Apr - Nov	Credit Cards	Yes
Pro	Michael Grover	Tee Times	7 days
Comments	Tree lined, large greens		
Directions	I-495, exit 51B, left, Rt 121, 2 mi, left Sawyer Ave		

Tee	Holes	Par	Rating	Slope	Yards
Red	9	72	NA	NA	6,585
White	9	72	NA	NA	6,585
Blue	NA	NA	NA	NA	NA

6 Balsams Panorama Golf Course
Route 26, Dixville Notch, NH 03576
603-255-4961

Weekend Fee	$60	Weekday Fee	$60
Power Cart Fee	$32	Pull Carts	Yes
Putting Green	Yes	Driving Range	Yes
Season	May 1 - Oct 15	Credit Cards	Yes
Pro	Bill Hamblen	Tee Times	3 days
Comments	Resort, deep bunkers, built 1912		
Directions	I-93N, exit 35, Rt 3N, Rt 26E, 10 mi		

Tee	Holes	Par	Rating	Slope	Yards
Red	18	72	69.9	124	5,069
White	18	72	70.5	130	6,097
Blue	18	72	73.9	136	6,804

NEW HAMPSHIRE

7 Beaver Meadow Golf Club
1 Beaver Meadow Drive, Concord, NH 03301
603-228-8954

Weekend Fee	$26	Weekday Fee	$24
Power Cart Fee	$22	Pull Carts	Yes
Putting Green	Yes	Driving Range	Yes
Season	Apr 15 - Nov 11	Credit Cards	Yes
Pro	Ed Deshaies	Tee Times	2 days
Comments	Oldest course in NH (1896), residents less $		
Directions	I-93, exit Rt 15W, right at 2nd light Rt 3N, 3.1 mi		

Tee	Holes	Par	Rating	Slope	Yards
Red	18	72	71.8	123	5,519
White	18	72	68.5	118	6,034
Blue	18	72	70.1	121	6,356

8 Bethlehem Country Club
Main Street, Route 302, Bethlehem, NH 03574
603-869-5745

Weekend Fee	$24	Weekday Fee	$20
Power Cart Fee	$22	Pull Carts	Yes
Putting Green	Yes	Driving Range	No
Season	May - Oct	Credit Cards	Yes
Pro	Wayne Natti	Tee Times	3 days
Comments	Built 1898		
Directions	I-93, exit 40 Rt 302, 2.5 mi		

Tee	Holes	Par	Rating	Slope	Yards
Red	18	70	63.0	98	5,008
White	18	70	68.2	114	5,619
Blue	NA	NA	NA	NA	NA

9 Bramber Valley Golf Course
Greenland, NH 03840
603-436-4288

Weekend Fee	$18	Weekday Fee	$18
Power Cart Fee	$18	Pull Carts	Yes
Putting Green	Yes	Driving Range	No
Season	Apr - Oct	Credit Cards	No
Pro	Jason Taylor	Tee Times	No
Comments	Executive style		
Directions	I-95S, exit 3A, Rt 33W, 2nd light left, right at fork		

Tee	Holes	Par	Rating	Slope	Yards
Red	9	64	60.8	99	4,228
White	9	64	60.8	99	4,228
Blue	NA	NA	NA	NA	NA

10 Bretwood Golf Course - North
East Surry Road, Keene, NH 03431
603-352-7626

Weekend Fee	$30	Weekday Fee	$25
Power Cart Fee	$20	Pull Carts	Yes
Putting Green	Yes	Driving Range	Yes
Season	Apr 1 - Nov 15	Credit Cards	Yes
Pro	Matt Barrett	Tee Times	3 days
Comments	Island green, 7 covered bridges		
Directions	I-91N, Rt 9E, Keene, follow signs for hospital to Court St, East Surry Rd		

Tee	Holes	Par	Rating	Slope	Yards
Red	18	72	70.1	120	5,140
White	18	72	71.0	128	6,434
Blue	18	72	73.9	134	6,979

11 Bretwood Golf Course - South
East Surry Road, Keene, NH 03431
603-352-7626

Weekend Fee	$30	Weekday Fee	$25
Power Cart Fee	$20	Pull Carts	Yes
Putting Green	Yes	Driving Range	Yes
Season	Apr 1 - Nov 15	Credit Cards	Yes
Pro	Matt Barrett	Tee Times	3 days
Comments	Island green, 7 covered bridges		
Directions	I-91N, Rt 9E, Keene, follow signs for hospital to Court St, East Surry Rd		

Tee	Holes	Par	Rating	Slope	Yards
Red	18	71	NA	NA	4,984
White	18	72	70.4	133	6,309
Blue	18	72	73.0	137	6,924

12 Buckmeadow Golf Course
Route 101A, Box 42, Amherst, NH 03031
603-881-7467

Weekend Fee	$28	Weekday Fee	$21
Power Cart Fee	$22	Pull Carts	Yes
Putting Green	Yes	Driving Range	Yes
Season	Apr - Nov	Credit Cards	No
Pro	V. Young	Tee Times	5 days
Comments	Semi-private, elevated greens		
Directions	Rt 3N, exit 7W, RT 101A west, 7.3 mi, right		

Tee	Holes	Par	Rating	Slope	Yards
Red	9	68	66.2	103	4,560
White	9	66	60.9	100	4,680
Blue	9	66	61.4	101	4,850

NEW HAMPSHIRE

13 Campbell's Scottish Highlands
79 Brady Avenue, Salem, NH 03079
603-894-4653

Weekend Fee	$30	*Weekday Fee*	$25
Power Cart Fee	$20	*Pull Carts*	Yes
Putting Green	Yes	*Driving Range*	Yes
Season	Apr 6 - Nov	*Credit Cards*	Yes
Pro	Tony Zdunko	*Tee Times*	3 days
Comments	Well marked, large greens		
Directions	I-93, exit 2, right, right 1st light S. Policy Rd, right Rt 38, 1.5 mi, left		

Tee	Holes	Par	Rating	Slope	Yards
Red	18	71	68.4	114	5,056
White	18	71	66.4	112	5,746
Blue	18	71	69.5	120	6,249

14 Candia Woods
313 South Road, Candia, NH 03034
603-483-2307

Weekend Fee	$30	*Weekday Fee*	$23
Power Cart Fee	$22	*Pull Carts*	Yes
Putting Green	Yes	*Driving Range*	Yes
Season	Mar 15 - Dec 1	*Credit Cards*	Yes
Pro	Rich Thibeault	*Tee Times*	5 days
Comments	Flat and wide fairways, open links style		
Directions	I-93, exit 7, Rt 101E, exit 3, straight through stop sign, right at stop sign		

Tee	Holes	Par	Rating	Slope	Yards
Red	18	73	71.7	127	5,582
White	18	71	69.4	118	6,307
Blue	18	71	70.9	121	6,558

15 Carter Country Club
257 Mechanic Street, West Lebanon, NH 03784
603-448-4483

Weekend Fee	$20	*Weekday Fee*	$18
Power Cart Fee	$20	*Pull Carts*	Yes
Putting Green	Yes	*Driving Range*	No
Season	Apr 1 - Nov 1	*Credit Cards*	Yes
Pro	Harold Webb	*Tee Times*	7 days
Comments	Hilly, small greens, narrow fairways		
Directions	I-89, exit 19, follow signs		

Tee	Holes	Par	Rating	Slope	Yards
Red	9	72	68.1	118	4,952
White	9	72	66.1	116	5,610
Blue	9	72	66.1	116	6,046

16 Claremont Country Club
Maple Avenue, Claremont, NH 03743
603-542-9550

Weekend Fee	$22	*Weekday Fee*	$18
Power Cart Fee	$20	*Pull Carts*	Yes
Putting Green	Yes	*Driving Range*	No
Season	Apr - Nov	*Credit Cards*	No
Pro	Craig Gardner	*Tee Times*	No
Comments	Small greens, hilly		
Directions	I-91, Claremont exit, Pleasant St, right Maple Ave, 0.5 mi		

Tee	Holes	Par	Rating	Slope	Yards
Red	9	72	67.6	113	4,830
White	9	68	64.7	104	5,419
Blue	NA	NA	NA	NA	NA

17 Colebrook Country Club
Route 26, Colebrook, NH 03576
603-237-5566

Weekend Fee	$18	*Weekday Fee*	$18
Power Cart Fee	$20	*Pull Carts*	Yes
Putting Green	No	*Driving Range*	No
Season	May - Nov	*Credit Cards*	Yes
Pro	None	*Tee Times*	1 day
Comments	Lodging, unlimited play, par 6 hole		
Directions	I-93, Rt 3N from Littleton, right to Colebrook, Rt 26E, 0.5 mi		

Tee	Holes	Par	Rating	Slope	Yards
Red	9	72	72.3	105	4,178
White	9	72	67.1	105	5,893
Blue	NA	NA	NA	NA	NA

18 Country Club of New Hampshire
Kearsarge Valley Road, North Sutton, NH 03260
603-927-4246

Weekend Fee	$32	*Weekday Fee*	$25
Power Cart Fee	$22	*Pull Carts*	Yes
Putting Green	Yes	*Driving Range*	Yes
Season	Apr 1 - Nov 30	*Credit Cards*	Yes
Pro	Kevin Gibson	*Tee Times*	7 days
Comments	Lodging, rated in top 5 in NH		
Directions	I-89, exit 10, follow signs to Winslow State Park		

Tee	Holes	Par	Rating	Slope	Yards
Red	18	72	71.7	127	5,446
White	18	72	69.6	122	6,226
Blue	18	72	71.6	125	6,727

NEW HAMPSHIRE

19 Countryside Golf Club
20 Country Club Drive, Rt 13, Dunbarton, NH 03045
603-774-5031

Weekend Fee	$22	Weekday Fee	$18	
Power Cart Fee	$22	Pull Carts	Yes	
Putting Green	Yes	Driving Range	Yes	
Season	Apr 15 - Nov 15	Credit Cards	Yes	
Pro	Chuck Urwin	Tee Times	7 days	
Comments	Mountain views			
Directions	Rt 101, Rt 114, Rt 13N at superette, 4 mi			

Tee	Holes	Par	Rating	Slope	Yards
Red	9	72	71.5	126	5,516
White	9	72	70.5	129	6,002
Blue	9	72	71.1	132	6,314

22 Duston Country Club
40 Country Club Road, Hopkinton, NH 03229
603-746-4234

Weekend Fee	$16	Weekday Fee	$14	
Power Cart Fee	$16	Pull Carts	Yes	
Putting Green	Yes	Driving Range	No	
Season	Apr 15 - Nov 1	Credit Cards	Yes	
Pro	Bob White	Tee Times	3 days	
Comments	Semi-private, Scottish bunkers, lush greens			
Directions	I-89, exit 5, Rt 202/9, 3 mi, Country Club Rd exit, follow signs			

Tee	Holes	Par	Rating	Slope	Yards
Red	9	64	63.7	101	4,194
White	9	64	59.2	99	4,194
Blue	NA	NA	NA	NA	NA

20 Den Brae Golf Course
110 Prescott Road, Sanbornton, NH 03269
603-934-9818

Weekend Fee	$20	Weekday Fee	$18	
Power Cart Fee	$20	Pull Carts	Yes	
Putting Green	Yes	Driving Range	Yes	
Season	Apr - Oct	Credit Cards	Yes	
Pro	Gordon Craig	Tee Times	Yes	
Comments	Excellent greens			
Directions	I-93, exit 22, Rt 127S, 1.5 mi, right Prescott Rd, 0.3 mi			

Tee	Holes	Par	Rating	Slope	Yards
Red	9	72	70.9	126	5,236
White	9	72	67.1	109	5,926
Blue	NA	NA	NA	NA	NA

23 Eagle Mountain Resort
Carter Notch Road, Jackson, NH 03846
603-383-9111

Weekend Fee	$26	Weekday Fee	$20	
Power Cart Fee	$20	Pull Carts	Yes	
Putting Green	Yes	Driving Range	No	
Season	May 1 - Oct 20	Credit Cards	Yes	
Pro	None	Tee Times	1 day	
Comments	Lodging, mountain views			
Directions	I-95N, Spaulding Turnpike, Rt 16N, to Jackson, Carter Notch Rd			

Tee	Holes	Par	Rating	Slope	Yards
Red	9	70	NA	NA	4,252
White	9	64	NA	NA	4,252
Blue	NA	NA	NA	NA	NA

21 Derryfield Country Club
625 Mammouth Road, Manchester, NH 03104
603-669-0235

Weekend Fee	$24	Weekday Fee	$24	
Power Cart Fee	$20	Pull Carts	No	
Putting Green	Yes	Driving Range	No	
Season	Apr - Dec	Credit Cards	No	
Pro	Tim Gianferante	Tee Times	2 days	
Comments	Small greens, hilly, open fairways			
Directions	I-93N, exit 8, right, left 2nd light			

Tee	Holes	Par	Rating	Slope	Yards
Red	18	74	71.0	125	5,535
White	18	70	68.2	112	6,000
Blue	18	70	71.2	114	6,134

24 East Kingston Golf Course
Route 107, East Kingston, NH 03827
603-642-4414

Weekend Fee	$23	Weekday Fee	$20	
Power Cart Fee	$20	Pull Carts	Yes	
Putting Green	Yes	Driving Range	Yes	
Season	Apr - Nov	Credit Cards	No	
Pro	Frank Colanton	Tee Times	No	
Comments	Scenic, homes around course			
Directions	I-95, exit 1, Rt 107, 6 mi			

Tee	Holes	Par	Rating	Slope	Yards
Red	18	70	NA	NA	5,219
White	18	69	68.1	116	5,957
Blue	18	69	69.5	119	6,281

25 Eastman Golf Links
Clubhouse Lane, Old Rt 10, Grantham, NH 03753
603-863-4500

Weekend Fee	$38	*Weekday Fee*		$38
Power Cart Fee	$31	*Pull Carts*		Yes
Putting Green	Yes	*Driving Range*		Yes
Season	May 1 - Nov 1	*Credit Cards*		Yes
Pro	Dick Tuxbury	*Tee Times*		2 days
Comments	Rated in top 10 in NH, carts required wknds			
Directions	I-89, exit 13, course at exit			

Tee	Holes	Par	Rating	Slope	Yards
Red	18	73	71.9	128	5,369
White	18	71	71.7	133	6,338
Blue	18	71	73.5	137	6,731

26 Exeter Country Club
Jady Hill Lane, Exeter, NH 03833
603-778-8080

Weekend Fee	$22	*Weekday Fee*	$20
Power Cart Fee	$20	*Pull Carts*	Yes
Putting Green	Yes	*Driving Range*	No
Season	Apr 1 - Dec 1	*Credit Cards*	Yes
Pro	Don Folsom	*Tee Times*	No
Comments	Semi-private, rolling terrain, built 1889		
Directions	I-95, Rt 51/101N, Rt 108, left, right 3rd light, 1st left, 1st right, right end		

Tee	Holes	Par	Rating	Slope	Yards
Red	9	64	70.5	125	5,006
White	9	70	67.8	115	5,800
Blue	NA	NA	NA	NA	NA

27 Farmington Country Club
Henry Wilson Highway, Farmington, NH 03835
603-755-2412

Weekend Fee	$20	*Weekday Fee*	$15
Power Cart Fee	$20	*Pull Carts*	Yes
Putting Green	Yes	*Driving Range*	No
Season	Apr 15 - Oct 31	*Credit Cards*	No
Pro	Bert Prenaveau	*Tee Times*	3 days
Comments	Tee 8th from wood platform on hill		
Directions	I-95, Spaulding Turnpike, exit 15, Rt 11N, Rt 153, 1 mi		

Tee	Holes	Par	Rating	Slope	Yards
Red	9	68	66.8	113	4,690
White	9	64	61.8	95	4,690
Blue	NA	NA	NA	NA	NA

28 Green Meadow Golf Course - North
59 Steele Road, Hudson, NH 03051
603-889-1555

Weekend Fee	$30	*Weekday Fee*	$24
Power Cart Fee	$22	*Pull Carts*	Yes
Putting Green	Yes	*Driving Range*	Yes
Season	Year-round	*Credit Cards*	Yes
Pro	Patrick O'Keefe	*Tee Times*	7 days
Comments	Wide open and straight		
Directions	Rt 3, exit 34, right, left 1st light, left over bridge, Rt 3A 2.5 mi, left Steele		

Tee	Holes	Par	Rating	Slope	Yards
Red	18	72	68.3	113	5,100
White	18	72	67.6	109	6,088
Blue	18	72	67.6	109	6,500

29 Green Meadow Golf Course - South
59 Steele Road, Hudson, NH 03051
603-889-1555

Weekend Fee	$30	*Weekday Fee*	$24
Power Cart Fee	$22	*Pull Carts*	Yes
Putting Green	Yes	*Driving Range*	Yes
Season	Year-round	*Credit Cards*	Yes
Pro	Patrick O'Keefe	*Tee Times*	7 days
Comments	Hilly		
Directions	Rt 3, exit 34, right, left 1st light, left over bridge, Rt 3A 2.5 mi, left Steele		

Tee	Holes	Par	Rating	Slope	Yards
Red	18	72	71.2	120	5,200
White	18	72	69.3	113	6,182
Blue	18	72	70.0	114	6,600

30 Hale's Location Country Club
Westside Road, North Conway, NH 03860
603-356-2140

Weekend Fee	$35	*Weekday Fee*	$33
Power Cart Fee	$20	*Pull Carts*	Yes
Putting Green	Yes	*Driving Range*	No
Season	May - Nov	*Credit Cards*	Yes
Pro	Jonathan Rivers	*Tee Times*	7 days
Comments	Semi-private, views, elevated greens		
Directions	Rt 16 to Conway, take Washington St, right West Side Rd, 5 mi		

Tee	Holes	Par	Rating	Slope	Yards
Red	9	72	67.4	113	5,016
White	9	72	66.8	117	5,632
Blue	9	72	68.2	122	6,050

NEW HAMPSHIRE

31 Hanover Country Club
Rope Ferry Road, Hanover, NH 03755
603-646-2000

Weekend Fee	$31	Weekday Fee	$31
Power Cart Fee	$28	Pull Carts	Yes
Putting Green	Yes	Driving Range	Yes
Season	Apr 1 - Nov 1	Credit Cards	Yes
Pro	Bill Johnson	Tee Times	2 days
Comments	Semi-private, built in 1899, 4 practice holes		
Directions	I-89, Dartmouth exit, town center, Main St north, on north side of college		

Tee	Holes	Par	Rating	Slope	Yards
Red	18	73	72.7	127	5,468
White	18	69	68.7	118	5,876
Blue	NA	NA	NA	NA	NA

32 Highlands Links Colony Golf Club
Mount Prospect Rd, Holderness, NH 03264
603-536-3452

Weekend Fee	$15	Weekday Fee	$15
Power Cart Fee	$18	Pull Carts	Yes
Putting Green	Yes	Driving Range	No
Season	May 1 - Oct 12	Credit Cards	No
Pro	Joe Clark	Tee Times	7 days
Comments	Scenic, small greens		
Directions	I-93N, exit 25, left Holderness Rd, Rt 175S, 1st left after stop Mt. Prospect		

Tee	Holes	Par	Rating	Slope	Yards
Red	9	64	NA	NA	2,700
White	9	54	56.7	92	3,000
Blue	NA	NA	NA	NA	NA

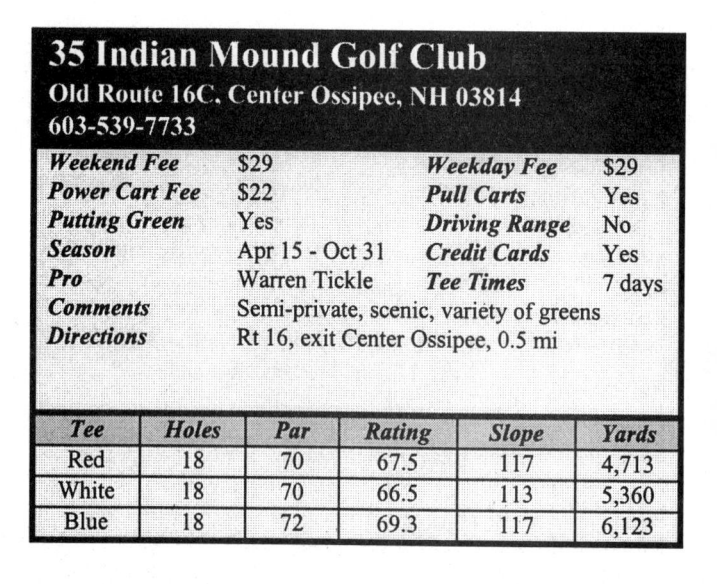

33 Hoodkroft Country Club
121 East Broadway, Derry, NH 03038
603-434-0651

Weekend Fee	$24	Weekday Fee	$22
Power Cart Fee	$24	Pull Carts	Yes
Putting Green	Yes	Driving Range	No
Season	Apr 1 - Nov 30	Credit Cards	No
Pro	Rich Berberian	Tee Times	4 days
Comments	Semi-private, flat, open, lots of water		
Directions	I-293, exit 4, Rt 102E, 2 mi		

Tee	Holes	Par	Rating	Slope	Yards
Red	9	70	70.1	117	5,152
White	9	71	70.1	121	6,466
Blue	NA	NA	NA	NA	NA

34 Hooper Golf Club
Prospect Hill Road, Walpole, NH 03608
603-756-4080

Weekend Fee	$22	Weekday Fee	$22
Power Cart Fee	$22	Pull Carts	Yes
Putting Green	Yes	Driving Range	No
Season	Apr 1 - Oct 31	Credit Cards	Yes
Pro	Jay Clace	Tee Times	No
Comments	Semi-private, fast greens, narrow fairways		
Directions	Rt 12N, right on South St, turns into Prospect Hill Rd		

Tee	Holes	Par	Rating	Slope	Yards
Red	9	72	73.5	132	5,522
White	9	72	69.3	122	6,038
Blue	NA	NA	NA	NA	NA

35 Indian Mound Golf Club
Old Route 16C, Center Ossipee, NH 03814
603-539-7733

Weekend Fee	$29	Weekday Fee	$29
Power Cart Fee	$22	Pull Carts	Yes
Putting Green	Yes	Driving Range	No
Season	Apr 15 - Oct 31	Credit Cards	Yes
Pro	Warren Tickle	Tee Times	7 days
Comments	Semi-private, scenic, variety of greens		
Directions	Rt 16, exit Center Ossipee, 0.5 mi		

Tee	Holes	Par	Rating	Slope	Yards
Red	18	70	67.5	117	4,713
White	18	70	66.5	113	5,360
Blue	18	72	69.3	117	6,123

36 Intervale Country Club
1491 Front Street, Manchester, NH 03102
603-647-6811

Weekend Fee	$25	Weekday Fee	$22
Power Cart Fee	$18	Pull Carts	Yes
Putting Green	Yes	Driving Range	No
Season	Apr - Dec	Credit Cards	No
Pro	Matt Thibeault	Tee Times	No
Comments	Semi-private, built 1903		
Directions	I-293N, exit 7, 0.8 mi		

Tee	Holes	Par	Rating	Slope	Yards
Red	9	76	71.4	120	5,676
White	9	72	68.8	107	6,074
Blue	NA	NA	NA	NA	NA

37 Jack O'Lantern Resort
Old Route 3, Box A, Woodstock, NH 03293
603-745-3636

Weekend Fee	$33	Weekday Fee	$30
Power Cart Fee	$24	Pull Carts	Yes
Putting Green	Yes	Driving Range	No
Season	May - Oct	Credit Cards	Yes
Pro	Fletcher Ivey	Tee Times	7 days
Comments	Mt scenery, small fast undulating greens		
Directions	I-93, exit 30		

Tee	Holes	Par	Rating	Slope	Yards
Red	18	70	68.9	114	4,725
White	18	70	67.5	113	5,829
Blue	NA	NA	NA	NA	NA

38 John H. Cain Golf Course
Unity Road, Newport, NH 03773
603-863-7787

Weekend Fee	$29	Weekday Fee	$25
Power Cart Fee	$24	Pull Carts	Yes
Putting Green	Yes	Driving Range	Yes
Season	Apr - Nov 1	Credit Cards	Yes
Pro	John Pawlak	Tee Times	7 days
Comments	Semi-private, lots of water		
Directions	I-89N, exit 9, Rt 103 to Newport, left Unity Rd, 1 mi		

Tee	Holes	Par	Rating	Slope	Yards
Red	18	71	69.1	123	4,738
White	18	71	68.3	127	6,005
Blue	18	71	71.4	133	6,415

39 Keene Country Club
755 West Hill Road, Keene, NH 03431
603-352-9722

Weekend Fee	$55	Weekday Fee	$55
Power Cart Fee	$20	Pull Carts	Yes
Putting Green	Yes	Driving Range	Yes
Season	Apr 15 - Nov 1	Credit Cards	Yes
Pro	Charlie Kamal	Tee Times	No
Comments	Semi-private, excellent greens, built 1900		
Directions	I-91, Keene exit, Rt 9, left flashing light West Hill Rd		

Tee	Holes	Par	Rating	Slope	Yards
Red	18	75	72.2	130	5,352
White	18	72	69.0	120	5,912
Blue	18	72	71.2	121	6,131

40 Kingswood Golf Club
Kingswood Road, Wolfeboro, NH 03894
603-569-3569

Weekend Fee	$35	Weekday Fee	$30
Power Cart Fee	$25	Pull Carts	Yes
Putting Green	Yes	Driving Range	Yes
Season	Apr - Oct 31	Credit Cards	No
Pro	David Pollini	Tee Times	3 days
Comments	Semi-private, hilly, 5 ponds, Ross design		
Directions	Rt 28N, 0.3 mi, left Kingswood Rd		

Tee	Holes	Par	Rating	Slope	Yards
Red	18	72	73.1	130	5,305
White	18	72	68.8	125	5,860
Blue	18	72	71.1	128	6,325

41 Kona Mansion Inn
Moultonboro Neck Road, Moultonboro, NH 03254
603-253-4900

Weekend Fee	$13	Weekday Fee	$13
Power Cart Fee	No carts	Pull Carts	Yes
Putting Green	No	Driving Range	No
Season	May 1 - Nov 1	Credit Cards	Yes
Pro	Kevin Crowley	Tee Times	No
Comments	Short par 3		
Directions	Rt 25E, take Moultonboro Neck Rd, 2 mi		

Tee	Holes	Par	Rating	Slope	Yards
Red	9	54	64.2	111	4,680
White	9	54	64.2	111	4,680
Blue	NA	NA	NA	NA	NA

42 Laconia Country Club
607 Elm Street, Laconia, NH 03246
603-524-1273

Weekend Fee	$65	Weekday Fee	$65
Power Cart Fee	Included	Pull Carts	No
Putting Green	Yes	Driving Range	Yes
Season	Apr 15 - Nov 15	Credit Cards	Yes
Pro	Mike Marquis	Tee Times	7 days
Comments	Long course		
Directions	I-93N, exit 20, left, 7 mi, left Elm St		

Tee	Holes	Par	Rating	Slope	Yards
Red	18	73	72.1	125	5,550
White	18	72	70.7	126	6,253
Blue	18	72	71.3	128	6,500

NEW HAMPSHIRE

43 Lakeview Golf Club
Ladd Hill Road, Belmont, NH 03220
603-524-2220

Weekend Fee	$20	Weekday Fee	$20
Power Cart Fee	$20	Pull Carts	Yes
Putting Green	Yes	Driving Range	No
Season	May - Oct	Credit Cards	No
Pro	None	Tee Times	No
Comments	Views of the Mts and lake		
Directions	I-93N, exit 20, Rt 3E, 1 mi after bridge, right at light across Belknap Mall		

Tee	Holes	Par	Rating	Slope	Yards
Red	NA	NA	NA	NA	NA
White	18	70	69.0	NA	6,220
Blue	NA	NA	NA	NA	NA

44 Lisbon Village Country Club
Bishop Road, Lisbon, NH 03053
603-838-6004

Weekend Fee	$20	Weekday Fee	$20
Power Cart Fee	$20	Pull Carts	Yes
Putting Green	Yes	Driving Range	No
Season	May - Oct	Credit Cards	Yes
Pro	Enie Lyndes	Tee Times	7 days
Comments	Accuracy a must		
Directions	I-93, exit 42, Rt 302W, 7 mi, right Lyman Rd, left Bishop Rd		

Tee	Holes	Par	Rating	Slope	Yards
Red	9	72	70.6	127	5,120
White	9	72	67.9	126	5,782
Blue	9	72	NA	NA	5,842

45 Lochmere Golf and Country Club
Rural Route 3, Tilton, NH 03276
603-528-4653

Weekend Fee	$24	Weekday Fee	$20
Power Cart Fee	$20	Pull Carts	Yes
Putting Green	Yes	Driving Range	Yes
Season	Apr 1 - Oct 1	Credit Cards	No
Pro	Vic Stanfield	Tee Times	2 days
Comments	10th hole part of future expansion		
Directions	I-93, exit 20, Rt 3E, 1.5 mi		

Tee	Holes	Par	Rating	Slope	Yards
Red	10	72	68.7	113	5,102
White	10	71	68.7	126	6,010
Blue	NA	NA	NA	NA	NA

46 Londonderry Country Club
56 Kimball Road, Londonderry, NH 03053
603-432-9789

Weekend Fee	$22	Weekday Fee	$20
Power Cart Fee	$16	Pull Carts	Yes
Putting Green	Yes	Driving Range	No
Season	Apr - Nov	Credit Cards	No
Pro	None	Tee Times	2 days
Comments	Executive par 3, excellent greens		
Directions	I-93, exit 4, left Rt 102, right Rt 128, 4 mi, Litchfield Rd, left Kimball Rd		

Tee	Holes	Par	Rating	Slope	Yards
Red	18	62	57.4	87	3,210
White	18	62	57.2	86	3,740
Blue	NA	NA	NA	NA	NA

47 Loudon Country Club
653 Route 106 North, Loudon, NH 03301
603-783-3372

Weekend Fee	$22	Weekday Fee	$20
Power Cart Fee	$18	Pull Carts	Yes
Putting Green	Yes	Driving Range	Yes
Season	Apr 15 - Nov 15	Credit Cards	Yes
Pro	Reggie Ridlon	Tee Times	7 days
Comments	Challenging, narrow fairways, ponds		
Directions	I-93, Rt 9/202E, Rt 106N		

Tee	Holes	Par	Rating	Slope	Yards
Red	9	72	NA	NA	4,352
White	9	70	69.2	123	5,534
Blue	9	70	NA	NA	6,008

48 Maplewood Casino & Golf Course
Main Street, Route 302, Bethlehem, NH 03574
603-869-3335

Weekend Fee	$22	Weekday Fee	$20
Power Cart Fee	$22	Pull Carts	Yes
Putting Green	Yes	Driving Range	Yes
Season	May 1 - Oct 15	Credit Cards	Yes
Pro	Roger Peabody	Tee Times	7 days
Comments	#16 is par 6 651 yards, D. Ross design		
Directions	I-93, exit 40, Rt 302E, 5 mi		

Tee	Holes	Par	Rating	Slope	Yards
Red	18	71	68.8	113	5,013
White	18	72	67.4	109	6,001
Blue	NA	NA	NA	NA	NA

49 Mojalaki Country Club
4653 Prospect Street, Franklin, NH 03235
603-934-3033

Weekend Fee	$22	*Weekday Fee*	$18
Power Cart Fee	$20	*Pull Carts*	Yes
Putting Green	Yes	*Driving Range*	No
Season	Apr - Nov	*Credit Cards*	No
Pro	Eleanor Pines	*Tee Times*	1 day
Comments	2 sets of tees, mountain views		
Directions	I-93, exit 20, Rt 3S, 4 mi, center Franklin, left Prospect St		

Tee	Holes	Par	Rating	Slope	Yards
Red	9	70	71.1	117	4,942
White	9	70	69.4	122	5,970
Blue	NA	NA	NA	NA	NA

50 Monadnock Country Club
49 High Street, Peterborough, NH 03458
603-924-7769

Weekend Fee	$15	*Weekday Fee*	$13
Power Cart Fee	No carts	*Pull Carts*	Yes
Putting Green	Yes	*Driving Range*	No
Season	Apr 15 - Nov 7	*Credit Cards*	Yes
Pro	None	*Tee Times*	No
Comments	Semi-private, scenic, built in 1901		
Directions	Rt 101, Peterborough, High St		

Tee	Holes	Par	Rating	Slope	Yards
Red	9	64	57.3	87	3,152
White	9	58	54.0	76	3,152
Blue	NA	NA	NA	NA	NA

51 Mountain View Golf & C. C.
Mountain View Road, Whitefield, NH 03598
603-837-3885

Weekend Fee	$20	*Weekday Fee*	$20
Power Cart Fee	$20	*Pull Carts*	Yes
Putting Green	Yes	*Driving Range*	No
Season	May - Oct	*Credit Cards*	No
Pro	Gary Roy	*Tee Times*	2 days
Comments	Semi-private, built in 1908, narrow course		
Directions	From main road thru Whitefield, take Rt 116, 2 mi		

Tee	Holes	Par	Rating	Slope	Yards
Red	9	70	71.9	103	5,740
White	9	70	67.3	109	5,874
Blue	9	70	69.7	112	6,240

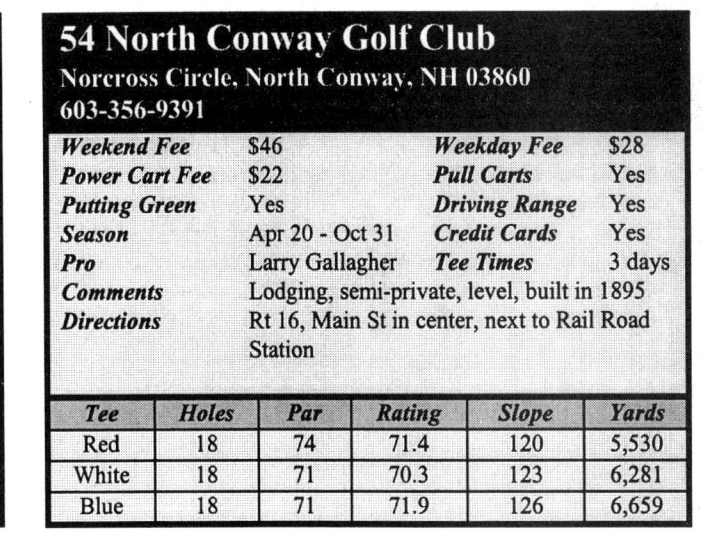

52 Mount Washington Golf Club
Route 302, Bretton Woods, NH 03575
603-278-1000

Weekend Fee	$29	*Weekday Fee*	$25
Power Cart Fee	$22	*Pull Carts*	Yes
Putting Green	Yes	*Driving Range*	No
Season	May - Oct	*Credit Cards*	Yes
Pro	Fran O'Brien	*Tee Times*	7 days
Comments	Lodging, 18 hole putting green		
Directions	I-93, exit 35, Rt 302 to Bretton Woods		

Tee	Holes	Par	Rating	Slope	Yards
Red	18	70	69.0	120	5,336
White	18	70	69.0	120	6,154
Blue	18	70	71.0	123	6,638

53 Nippo Lake Golf Club
550 Province Road, Barrington, NH 03825
603-664-7616

Weekend Fee	$20	*Weekday Fee*	$18
Power Cart Fee	$20	*Pull Carts*	Yes
Putting Green	Yes	*Driving Range*	Yes
Season	Apr 1 - Oct 31	*Credit Cards*	Yes
Pro	Geoff Williams	*Tee Times*	2 days
Comments	Semi-private, scenic, country setting		
Directions	Spaulding Turnpike north, exit 13 Rt 202N, right Rt 126, 0.2 mi, left		

Tee	Holes	Par	Rating	Slope	Yards
Red	9	70	65.8	103	4,746
White	9	68	64.5	105	5,172
Blue	NA	NA	NA	NA	NA

54 North Conway Golf Club
Norcross Circle, North Conway, NH 03860
603-356-9391

Weekend Fee	$46	*Weekday Fee*	$28
Power Cart Fee	$22	*Pull Carts*	Yes
Putting Green	Yes	*Driving Range*	Yes
Season	Apr 20 - Oct 31	*Credit Cards*	Yes
Pro	Larry Gallagher	*Tee Times*	3 days
Comments	Lodging, semi-private, level, built in 1895		
Directions	Rt 16, Main St in center, next to Rail Road Station		

Tee	Holes	Par	Rating	Slope	Yards
Red	18	74	71.4	120	5,530
White	18	71	70.3	123	6,281
Blue	18	71	71.9	126	6,659

NEW HAMPSHIRE

55 Oak Hill Golf Club
159 Pease Road, Meredith, NH 03253
603-279-4438

Weekend Fee	$17	*Weekday Fee*	$17
Power Cart Fee	$18	*Pull Carts*	Yes
Putting Green	Yes	*Driving Range*	No
Season	Apr 20 - Nov 20	*Credit Cards*	Yes
Pro	None	*Tee Times*	No
Comments	Semi-private, wooded, scenic		
Directions	I-93, Rt 104E, 8.5 mi, right Pease Rd		

Tee	Holes	Par	Rating	Slope	Yards
Red	9	68	64.6	107	3,962
White	9	68	60.6	90	4,468
Blue	NA	NA	NA	NA	NA

56 Overlook Country Club
5 Overlook Drive, Hollis, NH 03049
603-465-2909

Weekend Fee	$35	*Weekday Fee*	$28
Power Cart Fee	$22	*Pull Carts*	Yes
Putting Green	Yes	*Driving Range*	No
Season	Apr - Oct	*Credit Cards*	Yes
Pro	Dick Dichard	*Tee Times*	7 days
Comments	Bunkers throughout, flat, many trees		
Directions	Rt 3, exit 5W Rt 111W, 4 mi		

Tee	Holes	Par	Rating	Slope	Yards
Red	18	72	70.4	126	5,230
White	18	71	69.0	128	6,051
Blue	18	71	69.7	130	6,539

57 Passaconaway Country Club
12 Midway Avenue, Litchfield, NH 03103
603-424-4653

Weekend Fee	$35	*Weekday Fee*	$25
Power Cart Fee	$20	*Pull Carts*	Yes
Putting Green	Yes	*Driving Range*	Yes
Season	Apr 1 - Nov 30	*Credit Cards*	Yes
Pro	Eben Wheeler	*Tee Times*	5 days
Comments	Links, undulating greens, water hazards		
Directions	I-293, exit, Rt 3A, south 6 mi		

Tee	Holes	Par	Rating	Slope	Yards
Red	18	72	70.3	118	5,369
White	18	71	70.7	123	6,462
Blue	18	71	72.3	126	6,855

58 Pease Golf Course
2 Sherburne Road, Portsmouth, NH 03801
603-433-1331

Weekend Fee	$26	*Weekday Fee*	$26
Power Cart Fee	$20	*Pull Carts*	Yes
Putting Green	Yes	*Driving Range*	Yes
Season	Mar - Dec	*Credit Cards*	Yes
Pro	Chris Loch	*Tee Times*	3 days
Comments	Small and fast greens, narrow fairways		
Directions	I-95N, exit 3, Rt 101E, Sherbourne Rd		

Tee	Holes	Par	Rating	Slope	Yards
Red	18	71	69.9	115	5,291
White	18	70	67.8	114	5,820
Blue	18	70	68.7	116	6,228

59 Perry Hollow Golf & Country Club
Middleton Road, Wolfboro, NH 03894
603-569-3055

Weekend Fee	$30	*Weekday Fee*	$30
Power Cart Fee	$25	*Pull Carts*	Yes
Putting Green	Yes	*Driving Range*	Yes
Season	May 1 - Nov 15	*Credit Cards*	Yes
Pro	Karen Chase	*Tee Times*	7 days
Comments	Cut through woods, great views		
Directions	From Wolfboro, Rt 28S, 2.5 mi, Middleton Rd		

Tee	Holes	Par	Rating	Slope	Yards
Red	18	70	74.6	135	4,512
White	18	71	69.9	129	5,927
Blue	18	70	71.5	132	6,256

60 Pheasant Ridge Country Club
Frank Bean Road, Gilford, NH 03246
603-524-7808

Weekend Fee	$22	*Weekday Fee*	$20
Power Cart Fee	$20	*Pull Carts*	Yes
Putting Green	Yes	*Driving Range*	No
Season	Apr - Nov	*Credit Cards*	Yes
Pro	Jim Swarthout	*Tee Times*	4 days
Comments	Wide with mountain views		
Directions	I-93, exit 20, Rt 3N, 13 mi onto Rt 3/11, 2nd exit, right, right, 0.5 mi		

Tee	Holes	Par	Rating	Slope	Yards
Red	9	70	70.1	116	5,144
White	9	70	67.1	103	6,044
Blue	NA	NA	NA	NA	NA

NEW HAMPSHIRE

61 Pine Grove Springs Country Club
Route 9A, Spofford, NH 03462
603-363-4433

Weekend Fee	$20	Weekday Fee	$15
Power Cart Fee	$19	Pull Carts	Yes
Putting Green	Yes	Driving Range	No
Season	Apr 1 - Oct 31	Credit Cards	Yes
Pro	None	Tee Times	7 days
Comments	Tight fairways, fast greens, semi-private		
Directions	Rt 101, Rt 9W, 8 mi		

Tee	Holes	Par	Rating	Slope	Yards
Red	9	70	70.1	115	5,600
White	9	68	70.8	132	5,980
Blue	NA	NA	NA	NA	NA

62 Pine Valley Golf Links
246 Old Gage Hill Road, Pelham, NH 03076
603-635-8305

Weekend Fee	$22	Weekday Fee	$17
Power Cart Fee	$19	Pull Carts	Yes
Putting Green	Yes	Driving Range	No
Season	Mar - Dec	Credit Cards	Yes
Pro	Todd Madden	Tee Times	7 days
Comments	Semi-private, tight fairways, fast greens		
Directions	I-93, exit 1, Rt 38S, 5 mi		

Tee	Holes	Par	Rating	Slope	Yards
Red	9	72	70.0	125	5,410
White	9	70	67.0	119	5,820
Blue	9	70	68.9	120	6,030

63 Plausawa Valley Country Club
42 Whittemore Street, Pembroke, NH 03275
603-224-6267

Weekend Fee	$30	Weekday Fee	$27
Power Cart Fee	$24	Pull Carts	Yes
Putting Green	Yes	Driving Range	Yes
Season	Apr 1 - Dec 1	Credit Cards	Yes
Pro	Lionel Dupuis	Tee Times	7 days
Comments	Semi-private, undulating greens		
Directions	I-93, exit 3, Rt 3S, 4 mi		

Tee	Holes	Par	Rating	Slope	Yards
Red	18	73	71.5	128	5,416
White	18	72	70.6	131	6,162
Blue	18	72	72.6	137	6,572

64 Ponemah Greens
55 Ponemah Road, Amherst, NH 03031
603-672-4732

Weekend Fee	$23	Weekday Fee	$21
Power Cart Fee	$22	Pull Carts	Yes
Putting Green	Yes	Driving Range	Yes
Season	Apr 1 - Nov 1	Credit Cards	Yes
Pro	None	Tee Times	3 days
Comments	Scottish links course, 1 very large green		
Directions	I-293, Rt 101W, Amherst, Rt 122, 0.5 mi past Amherst Country Club		

Tee	Holes	Par	Rating	Slope	Yards
Red	9	68	71.0	104	3,608
White	9	68	59.7	97	4,042
Blue	NA	NA	NA	NA	NA

65 Portsmouth Country Club
1 Country Club Lane, Exeter, NH 03833
603-436-9719

Weekend Fee	$50	Weekday Fee	$50
Power Cart Fee	$20	Pull Carts	Yes
Putting Green	Yes	Driving Range	Yes
Season	Apr - Dec	Credit Cards	Yes
Pro	Joel St. Laurent	Tee Times	1 day
Comments	Semi-private, along coastal marsh		
Directions	I-95, Rt 101W Greenland exit, follow signs, 2 mi		

Tee	Holes	Par	Rating	Slope	Yards
Red	18	78	77.1	135	6,202
White	18	72	72	122	6,609
Blue	18	72	74.1	127	7,050

66 Profile Golf Club
Profile Road, Franconia, NH 03580
603-823-9568

Weekend Fee	$15	Weekday Fee	$14
Power Cart Fee	$18	Pull Carts	Yes
Putting Green	Yes	Driving Range	No
Season	May - Nov	Credit Cards	No
Pro	Chuck McLure	Tee Times	No
Comments	Semi-private		
Directions	I-93, exit 37, Rt 116 (Profile Rd)		

Tee	Holes	Par	Rating	Slope	Yards
Red	NA	NA	NA	NA	NA
White	9	72	70.2	129	6,003
Blue	NA	NA	NA	NA	NA

NEW HAMPSHIRE

67 Rochester Country Club
Church Street, Rochester, NH 03867
603-332-9892

Weekend Fee	$45	Weekday Fee	$40
Power Cart Fee	Included	Pull Carts	No
Putting Green	Yes	Driving Range	No
Season	May - Nov	Credit Cards	Yes
Pro	Ted Seavey	Tee Times	No
Comments	Semi-private, hilly, narrow		
Directions	Spaulding Turnpike, exit 12, Rt 125S, 1.5 mi		

Tee	Holes	Par	Rating	Slope	Yards
Red	18	73	70.4	123	5,414
White	18	72	68.7	123	6,317
Blue	18	72	72.2	125	6,596

68 Rockingham Country Club
200 Exeter Road, Newmarket, NH 03857
603-659-9956

Weekend Fee	$20	Weekday Fee	$20
Power Cart Fee	$20	Pull Carts	Yes
Putting Green	Yes	Driving Range	No
Season	May 1 - Oct 30	Credit Cards	No
Pro	Mark Taylor	Tee Times	5 days
Comments	Sloped greens, tree lined fairways		
Directions	I-95, Hampton exit, Rt 51E, Rt 108N		

Tee	Holes	Par	Rating	Slope	Yards
Red	9	70	64.2	111	6,102
White	9	70	65.3	113	6,150
Blue	NA	NA	NA	NA	NA

69 Sagamore-Hampton Golf Course
101 North Road, North Hampton, NH 03862
603-964-5341

Weekend Fee	$25	Weekday Fee	$25
Power Cart Fee	No carts	Pull Carts	Yes
Putting Green	No	Driving Range	No
Season	Apr 15 - Dec 24	Credit Cards	No
Pro	None	Tee Times	7 days
Comments	Organically maintained		
Directions	I-95, exit 2, right Rt 51W, 1.2 mi, right Rt 111, 2.5 mi, left Rt 151N		

Tee	Holes	Par	Rating	Slope	Yards
Red	18	71	67.1	101	5,822
White	18	71	70.5	101	6,489
Blue	NA	NA	NA	NA	NA

70 Shattuck Golf Course
P.O. Box 540, 28 Dublin Road, Jaffrey, NH 03452
603-532-4300

Weekend Fee	$35	Weekday Fee	$35
Power Cart Fee	$22	Pull Carts	Yes
Putting Green	Yes	Driving Range	Yes
Season	May - Dec 1	Credit Cards	Yes
Pro	Lyman Doane	Tee Times	4 days
Comments	Lots of water, rated #1 in NH		
Directions	Rt 202N, Rt 124 Jaffrey center, Rt 124W, 2.3 mi		

Tee	Holes	Par	Rating	Slope	Yards
Red	18	71	73.1	139	4,632
White	18	71	71	143	6,077
Blue	18	71	74.1	145	6,701

71 Sky Meadow Country Club
25 Sky Meadow Drive, Nashua, NH 03062
603-888-9000

Weekend Fee	$85	Weekday Fee	$65
Power Cart Fee	Included	Pull Carts	No
Putting Green	Yes	Driving Range	Yes
Season	Apr 15 - Nov 1	Credit Cards	Yes
Pro	Rich Ingraham	Tee Times	2 days
Comments	Semi-private, highly rated, beautiful views		
Directions	Rt 3N, exit 1, left Spitbrook Rd, 2 mi		

Tee	Holes	Par	Rating	Slope	Yards
Red	18	74	71.2	131	5,127
White	18	72	70.8	128	6,036
Blue	18	72	73.3	133	6,590

72 Souhegan Woods Golf Course
65 Thornton Ferry Road, Amherst, NH 03031
603-673-0200

Weekend Fee	$32	Weekday Fee	$25
Power Cart Fee	$22	Pull Carts	No
Putting Green	Yes	Driving Range	Yes
Season	Apr - Nov	Credit Cards	Yes
Pro	Bill Meier	Tee Times	5 days
Comments	70 sand bunkers, water on 5 holes		
Directions	Rt 3N, exit 11, left end of ramp, first right, 4 miles		

Tee	Holes	Par	Rating	Slope	Yards
Red	18	71	65.6	111	5,423
White	18	72	68.7	117	6,122
Blue	18	72	69.5	119	6,497

73 Sunningdale Golf Club
301 Green Street, Somersworth, NH 03878
603-742-8056

Weekend Fee	$24	Weekday Fee	$21
Power Cart Fee	$22	Pull Carts	Yes
Putting Green	Yes	Driving Range	Yes
Season	Apr - Nov	Credit Cards	No
Pro	Alan Richard	Tee Times	7 days
Comments	Semi-private, hilly and narrow		
Directions	Spaulding Turnpike, exit 9, Rt 9E, right Stackpole Rd past Walmart, right		

Tee	Holes	Par	Rating	Slope	Yards
Red	9	74	72.5	126	6,040
White	9	72	70.4	121	6,660
Blue	9	72	70.5	125	6,870

74 Sunset Hill Golf Links
Sunset Rd, Sugar Hill, NH 03585
603-823-8585

Weekend Fee	$20	Weekday Fee	$18
Power Cart Fee	$20	Pull Carts	Yes
Putting Green	Yes	Driving Range	Yes
Season	May 1 - Nov 1	Credit Cards	No
Pro	Richard Thomas	Tee Times	No
Comments	View White and Green Mts, built 1900		
Directions	I-93, exit 38, right over bridge, Sugar Hill Rd (Rt 117), left Sunset, 0.5 mi		

Tee	Holes	Par	Rating	Slope	Yards
Red	9	66	NA	NA	3,954
White	9	66	58.2	81	3,954
Blue	NA	NA	NA	NA	NA

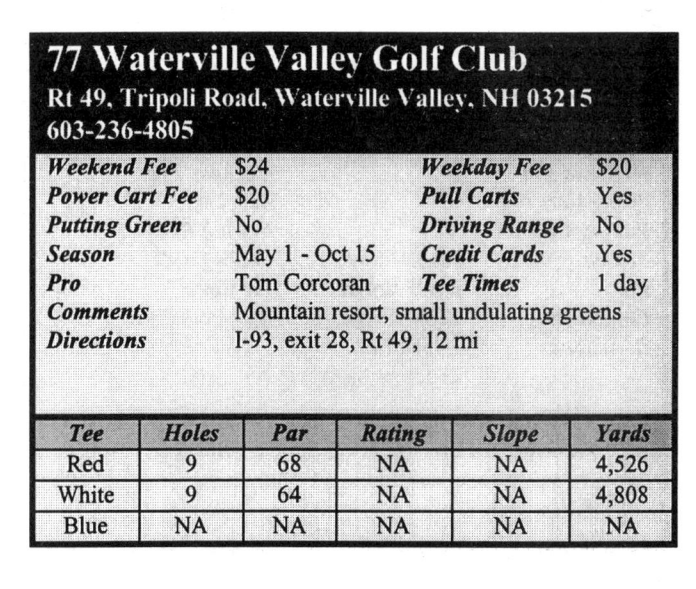

75 Tory Pines Resort
Box 655, Route 47, Francestown, NH 03043
603-588-2000

Weekend Fee	$32	Weekday Fee	$25
Power Cart Fee	$24	Pull Carts	Yes
Putting Green	Yes	Driving Range	Yes
Season	Apr 15 - Nov 15	Credit Cards	Yes
Pro	Peter Bonasia	Tee Times	3 days
Comments	Golf school, Ross design, elevated greens		
Directions	Rt 3N, Rt 101A W, right Rt 13, Rt 136 to Francestown, right Rt 47, 4 mi		

Tee	Holes	Par	Rating	Slope	Yards
Red	18	71	70.8	124	4,669
White	18	71	67.5	126	5,560
Blue	18	71	69.6	129	6,141

76 Twin Lake Village Golf Club
21 Twin Lake Village Road, New London, NH 03257
603-526-6460

Weekend Fee	$19	Weekday Fee	$16
Power Cart Fee	No carts	Pull Carts	Yes
Putting Green	Yes	Driving Range	No
Season	May 1 - Oct 31	Credit Cards	No
Pro	Carl Luthran	Tee Times	7 days
Comments	Easy par 3, mainly flat		
Directions	I-89, exit 11, Rt 11E, thru New London, take Little Lake Sunnapee Rd		

Tee	Holes	Par	Rating	Slope	Yards
Red	9	54	NA	NA	2,302
White	9	54	NA	NA	2,424
Blue	9	54	NA	NA	2,992

77 Waterville Valley Golf Club
Rt 49, Tripoli Road, Waterville Valley, NH 03215
603-236-4805

Weekend Fee	$24	Weekday Fee	$20
Power Cart Fee	$20	Pull Carts	Yes
Putting Green	No	Driving Range	No
Season	May 1 - Oct 15	Credit Cards	Yes
Pro	Tom Corcoran	Tee Times	1 day
Comments	Mountain resort, small undulating greens		
Directions	I-93, exit 28, Rt 49, 12 mi		

Tee	Holes	Par	Rating	Slope	Yards
Red	9	68	NA	NA	4,526
White	9	64	NA	NA	4,808
Blue	NA	NA	NA	NA	NA

78 Waukewan Golf Club
Waukewan Road, PO Box 403, Meredith, NH 03253
603-279-6661

Weekend Fee	$25	Weekday Fee	$25
Power Cart Fee	$20	Pull Carts	Yes
Putting Green	Yes	Driving Range	Yes
Season	Apr 15 - Nov 15	Credit Cards	Yes
Pro	Dexter Hale	Tee Times	2 days
Comments	Views of White Mts, narrow fairways		
Directions	I-93N, exit 23, Rt 104 to Meredith, Rt 3N Plymouth, 3 mi, left Waukewan		

Tee	Holes	Par	Rating	Slope	Yards
Red	18	73	68.7	112	5,010
White	18	71	67.1	120	5,735
Blue	NA	NA	NA	NA	NA

NEW HAMPSHIRE

79 Waumbek Inn & Country Club
Rt 2 (center of town), Jefferson, NH 03583
603-586-7777

Weekend Fee	$18	Weekday Fee	$18
Power Cart Fee	$18	Pull Carts	Yes
Putting Green	Yes	Driving Range	No
Season	Apr 1 - Nov 1	Credit Cards	No
Pro	Bob Dichard	Tee Times	No
Comments	Lodging, built 1895, fast large greens		
Directions	I-93, Twin Mountain, Rt 115, left Rt 2, past Six Gun Town		

Tee	Holes	Par	Rating	Slope	Yards
Red	18	73	66.0	107	4,772
White	18	71	69.9	107	5,874
Blue	NA	NA	NA	NA	NA

80 Wentworth-By-The-Sea
Wentworth Road, Rt 1B, Portsmouth, NH 03854
603-433-5010

Weekend Fee	$75	Weekday Fee	$75
Power Cart Fee	$28	Pull Carts	Yes
Putting Green	Yes	Driving Range	No
Season	Apr 1 - Nov 1	Credit Cards	Yes
Pro	Dan Franzoso	Tee Times	5 days
Comments	Semi-private, great views, built in 1897		
Directions	I-95N, exit 3, right, 1.7 mi, right fork, right 2nd light Sagamore Ave, 1st left		

Tee	Holes	Par	Rating	Slope	Yards
Red	18	70	70.5	119	6,000
White	18	70	66.7	121	6,100
Blue	18	70	67.8	123	6,300

81 Wentworth Resort Golf Club
Route 16A, Jackson, NH 03846
603-383-9641

Weekend Fee	$35	Weekday Fee	$25
Power Cart Fee	$22	Pull Carts	Yes
Putting Green	Yes	Driving Range	No
Season	May 10 - Oct 1	Credit Cards	Yes
Pro	Bob McGraw	Tee Times	5 days
Comments	2nd oldest in NH, carts required wknd am		
Directions	I-95, Spaulding Turnpike, Rt 16 to Jackson Village		

Tee	Holes	Par	Rating	Slope	Yards
Red	18	69	69.8	118	4,910
White	18	69	63.9	105	5,305
Blue	NA	NA	NA	NA	NA

82 Whip-Poor-Will Golf Club
55 Marsh Road, Hudson, NH 03051
603-889-9706

Weekend Fee	$24	Weekday Fee	$20
Power Cart Fee	$22	Pull Carts	Yes
Putting Green	Yes	Driving Range	No
Season	Apr 1 - Nov 25	Credit Cards	Yes
Pro	Phil Friel	Tee Times	7 days
Comments	Golf packages, small greens, hilly		
Directions	I-93, exit 4, Rt 102W, 7 mi, Marsh Rd right after High School		

Tee	Holes	Par	Rating	Slope	Yards
Red	9	72	69.9	119	5,094
White	9	72	67.8	120	5,980
Blue	NA	NA	NA	NA	NA

83 White Mountain Country Club
North Ashland Road, Ashland, NH 03217
603-536-2227

Weekend Fee	$29	Weekday Fee	$23
Power Cart Fee	$22	Pull Carts	Yes
Putting Green	Yes	Driving Range	Yes
Season	May - Oct	Credit Cards	Yes
Pro	Gregg Sufat	Tee Times	7 days
Comments	Small airport between 3rd and 5th holes		
Directions	I-93N, exit 24, left, 1 mi, right North Ashland Rd, 2.5 mi		

Tee	Holes	Par	Rating	Slope	Yards
Red	18	73	70.2	118	5,410
White	18	71	68.6	121	5,974
Blue	18	71	70.4	125	6,408

84 Windham Country Club
Londonderry Road, Windham, NH 03087
603-434-2093

Weekend Fee	$35	Weekday Fee	$30
Power Cart Fee	$24	Pull Carts	Yes
Putting Green	Yes	Driving Range	Yes
Season	Apr - Snow	Credit Cards	Yes
Pro	Bill Flynn	Tee Times	Yes
Comments	Lot of woods, narrow, tough course		
Directions	I-93N, exit 3 Rt 111, left, 1.8 mi, right Church St, right at end, 1.2 mi left		

Tee	Holes	Par	Rating	Slope	Yards
Red	18	72	67.3	128	5,584
White	18	72	69.1	132	6,013
Blue	18	72	71.3	136	6,442

NEW HAMPSHIRE

85 Woodbound Inn Golf Club
Woodbound Road, Jaffrey, NH 03452
603-532-8341

Weekend Fee	$12	*Weekday Fee*	$12
Power Cart Fee	No carts	*Pull Carts*	Yes
Putting Green	Yes	*Driving Range*	No
Season	Apr 1 - Oct 30	*Credit Cards*	Yes
Pro	Skip Sullivan	*Tee Times*	No
Comments	Semi-private, view of lake		
Directions	I-495, Rt 119W, 10 mi, follow signs		

Tee	Holes	Par	Rating	Slope	Yards
Red	9	54	NA	NA	1,956
White	9	54	NA	NA	1,956
Blue	NA	NA	NA	NA	NA

Blackmount
North Haverhill, NH
603-787-6564

Weekend Fee	$	*Weekday Fee*	$
Power Cart Fee	$	*Pull Carts*	
Putting Green		*Driving Range*	
Season		*Credit Cards*	
Pro		*Tee Times*	
Comments	Opened late 1996		
Directions			

Tee	Holes	Par	Rating	Slope	Yards
Red					
White					
Blue					

Information on several courses recently or soon to be opened was obtained too late to include them in the alphabetical listing or location maps in this book.

Atkinson Country Club & Resort
19 Providence Hill Road, Atkinson, NH 03811
603-362-5681

Weekend Fee	$27	*Weekday Fee*	$22
Power Cart Fee	$22	*Pull Carts*	Yes
Putting Green	Yes	*Driving Range*	No
Season	Apr 1 - Oct 30	*Credit Cards*	NA
Pro	Joe Healey	*Tee Times*	Yes
Comments	Built in 1996		
Directions	Call ahead for directions		

Tee	Holes	Par	Rating	Slope	Yards
Red	9	72	NA	NA	4,894
White	9	72	NA	NA	6,254
Blue	9	72	NA	NA	6,730

Fore-U-Golf Center
West Lebanon, NH
603-298-9702

Weekend Fee	$8	*Weekday Fee*	$8
Power Cart Fee	None	*Pull Carts*	Yes
Putting Green	Yes	*Driving Range*	Yes
Season	Mar 15 - Nov 1	*Credit Cards*	No
Pro	Mark Johnson	*Tee Times*	No
Comments	Night golf, artificial greens		
Directions	I-89, exit 20, Rt 12A south, 1 mi		

Tee	Holes	Par	Rating	Slope	Yards
Red	9	54	NA	NA	2,058
White	9	54	NA	NA	2,058
Blue	NA	NA	NA	NA	NA

Balsams - Coashaukee Golf Course
Route 26, Dixville Notch, NH 03576
603-255-4961

Weekend Fee	$25	*Weekday Fee*	$25
Power Cart Fee	$25	*Pull Carts*	Yes
Putting Green	Yes	*Driving Range*	No
Season	May 1 - Oct 15	*Credit Cards*	Yes
Pro	Bill Hamblen	*Tee Times*	No
Comments	Next to resort		
Directions	I-93N, exit 35, Rt 3N, Rt 26E, 10 mi		

Tee	Holes	Par	Rating	Slope	Yards
Red	9	64	57.2	78	3,834
White	9	64	57.2	78	3,834
Blue	NA	NA	NA	NA	NA

Kingston Fairways
Kingston, NH
603-642-7722

Weekend Fee	$23	*Weekday Fee*	$20
Power Cart Fee	$20	*Pull Carts*	Yes
Putting Green	Yes	*Driving Range*	Yes
Season	Apr 1 - Nov 1	*Credit Cards*	No
Pro	NA	*Tee Times*	No
Comments	Easy course		
Directions	I-95, Rt 107S, 8 mi		

Tee	Holes	Par	Rating	Slope	Yards
Red	9	68	NA	NA	4,856
White	9	66	NA	NA	5,288
Blue	NA	NA	NA	NA	NA

NEW HAMPSHIRE

Hickory Pond Golf Course
Durham, NH
603-659-2227

Weekend Fee	$	*Weekday Fee*	$	
Power Cart Fee	$	*Pull Carts*		
Putting Green		*Driving Range*		
Season		*Credit Cards*		
Pro		*Tee Times*		
Comments	No information yet available			
Directions				

Tee	Holes	Par	Rating	Slope	Yards
Red					
White					
Blue					

Hidden Valley Golf Course
Derry, NH
603-887-3767

Weekend Fee	$	*Weekday Fee*	$	
Power Cart Fee	$	*Pull Carts*		
Putting Green		*Driving Range*		
Season		*Credit Cards*		
Pro		*Tee Times*		
Comments	No information yet available			
Directions				

Tee	Holes	Par	Rating	Slope	Yards
Red					
White					
Blue					

52 Mount Washington Golf Club - 9
Route 302, Bretton Woods, NH 03575
603-278-1000

Weekend Fee	$29	*Weekday Fee*	$25
Power Cart Fee	$22	*Pull Carts*	Yes
Putting Green	Yes	*Driving Range*	No
Season	May - Oct	*Credit Cards*	Yes
Pro	Fran O'Brien	*Tee Times*	7 days
Comments	Lodging		
Directions	I-93, exit 35, Rt 302 to Bretton Woods		

Tee	Holes	Par	Rating	Slope	Yards
Red	9	71	NA	120	4,950
White	9	71	NA	120	5,980
Blue	9	71	NA	122	6,430

Bretwood Golf Cou...
Keene, New Hampsh...

RHODE ISLAND GOLF COURSES

Public Courses	29	Private Courses	20
Total Courses	49	Percent Public Courses	60%
18 Hole Public Courses	13	9 Hole Public Courses	16
Total Golfers	106,000	Total Rounds of Golf	2,618,200
Percent Female Golfers	19.2%	Percent Senior Golfers	21.6%
Rounds Per Course	54,546	Rounds Per Golfer	24.7
Golfers Per Course	2,208	Courses Per 100 Square Miles	3.96
Average Weekend Fee	$22.03	Average Weekday Fee	$19.10
Average Weekend Fee w/Power Cart	$31.36	Average Weekday Fee w/Power Cart	$28.39
Average Slope	115.9	Average Yardage	5,711

Rhode Island has the least number of golf courses in New England. There are 48 golf courses and only 29 courses are open to the public.

Over 10 percent of the population plays golf which translates into 106,000 golfers playing 2.6 million rounds of golf every year[1] (24.7 rounds per golfer). Over 21 percent of the golfers are senior citizens and 19 percent are women.

Because of the small number of courses, courses in Rhode Island tend to be crowded. Rhode Island has 2,208 golfers per golf course and 54,546 rounds of golf are played annually per golf course.

Most of the public courses are only 9 holes. Courses with 18 holes or more comprise 45% of the total public courses.

Greens Fees

Rhode Island is one of the least expensive states to play golf. On weekends, the average greens fees to play a round of 18 holes on public courses is $22.03 ($25.62 for 18 hole and $19.13 for 9 hole courses). (These costs include courses where power cart fees are part of the greens fees.) Golfers can save $2.93 by playing during the week when the average greens fee is $19.10 ($22.69 for 18 hole and $16.19 for 9 hole courses).

The courses with the most expensive greens fees are the 18 hole Montaup Country Club in Portsmouth ($42) and the 9 hole Boulder Hills Golf & Country Club in Richmond ($34). The least expensive courses are the 9 hole Bristol Golf Club ($10) and the 18 hole Meadow Brook Golf Course in Wyoming ($15).

A power cart rental for two players will cost $18.74 in Rhode Island. On weekends, a round of golf with a power cart will cost each golfer an average of $31.36.

Slope and Yardage

Rhode Island courses tend to be average in terms of average slope ratings. The average slope rating of all public courses from the white tees is 115.9 (117.4 for 18 hole and 113.1 for 9 hole courses). The courses with the highest slope rating from the white tees are the 18 hole Triggs Memorial Golf Club in Providence (126) and the 9 hole Pond View Golf Course in Westerly (120). The easiest 18 and 9 hole courses are the Winnapaug Golf Course in Westerly (118) and the Pocasset Country Club in Portsmouth (110), respectively.

Rhode Island courses are longer than courses in other New England states. The average yardage of all public courses from the white tees is 5,711 yards (6,113 yards for 18 hole and 5,385 yards for 9 hole

---

[1] The Complete Golfer's Almanac 1995

RHODE ISLAND

courses). The courses with the longest yardage from the white tees are the 18 hole Green Valley Country Club in Portsmouth (6,641) and the 9 hole Coventry Pines Golf Club in Coventry (6,340). The shortest 18 and 9 hole courses are the Country View Golf Club in Harrisville (5,721) and the Fairlawn Golf Course in Lincoln (2,534), respectively.

Public Courses Rated in Top 10 by Golf Digest

Rank	Course
1	Richmond Country Club
2	Exeter Country Club
3	North Kingstown Municipal Golf Course
4	Montaup Country Club
5	Triggs Memorial Golf Course

Rank	Course
6	Winnapaug Country Club
7	Laurel Lane Golf Course
8	Green Valley Country Club
9	Foster Country Club
10	Cranston Country Club

Oldest Golf Courses

Club	Year
Newport Country Club	1894
Jamestown Golf Club	1895
Agawam Hunt Club (private)	1897
Sakonnett Golf Club (private)	1899
Pawtucket Country Club (private)	1902

Golf Schools and Instruction

- Challenge Cup Junior Golf Foundation, 140 Waterman Street, Providence, 02906, 401-331-4653

Golf Associations and Touring Clubs

- Boston Amateur Golf Society, 401-621-1525
- The Greater Boston Amateur Golf Club (The Tour), 617-484-8687
- InterState Golf Association, 617-566-7723
- Ocean State Women's Golf Association, 401-353-7728
- Rhode Island Golf Association, 10 Orms Street, Suite 326, Providence, 401-272-1350
- Rhode Island Women's Golf Association, 40 Pinewood Drive, North Providence, 401-353-1025

Private Golf Courses

Course	Town
Agawam Hunt Club	East Providence
Alpine Country Club	Cranston
Gloucester Country Club	Harmony
Kirkbrae Country Club	Lincoln
Lincoln Country Club	Lincoln
Louisquisset Golf Course	N. Providence
Metacomet Country Club	East Providence
Misquamicut Club	Watch Hill
Newport Country Club	Newport
Pawtucket Country Club	Pawtucket

Course	Town
Point Judith Country Club	Narragansett
Potowomut Golf Club	East Greenwich
Quidnessett Country Club	North Kingstown
Rhode Island Country Club	Barrington
Sakonnet Golf Club	Little Compton
Valley Country Club	Warwick
Wannamoisett Country Club	Rumford
Wanumetonomy Golf and CC	Middletown
Warwick Country Club	Warwick
West Warwick Country Club	West Warwick

Driving Ranges and Practice Areas

Name	Address	Town	Phone
DOCTOR GOLF	279 School Street	Pawtucket	401-722-5440
Fiddlesticks	1300 Ten Rod Road	N. Kingstown	401-295-1519
Johnston Golf Center	1302 Hartford Avenue	Johnston	401-621-7232
New England Golf Center	6100 Post Road	North Kingstown	401-885-0214
Pond View Driving Range	252 Shore Road	Westerly	401-322-1777
Smithfield Driving Range	Douglas Turnpike	Smithfield	401-231-3726
Tee Time Golf Practice	1305 West Main Street	Middletown	401-841-8454

Retailers

- Alpine Country Club Pro Shop, 251 Pippin Orchard Road, Cranston, 401-944-9760
- Clones Golf, 780 Main Street, E. Greenwich, 02818, 401-886-4220
- Collect-a-Ball, 774 Main Street, E. Greenwich, 02818, 401-886-4220
- Golf Day, 1000 Bald Hill Road, Warwick, 401-828-1402
- Golfer's Warehouse, 60 Freeway Drive, Cranston, 401-467-8740
- Golf World, 6170 Post Road, North Kingstown, 401-884-3222
- Northeast Golf Sales, 1050 Main Street, East Greenwich, 401-884-1033
- Palumbo Golf Shop, 251 New London Avenue, W. Warwick, 02893, 401-822-1716
- Pier Golf Market, 14 Narragansett Avenue, Narragansett, 02882, 401-789-4140
- Play it Again Sports, 52 Frenchtown Road, N. Kingstown, 02852, 401-885-6760
- Second Time Around Sports, 334 Atwood Avenue, Cranston, 02920, 401-944-9380
- Smithfield Pro Shop, Douglas Pike Street, Smithfield, 02917, 401-231-3726
- The Golf Store, 400 Franklin Street, Bristol, 401-254-1273
- Warwick Golf, 903 Warwick Avenue, Warwick, 02888, 401-461-8590

Courses By Town

Course	Town	Holes
Bristol GC	Bristol	9
Coventry Pines GC	Coventry	9
Washington Village GC	Coventry	9
Cranston CC	Cranston	18
East Greenwich G & CC	East Greenwich	9
Silver Spring GC	East Providence	6
Exeter CC	Exeter	18
Foster CC	Foster	18
Melody Hill GC	Harmony	18
Country View GC	Harrisville	18
Lindhbrook CC	Hope Valley	9
Richmond CC	Hope Valley	18
Jamestown Golf & CC	Jamestown	9
Fairlawn GC	Lincoln	9
North Kingstown GC	North Kingstown	18

Course	Town	Holes
Rolling Greens GC	North Kingstown	9
Woodland Greens GC	North Kingstown	9
Green Valley CC	Portsmouth	18
Montaup CC	Portsmouth	18
Pocasset CC	Portsmouth	9
Triggs Memorial GC	Providence	18
Boulder Hills G & CC	Richmond	9
Goddard Park GC	Warwick	9
Seaview CC	Warwick	9
Laurel Lane GC	West Kingston	18
Midville CC	West Warwick	9
Pond View GC	Westerly	9
Winnapaug GC	Westerly	18
Meadow Brook GC	Wyoming	18

Easiest Courses

Course	Town	Slope	Holes
Jamestown Golf & CC	Jamestown	110	9
Pocasset CC	Portsmouth	110	9
Woodland Greens GC	North Kingstown	110	9
Winnapaug GC	Westerly	111	18

Hardest Courses

Course	Town	Slope	Holes
Cranston CC	Cranston	120	18
Green Valley CC	Portsmouth	120	18
Montaup CC	Portsmouth	123	18
Triggs Memorial GC	Providence	126	18

RHODE ISLAND

Least Expensive Courses

Course	Town	Holes	Fee
Bristol GC	Bristol	9	$10
Silver Spring GC	East Providence	6	$12
Fairlawn GC	Lincoln	9	$14
Lindhbrook CC	Hope Valley	9	$14

Shortest Courses

Course	Town	Holes	Distance
Fairlawn GC	Lincoln	9	2,534
Lindhbrook CC	Hope Valley	9	2,885
Washington Village GC	Coventry	9	4,846
Silver Spring GC	East Providence	6	4,936
Bristol GC	Bristol	9	5,030

Year-Round Courses

Course	Town	Holes
Lindhbrook CC	Hope Valley	9
Meadow Brook GC	Wyoming	18
Montaup CC	Portsmouth	18
Pocasset CC	Portsmouth	9
Pond View GC	Westerly	9
Rolling Greens GC	North Kingstown	9
Triggs Memorial GC	Providence	18
Washington Village GC	Coventry	9
Winnapaug GC	Westerly	18
Woodland Greens GC	North Kingstown	9

Most Expensive Courses

Course	Town	Holes	Fee
Winnapaug Golf Course	Westerly	18	$28
Richmond Country Club	Hope valley	18	$29
Boulder Hills Golf & CC	Richmond	9	$34
Montaup CC	Portsmouth	18	$42

Longest Courses

Course	Town	Holes	Distance
Pond View GC	Westerly	9	6,324
Coventry Pines GC	Coventry	9	6,340
Exeter CC	Exeter	18	6,390
Triggs Memorial GC	Providence	18	6,394
Green Valley CC	Portsmouth	18	6,641

Midville Country Club
West Warwick, Rhode Island

Richmond Country Club
Hope Valley, Rhode Island

Rhode Island

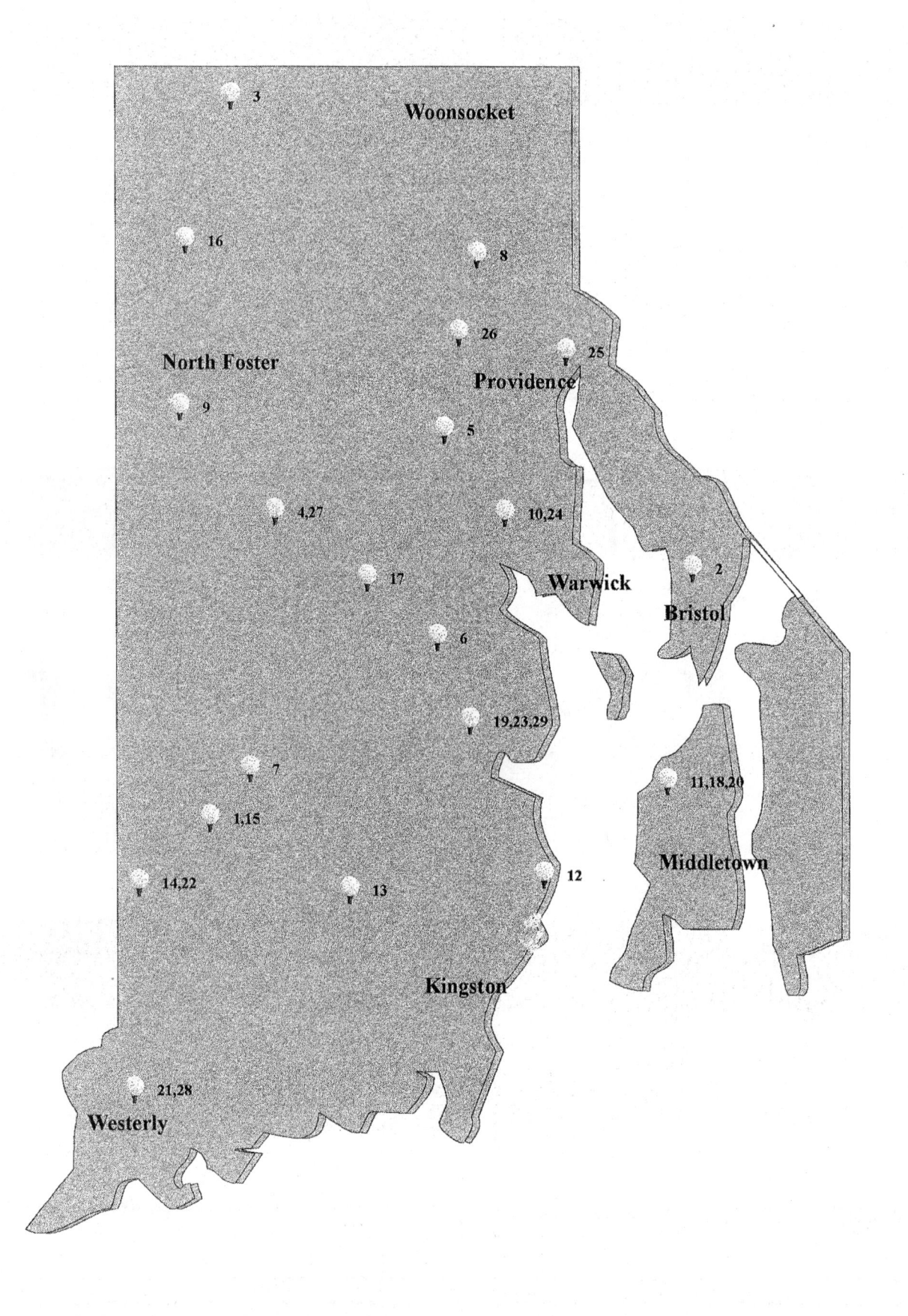

RHODE ISLAND

1 Boulder Hills Golf & Country Club
Route 138, Richmond, RI 02898
401-539-4653

Weekend Fee	$34	*Weekday Fee*	$25
Power Cart Fee	$22	*Pull Carts*	Yes
Putting Green	Yes	*Driving Range*	No
Season	Apr 1 - Nov 30	*Credit Cards*	Yes
Pro	Jim Calcione	*Tee Times*	7 days
Comments	Semi-private, built 1995, full restaurant		
Directions	I-95S, exit 3A, Rt 138E		

Tee	*Holes*	*Par*	*Rating*	*Slope*	*Yards*
Red	18	71	70.9	123	5,523
White	18	71	70.9	125	5,864
Blue	18	71	70.9	129	6,241

2 Bristol Golf Club
95 Tupelo Street, Bristol, RI 02809
401-253-9844

Weekend Fee	$10	*Weekday Fee*	$8
Power Cart Fee	$15	*Pull Carts*	Yes
Putting Green	Yes	*Driving Range*	No
Season	Apr 1 - Nov 1	*Credit Cards*	No
Pro	None	*Tee Times*	No
Comments	Beginner course, flat		
Directions	I-195E, exit 2, Rt 136, right on Tupelo St		

Tee	*Holes*	*Par*	*Rating*	*Slope*	*Yards*
Red	9	66	NA	NA	5,030
White	9	66	NA	NA	5,030
Blue	NA	NA	NA	NA	NA

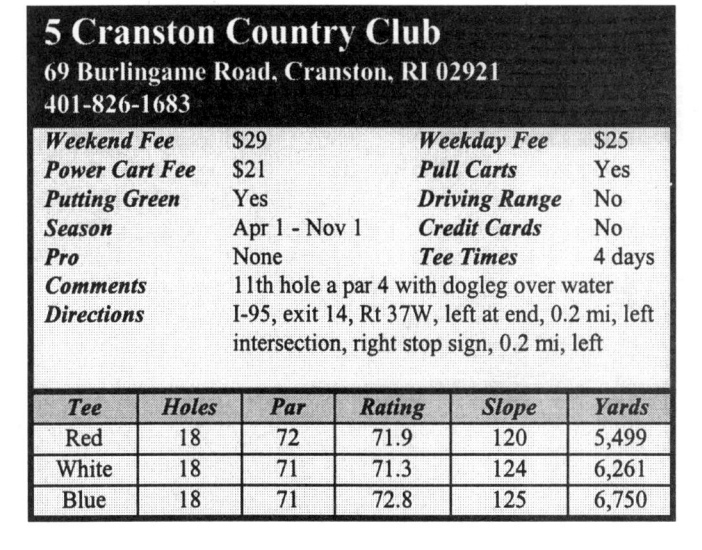

3 Country View Golf Club
Colwell Road, RR 4, Harrisville, RI 02830
401-568-7157

Weekend Fee	$24	*Weekday Fee*	$20
Power Cart Fee	$22	*Pull Carts*	Yes
Putting Green	Yes	*Driving Range*	No
Season	May 1 - Nov 30	*Credit Cards*	No
Pro	Bob Montanari	*Tee Times*	7 days
Comments	Plush fairways and small greens		
Directions	I-295, exit 8, Rt 7N, 6 mi, left Tarklin Rd, left Colwell Rd		

Tee	*Holes*	*Par*	*Rating*	*Slope*	*Yards*
Red	18	70	67.0	119	4,755
White	18	70	67.7	116	5,721
Blue	18	70	69.2	119	6,067

4 Coventry Pines Golf Club
1065 Harkney Hill Road, Coventry, RI 02816
401-397-9482

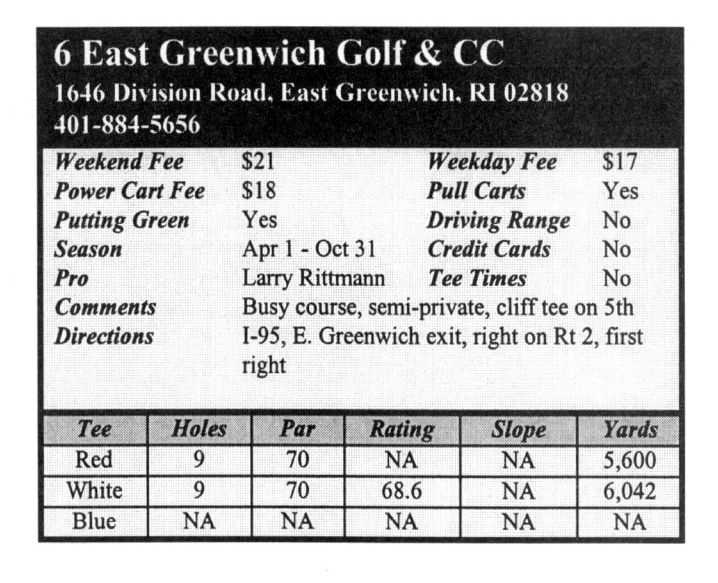

Weekend Fee	$20	*Weekday Fee*	$16
Power Cart Fee	$20	*Pull Carts*	Yes
Putting Green	Yes	*Driving Range*	No
Season	Apr 1 - Dec 1	*Credit Cards*	No
Pro	None	*Tee Times*	No
Comments	Par 5 6th hole has 2 separate greens		
Directions	I-95, exit 6, Rt 3N, 1 mi, left Harkney Hill Rd, 2 mi		

Tee	*Holes*	*Par*	*Rating*	*Slope*	*Yards*
Red	9	72	NA	113	5,860
White	9	70	NA	113	6,340
Blue	NA	NA	NA	NA	NA

5 Cranston Country Club
69 Burlingame Road, Cranston, RI 02921
401-826-1683

Weekend Fee	$29	*Weekday Fee*	$25
Power Cart Fee	$21	*Pull Carts*	Yes
Putting Green	Yes	*Driving Range*	No
Season	Apr 1 - Nov 1	*Credit Cards*	No
Pro	None	*Tee Times*	4 days
Comments	11th hole a par 4 with dogleg over water		
Directions	I-95, exit 14, Rt 37W, left at end, 0.2 mi, left intersection, right stop sign, 0.2 mi, left		

Tee	*Holes*	*Par*	*Rating*	*Slope*	*Yards*
Red	18	72	71.9	120	5,499
White	18	71	71.3	124	6,261
Blue	18	71	72.8	125	6,750

6 East Greenwich Golf & CC
1646 Division Road, East Greenwich, RI 02818
401-884-5656

Weekend Fee	$21	*Weekday Fee*	$17
Power Cart Fee	$18	*Pull Carts*	Yes
Putting Green	Yes	*Driving Range*	No
Season	Apr 1 - Oct 31	*Credit Cards*	No
Pro	Larry Rittmann	*Tee Times*	No
Comments	Busy course, semi-private, cliff tee on 5th		
Directions	I-95, E. Greenwich exit, right on Rt 2, first right		

Tee	*Holes*	*Par*	*Rating*	*Slope*	*Yards*
Red	9	70	NA	NA	5,600
White	9	70	68.6	NA	6,042
Blue	NA	NA	NA	NA	NA

RHODE ISLAND

7 Exeter Country Club
320 Ten Rod Road, Exeter, RI 02822
401-295-8212

Weekend Fee	$26	Weekday Fee	$21
Power Cart Fee	$20	Pull Carts	Yes
Putting Green	Yes	Driving Range	No
Season	Mar 15 - Nov 1	Credit Cards	Yes
Pro	None	Tee Times	1 day
Comments	Covered bridge, semi-private, Cornish		
Directions	I-95, exit 9S, Rt 4, 4-5 mi, Rt 102N, on left		

Tee	Holes	Par	Rating	Slope	Yards
Red	18	72	72.1	115	5,733
White	18	72	69.9	118	6,390
Blue	18	72	72.3	123	6,911

8 Fairlawn Golf Course
2 Sherman Avenue, Lincoln, RI 02865
401-334-3937

Weekend Fee	$14	Weekday Fee	$12
Power Cart Fee	No carts	Pull Carts	Yes
Putting Green	Yes	Driving Range	No
Season	Apr 1 - Nov 30	Credit Cards	No
Pro	None	Tee Times	No
Comments	Easy walker, many sand traps		
Directions	I-95N, Rt 146N (Sherman Ave exit), 1.5 mi		

Tee	Holes	Par	Rating	Slope	Yards
Red	9	54	52.2	NA	2,534
White	9	54	52.2	NA	2,534
Blue	NA	NA	NA	NA	NA

9 Foster Country Club
67 Johnson Road, Foster, RI 02825
401-397-7750

Weekend Fee	$20	Weekday Fee	$18
Power Cart Fee	$18	Pull Carts	Yes
Putting Green	Yes	Driving Range	Nets
Season	Mar 1 - Nov 15	Credit Cards	Yes
Pro	Bob Di Pauda	Tee Times	3 days
Comments	Blind shots, doglegs, semi-private, Cornish		
Directions	I-95, Rt 102N, left Rt 14, right Moosup Valley Rd, right Johnson Rd		

Tee	Holes	Par	Rating	Slope	Yards
Red	18	74	70.0	112	5,499
White	18	72	69.5	114	6,187
Blue	NA	NA	NA	NA	NA

10 Goddard State Park Golf Course
Ives Road, Warwick, RI 02886
401-884-9834

Weekend Fee	$16	Weekday Fee	$12
Power Cart Fee	$20	Pull Carts	Yes
Putting Green	No	Driving Range	No
Season	Apr 1 - Nov 26	Credit Cards	Yes
Pro	None	Tee Times	No
Comments	Inside park, beach, jogging and horse trails		
Directions	I-95S, Rt 4 cutoff, 1st exit (E. Greenwich), Rt 401, signs		

Tee	Holes	Par	Rating	Slope	Yards
Red	9	72	NA	NA	6,042
White	9	72	NA	NA	6,042
Blue	NA	NA	NA	NA	NA

11 Green Valley Country Club
371 Union Street, Portsmouth, RI 02871
401-847-9543

Weekend Fee	$30	Weekday Fee	$30
Power Cart Fee	$22	Pull Carts	Yes
Putting Green	Yes	Driving Range	Yes
Season	Apr 1 - Nov 1	Credit Cards	Yes
Pro	Gary Dorsi	Tee Times	2 days
Comments	On Aquidneck Island, windy, semi-private		
Directions	I-195, Rt 24S, Rt 114S, several miles after Raytheon left Union St		

Tee	Holes	Par	Rating	Slope	Yards
Red	18	71	69.5	113	5,459
White	18	71	71.6	120	6,641
Blue	18	71	72.0	122	6,830

12 Jamestown Golf & Country Club
245 Conanicus Avenue, Jamestown, RI 02835
401-423-9930

Weekend Fee	$17	Weekday Fee	$17
Power Cart Fee	$15	Pull Carts	Yes
Putting Green	Yes	Driving Range	No
Season	Apr 1 - Dec 31	Credit Cards	No
Pro	Lou Vecchia	Tee Times	No
Comments	One of oldest 9 hole courses (1895)		
Directions	I-95, Rt 138E, over Jamestown bridge, follow signs Newport bridge, stay right before bridge		

Tee	Holes	Par	Rating	Slope	Yards
Red	9	76	NA	NA	5,636
White	9	72	69.7	110	5,998
Blue	NA	NA	NA	NA	NA

RHODE ISLAND

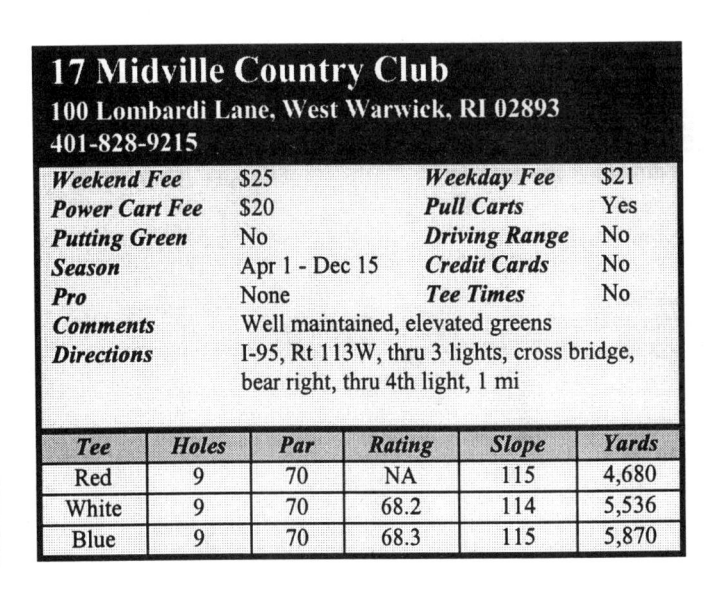

13 Laurel Lane Golf Club
309 Laurel Lane, West Kingston, RI 02892
401-783-3844

Weekend Fee	$20	*Weekday Fee*	$18
Power Cart Fee	$20	*Pull Carts*	Yes
Putting Green	Yes	*Driving Range*	No
Season	Mar 1 - Dec 31	*Credit Cards*	No
Pro	None	*Tee Times*	No
Comments	Open front 9, tight back 9, semi-private		
Directions	I-95N, Rt 38, Rt 138E, 7 mi		

Tee	Holes	Par	Rating	Slope	Yards
Red	18	70	70.8	115	5,381
White	18	71	68.1	113	5,806
Blue	18	71	NA	NA	6,215

14 Lindhbrook Country Club
299 Woodville Alton Road, Hope Valley, RI 02832
401-539-8641

Weekend Fee	$15	*Weekday Fee*	$13
Power Cart Fee	$12	*Pull Carts*	Yes
Putting Green	Yes	*Driving Range*	No
Season	Year-round	*Credit Cards*	Yes
Pro	Sam Toscano	*Tee Times*	3 days
Comments	Many water holes, executive course		
Directions	I-95N, exit 2, bear right, 0.5 mi on right		

Tee	Holes	Par	Rating	Slope	Yards
Red	18	54	NA	NA	2,682
White	18	54	NA	NA	2,885
Blue	NA	NA	NA	NA	NA

15 Meadow Brook Golf Course
163 Kingstown Road, Wyoming, RI 02898
401-539-8491

Weekend Fee	$15	*Weekday Fee*	$12
Power Cart Fee	$15	*Pull Carts*	Yes
Putting Green	Yes	*Driving Range*	Yes
Season	Year-round	*Credit Cards*	No
Pro	Joe Videita	*Tee Times*	Yes
Comments	Level, undulating greens, some hazards		
Directions	I-95, exit 3, Rt 138E, 1.5 mi		

Tee	Holes	Par	Rating	Slope	Yards
Red	18	73	NA	NA	5,605
White	18	71	70.1	118	6,075
Blue	NA	NA	NA	NA	NA

16 Melody Hill Golf Course
55 Melody Hill Road, Harmony, RI 02829
401-949-9851

Weekend Fee	$19	*Weekday Fee*	$16
Power Cart Fee	$20	*Pull Carts*	Yes
Putting Green	Yes	*Driving Range*	No
Season	Mar 1 - Nov 30	*Credit Cards*	No
Pro	None	*Tee Times*	No
Comments	Scenic, rolling hills, wooded, doglegs		
Directions	Rt 44W, 1st left after fire station in center		

Tee	Holes	Par	Rating	Slope	Yards
Red	18	71	69.0	113	6,185
White	18	71	69.0	113	6,185
Blue	NA	NA	NA	NA	NA

17 Midville Country Club
100 Lombardi Lane, West Warwick, RI 02893
401-828-9215

Weekend Fee	$25	*Weekday Fee*	$21
Power Cart Fee	$20	*Pull Carts*	Yes
Putting Green	No	*Driving Range*	No
Season	Apr 1 - Dec 15	*Credit Cards*	No
Pro	None	*Tee Times*	No
Comments	Well maintained, elevated greens		
Directions	I-95, Rt 113W, thru 3 lights, cross bridge, bear right, thru 4th light, 1 mi		

Tee	Holes	Par	Rating	Slope	Yards
Red	9	70	NA	115	4,680
White	9	70	68.2	114	5,536
Blue	9	70	68.3	115	5,870

18 Montaup Country Club
500 Anthony Road, Portsmouth, RI 02871
401-683-9107

Weekend Fee	$42	*Weekday Fee*	$42
Power Cart Fee	Included	*Pull Carts*	No
Putting Green	Yes	*Driving Range*	No
Season	Year-round	*Credit Cards*	No
Pro	Stephen Diemoz	*Tee Times*	1 day
Comments	Green side traps, ponds, semi-private		
Directions	Rt 24, exit 1 in RI, right		

Tee	Holes	Par	Rating	Slope	Yards
Red	18	73	72.3	120	5,473
White	18	71	71.4	123	6,236
Blue	18	71	NA	NA	6,500

RHODE ISLAND

19 N. Kingstown Municipal G. Course
1 Callahan Road, North Kingstown, RI 02852
401-294-4051

Weekend Fee	$24	Weekday Fee	$21	
Power Cart Fee	$20	Pull Carts	Yes	
Putting Green	Yes	Driving Range	Yes	
Season	Mar 1 - Jan 1	Credit Cards	No	
Pro	Fran O'Keefe	Tee Times	2 days	
Comments	Seaside links course, windy, Cornish design			
Directions	I-95, exit 9, Rt 4, exit Rt 403S, 3 mi into military base, 1st right			

Tee	Holes	Par	Rating	Slope	Yards
Red	18	70	69.5	115	5,227
White	18	70	68.3	116	5,848
Blue	18	70	69.7	119	6,161

20 Pocasset Country Club
807 Bristol Ferry Road, Portsmouth, RI 02871
401-683-2266

Weekend Fee	$22	Weekday Fee	$18	
Power Cart Fee	$16	Pull Carts	Yes	
Putting Green	Yes	Driving Range	No	
Season	Year-round	Credit Cards	Yes	
Pro	None	Tee Times	No	
Comments	Under Mt. Hope Bridge, bay views			
Directions	Rt 24S, Bristol exit, right, right at light			

Tee	Holes	Par	Rating	Slope	Yards
Red	9	68	NA	NA	5,230
White	9	68	67.0	110	5,590
Blue	NA	NA	NA	NA	NA

21 Pond View Golf Course
265 Shore Road, Westerly, RI 02891
401-322-7870

Weekend Fee	$20	Weekday Fee	$20	
Power Cart Fee	$20	Pull Carts	Yes	
Putting Green	Yes	Driving Range	Yes	
Season	Year-round	Credit Cards	Yes	
Pro	Andy Rushford	Tee Times	No	
Comments	2 holes on shore, small greens, semi-private			
Directions	I-95S, exit 1, Rt 3, Rt 78E, left Rt 1, 2 mi, right at light, right Shore Rd			

Tee	Holes	Par	Rating	Slope	Yards
Red	9	72	67.6	110	5,680
White	9	72	70.0	118	6,324
Blue	9	72	NA	NA	6,600

22 Richmond Country Club
74 Sandy Pond Road, Hope Valley, RI 02832
401-364-9292

Weekend Fee	$29	Weekday Fee	$24	
Power Cart Fee	$20	Pull Carts	Yes	
Putting Green	Yes	Driving Range	No	
Season	Apr 1 - Dec 31	Credit Cards	No	
Pro	Peter Hendrick	Tee Times	1 day	
Comments	Narrow fairways through pine forest			
Directions	I-95, exit 3B, 2 mi, left at light Mechanic St, 2.5 mi, right on Sandy Pond Rd			

Tee	Holes	Par	Rating	Slope	Yards
Red	18	71	67.0	113	4,974
White	18	71	68.5	114	5,827
Blue	18	71	69.9	117	6,515

23 Rolling Greens Golf Club
1625 Ten Rod Road, North Kingstown, RI 02852
401-294-9859

Weekend Fee	$15	Weekday Fee	$13	
Power Cart Fee	$16	Pull Carts	Yes	
Putting Green	No	Driving Range	No	
Season	Year-round	Credit Cards	No	
Pro	None	Tee Times	No	
Comments	Hilly			
Directions	I-95S, Rt 4 N. Kingstown, Rt 102W, 1.3 mi			

Tee	Holes	Par	Rating	Slope	Yards
Red	9	74	NA	NA	NA
White	9	70	NA	NA	6,144
Blue	NA	NA	NA	NA	NA

24 Seaview Country Club
150 Grey Street, Warwick, RI 02889
401-739-6311

Weekend Fee	$24	Weekday Fee	$20	
Power Cart Fee	$20	Pull Carts	Yes	
Putting Green	Yes	Driving Range	Yes	
Season	Mar 1 - Nov 1	Credit Cards	Yes	
Pro	Bill D'Angelos	Tee Times	1 day	
Comments	Many hazards, narrow, semi-private			
Directions	I-95, Rt 117E, 5 mi, right Warwick Neck Ave, right Meadow View Ave, 1 mi			

Tee	Holes	Par	Rating	Slope	Yards
Red	9	72	64.0	110	5,144
White	9	72	66.8	117	5,646
Blue	NA	NA	NA	NA	NA

25 Silver Spring Golf Club
3303 Pawtucket Avenue, East Providence, RI 02915
401-434-9697

Weekend Fee	$13	*Weekday Fee*	$12
Power Cart Fee	$12	*Pull Carts*	Yes
Putting Green	No	*Driving Range*	No
Season	Apr 1 - Dec 1	*Credit Cards*	No
Pro	None	*Tee Times*	No
Comments	Hilly, trees, small undulating greens		
Directions	I-195, exit 4, south Veterans Memorial Parkway, 3 mi, Pawtucket Ave		

Tee	Holes	Par	Rating	Slope	Yards
Red	6	69	NA	NA	4,936
White	6	69	NA	NA	4,936
Blue	NA	NA	NA	NA	NA

26 Triggs Memorial Golf Club
1533 Chalkstone Avenue, Providence, RI 02909
401-521-8460

Weekend Fee	$26	*Weekday Fee*	$23
Power Cart Fee	$20	*Pull Carts*	Yes
Putting Green	Yes	*Driving Range*	No
Season	Year-round	*Credit Cards*	Yes
Pro	Charlie Smith	*Tee Times*	3 days
Comments	Ross design, undulating greens with bunkers		
Directions	I-95, exit 21, Mt. Pleasant Ave, right light, left 1st light		

Tee	Holes	Par	Rating	Slope	Yards
Red	18	72	NA	123	5,596
White	18	72	71.7	126	6,394
Blue	18	72	72.8	128	6,596

27 Washington Village Golf Course
174 Station Street, Coventry, RI 02816
401-823-0010

Weekend Fee	$18	*Weekday Fee*	$15
Power Cart Fee	$20	*Pull Carts*	Yes
Putting Green	Yes	*Driving Range*	No
Season	Year-round	*Credit Cards*	No
Pro	None	*Tee Times*	No
Comments	Easy to walk, sand traps throughout		
Directions	I-95, Rt 117W, 5 mi, follow signs		

Tee	Holes	Par	Rating	Slope	Yards
Red	9	66	NA	NA	3,986
White	9	66	NA	NA	4,846
Blue	NA	NA	NA	NA	NA

28 Winnapaug Golf Course
184 Shore Road, Westerly, RI 02891
401-596-1237

Weekend Fee	$29	*Weekday Fee*	$25
Power Cart Fee	$22	*Pull Carts*	Yes
Putting Green	Yes	*Driving Range*	No
Season	Year-round	*Credit Cards*	Yes
Pro	Kirk Strong	*Tee Times*	7 days
Comments	Ocean views, short, tight, semi-private, Ross		
Directions	I-95N, exit 92, right on Rt 2, Rt 78 towards beaches, left Rt 1A, 1 mi		

Tee	Holes	Par	Rating	Slope	Yards
Red	18	72	69.0	110	5,113
White	18	72	67.9	111	5,914
Blue	18	72	68.9	113	6,337

29 Woodland Greens Golf Club
655 Old Baptist Road, North Kingstown, RI 02852
401-294-2872

Weekend Fee	$22	*Weekday Fee*	$20
Power Cart Fee	$20	*Pull Carts*	Yes
Putting Green	Yes	*Driving Range*	No
Season	Year-round	*Credit Cards*	No
Pro	Dave Creta	*Tee Times*	No
Comments	Tight fairways		
Directions	I-95S, Rt 4S, left 2nd light Stony Lane, left 1st intersection		

Tee	Holes	Par	Rating	Slope	Yards
Red	9	70	67.1	110	6,046
White	9	70	67.1	110	6,046
Blue	NA	NA	NA	NA	NA

The following course information was received too late to include in the alphabetical listing or the location map.

West Warwick Golf Course
West Warwick, RI
401-821-9789

Weekend Fee	$	*Weekday Fee*	$
Power Cart Fee	$	*Pull Carts*	
Putting Green		*Driving Range*	
Season		*Credit Cards*	
Pro		*Tee Times*	
Comments	No information yet available		
Directions			

Tee	Holes	Par	Rating	Slope	Yards
Red					
White					
Blue					

Haystack Golf Course
Wilmington, Vermont

VERMONT GOLF COURSES

Public Courses	61	Private Courses	4
Total Courses	65	Percent Public Courses	94%
18 Hole Public Courses	33	9 Hole Public Courses	28
Total Golfers	42,000	Total Rounds of Golf	978,600
Percent Female Golfers	16.2%	Percent Senior Golfers	23.7%
Rounds Per Course	15,055	Rounds Per Golfer	23.3
Golfers Per Course	646	Courses Per 100 Square Miles	0.68
Average Weekend Fee	$30.66	Average Weekday Fee	$27.97
Average Weekend Fee w/Power Cart	$43.13	Average Weekday Fee w/Power Cart	$40.01
Average Slope	116.2	Average Yardage	5,531

Vermont has a small number of golf courses. There are 65 golf courses and the majority (94%) of the courses are open to the public.

Only 7 percent of the population plays golf which translates into 42,000 golfers playing 1 million rounds of golf every year[1] (23.3 rounds per golfer). Almost one quarter of the golfers are senior citizens and only 16 percent are women.

Since Vermont has few golfers and a short golf season, this state is one of the least crowded to play golf. Vermont has 646 golfers per golf course and only 15,055 golf rounds are played per golf course.

Vermont has a high percentage of 9 hole courses. Courses with 18 holes or more comprise 54% of the total public courses.

Greens Fees

It costs more to play in Vermont than any other New England state. On weekends, the average greens fees to play a round of 18 holes on public courses is $30.66 ($38.56 for 18 hole courses and $21.30 for 9 hole courses). (These costs include courses where power cart fees are part of the greens fees.) Golfers can save $2.69 by playing during the week when the average greens fee is $27.97 ($35.76 for 18 hole and $18.79 for 9 hole courses).

The courses with the most expensive greens fees are the 18 hole Gleneagles Golf Course at the Equinox Hotel in Manchester Village ($80) and the 9 hole Someday Golf Resort in West Dover ($47). The least expensive courses are the 9 hole Granddad's Invitational Golf Course in Newark ($5) and the 18 hole Sitzmark Golf Course in Wilmington ($12).

A power cart rental for two players will cost $22.85 in Vermont. On weekends, a round of golf with a power cart will cost each golfer an average of $43.13.

Slope and Yardage

Vermont courses tend to be harder than courses in other states. The average slope rating of all public courses from the white tees is 116.2 (119.7 for 18 hole and 111.1 for 9 hole courses). The courses with the highest slope rating from the white tees are the 18 hole Mount Snow Golf Course (127) and the 9 hole Mount Anthony Country Club in Bennington (125). The easiest 18 hole course is the West Bolton Golf Club (109). The easiest 9 hole courses are the Blush Hill Country Club in Waterbury and the White River Golf Club in Rochester (101).

---

[1] The Complete Golfer's Almanac 1995

VERMONT

Vermont courses are average in terms of distance from the white tees. The average yardage of all public courses from the white tees is 5,531 yards (5,885 yards for 18 hole and 5,115 yards for 9 hole courses). The courses with the longest yardage from the white tees are the 18 hole Kwiniaska Golf Club in Shelburne (6,796) and the 9 hole Brattleboro Country Club (6,265). The shortest 18 and 9 hole courses are the Sitzmark Golf Course in Wilmington (2,643) and the Stonehedge Country Club in North Claredon (2,214), respectively.

Public Courses Rated in Top 10 by Golf Digest

Rank	Course
1	Gleneagles Golf Course
2	Rutland Country Club
3	Stratton Mountain CC
4	Mount Snow Golf Course
5	Sugarbush Golf Course

Rank	Course
6	Woodstock Country Club
7	Country Club of Barre
8	Haystack Golf Course
9	Crown Point Country Club
10	Killington Golf Course

Oldest Golf Courses

Club	Year
The Equinox Hotel	1894
Dummerston	1894
Dorset Field Club	1886
Woodstock Country Club	1896

Club	Year
Buena Vista	1896
Mount Anthony Club	1897
Rutland Golf Club	1897

Golf Schools and Instruction

- Marty Keene's Golf World, 9 Blair Park Road, Williston, 05495, 802-879-4005
- Mountain Top Inn and Resort, Mountain Top Road, Chittenden, 800-445-2100
- The Golf School, Mt. Snow Resort, Mt. Snow, 802-464-3333
- The Mountain Golf School at Killington, 802-422-3101
- The Stratton Golf School, Stratton Mountain, 802-297-2200
- Natural Asset Golf Program, Stoweflake Golf School, 1746 Mountain Road, Stowe, 802-253-7355
- Quechee Country Club Golf School, 1 River Road, Quechee, 802-295-6245

Golf Associations and Touring Clubs

- Vermont Golf Association, PO Box 1612, Station A, Rutland, 05701, 802-773-7180
- Vermont State Women's Golf Association, 603-469-3487

Private Golf Courses

Course	Town
Burlington Country Club	Burlington
Dorset Field Club	Dorset
Ekwanok Country Club	Manchester
Manchester Country Club	Manchester

Retailers

- Golf & Ski Warehouse, 123 Industrial Parkway, Burlington, 802-660-2515
- John Paul's Golf Shop, 568 South Prospect Street, Burlington, 802-658-3856
- John's Golf Supply, 152 Woodstock Avenue, Rutland, 802-773-8917
- Keith's Golf Shop, Route 7, Pittsford, 05763, 800-483-6341
- Ken's Golf Shop, 11 Center Street, Burlington, 802-862-5034
- Lefties Only Golf Shop, 1972 Williston Road, S. Burlington, 05403, 802-862-1114
- Lindholm Sports Center, 2 S. Main Street, Rutland, 05701, 802-773-6000
- Marilyn's Place for Golf, Derby Road, Newport, 802-626-9637
- Marty Keene's Golf World, Blair Park, Williston, 802-879-4005
- New England Discount Golf, 259 North Main Street, Rutland, 802-773-4382
- Sports Connection, 38 S. Main Street, Saint Albans, 05478, 802-524-3312
- The Golf Shop, Plainfield Road, Barre, 802-479-2312
- Village Golf Shop, Depot Street, Stowe, 802-253-4040

Driving Ranges and Practice Areas

Name	Address	Town	Phone
Airport Driving Range	Old Route 7B	Clarendon	802-773-1315
Bolton Driving Range	Route 2	Bolton Flats	802-434-4219
Bomoseen Golfland	Route 30	Bomoseen	802-468-2975
Frenchie's Driving Range	Route 5	Dummarston	802-254-6077
Georgia Farmhouse Driving Range	Route 7	Milton	802-524-5890
Pinewoods Driving Range	Route 7 North	North Pittsford	802-775-6623
Place Driving Range	Route 116	Hinesburg	802-482-2266
Pro Line Driving Range	Route 7	St. Albans	802-527-0337
Quarry Hill Driving Range	Spear Street	South	802-862-5200
Tee-Off Driving Range	Victory Road	Lyndonville	802-626-9666
The Practice Tee	Route 7A	Manchester	802-362-3100
Three Stallion Driving Range	Exit 4 off I-89	Randolph	802-728-5575
Towers Driving Range	Call for address	Richmond	802-434-2412
Townshend Golf	Route 30	Townshend	802-365-7839
White River Practice Area	Route 100	Rochester	802-767-3211
Williston Driving Range	Route 2	Williston	802-879-0266

Shortest Courses

Course	Town	Distance	Holes
Stonehedge CC	North	2,214	9
Appletree Bay GC	South Hero	2,264	9
Sitzmark GC	Wilmington	2,643	18
Wilcox Cove Cottages & GC	Grand Isle	3,410	9
Bradford GC	Bradford	4,260	9
White River GC	Rochester	4,518	9
Granddad's Invitational GC	Newark	4,568	9

Longest Courses

Course	Town	Distance	Holes
Basin Harbor GC	Vergennes	6,232	18
Brattleboro CC	Brattleboro	6,265	9
Essex CC	Essex Junction	6,310	18
Quechee Resort -	Quechee	6,342	18
Alburg CC	South Alburg	6,388	18
Mount Snow GC	Mount Snow	6,443	18
Kwiniaska GC	Shelburne	6,796	18

VERMONT

Courses By Town

Course	Town	Holes
Bakersfield GC	Bakersfield	9
Wolf Run GC	Bakersfield	9
Barre GC	Barre	18
Barton GC	Barton	9
Bellows Falls GC	Bellows Falls	9
Mount Anthony GC	Bennington	9
Prospect Bay GC	Bomoseen	9
Bradford GC	Bradford	9
Neshobe GC	Brandon	9
Brattleboro GC	Brattleboro	9
Rocky Ridge GC	Burlington	18
Tater Hill Resort	Chester	18
Enosberg Falls GC	Enosberg Falls	9
Essex GC	Essex Junction	18
Lake Morey GC	Fairlee	18
Wilcox Cove Cottages and GC	Grand Isle	9
Mountain View GC	Greensboro	9
Cedar Knoll GC	Hinesburg	18
Killington Golf Resort	Killington	18
Fox Run GC	Ludlow	9
Marble Island GC	Mallets Bay	9
Gleneagles GC at Equinox Hotel	Manchester Village	18
Ralph Myhre GC	Middlebury	18
Montpelier GC	Montpelier	9
Farm Resort GC	Morisville	9
Copley GC	Morrisville	9
Mount Snow GC	Mount Snow	18
Granddad's Invitational GC	Newark	9
Newport GC	Newport	18
Stonehedge GC	North Claredon	9
Northfield GC	Northfield	9

Course	Town	Holes
Orleans GC	Orleans	18
Proctor Pittsford GC	Pittsford	18
Lake St. Catherine GC	Poultney	9
Quechee Club Resort -	Quechee	18
Quechee Club Resort -	Quechee	18
Montague GC	Randolph	18
Richford GC	Richford	9
White River GC	Rochester	9
Rutland GC	Rutland	18
Champlain GC	Saint Albans	18
Kwiniaska GC	Shelburne	18
Alburg GC	South Alburg	18
Appletree Bay GC	South Hero	9
Crown Point GC	Springfield	18
St. Johnsbury GC	St. Johnsbury	18
Stamford Valley GC	Stamford	9
Stowe GC	Stowe	18
Stratton Mt. GC (Forest)	Stratton	18
Stratton Mt. GC (Lake)	Stratton	18
Stratton Mt. GC (Mountain)	Stratton	18
Basin Harbor GC	Vergennes	18
Sugarbush GC	Warren	18
Blush Hill GC	Waterbury	9
West Bolton GC	West Bolton	18
Someday Golf Resort	West Dover	9
Williston GC	Williston	18
Haystack GC	Wilmington	18
Sitzmark GC	Wilmington	18
Windsor GC	Windsor	9
Woodstock Inn and Resort	Woodstock	18

Least Expensive Courses

Course	Town	Holes	Fee
Granddad's Invitational GC	Newark	9	$5
Appletree Bay GC	South Hero	9	$8
Stamford Valley CC	Stamford	9	$10
Wilcox Cove Cottages and	Grand Isle	9	$11
Sitzmark GC	Wilmington	18	$12
Barton GC	Barton	9	$15
Stonehedge CC	North Claredon	9	$15
Wolf Run CC	Bakersfield	9	$15
Bakersfield GC	Bakersfield	9	$16

Most Expensive Courses

Course	Town	Holes	Fee
Woodstock Inn and Resort	Woodstock	18	$59
Mount Snow GC	Mount Snow	18	$59
Quechee Resort - Highland	Quechee	18	$60
Quechee Resort - Lakeland	Quechee	18	$60
Tater Hill Resort	Chester	18	$64
Stratton Mt. GC (Forest)	Stratton	18	$66
Stratton Mt. GC (Lake)	Stratton	18	$66
Stratton Mt. GC (Mountain)	Stratton	18	$66
Gleneagles GC at Equinox	Manchester	18	$80

Easiest Courses

Course	Town	Holes	Slope
Blush Hill CC	Waterbury	9	101
White River GC	Rochester	9	101
Bradford GC	Bradford	9	102
Stamford Valley CC	Stamford	9	104
Windsor CC	Windsor	9	105
Copley CC	Morrisville	9	106
Fox Run GC	Ludlow	9	106
Newport CC	Newport	18	106
Prospect Bay CC	Bomoseen	9	107

Hardest Courses

Course	Town	Holes	Slope
Quechee Club Resort -	Quechee	18	124
Rocky Ridge GC	Burlington	18	124
Tater Hill Resort	Chester	18	124
Gleneagles GC at Equinox	Manchester	18	125
Haystack CC	Wilmington	18	125
Mount Anthony CC	Bennington	9	125
St. Johnsbury CC	St. Johnsbury	18	125
Ralph Myhre GC	Middlebury	18	126
Mount Snow GC	Mount Snow	18	127

Woodstock Country Club
Woodstock, Vermont

Vermont

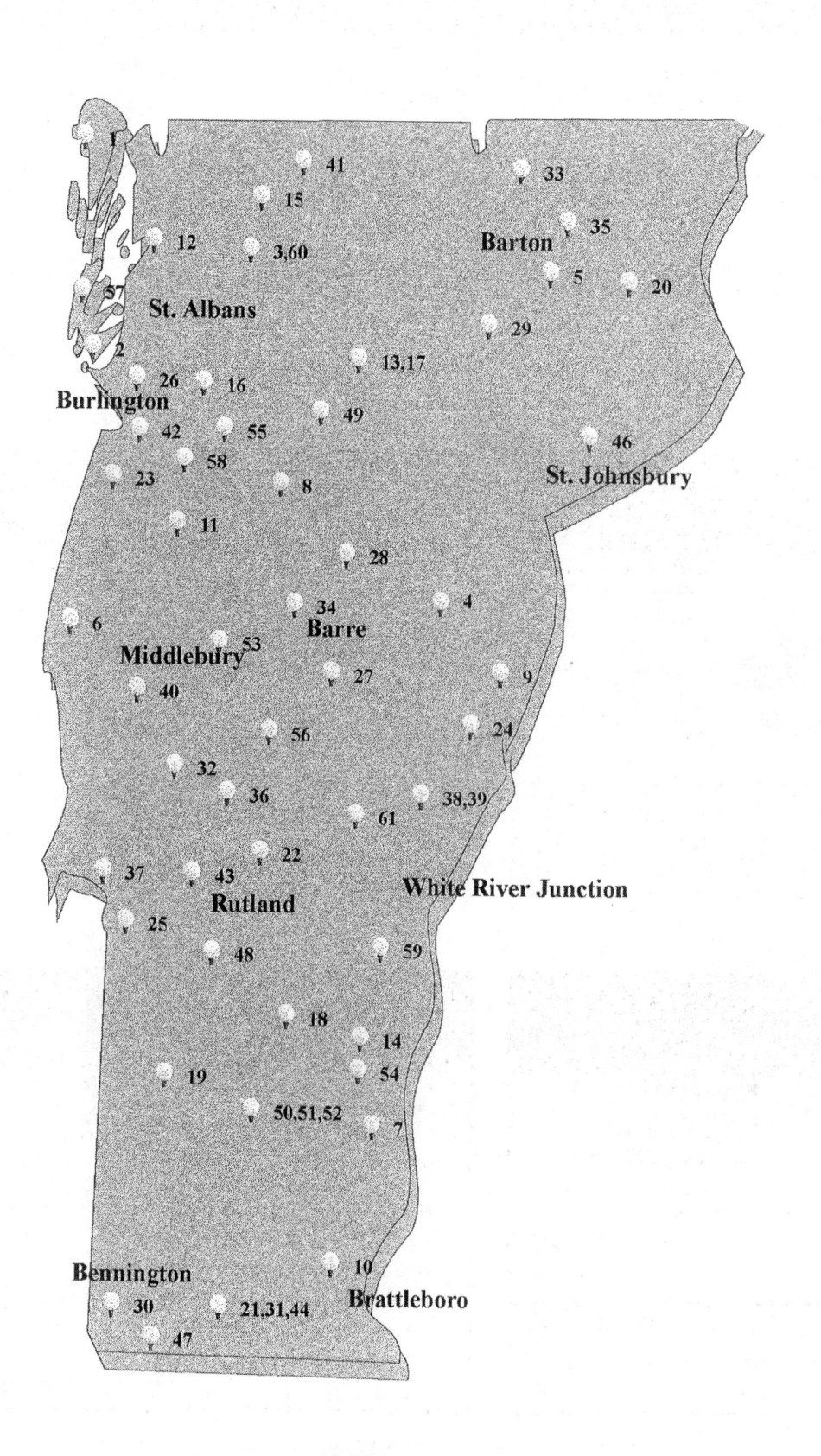

VERMONT

1 Alburg Country Club
Route 129, South Alburg, VT 05440
802-796-3586

Weekend Fee	$25	Weekday Fee	$20
Power Cart Fee	$20	Pull Carts	Yes
Putting Green	Yes	Driving Range	Yes
Season	May 1 - Oct 18	Credit Cards	No
Pro	None	Tee Times	3 days
Comments	Easy course, semi-private, undulating greens		
Directions	I-89, exit 17, Rt 2 to Alburg, Rt 129		

Tee	Holes	Par	Rating	Slope	Yards
Red	18	75	70.8	106	5,621
White	18	72	69.4	110	6,388
Blue	NA	NA	NA	NA	NA

2 Appletree Bay Golf Club
Route 2, South Hero, VT 05486
802-372-5398

Weekend Fee	$8	Weekday Fee	$7
Power Cart Fee	No carts	Pull Carts	Yes
Putting Green	Yes	Driving Range	No
Season	Apr 1 - Oct 22	Credit Cards	No
Pro	None	Tee Times	No
Comments	Short par 3		
Directions	I-89N, exit 17, Rt 2N, 6 mi, look for signs		

Tee	Holes	Par	Rating	Slope	Yards
Red	9	54	NA	NA	2,264
White	9	54	NA	NA	2,264
Blue	NA	NA	NA	NA	NA

3 Bakersfield Golf Club
Boston Post Road, Bakersfield, VT 05441
802-933-5100

Weekend Fee	$16	Weekday Fee	$14
Power Cart Fee	$16	Pull Carts	Yes
Putting Green	Yes	Driving Range	No
Season	Apr 1 - Oct 15	Credit Cards	No
Pro	None	Tee Times	No
Comments	Many bunkers, 3 water holes		
Directions	Rt 105 to N. Enosburg, south on Boston Post Rd		

Tee	Holes	Par	Rating	Slope	Yards
Red	9	70	NA	NA	5,220
White	9	70	69.0	115	5,960
Blue	NA	NA	NA	NA	NA

4 Barre Country Club
Plainfield Road, P.O. Box 298, Barre, VT 05641
802-476-7658

Weekend Fee	$30	Weekday Fee	$30
Power Cart Fee	$28	Pull Carts	Yes
Putting Green	Yes	Driving Range	No
Season	Apr 20 - Oct 31	Credit Cards	Yes
Pro	David Christy	Tee Times	7 days
Comments	Scenic, hilly, tight fairways, semi-private		
Directions	I-89, exit 7, Rt 14N, 4 mi, follow signs		

Tee	Holes	Par	Rating	Slope	Yards
Red	18	71	72.0	120	5,515
White	18	71	69.2	119	5,986
Blue	18	71	70.2	123	6,191

5 Barton Golf Club
Telefer Hill, Route 1 Box 186, Barton, VT 05822
802-525-1126

Weekend Fee	$15	Weekday Fee	$15
Power Cart Fee	$15	Pull Carts	Yes
Putting Green	Yes	Driving Range	No
Season	May 10 - Oct 31	Credit Cards	No
Pro	None	Tee Times	7 days
Comments	Small greens, view of Jay Peak, new course		
Directions	I-91N, exit 25, Rt 5N, fast left after RR crossing, 1.5 mi		

Tee	Holes	Par	Rating	Slope	Yards
Red	9	74	66.0	113	5,322
White	9	71	66.0	113	5,800
Blue	NA	NA	NA	NA	NA

6 Basin Harbor Golf Club
Basin Harbor Road, Vergennes, VT 05491
802-475-2309

Weekend Fee	$35	Weekday Fee	$35
Power Cart Fee	$24	Pull Carts	Yes
Putting Green	Yes	Driving Range	Yes
Season	May 1 - Oct 15	Credit Cards	Yes
Pro	John Uzdilla	Tee Times	2 days
Comments	Lake and Mt views, Cornish design, resort		
Directions	Rt 7, Vergennes exit, Rt 22A thru town, right to Basin Harbor, 1 mi, right		

Tee	Holes	Par	Rating	Slope	Yards
Red	18	72	72.2	118	5,745
White	18	72	70.4	120	6,232
Blue	18	72	71.5	122	6,513

VERMONT

7 Bellows Falls Country Club
Rockingham Road, Bellows Falls, VT 05101
802-463-4742

Weekend Fee	$24	Weekday Fee	$18
Power Cart Fee	$21	Pull Carts	Yes
Putting Green	Yes	Driving Range	No
Season	Apr 15 - Nov 1	Credit Cards	Yes
Pro	None	Tee Times	No
Comments	Opened 1921, elevated greens, semi-private		
Directions	I-91, exit 6, Rt 103N, 3 mi		

Tee	Holes	Par	Rating	Slope	Yards
Red	9	72	70.1	112	5,138
White	9	70	68.5	111	5,752
Blue	NA	NA	NA	NA	NA

10 Brattleboro Country Club
Upper Dummerston Rd, Brattleboro, VT 05301
802-257-7380

Weekend Fee	$25 w/members	Weekday Fee	$25
Power Cart Fee	$25	Pull Carts	Yes
Putting Green	No	Driving Range	No
Season	Apr 11 - Nov 1	Credit Cards	No
Pro	802-257-7380	Tee Times	2 days
Comments	Opened in 1914, semi-private		
Directions	I-91S, exit 2, Rt 9W, right Orchard St across from Texaco, 1.5 mi, bear right, right		

Tee	Holes	Par	Rating	Slope	Yards
Red	9	72	71.0	115	5,380
White	9	70	69.8	117	6,265
Blue	NA	NA	NA	NA	NA

8 Blush Hill Country Club
Blush Hill Road, P.O. Box 396, Waterbury, VT 05676
802-244-8974

Weekend Fee	$21	Weekday Fee	$16
Power Cart Fee	$20	Pull Carts	Yes
Putting Green	Yes	Driving Range	Yes
Season	May 1 - Oct 15	Credit Cards	Yes
Pro	Dennis Grasso	Tee Times	No
Comments	Very scenic, semi-private		
Directions	I-89, Rt 100N, 0.5 mi, Blush Hill Rd, 1 mi		

Tee	Holes	Par	Rating	Slope	Yards
Red	9	66	61.6	101	4,730
White	9	66	63.0	101	4,730
Blue	NA	NA	NA	NA	NA

11 Cedar Knoll Country Club
Route 116, Hinesboro, VT 05461
802-482-3816

Weekend Fee	$18	Weekday Fee	$18
Power Cart Fee	$19	Pull Carts	Yes
Putting Green	Yes	Driving Range	Yes
Season	Apr 10 - Oct 31	Credit Cards	No
Pro	None	Tee Times	4 days
Comments	New course, scenic, open		
Directions	I-89, exit 12, 5 mi, left at intersection Rt 2A and 116, 5 mi		

Tee	Holes	Par	Rating	Slope	Yards
Red	18	72	64.1	110	5,179
White	18	72	67.4	117	5,903
Blue	18	72	69.0	120	6,245

9 Bradford Golf Club
Route 5, P.O. Box 315, Bradford, VT 05033
802-222-5207

Weekend Fee	$18	Weekday Fee	$15
Power Cart Fee	$18	Pull Carts	Yes
Putting Green	Yes	Driving Range	No
Season	May 1 - Nov 1	Credit Cards	No
Pro	David McGinn	Tee Times	No
Comments	Mostly flat, 2 ponds		
Directions	I-91N, exit 16, Rt 5N, look for signs		

Tee	Holes	Par	Rating	Slope	Yards
Red	9	64	60.6	89	4,260
White	9	64	60.4	102	4,260
Blue	NA	NA	NA	NA	NA

12 Champlain Country Club
Route 7, Saint Albans, VT 05478
802-527-1187

Weekend Fee	$24	Weekday Fee	$21
Power Cart Fee	$22	Pull Carts	Yes
Putting Green	Yes	Driving Range	No
Season	Apr 15-Oct 15	Credit Cards	Yes
Pro	Gary Munano	Tee Times	1 day
Comments	Tree lined, small and undulating greens		
Directions	I-89, exit 20, Rt 7N, 0.5 mi		

Tee	Holes	Par	Rating	Slope	Yards
Red	18	68	69.4	106	5,217
White	18	70	69.0	119	5,976
Blue	18	70	69.6	120	6,145

VERMONT

13 Copley Country Club
Maple Road, P.O. Box 51, Morrisville, VT 05661
802-888-3013

Weekend Fee	$20	*Weekday Fee*	$20
Power Cart Fee	$25	*Pull Carts*	Yes
Putting Green	Yes	*Driving Range*	No
Season	Apr 15 - Oct 15	*Credit Cards*	Yes
Pro	Tom Beck	*Tee Times*	No
Comments	Level course built in 1932, links style		
Directions	I-89, Waterbury exit, 18 mi to Morrisville		

Tee	Holes	Par	Rating	Slope	Yards
Red	9	72	67.1	104	5,000
White	9	70	66.5	106	5,549
Blue	NA	NA	NA	NA	NA

14 Crown Point Country Club
Weathersfield Center Road, Springfield, VT 05156
802-885-1010

Weekend Fee	$39	*Weekday Fee*	$32
Power Cart Fee	$27	*Pull Carts*	Yes
Putting Green	Yes	*Driving Range*	Yes
Season	Apr 15 - Nov 1	*Credit Cards*	Yes
Pro	D. Pfannenstein	*Tee Times*	3 days
Comments	Many sidehill lies, views of Mts		
Directions	I-91, exit 8, Rt 131W, left Center Rd, 5 mi		

Tee	Holes	Par	Rating	Slope	Yards
Red	18	72	71.3	117	5,542
White	18	72	70.0	119	6,120
Blue	18	72	72.0	123	6,572

15 Enosberg Falls Country Club
108 Main Street, Enosberg Falls, VT 05450
802-933-2296

Weekend Fee	$19	*Weekday Fee*	$17
Power Cart Fee	$15	*Pull Carts*	Yes
Putting Green	Yes	*Driving Range*	No
Season	Apr 15 - Oct 15	*Credit Cards*	Yes
Pro	None	*Tee Times*	1 day
Comments	Some long par 5s, hilly, expanding to 18		
Directions	St. Albans exit, Rt 105N, to Enosberg Falls, left Rt 108		

Tee	Holes	Par	Rating	Slope	Yards
Red	9	72	NA	NA	4,876
White	9	72	NA	117	5,568
Blue	9	72	NA	NA	5,668

16 Essex Country Club
332 Old Stage Road, Essex Junction, VT 05452
802-879-3232

Weekend Fee	$18	*Weekday Fee*	$18
Power Cart Fee	$19	*Pull Carts*	Yes
Putting Green	Yes	*Driving Range*	No
Season	Apr 15 - Nov 15	*Credit Cards*	Yes
Pro	John Chadwick	*Tee Times*	1 day
Comments	Mountain views, sand traps throughout		
Directions	I-89, Williston exit, Rt 2A to Essex Junction, Rt 15, Old Stage Rd, 3 mi		

Tee	Holes	Par	Rating	Slope	Yards
Red	18	72	70.7	114	5,890
White	18	72	68.6	114	6,310
Blue	NA	NA	NA	NA	NA

17 Farm Resort Golf Club
Route 2 Box 6335, Route 100, Morrisville, VT 05661
802-888-3525

Weekend Fee	$22	*Weekday Fee*	$20
Power Cart Fee	$18	*Pull Carts*	Yes
Putting Green	Yes	*Driving Range*	Yes
Season	Apr 15 - Oct 22	*Credit Cards*	Yes
Pro	A. Schuermann	*Tee Times*	2 days
Comments	Scenic, hilly, 3 water holes, Cornish design		
Directions	I-89, exit 10, Rt 100N, 15 mi		

Tee	Holes	Par	Rating	Slope	Yards
Red	9	72	69.2	116	5,198
White	9	72	67.6	112	5,798
Blue	9	72	68.4	114	6,038

18 Fox Run Golf Course
Fox Lane, Route 103, Ludlow, VT 05149
802-228-8871

Weekend Fee	$30	*Weekday Fee*	$25
Power Cart Fee	$25	*Pull Carts*	Yes
Putting Green	Yes	*Driving Range*	No
Season	Apr 15 - Nov 1	*Credit Cards*	Yes
Pro	None	*Tee Times*	1 day
Comments	Semi-private, hazards every hole		
Directions	I-91N, Ludlow exit, Rt 103N, 40 minutes, at intersection with Rt 100		

Tee	Holes	Par	Rating	Slope	Yards
Red	9	70	68.5	109	4,840
White	9	70	65.6	106	5,124
Blue	9	70	67.2	108	5,402

VERMONT

19 Gleneagles Golf Course
Union Street, Route 7A, Manchester Village, VT 05254
802-879-3232

Weekend Fee	$80	Weekday Fee	$70
Power Cart Fee	$36 required	Pull Carts	Yes
Putting Green	Yes	Driving Range	No
Season	Mar 1 - Jan 1	Credit Cards	Yes
Pro	Richard Wood	Tee Times	2 days
Comments	Resort, built 1896, carts required before 11		
Directions	Rt 7N, exit 3, Rt 7A north, look for signs, across from hotel		

Tee	Holes	Par	Rating	Slope	Yards
Red	18	71	65.2	117	5,082
White	18	71	69.1	125	6,069
Blue	18	71	71.3	129	6,423

20 Granddad's Invitational GC
Newark, VT 05871
802-467-3739

Weekend Fee	$5	Weekday Fee	$5
Power Cart Fee	No carts	Pull Carts	Yes
Putting Green	Yes	Driving Range	No
Season	May 1 - Nov 1	Credit Cards	No
Pro	None	Tee Times	No
Comments	Easy course		
Directions	West Burke, Rt 5A to Newark, 4 mi, right, right at 4 corners		

Tee	Holes	Par	Rating	Slope	Yards
Red	9	60	NA	NA	4,568
White	9	60	NA	NA	4,568
Blue	NA	NA	NA	NA	NA

21 Haystack Golf Course
Mann Road, Wilmington, VT 05356
800-845-7690

Weekend Fee	$45	Weekday Fee	$39
Power Cart Fee	$30	Pull Carts	Yes
Putting Green	Yes	Driving Range	Yes
Season	May 16 - Nov 1	Credit Cards	Yes
Pro	Mark Bradley	Tee Times	3 days
Comments	Hilly, narrow, views, carts needed weekend		
Directions	I-91, Brattleboro, Rt 9W, Rt 100N, 3 mi, left Coldbrook Rd, left Mann Road		

Tee	Holes	Par	Rating	Slope	Yards
Red	18	74	71.4	122	5,396
White	18	72	69.8	125	6,164
Blue	18	72	71.1	128	6,549

22 Killington Golf Resort
Killington Road, Killington, VT 05751
802-422-4100

Weekend Fee	$44	Weekday Fee	$44
Power Cart Fee	$28	Pull Carts	Yes
Putting Green	Yes	Driving Range	Yes
Season	May 1 - Oct 31	Credit Cards	Yes
Pro	James Remy	Tee Times	5 days
Comments	Wooded, tight, 200 ft drops, great views		
Directions	I-89, exit 1, Rt 4W, left on Killington Rd		

Tee	Holes	Par	Rating	Slope	Yards
Red	18	72	71.2	123	5,108
White	18	72	69.6	123	5,876
Blue	18	72	70.6	126	6,326

23 Kwiniaska Golf Club
Spear Street, P.O. Box 129, Shelburne, VT 05482
802-985-3672

Weekend Fee	$24	Weekday Fee	$24
Power Cart Fee	$20	Pull Carts	Yes
Putting Green	Yes	Driving Range	No
Season	Apr 15 - Nov 15	Credit Cards	Yes
Pro	Michael Bailey	Tee Times	1 day
Comments	View Lk Champlain, Green/Adirondack Mts		
Directions	I-89, exit 14W, follow signs to Spear St, 5 mi south		

Tee	Holes	Par	Rating	Slope	Yards
Red	18	72	72.6	119	5,670
White	18	72	71.2	122	6,796
Blue	18	72	72.7	125	7,067

24 Lake Morey Country Club
Lake Road, P. O. Box 326, Fairlee, VT 05045
802-333-4800

Weekend Fee	$31	Weekday Fee	$26
Power Cart Fee	$26	Pull Carts	Yes
Putting Green	Yes	Driving Range	No
Season	May 1 - Oct 30	Credit Cards	Yes
Pro	Bill Ross	Tee Times	4 days
Comments	Hilly back, level front, elevated par 5 green		
Directions	I-91N, exit 15, left, follow signs		

Tee	Holes	Par	Rating	Slope	Yards
Red	18	70	67.8	106	4,942
White	18	70	68.4	118	5,807
Blue	18	70	69.4	120	6,024

25 Lake St. Catherine Country Club

Route 30, Poultney, VT 05764
802-287-9341

Weekend Fee	$30	*Weekday Fee*	$25
Power Cart Fee	$25	*Pull Carts*	Yes
Putting Green	Yes	*Driving Range*	No
Season	Apr 15 - Oct 15	*Credit Cards*	No
Pro	Kevin Bessonen	*Tee Times*	3 days
Comments	New 9 being built presently, semi-private		
Directions	Rt 149, Rt 4N, Rt 30N, 4 mi south of Poultney		

Tee	Holes	Par	Rating	Slope	Yards
Red	9	72	66.2	112	5,156
White	9	70	68.8	119	5,996
Blue	9	70	69.8	120	6,204

26 Marble Island Country Club

150 Marble Island Road, Mallets Bay, VT 05446
802-864-6800

Weekend Fee	$16	*Weekday Fee*	$12
Power Cart Fee	$18	*Pull Carts*	Yes
Putting Green	Yes	*Driving Range*	No
Season	May 1 - Oct 15	*Credit Cards*	Yes
Pro	Bill Currier	*Tee Times*	1 day
Comments	View Lake Champlain, Tillinghast design		
Directions	I-89, Colchester exit, Rt 7, left Rt 127, 2.8 mi, right Marble Island Rd		

Tee	Holes	Par	Rating	Slope	Yards
Red	9	66	62.6	103	4,436
White	9	66	65.6	110	5,086
Blue	9	66	66.2	111	5,228

27 Montague Golf Club

Randolph Avenue, P.O. Box 178, Randolph, VT 05060
802-728-3806

Weekend Fee	$26	*Weekday Fee*	$20
Power Cart Fee	$20	*Pull Carts*	Yes
Putting Green	Yes	*Driving Range*	No
Season	Apr 1 - Nov 1	*Credit Cards*	Yes
Pro	Matt Engberg	*Tee Times*	3 days
Comments	Small greens, semi-private, Cornish design		
Directions	I-89N, exit 4, Rt 66, Rt 12S, left after Ben Franklin, left Randolph Ave		

Tee	Holes	Par	Rating	Slope	Yards
Red	18	71	68.7	111	5,064
White	18	70	67.2	117	5,596
Blue	18	70	68.6	120	5,910

28 Montpelier Country Club

Country Club Drive, Drawer E, Montpelier, VT 05602
802-223-7457

Weekend Fee	$21	*Weekday Fee*	$18
Power Cart Fee	$20	*Pull Carts*	Yes
Putting Green	Yes	*Driving Range*	No
Season	Apr 1 - Oct 31	*Credit Cards*	No
Pro	Brian Haley	*Tee Times*	1 day
Comments	Undulating greens, members only before 12		
Directions	I-89, Rt 2 exit, follow signs to Montpelier		

Tee	Holes	Par	Rating	Slope	Yards
Red	9	70	67.9	112	4,846
White	9	70	66.6	114	5,226
Blue	9	70	67.0	117	5,380

29 Mountain View Country Club

Country Club Road, Greensboro, VT 05841
802-533-7477

Weekend Fee	Members only	*Weekday Fee*	$21
Power Cart Fee	$17	*Pull Carts*	Yes
Putting Green	Yes	*Driving Range*	No
Season	May 15 - Oct 15	*Credit Cards*	No
Pro	Barb Newhouse	*Tee Times*	No
Comments	Open fairways, tree lined, semi-private		
Directions	Rt 7, Bennington center, right West Main St, right Convent Ave, left at end of street		

Tee	Holes	Par	Rating	Slope	Yards
Red	9	70	70.4	105	4,878
White	9	70	67.3	112	5,592
Blue	NA	NA	NA	NA	NA

30 Mount Anthony Country Club

943 Bank Street, P.O. Box 947, Bennington, VT 05201
802-442-2617

Weekend Fee	$30	*Weekday Fee*	$25
Power Cart Fee	$22	*Pull Carts*	Yes
Putting Green	Yes	*Driving Range*	Yes
Season	Apr 15 - Nov 1	*Credit Cards*	Yes
Pro	Leo Reynolds	*Tee Times*	7 days
Comments	Small greens, views, semi-private, 1897		
Directions	Rt 7, Bennington center, right West Main St, right Convent Ave, left at St end		

Tee	Holes	Par	Rating	Slope	Yards
Red	9	72	67.7	122	4,570
White	9	71	69.2	125	5,941
Blue	NA	NA	NA	NA	NA

VERMONT

31 Mount Snow Golf Course
Crosstown Road, Mount Snow, VT 05356
800-845-7690

Weekend Fee	$59	Weekday Fee	$49
Power Cart Fee	Included	Pull Carts	No
Putting Green	No	Driving Range	No
Season	May 1 - Oct 1	Credit Cards	Yes
Pro	Jay Morelli	Tee Times	Yes
Comments	Golf school, resort, Cornish design		
Directions	I-91, exit 2, Rt 9W, 20 mi, right Rt 100N, 6 mi, left Crosstown Rd		

Tee	Holes	Par	Rating	Slope	Yards
Red	18	73	72.5	118	5,666
White	18	72	70.3	127	6,443
Blue	18	72	72.3	130	6,894

32 Neshobe Country Club
Town Farm Road, P.O. Box 205, Brandon, VT 05733
802-247-3611

Weekend Fee	$35	Weekday Fee	$32
Power Cart Fee	$22	Pull Carts	Yes
Putting Green	Yes	Driving Range	Yes
Season	Apr 1 - Oct 31	Credit Cards	Yes
Pro	Bill Youse	Tee Times	No
Comments	Trout brook, uneven lies, all day play		
Directions	Rt 7, left on Rt 73E, 2 mi, located 1 mi east of Brandon		

Tee	Holes	Par	Rating	Slope	Yards
Red	9	70	70.2	120	5,090
White	9	71	66.8	120	5,592
Blue	NA	NA	NA	NA	NA

33 Newport Country Club
Pine Hill Road, P.O. Box 434, Newport, VT 05855
802-334-7715

Weekend Fee	$21	Weekday Fee	$21
Power Cart Fee	$21	Pull Carts	Yes
Putting Green	Yes	Driving Range	Yes
Season	Apr 15 - Nov 15	Credit Cards	Yes
Pro	Peter Mathews	Tee Times	No
Comments	Contoured fairways, lake view, semi-private		
Directions	I-91, exit 27, towards Newport, 0.5 mi, left, follow signs		

Tee	Holes	Par	Rating	Slope	Yards
Red	18	72	69.3	111	5,312
White	18	72	69.2	106	6,117
Blue	18	72	69.4	109	6,453

34 Northfield Country Club
Roxbury Road, P.O. Box 306, Northfield, VT 05663
802-485-4515

Weekend Fee	$22	Weekday Fee	$18
Power Cart Fee	$18	Pull Carts	Yes
Putting Green	Yes	Driving Range	No
Season	Apr 15 - Oct 15	Credit Cards	No
Pro	John Laveroni	Tee Times	7 days
Comments	Many water holes, hilly, bunkered greens		
Directions	I-89, exit 5, Rt 12, Rt 12A, 4 mi north of center		

Tee	Holes	Par	Rating	Slope	Yards
Red	9	68	67.4	105	4,986
White	9	70	68.8	115	5,712
Blue	9	70	69.3	119	5,924

35 Orleans Country Club
Willoughby Lake Road, Route 58, Orleans, VT 05860
802-754-2333

Weekend Fee	$20	Weekday Fee	$20
Power Cart Fee	$20	Pull Carts	Yes
Putting Green	Yes	Driving Range	Yes
Season	Apr 15 - Nov 1	Credit Cards	Yes
Pro	Robert Silvester	Tee Times	1 day
Comments	#13 surrounded by moguls and hazards		
Directions	I-91, exit 26, Rt 58E, 1.5 mi, right Country Club Rd		

Tee	Holes	Par	Rating	Slope	Yards
Red	18	72	70.5	111	5,545
White	18	72	68.5	115	5,938
Blue	18	72	69.3	117	6,123

36 Proctor Pittsford Country Club
Corn Hill Road, Pittsford, VT 05763
802-483-9379

Weekend Fee	$27	Weekday Fee	$27
Power Cart Fee	$21	Pull Carts	Yes
Putting Green	Yes	Driving Range	No
Season	Apr 15 - Oct 31	Credit Cards	Yes
Pro	Merl Schoenfeld	Tee Times	7 days
Comments	Views, small bunkered greens, semi-private		
Directions	Rt 7N, left after Nissan dealer, 0.5 mi, right, 3 mi		

Tee	Holes	Par	Rating	Slope	Yards
Red	18	72	70.4	115	5,446
White	18	70	67.9	118	5,728
Blue	18	70	69.4	121	6,052

37 Prospect Bay Country Club
Route 30, P.O. Box 90, Bomoseen, VT 05732
802-468-5581

Weekend Fee	$20	*Weekday Fee*	$17
Power Cart Fee	$22	*Pull Carts*	Yes
Putting Green	Yes	*Driving Range*	No
Season	Apr 1 - Oct 15	*Credit Cards*	Yes
Pro	Thea Baker	*Tee Times*	No
Comments	Hilly, wooded		
Directions	Rutland, Rt 4W, exit 4, Rt 30N, look for signs		

Tee	Holes	Par	Rating	Slope	Yards
Red	9	70	66.4	101	4,420
White	9	70	64.0	107	5,010
Blue	NA	NA	NA	NA	NA

38 Quechee Club Resort - Highland
1 River Road, Quechee, VT 05059
802-295-6245

Weekend Fee	$60	*Weekday Fee*	$60
Power Cart Fee	$28 required	*Pull Carts*	No
Putting Green	Yes	*Driving Range*	No
Season	May 1 - Oct 31	*Credit Cards*	Yes
Pro	Lettie Trespasz	*Tee Times*	3 days
Comments	Wildlife, need to be resort guest to play		
Directions	Rt 100N, Rt 4E, 12 mi, left River Rd		

Tee	Holes	Par	Rating	Slope	Yards
Red	18	72	71.3	125	5,439
White	18	72	70.4	123	6,342
Blue	18	72	73.1	129	6,765

39 Quechee Club Resort - Lakeland
1 River Road, Quechee, VT 05059
802-295-6245

Weekend Fee	$60	*Weekday Fee*	$60
Power Cart Fee	$28 required	*Pull Carts*	No
Putting Green	Yes	*Driving Range*	No
Season	May 1 - Oct 31	*Credit Cards*	Yes
Pro	Lettie Trespasz	*Tee Times*	3 days
Comments	Wildlife, need to be resort guest to play		
Directions	Rt 100N, Rt 4E, 12 mi, left River Rd		

Tee	Holes	Par	Rating	Slope	Yards
Red	18	72	70.7	116	5,370
White	18	72	69.8	124	6,016
Blue	18	72	72.2	129	6,569

40 Ralph Myhre Golf Club
Middlebury College, Route 1, Middlebury, VT 05753
802-388-3711

Weekend Fee	$28	*Weekday Fee*	$28
Power Cart Fee	$27	*Pull Carts*	Yes
Putting Green	Yes	*Driving Range*	No
Season	Apr 1 - Nov 1	*Credit Cards*	Yes
Pro	George Phinney	*Tee Times*	1 day
Comments	Open fairways, picturesque college town		
Directions	Rt 7, Rt 30S, right after college field house		

Tee	Holes	Par	Rating	Slope	Yards
Red	18	71	66.9	120	5,309
White	18	71	69.6	126	6,014
Blue	18	71	71.3	129	6,379

41 Richford Country Club
Golf Course Road, Route 106, Richford, VT 05476
802-848-3527

Weekend Fee	$34	*Weekday Fee*	$30
Power Cart Fee	$30	*Pull Carts*	Yes
Putting Green	Yes	*Driving Range*	No
Season	May 1 - Oct 31	*Credit Cards*	Yes
Pro	Flo Cheeseman	*Tee Times*	7 days
Comments	Hills and trees, views of Green Mts		
Directions	I-89, exit St. Albans, Rt 105N, 28 mi, right opposite Blue Seal Feeds, 1 mi		

Tee	Holes	Par	Rating	Slope	Yards
Red	9	74	72.2	117	5,202
White	9	74	68.2	113	6,006
Blue	NA	NA	NA	NA	NA

42 Rocky Ridge Golf Club
68 Ledge Road, Route 116, Burlington, VT 05401
802-482-2191

Weekend Fee	$20	*Weekday Fee*	$20
Power Cart Fee	$21	*Pull Carts*	Yes
Putting Green	Yes	*Driving Range*	Yes
Season	Apr 1 - Nov 1	*Credit Cards*	No
Pro	Ken Rachliss	*Tee Times*	2 days
Comments	100 foot drop on 15th hole, narrow fairways		
Directions	I-89, exit 12, Rt 2A south, 7 mi, at junction with Rt 116		

Tee	Holes	Par	Rating	Slope	Yards
Red	18	72	65.6	117	5,230
White	18	72	69.1	124	5,933
Blue	18	72	70.3	126	6,282

VERMONT

43 Rutland Country Club
North Grove Street, P.O. Box 195, Rutland, VT 05701
802-773-3254

Weekend Fee	Members only	Weekday Fee	$64
Power Cart Fee	Included	Pull Carts	No
Putting Green	Yes	Driving Range	No
Season	Apr 1 - Oct 31	Credit Cards	Yes
Pro	Bill Andrews	Tee Times	1 day
Comments	Accuracy, fast greens, semi-private, 1896		
Directions	I-89, exit 1, Rt 4W to Rutland, right Grove St		

Tee	Holes	Par	Rating	Slope	Yards
Red	18	71	71.6	125	5,368
White	18	70	67.9	122	5,761
Blue	18	70	67.9	125	6,134

46 St. Johnsbury Country Club
Route 15 & Memorial Drive, St. Johnsbury, VT 05819
802-748-9894

Weekend Fee	$32	Weekday Fee	$28
Power Cart Fee	$24	Pull Carts	Yes
Putting Green	Yes	Driving Range	No
Season	Apr 15 - Oct 31	Credit Cards	Yes
Pro	Denis Blanc	Tee Times	4 days
Comments	Cornish design, hosted Amateur Champnshp		
Directions	I-91N, exit 23, Rt 15, 3 mi		

Tee	Holes	Par	Rating	Slope	Yards
Red	18	71	67.7	123	5,480
White	18	70	68.6	125	5,860
Blue	18	70	70.4	129	6,373

44 Sitzmark Golf Course
East Dover Road, Route 100, Wilmington, VT 05363
802-464-3384

Weekend Fee	$12	Weekday Fee	$12
Power Cart Fee	$15	Pull Carts	Yes
Putting Green	Yes	Driving Range	No
Season	Apr 1 - Dec 1	Credit Cards	Yes
Pro	None	Tee Times	No
Comments	Holes from 90-155 yards, undulating greens		
Directions	I-91, Brattleboro, Rt 9 towards Wilmington, Rt 100, 5 mi		

Tee	Holes	Par	Rating	Slope	Yards
Red	18	54	NA	NA	2,643
White	18	54	NA	NA	2,643
Blue	NA	NA	NA	NA	NA

47 Stamford Valley Country Club
Box 825 East Road, Route 9, Stamford, VT 05352
802-694-9144

Weekend Fee	$10	Weekday Fee	$10
Power Cart Fee	No carts	Pull Carts	Yes
Putting Green	Yes	Driving Range	No
Season	Apr 1 - Dec 1	Credit Cards	No
Pro	None	Tee Times	No
Comments	Very level course, large greens		
Directions	North Adams, Rt 8N, approximately 5 mi		

Tee	Holes	Par	Rating	Slope	Yards
Red	9	72	NA	NA	4,690
White	9	72	66.6	104	5,418
Blue	9	72	NA	NA	5,910

45 Someday Golf Resort
Highway 100/Bluebrook Road, West Dover, VT 05356
802-464-5807

Weekend Fee	$47	Weekday Fee	$47
Power Cart Fee	Included	Pull Carts	No
Putting Green	Yes	Driving Range	No
Season	Jun 15 - Oct 15	Credit Cards	Yes
Pro	None	Tee Times	7 days
Comments	1 island green, resort quests only		
Directions	I-91N, exit 2, Rt 9W, Rt 100N, look for signs		

Tee	Holes	Par	Rating	Slope	Yards
Red	9	72	NA	NA	4,034
White	9	72	NA	NA	4,716
Blue	9	72	NA	NA	4,910

48 Stonehedge Country Club
Town Highway 19, North Claredon, VT 05759
802-773-2666

Weekend Fee	$15	Weekday Fee	$12
Power Cart Fee	$15	Pull Carts	Yes
Putting Green	No	Driving Range	No
Season	Apr 1 - Oct 31	Credit Cards	No
Pro	Bob Matson	Tee Times	Yes
Comments	Executive course		
Directions	Rutland, Rt 7S, junction of Rt 103 and Rt 7		

Tee	Holes	Par	Rating	Slope	Yards
Red	9	54	NA	NA	2,214
White	9	54	NA	NA	2,214
Blue	NA	NA	NA	NA	NA

VERMONT

49 Stowe Country Club
5781 Mountain Road, Stowe, VT 05672
802-252-4895

Weekend Fee	$50	Weekday Fee	$50
Power Cart Fee	$30	Pull Carts	Yes
Putting Green	Yes	Driving Range	Yes
Season	May - Oct 15	Credit Cards	Yes
Pro	Chris Hedges	Tee Times	7 days
Comments	Resort, scenic		
Directions	I-89, exit 10, Rt 90N, Rt 100, 10 mi, left at blinking light, right Cape Cod Rd		

Tee	Holes	Par	Rating	Slope	Yards
Red	18	74	69.7	112	5,346
White	18	72	68.5	121	5,851
Blue	18	72	70.4	122	6,206

50 Stratton Mt. Golf Club (Forest)
Stratton Mountain Access Road, Stratton, VT 05155
802-297-4114

Weekend Fee	$66	Weekday Fee	$56
Power Cart Fee	$32	Pull Carts	Yes
Putting Green	Yes	Driving Range	Yes
Season	May 1 - Oct 31	Credit Cards	Yes
Pro	David Rihm	Tee Times	1 day
Comments	Three 9 holes played in combinations of 18		
Directions	I-91, Brattleboro exit, Rt 30E, 30 mi, look for signs		

Tee	Holes	Par	Rating	Slope	Yards
Red	18	74	69.8	123	5,153
White	18	72	69.4	122	6,044
Blue	18	72	71.2	125	6,526

51 Stratton Mt. Golf Club (Lake)
Stratton Mountain Access Road, Stratton, VT 05155
802-297-4114

Weekend Fee	$66	Weekday Fee	$56
Power Cart Fee	$32	Pull Carts	Yes
Putting Green	Yes	Driving Range	Yes
Season	May 1 - Oct 31	Credit Cards	Yes
Pro	David Rihm	Tee Times	1 day
Comments	Three 9 holes played in combinations of 18		
Directions	I-91, Brattleboro exit, Rt 30E, 30 mi, look for signs		

Tee	Holes	Par	Rating	Slope	Yards
Red	18	74	71.1	124	5,410
White	18	72	70.3	123	6,107
Blue	71	72	72.0	125	6,602

52 Stratton Mt. Golf Club (Mountain)
Stratton Mountain Access Road, Stratton, VT 05155
802-297-4114

Weekend Fee	$66	Weekday Fee	$56
Power Cart Fee	$32	Pull Carts	Yes
Putting Green	Yes	Driving Range	Yes
Season	May 1 - Oct 31	Credit Cards	Yes
Pro	David Rihm	Tee Times	1 day
Comments	Three 9 holes played in combinations of 18		
Directions	I-91, Brattleboro exit, Rt 30E, 30 mi, look for signs		

Tee	Holes	Par	Rating	Slope	Yards
Red	18	74	69.9	123	5,163
White	18	72	69.3	123	6,019
Blue	18	72	71.2	126	6,478

53 Sugarbush Golf Course
Sugarbush Access Road, Warren, VT 05674
802-583-2301

Weekend Fee	$49	Weekday Fee	$40
Power Cart Fee	$30	Pull Carts	Yes
Putting Green	Yes	Driving Range	Yes
Season	May 15 - Oct 15	Credit Cards	Yes
Pro	Mike Aldridge	Tee Times	1 day
Comments	Great views, resort, target golf, Trent design		
Directions	I-89S, exit 10, Rt 100S, Sugarbush Access Rd		

Tee	Holes	Par	Rating	Slope	Yards
Red	18	72	70.4	119	5,187
White	18	72	69.0	122	5,886
Blue	18	72	71.7	128	6,524

54 Tater Hill Resort
Popple Dungeon Road, RFD 1, Chester, VT 05143
802-875-2517

Weekend Fee	$64	Weekday Fee	$55
Power Cart Fee	Included	Pull Carts	Yes
Putting Green	Yes	Driving Range	Yes
Season	May 1 - Oct 31	Credit Cards	Yes
Pro	Mike Higuera	Tee Times	4 days
Comments	Par 5 599 yard hole		
Directions	I-91, exit 6, left, Rt 103, Rt 11W, 7 mi near Chester look for course signs		

Tee	Holes	Par	Rating	Slope	Yards
Red	18	72	71.3	116	4,979
White	18	72	71.4	124	6,015
Blue	18	72	72.5	126	6,801

VERMONT

55 West Bolton Golf Club
Box 305 West Bolton Road, West Bolton, VT 05465
802-434-4321

Weekend Fee	$17	*Weekday Fee*	$15
Power Cart Fee	$18	*Pull Carts*	Yes
Putting Green	Yes	*Driving Range*	No
Season	May 1 - Nov 1	*Credit Cards*	Yes
Pro	Marty Keene	*Tee Times*	7 days
Comments	Small greens, mountain views		
Directions	I-89, exit 11, towards Richmond, left light, 7 mi, right at course sign, 4 mi		

Tee	Holes	Par	Rating	Slope	Yards
Red	18	71	67.4	103	5,017
White	18	69	66.3	109	5,432
Blue	NA	NA	NA	NA	NA

58 Williston Golf Club
North Williston Road, Williston, VT 05495
802-878-3747

Weekend Fee	$19	*Weekday Fee*	$19
Power Cart Fee	$20	*Pull Carts*	Yes
Putting Green	Yes	*Driving Range*	No
Season	May 1 - Nov 12	*Credit Cards*	Yes
Pro	Wesley Olson	*Tee Times*	2 days
Comments	Well kept up, tree lined fairways		
Directions	I-89, exit 11, Rt 2E, North Williston Rd		

Tee	Holes	Par	Rating	Slope	Yards
Red	18	72	64.1	106	4,753
White	18	69	66.6	113	5,262
Blue	18	69	68.0	118	5,651

56 White River Golf Club
RD 1 Box 137, Route 100, Rochester, VT 05767
802-767-4653

Weekend Fee	$22	*Weekday Fee*	$22
Power Cart Fee	$20	*Pull Carts*	Yes
Putting Green	Yes	*Driving Range*	Yes
Season	May 1 - Oct 31	*Credit Cards*	Yes
Pro	Don Bank	*Tee Times*	No
Comments	Sand traps and water throughout		
Directions	I-89, Rt 107W, Rt 100N, 10 mi		

Tee	Holes	Par	Rating	Slope	Yards
Red	9	66	60.2	96	4,004
White	9	66	62.6	101	4,518
Blue	NA	NA	NA	NA	NA

59 Windsor Country Club
North Main Street, P.O. Box 263, Windsor, VT 05089
802-674-6491

Weekend Fee	$24	*Weekday Fee*	$19
Power Cart Fee	$20	*Pull Carts*	Yes
Putting Green	Yes	*Driving Range*	No
Season	Apr 15 - Nov 1	*Credit Cards*	Yes
Pro	None	*Tee Times*	3 days
Comments	Small elevated greens, view CT River		
Directions	I-91, exit 9, left Rt 5, 3.5 mi		

Tee	Holes	Par	Rating	Slope	Yards
Red	9	72	68.2	109	4,902
White	9	68	65.1	105	5,286
Blue	9	68	NA	NA	5,478

57 Wilcox Cove Cottages and Golf Club
3 Camp Vermont Court, Grand Isle, VT 05458
802-372-8343

Weekend Fee	$11	*Weekday Fee*	$9
Power Cart Fee	No carts	*Pull Carts*	Yes
Putting Green	Yes	*Driving Range*	No
Season	Apr 1 - Nov 1	*Credit Cards*	No
Pro	None	*Tee Times*	No
Comments	Shore of Lake Champlain, narrow fairways		
Directions	I-89, exit 17, Rt 2N, Rt 314 to Grand Isle ferry		

Tee	Holes	Par	Rating	Slope	Yards
Red	9	64	NA	NA	3,410
White	9	64	NA	NA	3,410
Blue	NA	NA	NA	NA	NA

60 Wolf Run Country Club
Route 109, Boston Post Road, Bakersfield, VT 05441
802-933-5100

Weekend Fee	$15	*Weekday Fee*	$12
Power Cart Fee	$16	*Pull Carts*	Yes
Putting Green	Yes	*Driving Range*	No
Season	Apr 1 - Nov 1	*Credit Cards*	Yes
Pro	None	*Tee Times*	No
Comments	Wildlife		
Directions	Rt 108, Bakersfield, right Boston Post Rd, follow signs		

Tee	Holes	Par	Rating	Slope	Yards
Red	9	70	NA	NA	5,220
White	9	70	NA	NA	5,940
Blue	NA	NA	NA	NA	NA

61 Woodstock Inn and Resort
14 The Green, Woodstock, VT 05091
802-457-6674

Weekend Fee	$59	*Weekday Fee*	$49
Power Cart Fee	$30	*Pull Carts*	Yes
Putting Green	Yes	*Driving Range*	Yes
Season	May 1 - Oct 31	*Credit Cards*	Yes
Pro	Jim Gunnare	*Tee Times*	1 day
Comments	Built 1895, 14 water holes, sports center		
Directions	I-89, Rt 4W to Woodstock, Rt 106S, 1 mi		

Tee	Holes	Par	Rating	Slope	Yards
Red	18	71	67.0	113	4,924
White	18	69	67.0	117	5,555
Blue	18	69	69.0	121	6,001

Information on the following course recently opened was obtained too late to include in the alphabetical listing or the location maps in this book.

Green Mountain National Golf Course
Barrows-Towne Road, Killington, VT
802-422-4653

Weekend Fee	$ 45	*Weekday Fee*	$ 40
Power Cart Fee	$ 14	*Pull Carts*	Yes
Putting Green	Yes	*Driving Range*	Yes
Season	Apr 1 - Nov 1	*Credit Cards*	Yes
Pro	Jeffrey Hadley	*Tee Times*	Yes
Comments	Opened 1996		
Directions	I-91, exit 6, Rt 103N, Rt 100N		

Tee	Holes	Par	Rating	Slope	Yards
Red	18	71	63.9	118	4,740
White	18	71	70.2	132	6,164
Blue	18	71	72.6	139	6,589

Woodstock Country Club
Woodstock, Vermont

Bibliography

Books and References

Apfelbaum, Jim. Golf on $30 A Day. Villard Books. 1995
Cornish, Geoffrey S. and Ronald E. Whitten. The Golf Course. Rutledge. 1987
Cornish, Geoffrey S. and Ronald E. Whitten. The Architects of Golf: A Survey of Course Design From Its Beginnings to the Present.
Curhan, Leona and Irwin Garfinkle. New England Golf Guide. 1996.
Doak, Tom. The Anatomy of a Golf Course. 1992
Garrity, John. America's Worst Golf Courses.
Golf America. Eastern Region Golf Guide. Cy DeCosse Incorporated. 1996.
Graham, David. David Graham's Guide to Golf Equipment. 1993
Harber, Paul. The Complete Guide to Golf on Cape Cod, Nantucket, and Martha's Vineyard. 1993
Huggins, Percy. The Golfer's Miscellaney. Harper & Row. 1970
International Federation of Golf. 1994 Yellow Pages of Golf. Activities Directories International. 1993
Jones Jr., Robert Trent. Golf by Design. 1993
Labance, Bob and David Cornwell. Vermont Golf Courses: A Players Guide.
Lane, James. The Complete Golfer's Almanac 1995. A Perigee Book. 1995
Lanier, Pamela. Golf Resorts. Lanier Publishing International. 1989
Kelly, Leo. Antique Golf Ball Reference and Price Guide. Old Chicago Golf Shop. 1993
Maltby, Ralph. The Complete Golf Club Fitting Plan. The Golf Works. 1986
McMillan, Robin. The Golfer's Home Companion. 1993
Pedroli, Hubert. The American Golfer's Guide. 1992
Powers. Northeast Region Golf Guide. Briarcliff Press, Inc., 1995.
Scharff, Robert. The Encyclopedia of Golf. Harper & Row. 1970
Smith, Peter. The Guinness Book of Golf. 1992
USA Today, Golf Atlas, Simon & Schuster, 1995
Ward-Thomas, Pat. The World Atlas of Golf. Random House. 1976
Wind, Herbert Warren. The Story of American Golf. Simon and Schuster. 1956

Ballymeade Country Club, Falmouth, Massachusetts

Magazines and Periodicals

Al Barlow's Golf Report, 444 Bedford Road, Pleasantville, NY 10570, 914-747-4716
Clubmakers Digest, 71 Maholm Street, Newark, OH 43055, 614-344-1191
The Country Club, 16 Forest Street, New Canaan, CT, 203-972-3892
Discover Golf, 420 Boyd Street, #502, Los Angeles, CA 90013 213-680-9101
Eastern Golfer, PO Box 134, West End Station, West End, NJ 07740, 201-222-4877
Executive Golfer, 21771 Campus Drive, Irvine, CA 92715
Fairway, Two Park Avenue, New York, NY 10016, 212-779-5000
Golf and Turf Annual, 1500 NE 131st Street, North Miami, FL 33161 305-893-9600
Golf Course Development and Operations Quality, 1150 S. US Hghwy 1, Jupiter, FL 33477 407-744-6006
Golf Course Management, 1421 Research Park Drive, Lawrence, KS 66049, 913-832-4490
Golf Course News, 38 Lafayette Street, Box 997, Yarmouth, ME 04096
Golf Development, 250 Bel Marin Keys, #A, Novata, CA 94949, 415-382-2490
Golf Digest, 5520 Park Avenue, Box 395, Trumbull, CT 06611, 203-373-7000
Golf for Women, All American Plaza, 2130 Jackson Avenue, West Oxford, MS 38655, 515-284-2484
Golf Illustrated, 5050 North 40th Street, Suite 250, Phoenix, AZ 85018, 602-955-3332
Golf Journal, Golf House, Liberty Corner, Far Hills, NJ 07931, 908-234-2300
Golf Magazine, Two Park Avenue, New York, NY 10016, 212-779-5000
Golf Market Today, 1150 South US Highway 1, Jupiter, FL 33477, 407-744-6006
Golf Network, 6230 Buson Boulevard, #444, Columbus, OH, 614-433-6393
Golf Pro, 7 West 34th Street, New York, NY 10001, 212-630-3738
Golf Products News, 1522 Fair Lawn Avenue, Fair Lawn, NJ 07410, 201-796-6031
Golf Shop Operations, 5520 Park Avenue, Trumbull, CT 06611, 203-373-7232
Golf Tips, 12121 Wilshire Boulevard, #1220, Los Angeles, CA 90025, 310-820-1500
Golf Today, 650 Bair Island Road, Redwood City, CA, 94063, 415-306-0122
Golf Travel, PO Box 3485, Charlottesville, VA 22907, 800-225-7825
Golf Traveler, 1637 Metropolitan Boulevard, Suite C, Tallahassee, FL 32308, 800-522-9232
GolfWeek, 175 5th Street SW, Winter Haven, FL 33880, 813-294-5511
Golf World, 5520 Park Avenue, Trumbull, CT 06611, 203-373-7000
Great Golf Resorts of the World, 111 Presidential Blvd, Bala Cynwyd, PA 19004, 610-668-3564
Links - The Best of Golf, 1040 William Hilton Parkway, Hilton Head, SC 29928, 803-842-6200
National Golfer, 57 North Washington Street, Plainville, CT 06062, 203-747-4404
New England Golf Magazine, 120 Boylston Street, Boston, MA 02116, 617-482-3434
Ocean State Golf, 1665 Hartford Avenue, Johnston, RI, 401-421-4653
The Massachusetts Golfer, 670 Centre Street, Boston, MA 02130
Petersen's Golfing, 6420 Wilshire Boulevard, Los Angeles, CA 90048, 213-782-2800
PGA Magazine, 2155 Butterfield, #200, Troy, MI 48084, 313-649-1110
Senior Golfer, One Exeter Plaza, Boston, MA 02116, 617-266-2600
Tee Time, P.O. Box 225, Whitman, MA 02382, 617-447-2299
The Massachusetts Golfer, 670 Centre Street, Boston, MA 02130, 617-522-3267
TOUR, 2 Park Avenue, New York, NY 10016, 212-779-5000
S.E. MA/RI Golfer Magazine, 9 Prince Street, Fairhaven, MA 02719, 508-994-1223
Vermont Golf Journal and Directory, 431 Pine Street, Burlington, VT 05401 802-864-6115

New England Cartographics
Order Form

Maps

Holyoke Range State Park (Eastern Section)	$3.50	_____
Holyoke Range/Skinner State Park (Western Section)	$3.50	_____
Mt. Greylock Reservation Trail Map	$3.50	_____
Mt. Toby Reservation Trail Map	$3.50	_____
Mt. Tom Reservation Trail Map	$3.50	_____
Mt. Wachusett and Leominster State Forest Trail Map	$3.50	_____
Western Massachusetts Trail Map Pack (all 6 listed above)	$13.95	_____
Quabbin Reservation Guide	$3.95	_____
Quabbin Reservation Guide (waterproof version)	$5.95	_____
New England Trails (general locator map)	$2.00	_____
Grand Monadnock Trail Map	$3.50	_____
Connecticut River Map (in Massachusetts)	$5.95	_____

Books

Guide to the Metacomet-Monadnock Trail	$6.95	_____
Hiking the Pioneer Valley	$10.95	_____
Hiking the Monadnock Region	$10.95	_____
Deerfield River Guide	$11.95	_____
High Peaks of the Northeast	$12.95	_____
Great Rail Trails of the Northeast	$14.95	_____
Skiing the Pioneer Valley	$10.95	_____
Golfing in New England	$16.95	_____

Subtotal _____

Please include postage/handling:
$0.75 for the first single map and $0.25 for each additional map;
$1.00 for the Western Mass. Map Pack;
$2.00 for the first book and $1.00 for each additional book.

Mailing _____

Total Enclosed _____

To order, call or write: *New England Cartographics*
P.O. Box 9369
North Amherst MA 01059
(413) - 549-4124
FAX orders: (413) - 549-3621

Circle one: **Mastercard**   *Visa*   *Check*   *Money Order*

Card Number _____   **Expiration Date** _____
Signature _____   **Telephone (optional)** _____

Please send my order to:

    Name   _____
    Address   _____
    Town/City _____   State _____ Zip _____

Comments, Additions, and Corrections

I will be updating **Golfing in New England** on a regular basis by contacting golf courses directly. However, due to the large amount of information in this book, it is very likely that at various points in time some of the information will be outdated (fee changes, number of holes, new courses, etc.). Also, I am always looking for new ideas on how to make the book more valuable to you and better organized. With that in mind, I would appreciate your feedback. If you have any ideas, suggestions, or corrections, please make a copy of this page, fill in the appropriate sections, and send to:

New England Cartographics
PO Box 9369
North Amherst, MA 01059

Your Name (optional)	
Your Address (optional)	
Your Phone # (optional)	

Corrections to Existing Golf Courses or Additional Courses Not in the Book

Course Name	
Street	
Town	
State	
Zip Code	
Phone Number	
Pro	
Season	
Putting Green	
Driving Range	
Pull Carts Allowed	
Tee Times	
Weekend 18 Holes	
Weekday 18 Holes	
Power Cart Fee	
Credit Cards	
Comments	
Directions	

Tee	Holes	Par	Rating	Slope	Yards
Red					
White					
Blue					

Other Corrections or Suggestions on How to Improve the Book